# MAJOR POEMS AND SELECTED PROSE

# *Algernon Charles Swinburne*

# *Major Poems and Selected Prose*

EDITED BY JEROME McGANN
AND CHARLES L. SLIGH

Yale University Press / New Haven & London

Set in Galliard type by Integrated Publishing Solutions.
Printed in the United States of America.

Library of Congress Cataloging-in-Publication Data

Swinburne, Algernon Charles, 1837–1909.
[Selections. 2004]
Algernon Charles Swinburne : major poems and selected prose / edited by Jerome McGann and Charles L. Sligh.
p. cm.
Includes bibliographical references (p. ) and indexes.
ISBN 0-300-10499-5 (pb: alk. paper)
I. McGann, Jerome J. II. Sligh, Charles L. III. Title.
PR5502.M35 2004
821′.8—dc22 2004043062

A catalogue record for this book is available from the British Library.

The paper in this book meets the guidelines for permanence and durability of the Committee on Production Guidelines for Book Longevity of the Council on Library Resources.

10 9 8 7 6 5 4 3 2 1

## CONTENTS

*Part Four • Uncollected Prose*

In Memoriam

Cecil Y. Lang

*accipe*

*atque in perpetuum, frater, ave atque vale*

# ACKNOWLEDGMENTS

First of all we have an unpayable debt to the work and the generosity of the great scholar to whom this edition is dedicated. Cecil Y. Lang kept a human vision in a time of trouble. That having been so, "how should we living fear to call thee dead"?

We must as well thank Violette Lang, Cecil's wife, for the encouragement and help she gave us in preparing this work. We are especially pleased to print in this book her translation of a key passage of Swinburne's French prose that Swinburne imbedded in his review of Matthew Arnold.

Several other scholars have been extremely generous of their knowledge and expertise: Terry Meyers most of all, whose edition of Swinburne's uncollected letters is a major addition to scholarship; and Rikky Rooksby, who has written what is in our view the most readable and the liveliest biography of the poet. Special thanks go as well to the acute readers Virgil Burnett, Johanna Drucker, John Hollander, Catherine Maxwell, Marjorie Perloff, Lawrence Rainey, Herbert Tucker, and John Walsh.

# INTRODUCTION

Neither Swinburne nor his writings are normal or ordinary. "Demoniac youth," Ruskin called him, and to Maupassant he was "the most extravagant artistic person alive in the world today." Descriptions like that recur in the numerous contemporary reports, though many also express horror at the person Edward Burne-Jones called "the most poetic personality I have ever known." So Bayard Taylor observes that "I admire in him . . . the mad, unrestrained preponderance of the imagination. It is a god-like quality, but he sometimes uses it like the devil. . . . He told me some things, unspeakably shocking, which he had omitted from his last volume." Excepting his love for children and old people, few things about Swinburne seemed appropriate, to appropriate a commonplace of our preposterously careful and standardized age. He even looked odd. Burne-Jones's wife, Georgiana, recalled "the flame-like beauty of his wavy mass of hair, his swift speech and extraordinary swiftness of thought and apprehension, and a certain delightful inconsequence all his own." Most unforgettable were his piercing green eyes and the ways he moved: "When repeating poetry he had a perfectly natural way of lifting [his eyes] in a rapt, unconscious gaze. . . . 'Looks commencing with the skies' expresses it without exaggeration. He was restless beyond words, scarcely standing still at all and almost dancing as he walked."

The writings are as arresting as the man. He composed as easily in French as in English, and nearly as easily in Greek, Latin, and Italian. Probably Tennyson is the only poet after Pope who possessed his extraordinary prosodic skills, and Tennyson cannot match the range of Swinburne's literary work. His critical and speculative prose, though still largely inviolate, is seminal and made Pater's and Wilde's work possible; he is a major writer of fiction, as Edmund Wilson would discover late in his life; and with his friend Dante Gabriel Rossetti, he passed along to Ezra Pound a theory and practice of poetic translation that was crucial for the Modernist program. All this is accomplished within a clearly defined intellectual framework that was also, for him, a mission. He meant to establish the practice of Imagination at the center of cultural life. His idea of Imagination is Shelleyan—that is to say, it is moral, comprehensive, and committed to social transformation. Also like Shelley, he directed his work to the arena of ideology and the forms of belief that society's ideological apparatuses, especially the schools and the churches, promote and maintain. But he is far more like Byron in seeking a broad public engagement with his secular humanism. He made himself and his work a sign of contention.

He was fearless, immensely gifted, and unswerving in this work. But he was expelled from our schools in the twentieth century. The expulsion was understandable given the cultural program to which academic Modernism devoted itself between approximately 1920 and 1965. Later well-known reevaluations of that program have begun to study its police-keeping work and restore attention to the true range of what is involved—is still involved—in Modernism and Modernity. In that context Swinburne's aesthetic program, both theory and practice, is a great, neglected cultural and scholarly obligation.

## THE LIFE

In February 1875 the American poet and critic E. C. Stedman asked Swinburne for an account of his "birth and career." Swinburne was then the most celebrated (and excoriated) poet in England, and his fame on the Continent and the United States was equally broadcast.

The poet replied with a long letter—an impressive example of his marvelous prose and important as an index to the salient features of his life as he saw them or wanted them seen. The letter is a kind of midlife memoir written neither as an advertisement for himself nor as a scandalous confidence. For persons interested in Swinburne today, it should probably be read before any other account of the man. While the letter refers to Byron several times, Swinburne is aware that his is not, like Byron's, an eventful life. What concerns him are ideas, writing (poetry in particular), and issues of character (especially as these descend to him through his family). With quiet verve Swinburne declines any "Rousseau-like record of . . . emotions." As to important dates he simply remarks, "Knowing as you do the dates and sequence of my published books you know every event of my life." To this one might add only that Swinburne's unpublished work—much of it even yet unprinted—would also interest an interested person.

Swinburne did not wake on 16 July 1866—the day his *Poems and Ballads* appeared—to find himself instantly famous, as Byron had on the day *Childe Harold. A Romaunt* was issued in 1812. But the mixed blessing of his fame spread quickly from that day—from that book—forward. "A very great poet has arisen in England," the historian W. E. H. Lecky wrote to a cousin shortly after the book appeared. "All literary London is now ringing with [the book's] genius . . . blasphemies and indecencies." He became a wonder, a terror, and finally a catalyst for great social and cultural change. Ruskin's ambivalence is worth recalling: "For the matter of it—I consent to much—I regret much—I blame or reject nothing. I should as soon think of finding fault with you as with a thundercloud or a nightshade blossom. All I can say of you or them—is that God made you, and that you are very wonderful and beautiful. To me it may be dreadful or deadly—it may be in a deeper sense, or in certain relations, helpful and medicinal. There is assuredly something wrong with you—awful in proportion to the great powers it affects, and renders (nationally) at present useless."

Most readers troubled by the book had lost such power of reflection. The *London Review* called it "depressing and misbegotten—in many of its constituents . . . utterly revolting." The *Athenaeum*: "Unclean for the sake of uncleanness." The *Pall Mall Gazette*: "Mad . . . indecency." And so forth. Swinburne's publisher (Edward Moxon) was so frightened by the virulence of the abuse that he broke off publication and passed the copies on hand to John Camden Hotten, who brought out five more editions. (At that point, 1875, Swinburne turned to a new publisher, Chatto and Windus, who would reprint the book no fewer than forty times between 1875 and 1916.)

The scandalous success of *Poems and Ballads* is precisely the *text*onic center of "The Life of Algernon Charles Swinburne" both in its contemporary and in its posthumous unfolding. His life in letters was his life, as he told Stedman. But so shocking was the advent of this epochal book that it would come to obscure the range of Swinburne's work—a range so extensive that one can sometimes scarcely imagine how it came to be thought narrow or precious.

To many the book represented the best that was known and being thought in the world at that moment in history. William Michael Rossetti, that steady and sane radical, spoke this point of view better than most:

> Swinburne's superiority over his contemporary poets, with the sole possible exception of Tennyson . . . lie[s] in his mastery of all the literary or artistic resources of poetry. . . . As to blasphemy, Swinburne is certainly a pronounced antichristian, and something very closely resembling an atheist; I consider that he is right in entertaining these or any other speculative opinions which commend themselves to his own mind, and expressing them as freely as Christians, Mohammedans, etc., express their speculative or traditional opinions. As to indecency [I do not think] his writings are likely to do any practical harm to anybody fitted by taste and training to admire them.

The intensity of Swinburne's work does not encourage that kind of intellectual clarity, though in many respects it does assume it. In this respect—as in some others—Swinburne comes to his age as Jesus came to his, bringing not peace, but a sword. Unlike Rossetti, he took a mischievous delight in upending settled minds, as one sees in his superb comic, satiric, and parodic verse. Writing to Joseph Knight about the attack in the *Athenaeum,* Swinburne says, "I have exhausted myself with a quasi-venereal enjoyment of th[at] incomparable article." Rossetti wrote a judicious pamphlet in praise and defense of his friend, *Swinburne's Poems and Ballads*. Swinburne's reply, the unrepentant and derisory *Notes on Poems and Reviews*, simply institutionalized himself with his antagonists as the figure John Morley called "the libidinous laureate of a pack of satyrs."

Two other related sets of events pivoting around the year 1878 are also intrinsic to the mythology of Swinburne's life. In June 1879 Theodore Watts, (later Watts-Dunton), finding the poet in a desperate physical state, took him from his rooms in London to Watts's house in Putney. The action probably saved Swinburne's life. His health had been deteriorating for some years, largely from his reckless abuse of alcohol. Stories about his outrageous public behavior were circulating from the midsixties, and gossip carried further tales of moral depravity. Many of his friends and acquaintances were notorious characters themselves, like Richard Monckton-Milnes, the sophisticated collector of strange books and strange persons and the man who introduced Swinburne to the works of Sade. Rumor had it (correctly) that Swinburne liked to frequent a certain brothel in St. John's Wood where flagellation was a specialty of the house. Swinburne was, it seems, never the worse for these visits, but his drunkenness was another matter.

Contemporary scandal grew rife during the seventies and did much to convince a public mind that Swinburne was simply a diseased creature, body and soul. The disease took one form in Swinburne's writings and conversation, another in a disgraceful life, and the gathering set of scandalous events came to define the man and, through that definition, the work. To the practical friend and lawyer Watts, however, Swinburne in 1879 was simply in mortal physical danger from his alcoholism. So he took Swinburne to his house and initiated what would come to be known as the Putney years, which lasted till the poet's death in 1909. Admirers of Swinburne's work often bemoan the bland regimen that Watts installed for his friend over the next thirty years, but few doubt that he saved the poet from untimely death. If his gift of imagination after the early eighties shows a tailing off, as it does, the Putney years nonetheless produced a handful of marvelous and even innovative works, and they left Swinburne the opportunity to set his literary house in order, which he did when he carefully prepared his collected edition of the poems and plays (1904).

To study Swinburne's personal life is to study a soul that looms strange even today. Such investigations doubtless have use, though they can impede our view of Swinburne's literary and cultural significance. Yet two distinctively personal matters are important even in the latter context.

First, Swinburne had a capacity for ecstatic, physical sympathy with elemental nature. His love of swimming and especially of "the unplumbed, salt estranging sea" was boundless and it supplied him with a type of phenomenal awareness that is perhaps unique in English literature. Only Ovid and Lucretius have left us equivalent literary records of the infinite, majestic universe that quantum mechanics would shortly begin to explore in functional terms.

Second, Swinburne was a quick scholar and a refractory student. He never finished his schooling at Eton or Oxford. What Captain Harewood says to his son Reginald in Swinburne's remarkable novel *A Year's Letters* (written 1861–62) is brief and to the point: "You set at nought all guidance." His command of language, of many languages ancient and modern, was complete, and while he endured instruction in those quarters as a boy, he broke for independent study as quickly as he could.

In intellectual matters Swinburne frightened and appalled partly because he was so formidably armed for discussion and dispute and partly because he had, as everyone reports, a dauntless spirit. We want to remember that he set a face of flint against an immensely powerful ideological regime. Religion, in particular Christianity, dominated English society and culture in the nineteenth century, and England dominated the world. Those who chafed against these spiritual dominions hailed the lucid force of Swinburne's *non serviam*, which even yet has a majesty about it and continued importance. "Reckless and ungoverned" was the judgment of those who lacked his purpose "to follow knowledge like a sinking star/Beyond the utmost bound of human thought." He undertook that pursuit by plunge and engulfment. Knowing "at an inner standing-point" was how his friend Dante Gabriel Rossetti described this kind of intellectual discipline. To think and to write from that vantage entails—we see this clearly in Swinburne's writing—the near complete disappearance, absorption or extinction, of Romantic subjectivity. Swinburne's work is Romantic, but it is not subjective.

All of this impinges directly on Swinburne's writing and cultural significance, as T. S. Eliot understood. In 1920 Eliot published a brilliant and influential critique of Swinburne's poetry in order to exorcise the demon of Swinburne's "genius," which remained at that time a commonplace word to describe Swinburne. "Only a man of genius could dwell so exclusively and consistently among words as Swinburne," Eliot observed. But because "language in a healthy state presents the object, is so close to the object that the two are identified," Swinburne's language is astonishing but decadent: "merely the hallucination of meaning . . . , language . . . uprooted." A critical sleight of hand returns us to the diseased Swinburne, the affront to "current notions of decency and dignity and social duty." Those are Morley's words in 1866. But the health of culture is always in jeopardy from unheard melodies, and Swinburne was not a normal or ordinary poet. So against Swinburne's "morbidity of language" Eliot sets "the language which is most important to us [and] which is struggling to digest and express" itself in 1920. In our hindsight we have come to understand the language prized by Eliot as "High Modernism": that is to say, a Modernism as intent on purity as were the hostile reviewers of *Poems and Ballads*. Always a certain kind of purity. Gertrude Stein, key Modernist though she is, did not write in Eliot's language, and her case is far from a special one.

Eliot's essay is a reading of Swinburne's life very much in the same spirit that the author lived it. Eliot reads him, that is to say, for his cultural significance. It is a highly critical reading—as we should expect from a man who had his own (Anglo-Catholic) cultural program to promote. That was the center of his life.

The reading that may be most important to us now, however, at a new century's turn, is perhaps Henry Adams's reading. Adams met Swinburne in 1862 at one of Monkton Milnes's famous dinner parties. Milnes had just discovered Swinburne, who had to that point published only some undergraduate work, a book of verse plays, *The Queen Mother and Rosamund* (1860), and a few recent poems. No expectations, friendly or hostile, set Adams up for this encounter with the poet just coming into full command of his powers. Adams recounted the event in a book full of memorable passages and events, none more so than this one. Swinburne held the five dinner guests spellbound "far into the night, listening to the rush of [his] talk. In a long experience, before or after, no one ever approached it; yet one had heard accounts of the best talking of the time, and read accounts of talkers in all time, among the rest, of Voltaire, who seemed to approach nearest the pattern." Voltaire! How *could* Adams have seen the poet so clearly. Swinburne held forth with commentary and recitation, his own poetry as well as declamations of "a play of Sophocles or a play of Shakespeare, forward or backward, from end to beginning; or Dante, or Villon, or Victor Hugo." For Adams, it was like hearing a voice from "millions of ages" beyond them. The experience was a defining event for Adams and for *The Education of Henry Adams* as well. In Swinburne Adams saw that a human being might possess the kind of cultural power he glimpsed in Dynamo and Virgin. His sense of his own insignificance set a measure for what Swinburne represented: "Adams could no more interest Algernon Swinburne than he could interest Encke's comet. . . . The quality of genius was an education almost ultimate, for one touched there the limits of the human mind on that side; but one could only receive; one had nothing to give — nothing even to offer." The comment and reaction recall Ruskin's. More to the point, they reflect a central feature of Swinburne's greatest poetry, which is intense, overwhelming, and — as Eliot said — "impersonal." The work comes as if overtaken by some transhuman force, with the poet, in Swinburne's own words, "Now no more a singer but a song." Ruskin judged that in 1866 the voice could scarcely be heard, was "(nationally) quite useless." At the limit of the human mind, millions of ages beyond Ruskin and Adams. Swinburne's subjects no longer terrorize, however — "Thank Somebody," as he used to say. So the writing is there, unburdened, "free at last," and perhaps finally useful to tormented nations that long ago found a place for the tormented Ruskin.

## THE WRITING

Neither Eliot nor William Empson was so interested in the high artifice of a poetry like Swinburne's as they were in the artifices of sixteenth- and seventeenth-century English verse. Nonetheless, these two exemplary English Modernists understood the core features of Swinburne's work, though both warned people away from it because (Empson observed) "its effects depended on a tradition that its [own] example was destroying." He is speaking of the tradition of Metaphysical poetry. But as a long line of inheritors shows, Swinburne was for that tradition, as Shelley might have said, both "destroyer and preserver." When Eliot remarked upon the impersonal character of Swinburne's writing and its immersion in words and language as such, he was connecting Swinburne to a tradition that Veronica Forrest-Thomson would later recall and recast in her brilliant revisionary presentation of twentieth-century poetry, *Poetic Artifice*. Christina and Dante Gabriel Rossetti were also conscious practitioners of the same late nineteenth-century revival of a poetic artifice they derived, in great part, from a study of Dante,

Petrarch, and their circles — and in Swinburne's case, from the classical tradition that supported and the Elizabethan tradition that studied them. To Empson and Eliot these derivations seemed enervated and decadent. Late twentieth-century poets — formalists like James Merrill and John Hollander as well as experimental writers like J. H. Prynne, Charles Bernstein, Susan Howe, and Forrest-Thomson — take a very different view. For them, Swinburne in particular is decisively important, even a kind of touchstone.

"People are oddly determined to regard Swinburne as an exponent of Pure Sound with no intellectual content," Empson dryly remarked. But the truth is that "as a matter of technique" Swinburne "is full of subdued conceits and ambiguities," and "as a matter of content, his sensibility was of the intellectual sort which proceeds by a process of analysis." Empson is right on both counts, as he is also correct to suggest that Swinburne (like Byron, we might observe) inherited and honored a legacy that his own practice was putting through a metabolic shift.

To recover Empson's clarity we might begin with the most apparent of Swinburne's intellectual frames of reference: his large critical-historical analysis of Western culture. This analysis centers in a broad study of the cultural damage that followed upon the institutionalization of monotheist ideas and of Christian ideas in particular. Because Neo-Christianities define so much of Modernism, particularly academic Modernism, Swinburne represented a key ideological antithesis — and a special abhorrence because his views were so clearly articulated.

His Shelleyan/Hugolian thought is that poets are the unacknowledged legislators of the world. As such, they regularly stand in opposition to what St. Paul called the "thrones, principalities, powers, and dominions" that seek to control and rule the world. A paradoxical historical inversion turned the Church that Paul helped to establish into Western culture's governing ideological dominion.

This view of Christianity was shared alike by Blake, Marx, and Swinburne. But whereas Marx followed Hegel in seeking emancipation through the social enactment of enlightened thought, Swinburne pledged allegiance to Blake and aesthetic tradition, where forces of ideology could be most sharply engaged. Not without reason did he stake his philosophical ground in the enlightened action of Sade, Blake, and Byron — emancipators whose "sincerity and strength," as Swinburne remarked, are as much a function of their tragedies as of their triumphs and should always be understood in aesthetic terms. Both Sade and Byron lived legendary and (in Shelley's sense) Imaginative lives, of which their writings are in a sense the sacramental signs.

Poetry is the chief means for securing freedom (a talismanic Swinburnean word and idea) from forces that darken the spirit. Like Shelley, Swinburne constructs a history of the world through a recovery of its poetical touchstones. So he sees the period between the installation of official Christianity at Rome and the reemergence of classical, humanist, and even pagan culture in the Italian Renaissance as a long, dark age. The Borgias and Villon are thus exemplary historical figures, forecasting the humanist pagan renaissance that captured the imaginations of so many nineteenth-century Europeans: Heine, Hugo, Baudelaire, Wagner, Nietzsche, to name only the most prominent. Sade, Blake, and Byron are also key historical figures for Swinburne: recent prophets of a freedom they foresee but, because of their socio-ideological inheritances, cannot fully possess.

Sappho is pivotal for several reasons. Her historical position signifies that the humanist ideal is literally primal—the true Alpha and Omega that monotheists would later refashion as the Lord. The sexual translation of primal imagination from motherhood to fatherhood was as significant for Swinburne as the fragmentary condition of Sappho's poetical remains, left in tatters by the long Dark Age of Christian worship. Equally important was the shift of primal power from a mortal poet, Sappho, to an immaterial idea, God. For Swinburne (as for Blake), the worst consequence of Christianity was the substitution of institutional religion for individual imaginative life at the center of human social and interpersonal exchange. Swinburne regarded Blake's *The Marriage of Heaven and Hell* as the greatest poem of the eighteenth century in large part because it had recovered a core truth: that God did not make the world but that human beings "animated . . . sensible objects" as gods and divinities and later, literally benighted, fell down and worshiped their own imaginative creations. "Thus began Priesthood," as Blake observes, "Choosing forms of worship from poetic tales" (plate 11). Swinburne's remarkable study *William Blake* develops its theoretical polemic for poetry out of a complex meditation on those basic ideas.

While Swinburne's writing is fundamentally about writing, poetry, and language, then, as Eliot remarks, it could only be called "uprooted" in the specialized sense promoted by Eliot in works like *Christianity and Culture* and *Notes toward a Definition of Culture*. A poem like "Hertha" explicitly offers imaginative expression, including the poem's own expression, as "the tree many-rooted" that encompasses all of reality. Two features of poetry are especially crucial.

First are its Ovidian capacities for infinite metamorphic change and transformation. Poetry is what Humberto Maturana and Francesco Varela have more recently described as an autopoietic system—a living form that maintains itself by a continual process of self-extrusion. Poetry's reception history sets out the record of that process and is itself an essential part of the process. Swinburne's writing practice is thus "performative" of an autopoiesis whose "growth [has] no guerdon/But only to grow." The contemporary relevance of Swinburne's work springs from its intellectual affinities with a quantum mechanical model of reality, on one hand, and postmodern autopoietical ideas on the other.

Autopoietic processes develop through elaborate feedback loopings, of which self-awareness is the most complex and important. Poetry's second great feature, dialectically related to the first, lies in its ability to reflect on itself, as it were. For Swinburne, no other human activity commands this power so fully as poetic work. Poetry's special privilege lies in what his friend and fellow artist Dante Gabriel Rossetti called poetry's "motive power": its obligation to approach its subjects from an "inner standing-point." In that view, enlightenment and understanding do not stand upon the ceremonies of ultimate meanings and ideas (the weak point in science and philosophy); they turn upon themselves, being part of an emergent poetic process. Swinburne's critique of Christianity, like Sade's late enlightenment, is historically determinate.

This process of self-reflection has been traditionally marked by what we call the poet's intentions and the reader's interpretations. In Swinburne's view, because intention and interpretation are themselves momentary and transformational events, imaginative writing exposes itself to its own impersonal character. In Swinburne we observe a drama of poetic subjectivity diffusing into the language as such—a startling effect in his work (it is less so in Dante's) precisely because Swinburne consciously situates his writing in the historical afterlife of Romanticism. The conclusion to "Anactoria"—one of Swinburne's, and the nineteenth century's, greatest poems—explicitly argues and demonstrates this view of poetry.

This signature poem illustrates much that is characteristic of Swinburne's work. Like Rossetti, Swinburne brought his writing to maturity by radically modifying the dramatic monologue—a verse procedure that dominates his *Poems and Ballads* volume. The form possesses two salient properties: an immersive textual environment defined as the inner standing-point of the poetic speaker; a nonsubjective frame of reference. These features clear the poetic space for the reader, who is shifted slightly but significantly away from the kind of sympathetic encounter set up by the conventions of a Romantic poem.

Swinburne wanted to devise a more engulfing poetic space in which the three possible forms of poetic consciousness—authorial, readerly, and fictive—would gain their identities, paradoxically, by a process of regular loss and transformation. In "Anactoria," Sappho as dramatic speaker is the primary exponent of such a process through her desire for complete union with Anactoria. But in the poem's climax (lines 259–304) her ecstatic declaration reveals her personal desire to be an index or symbol of a world-encompassing union in which she too is absorbed. Sappho is swept up into her own vision of "memories," "metaphors," and a host of "travailing . . . New Things and old things" so that she can finally declare, "I Sappho shall be one with all these things." The future tense is crucial, collapsing as it does the space between the historical Sappho and this nineteenth-century resurrection poem in which her prophecy gets fulfilled and literalized.

Were this a traditional dramatic monologue, that literalizing process would abstract the poet from the poetic space and remove the reader to a position of judgment, a *spectator ab extra*—as we see in that exemplary example of the form, Browning's "My Last Duchess." An economy of sociopsychological realism organizes this poetic space. Swinburne prevents that from happening by breaking the spell of the realist convention and establishing the work in an order of what Marjorie Perloff has called *Radical Artifice*. The poem's tropic extravagance and "Pure Sound" are the most recognizable signs of this radical artifice. So too are the repetitive set of rhymes that control the poem. But two outstanding moments are particularly spell-breaking, at the realist order, and spellbinding at the order of artifice.

The most famous is lines 155–88, which were in fact not part of the poem as Swinburne originally wrote it. Often criticized as a gratuitous attack on Christianity, apt for Swinburne but out of character for Sappho, the passage is in fact a key poetic device for connecting Sappho to her nineteenth-century resurrection and inheritance. The passage is there to draw the (contemporary) reader into the poem's action, whether in sympathy or in horror does not matter. Like Sappho, the reader must become, this way or that, "one with all these things."

The other passage, even more remarkable, has yet (remarkably) never been commented upon. In a dazzling spectacle of prosodic wit, Swinburne fashions lines 47–58 as a kind of mirror image and repetition of the immediately preceding lines 35–46. (He repeated this kind of tour de force on a more grand scale in *Tristram of Lyonesse*, a poem that, he said, was written on the same principles worked out in "Anactoria.") Reading the poem, are we to think that the passage illustrates Sappho at the magical height of her powers? As Swinburne showing off? Either interpretation might be offered but both point toward a third that encompasses and transcends them. As in a sestina or other intricate poetic form, the lines suggest that language itself, as it were, possesses within itself an infinite capacity for mutation and transformation.

Accompanying this diffusion of poetic subjectivity into the energy field of the poem is a dissolution that threatens and challenges the reader as well. Readers mark their drunken passages through the verse as "Pure Sound"—a remorselessly self-involved prosodic spectacle. This response, while true in a sense, is impercipient. The work might better be viewed in terms of Arnold's comment on Shakespeare, so much admired by Swinburne: "Others abide our question, thou art free." Readers will look (in vain) for "meaning" if they believe that meanings should stay for readerly determinations. Swinburne's poetry regularly imitates life because, as in life, its meanings spread and mutate and transform under our own pursuit. Negotiating a poem by Swinburne requires a state of attention that can scarcely be maintained and that is, in any case, never sufficient. Even the simplest poems, like "The Garden of Proserpine," run away with us:

Here, where the world is quiet;
  Here, where all trouble seems
Dead winds' and spent waves' riot
  In doubtful dreams of dreams;
I watch the green field growing
For reaping folk and sowing,
For harvest-time and mowing,
  A sleepy world of streams.

The poem's rhythm, stately but inexorable, locates places and things that immediately prove "doubtful: "Here"? Where is that? Is it the Garden of Proserpine—

and if we take it so, what is that garden, and where is it: in Sicilian fields of Enna, in the kingdom of Hades, in Italy, in Greece? Perhaps it is here in this poem—or in poetry as such?—that we are to locate ourselves. And who is speaking, who is this "I"? Proserpine? "The poet" ("Swinburne"?)? Besides, if the referential dimensions of the verse slip through our minds, what of the syntax? "Riot" is marked primarily as a noun but the play of syntax and line-termination suggest it might have been—might still be—a verb. And what do we—what can we—make of those possibilities? The enjambment at "seems" is another syntactic multiplier. Or consider the cunning ambiguities in lines 5–7: are those green fields (what fields?) being worked by these "folk" or are the fields active agents, growing in order to sow and reap the folk who are working them? And what of such "folk," what do they know of these "doubtful dreams of dreams"? Are we (readers) to take those metadreams as poetry? This poem? And if we do, what good is it to know of such metadreams, to enter them? What good is it not to know or enter?

This text is relatively simple. Compared with, say, "Anactoria" it seems a mere piano exercise. Still, it exemplifies the all but intolerable demand made upon the reader by a typical Swinburne poem. To read him is to be reminded that a full awareness of even the simplest human experience is unachievable. One thinks of Blake: "If the doors of perception were cleansed, every thing would appear to man as it is: infinite" (plate 14).

Poetry is a machine for cleansing doors of perception. Swinburne is special not because he makes us acutely aware of, say, those "infinite mountains of light" perceived by the visionary Blake (*The Marriage of Heaven and Hell* plate 25), but because he makes a drama of our experience—our knowledge—of the apparition and evanishment of such phenomena. This drama involves curtailing the power of poetry's visual illusions—that special door of perception, the eye, that had itself become a stumbling block by dominating, even (as in Blake) defining, perceptual experience. An inner standing-point is difficult to access through language when the perception's doors are patrolled by the eyes. In language, accessing the world through the eye—what Pound called *phanopoiea*—is to hold it at some kind of reflective distance. Swinburne's poetry of course deploys visual imagination everywhere. But if visualization is the sensory foundation for intellectual reflection in verse, as it is, the other senses are far more immersive and unmediated. When Swinburne forces the reader to negotiate language through its tactility and sound, he is moving to enlarge our perceptual resources. To speak of his verse as "Pure Sound" is to register Swinburne's critique of the dominance that visual imagination had gained in poetic theory and practice.

That critique, along with the reforming practices entailed by it, is perhaps Swinburne's greatest legacy to poetic tradition. Wallace Stevens's *Harmonium* is in large measure a lesson learned from Swinburne. The eye in that splendid book has become a moving point in a turning world, as "Thirteen Ways of Looking at a Blackbird" shows. It moves because it has been distracted to greater awareness by a pervading sensorium of other senses and sounds. And so Stevens can say, explicitly, that the "Theory" of his book is this: "I am what is around me." That is pure Swinburne:

I the mark that is missed,
  And the arrows that miss,
I the mouth that is kissed,
  And the breath in the kiss,
The search, and the sought, and the seeker, the soul and the body that is.
  ("Hertha" 21–25)

Swinburne's late so-called nature poetry—works like "A Nympholept," "Neap-Tide," and "The Lake of Gaube"—exhibits this immersive imagination in unmistakable terms. These poems recall what later scholars have named the "Greater Romantic Lyric," but they recall to recast, for when Swinburne's eye/I enters the natural world it gets engulfed. In that experience one does not so much "see into the life of things" as one is seen through that pervading life, the way Beatrice is finally seen through the pervading light of Dante's Paradise.

The dissolution is scarcely to be observed, however, lest one imagine that it could be understood by being *seen*. It is understood, rather, by being undergone. To read these poems is necessarily to be swept away by tactile and auditional immediacies, which here assume the status of what Eliot famously called an objective correlative. The correlated object of the poem is elemental, "great creating Nature" as it is known not by a God-like observer but by a percipient creature plunged within. The Nature known is a quantum, not a Newtonian, Nature.

As demonstrative of Swinburne's work as those late poems are, his lighter verse, so-called, may be more enlightening. The preeminent Swinburne scholar Cecil Y. Lang regarded Swinburne as "the greatest parodist that English poetry has ever seen" (Lang, *Pre-Raphaelites and their Circle,* 519). There is more to this judgment than might immediately catch the eye since a great deal of Swinburne's work is clear parody. *Atalanta in Calydon*, for example, is a serious parody, as are most of the poems in *Poems and Ballads.* The parody "Dolores" is striking exactly because it balances so delicately (and forcefully) between earnest and jest.

But the parodies Lang had in mind were masterpieces like "The Higher Pantheism in a Nutshell," "Sonnet for a Picture," and "Nephelidia" (which Swinburne published in his famous *Heptalogia*) as well as several others not included there, like "Poeta Loquitur" and "Disgust. A Dramatic Monologue." All this is very high order nonsense verse, which Swinburne often also practiced in private: in his unpublished flagellation farces, for instance, and in impish *jeux d'esprit* like his "Fragment of an address from S. Joseph to S. Mary":

So *this* is your bloody religion—
To father your kid on a pigeon?

Brilliant wit pervades even this little epigram, which is quite worthy of what Byron mock-seriously called "all those nauseous epigrams of Martial" (*Don Juan,* I. st. 43). The couplet's domestic vulgate works the words "bloody," "kid" and "pigeon" into a critical travesty of the Christian economy and one of its central ideas: Jesus as sacrificial scapegoat.

Like "Dolores," "Poeta Loquitur" is parody raised to another order entirely. Great parody, Lang observed, does not involve simply a critique of its source. It becomes in a sense *one* with that source, in a fusion "like that of anti-matter to matter." The fusing culminates in Swinburne's self-parodies "Nephelidia" and "Poeta Loquitur," in which an authoritative idea about poetry—that it should achieve a perfect unity of sound and sense, of form and content—becomes comically realized. The consequence is an apparition of writing as pure performance, writing that seems—we remember Auden—to make nothing happen but itself. Playing that game with his language, Swinburne achieves what few poets would dare to (or know how to) undertake: a critical satire of poetry itself from an inner standing-point, that is, taking itself as exemplum. The theory of poetry motivated at an inner standing-point here discovers a kind of perfect form—at once completely expressive and completely self-aware. These works do not "dwell in possibility," as Dickinson splendidly imagined for herself; they dwell in an actuality Stevens celebrated and longed for. They demonstrate/argue/perform autopoietic action, they make *Nothing happen*: as Stevens once observed, "The nothing that is not there and the nothing that is."

Comic writing is alone equal to such an aspiration, as we know from Ovid and Rabelais, from Chaucer, from Byron—in our own day, from Ashbery, Merrill, Bernstein. Searching poems for their meanings, we often forget that in poetry, language is not a vehicle of reference but a figural gesture. To make that gesture is to give momentary form to a reality that persists "beyond the singing of the sea." The cunning prepositional wordplay in that famous line from Stevens could scarcely be more Swinburnean.

## NOTE ON THE TEXTS

The poet himself established authoritative texts for most of his poetical works when he carefully oversaw the publication of the 1904–5 Chatto and Windus edition of the *Poems* and the *Tragedies*. The texts of works printed there are reprinted here. ACS never collected his prose works, critical or imaginative. For prose works that ACS published in his lifetime, the texts here are taken from those publications. Because a good deal of ACS's work had been left unpublished at his death in 1909, Edmund Gosse and T. J. Wise published a series of posthumous books containing a large corpus of this unpublished prose and poetry, and in 1925–27 they included these works in their twenty-volume *Complete Works* (the Bonchurch Edition). Because the Gosse and Wise texts, including the texts in the

Bonchurch Edition, are notoriously unreliable, we have returned to the manuscripts for texts left unpublished by ACS, and we have proceeded in the same way, and for the same reasons, with Randolph Hughes's later editions of important unpublished material. We have, however, with his widow's permission, used the texts established by Cecil Y. Lang in his edition of the *Letters* and his *New Writings by Swinburne*.

—Jerome McGann

# CHRONOLOGY

1837 Born in London, 5 April, to Captain (later Admiral) Charles Henry Swinburne and Lady Jane Swinburne. Spends formative years swimming and riding at Bonchurch, his home on the Isle of Wight, and visiting other family seats at Capheaton, Northumberland, and Ashburnham Place, Sussex.

1849 Enters Eton. Takes refuge from schoolboy traumas by immersing himself in readings of Elizabethan dramatists, Sappho, Landor, and Hugo. Meets Wordsworth at Rydal Mount during family holiday to the Lakes.

1856–60 Attends Balliol College, Oxford. Studies Classics with Benjamin Jowett, who exerts a steadying influence over the young poet's impulsive nature. Helps to found Old Mortality society. Meets Edward Burne Jones, William Morris, and Dante Gabriel Rossetti in 1857, all then at work on the Arthurian frescoes for the Union Debating Hall. Provisionally withdraws from Oxford in 1859.

1860–61 Relocates to London. Associates with Richard Monckton-Milnes (later Lord Houghton), who shares his encyclopedic collection of erotica—including the works of de Sade—and provides introductions to Ruskin, Browning, and, fatefully, Captain Sir Richard Francis Burton. Publishes *The Queen Mother* and *Rosamund*.

1862 Death of Elizabeth Siddal, Rossetti's wife. Lodges with Rossetti at No. 16, Cheyne Walk, Chelsea. Reports of irregular behavior and heavy drinking alarm friends and family.

1863 Travels with James McNeil Whistler to Paris, where he meets Manet. Death of beloved sister, Edith. Intensification of relationship with cousin, Mary Gordon, to whom he reads choruses from *Atalanta in Calydon*.

1864 Travels through France with Monckton-Milnes, and is granted an audience with Landor while visiting Florence. Experiences distress when Mary Gordon announces engagement to Colonel Disney-Leith.

1865 Publishes *Atalanta in Calydon*, to widespread acclaim.

1866 Publishes *Poems and Ballads*. Breaks with his publisher, Moxon, over hostile reviews. Responds to critics with *Notes on Poems and Reviews*, published by Hotten.

1867 Introduced to his hero, Mazzini. Memorializes Baudelaire in "Ave atque Vale." At the suggestion of Rossetti and others, engages in affair with Adah Isaacs Mencken ("Dolores"), American poet, theatre performer, and social adventuress.

1868 Publishes *William Blake: A Critical Essay*.

1871 Publishes *Songs Before Sunrise*. Appearance of Robert Buchanan's attack on ACS and Rossetti, *The Fleshly School of Poetry*.

1872 Publishes *Under the Microscope*, his reply to Buchanan. Rossetti suffers breakdown and ends friendship.

1877 Death of Admiral Swinburne. Publishes *A Year's Letters* in serial form.

1878 Publishes *Poems and Ballads, Second Series*.

1879 Alcohol abuse reaches crisis point in June. Theodore Watts, solicitor and friend of the Rossettis, removes ACS to seclusion at his home, "The Pines," in Putney.

1880 Publishes *A Study of Shakespeare*, *Songs of the Springtides*, *Studies in Song*, and (anonymously) a book of parodies, *The Heptalogia, or The Seven Against Sense*.

1882 Publishes *Tristram of Lyonesse and Other Poems*. Death of Dante Gabriel Rossetti.

1892 Mentioned as potential Poet Laureate following death of Tennyson. Appointment opposed by Gladstone.

1896 Death of Lady Jane Swinburne.

1904 Publishes *A Channel Passage and Other Poems*. Collects and publishes poetry in six-volume edition of *Poems*.

1909 Dies of pneumonia, April 10, at Putney. Buried at Bonchurch, Isle of Wight.

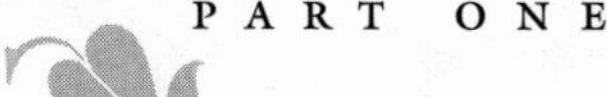

PART ONE

# *Poetry*

# ATALANTA IN CALYDON

## A Tragedy

*Τοὺς ζῶντας εὖ δρᾶν· κατθανὼν δὲ πᾶς ἀνὴρ*
*Γῆ καὶ σκιά· τὸ μηδὲν εἰς οὐδὲν ῥέπει*
*Eur.* Fr. Mel. *20 (537)*

TO THE MEMORY OF WALTER SAVAGE LANDOR I NOW DEDICATE, WITH EQUAL AFFECTION, REVERENCE, AND REGRET, A POEM INSCRIBED TO HIM WHILE YET ALIVE IN WORDS WHICH ARE NOW RETAINED BECAUSE THEY WERE LAID BEFORE HIM; AND TO WHICH, RATHER THAN CANCEL THEM, I HAVE ADDED SUCH OTHERS AS WERE EVOKED BY THE NEWS OF HIS DEATH: THAT THOUGH LOSING THE PLEASURE I MAY NOT LOSE THE HONOUR OF INSCRIBING IN FRONT OF MY WORK THE HIGHEST OF CONTEMPORARY NAMES.

*THE ARGUMENT*

*Althæa, daughter of Thestius and Eurythemis, queen of Calydon, being with child of Meleager her first-born son, dreamed that she brought forth a brand burning; and upon his birth came the three Fates and prophesied of him three things, namely these; that he should have great strength of his hands, and good fortune in this life, and that he should live no longer when the brand then in the fire were consumed: wherefore his mother plucked it forth and kept it by her. And the child being a man grown sailed with Jason after the fleece of gold, and won himself great praise of all men living; and when the tribes of the north and west made war upon Ætolia, he fought against their army and scattered it. But Artemis, having at the first stirred up these tribes to war against OEneus king of Calydon, because he had offered sacrifice to all the gods saving her alone, but her he had forgotten to honour, was yet more wroth because of the destruction of this army, and sent upon the land of Calydon a wild boar which slew many and wasted all their increase, but him could none slay, and many went against him and perished. Then were all the chief men of Greece gathered together, and among them Atalanta daughter of Iasius the Arcadian, a virgin; for whose sake Artemis let slay the boar, seeing she favoured the maiden greatly; and Meleager having despatched it gave the spoil thereof to Atalanta, as one beyond measure enamoured of her; but the brethren of Althæa his mother, Toxeus and Plexippus, with such others as misliked that she only should bear off the praise whereas many had borne the labour, laid wait for her to take away her spoil; but Meleager fought against them and slew them: whom when Althæa their sister beheld and knew to be slain of her son, she waxed for wrath and sorrow like as one mad, and taking the brand whereby the measure of her son's life was meted to him, she cast it upon a fire; and with the wasting thereof his life likewise wasted away, that being brought back to his father's house he died in a brief space; and his mother also endured not long after for very sorrow; and this was his end, and the end of that hunting.*

ὶστω δ̓ ὅστις οὐχ ὑπόπερος
φροντίσιν δαεὶς,
τὰν ά παιδολύμας τάλαινα θεστιὰς μήσατο
πυρδαῆ τινα πρόνοιαν,
καταίθουςα παιδὸς δαφοινὸν
δαλὸν ήλικ᾽, έπεὶ μολὼν
χατρόθεν κελάδησε;
σύμμετρόν τε διαὶ βίου
μοιρόκραντον ὲς άμαρ.

Æsch. *Cho.* 602–12

THE PERSONS

*CHIEF HUNTSMAN*
*CHORUS*
*ALTHÆA*
*MELEAGER*
*OENEUS*
*ATALANTA*
*TOXEUS*
*PLEXIPPUS*
*HERALD*
*MESSENGER*
*SECOND MESSENGER*

*CHIEF HUNTSMAN*

Maiden, and mistress of the months and stars
Now folded in the flowerless fields of heaven,
Goddess whom all gods love with threefold heart,
Being treble in thy divided deity,
A light for dead men and dark hours, a foot
Swift on the hills as morning, and a hand
To all things fierce and fleet that roar and range

Mortal, with gentler shafts than snow or sleep;
Hear now and help and lift no violent hand,
But favourable and fair as thine eye's beam
Hidden and shown in heaven; for I all night
Amid the king's hounds and the hunting men
Have wrought and worshipped toward thee; nor shall man
See goodlier hounds or deadlier edge of spears;
But for the end, that lies unreached at yet
Between the hands and on the knees of gods.
O fair-faced sun, killing the stars and dews
And dreams and desolation of the night!
Rise up, shine, stretch thine hand out, with thy bow
Touch the most dimmest height of trembling heaven,
And burn and break the dark about thy ways,
Shot through and through with arrows; let thine hair
Lighten as flame above that flameless shell
Which was the moon, and thine eyes fill the world
And thy lips kindle with swift beams; let earth
Laugh, and the long sea fiery from thy feet
Through all the roar and ripple of streaming springs
And foam in reddening flakes and flying flowers
Shaken from hands and blown from lips of nymphs
Whose hair or breast divides the wandering wave
With salt close tresses cleaving lock to lock,
All gold, or shuddering and unfurrowed snow;
And all the winds about thee with their wings,
And fountain-heads of all the watered world;
Each horn of Acheloüs, and the green
Euenus, wedded with the straitening sea.
For in fair time thou comest; come also thou,
Twin-born with him, and virgin, Artemis,
And give our spears their spoil, the wild boar's hide,
Sent in thine anger against us for sin done
And bloodless altars without wine or fire.
Him now consume thou; for thy sacrifice
With sanguine-shining steam divides the dawn,
And one, the maiden rose of all thy maids,
Arcadian Atalanta, snowy-souled,
Fair as the snow and footed as the wind,
From Ladon and well-wooded Mænalus
Over the firm hills and the fleeting sea
Hast thou drawn hither, and many an armed king,
Heroes, the crown of men, like gods in fight.

Moreover out of all the Ætolian land,
From the full-flowered Lelantian pasturage
To what of fruitful field the son of Zeus
Won from the roaring river and labouring sea
When the wild god shrank in his horn and fled
And foamed and lessened through his wrathful fords
Leaving clear lands that steamed with sudden sun,
These virgins with the lightening of the day
Bring thee fresh wreaths and their own sweeter hair,
Luxurious locks and flower-like mixed with flowers,
Clean offering, and chaste hymns; but me the time
Divides from these things; whom do thou not less
Help and give honour, and to mine hounds good speed,
And edge to spears, and luck to each man's hand.

*CHORUS*

When the hounds of spring are on winter's traces,
The mother of months in meadow or plain
Fills the shadows and windy places
With lisp of leaves and ripple of rain;
And the brown bright nightingale amorous
Is half assuaged for Itylus,
For the Thracian ships and the foreign faces,
The tongueless vigil, and all the pain.

Come with bows bent and with emptying of quivers,
Maiden most perfect, lady of light,
With a noise of winds and many rivers,
With a clamour of waters, and with might;
Bind on thy sandals, O thou most fleet,
Over the splendour and speed of thy feet;
For the faint east quickens, the wan west shivers,
Round the feet of the day and the feet of the night.

Where shall we find her, how shall we sing to her,
Fold our hands round her knees, and cling?
O that man's heart were as fire and could spring to her,
Fire, or the strength of the streams that spring!
For the stars and the winds are unto her
As raiment, as songs of the harp-player;
For the risen stars and the fallen cling to her,
And the southwest-wind and the west-wind sing.

For winter's rains and ruins are over,
And all the season of snows and sins;

The days dividing lover and lover,
  The light that loses, the night that wins;
And time remembered is grief forgotten,
And frosts are slain and flowers begotten,
And in green underwood and cover
  Blossom by blossom the spring begins.

The full streams feed on flower of rushes,
  Ripe grasses trammel a travelling foot,
The faint fresh flame of the young year flushes
  From leaf to flower and flower to fruit;
And fruit and leaf are as gold and fire,
And the oat is heard above the lyre,
And the hoofèd heel of a satyr crushes
  The chestnut-husk at the chestnut-root.

And Pan by noon and Bacchus by night,
  Fleeter of foot than the fleet-foot kid,
Follows with dancing and fills with delight
  The Mænad and the Bassarid;
And soft as lips that laugh and hide
The laughing leaves of the trees divide,
And screen from seeing and leave in sight
  The god pursuing, the maiden hid.

The ivy falls with the Bacchanal's hair
  Over her eyebrows hiding her eyes;
The wild vine slipping down leaves bare
  Her bright breast shortening into sighs;
The wild vine slips with the weight of its leaves,
But the berried ivy catches and cleaves
To the limbs that glitter, the feet that scare
  The wolf that follows, the fawn that flies.

*ALTHÆA*
What do ye singing? what is this ye sing?

*CHORUS*
Flowers bring we, and pure lips that please the gods,
And raiment meet for service: lest the day
Turn sharp with all its honey in our lips.

*ALTHÆA*
Night, a black hound, follows the white fawn day,
Swifter than dreams the white flown feet of sleep;
Will ye pray back the night with any prayers?

And though the spring put back a little while
Winter, and snows that plague all men for sin,
And the iron time of cursing, yet I know
Spring shall be ruined with the rain, and storm
Eat up like fire the ashen autumn days.
I marvel what men do with prayers awake
Who dream and die with dreaming; any god,
Yea the least god of all things called divine,
Is more than sleep and waking; yet we say,
Perchance by praying a man shall match his god.
For if sleep have no mercy, and man's dreams
Bite to the blood and burn into the bone,
What shall this man do waking? By the gods,
He shall not pray to dream sweet things to-night,
Having dreamt once more bitter things than death.

*CHORUS*
Queen, but what is it that hath burnt thine heart?
For thy speech flickers like a blown-out flame.

*ALTHÆA*
Look, ye say well, and know not what ye say;
For all my sleep is turned into a fire,
And all my dreams to stuff that kindles it.

*CHORUS*
Yet one doth well being patient of the gods.

*ALTHÆA*
Yea, lest they smite us with some four-foot plague.

*CHORUS*
But when time spreads find out some herb for it.

*ALTHÆA*
And with their healing herbs infect our blood.

*CHORUS*
What ails thee to be jealous of their ways?

*ALTHÆA*
What if they give us poisonous drinks for wine?

*CHORUS*
They have their will; much talking mends it not.

*ALTHÆA*
And gall for milk, and cursing for a prayer?

*CHORUS*
Have they not given life, and the end of life?

*ALTHÆA*
Lo, where they heal, they help not; thus they do,
They mock us with a little piteousness,
And we say prayers, and weep; but at the last,
Sparing awhile, they smite and spare no whit.

*CHORUS*
Small praise man gets dispraising the high gods:
What have they done that thou dishonourest them?

*ALTHÆA*
First Artemis for all this harried land
I praise not, and for wasting of the boar
That mars with tooth and tusk and fiery feet
Green pasturage and the grace of standing corn
And meadow and marsh with springs and unblown leaves,
Flocks and swift herds and all that bite sweet grass,
I praise her not; what things are these to praise?

*CHORUS*
But when the king did sacrifice, and gave
Each god fair dues of wheat and blood and wine,
Her not with bloodshed nor burnt-offering
Revered he, nor with salt or cloven cake;
Wherefore being wroth she plagued the land; but now
Takes off from us fate and her heavy things.
Which deed of these twain were not good to praise?
For a just deed looks always either way
With blameless eyes, and mercy is no fault.

*ALTHÆA*
Yea, but a curse she hath sent above all these
To hurt us where she healed us; and hath lit
Fire where the old fire went out, and where the wind
Slackened, hath blown on us with deadlier air.

*CHORUS*
What storm is this that tightens all our sail?

*ALTHÆA*
Love, a thwart sea-wind full of rain and foam.

*CHORUS*
Whence blown, and born under what stormier star?

*ALTHÆA*
Southward across Euenus from the sea.

*CHORUS*
Thy speech turns toward Arcadia like blown wind.

*ALTHÆA*
Sharp as the north sets when the snows are out.

*CHORUS*
Nay, for this maiden hath no touch of love.

*ALTHÆA*
I would she had sought in some cold gulf of sea
Love, or in dens where strange beasts lurk, or fire,
Or snows on the extreme hills, or iron land
Where no spring is; I would she had sought therein
And found, or ever love had found her here.

*CHORUS*
She is holier than all holy days or things,
The sprinkled water or fume of perfect fire;
Chaste, dedicated to pure prayers, and filled
With higher thoughts than heaven; a maiden clean,
Pure iron, fashioned for a sword; and man
She loves not; what should one such do with love?

*ALTHÆA*
Look you, I speak not as one light of wit,
But as a queen speaks, being heart-vexed; for oft
I hear my brothers wrangling in mid hall,
And am not moved; and my son chiding them,
And these things nowise move me, but I know
Foolish and wise men must be to the end,
And feed myself with patience; but this most,
This moves me, that for wise men as for fools
Love is one thing, an evil thing, and turns
Choice words and wisdom into fire and air.
And in the end shall no joy come, but grief,
Sharp words and soul's division and fresh tears
Flower-wise upon the old root of tears brought forth,
Fruit-wise upon the old flower of tears sprung up,
Pitiful sighs, and much regrafted pain.
These things are in my presage, and myself
Am part of them and know not; but in dreams
The gods are heavy on me, and all the fates

Shed fire across my eyelids mixed with night,
And burn me blind, and disilluminate
My sense of seeing, and my perspicuous soul
Darken with vision; seeing I see not, hear
And hearing am not holpen, but mine eyes
Stain many tender broideries in the bed
Drawn up about my face that I may weep
And the king wake not; and my brows and lips
Tremble and sob in sleeping, like swift flames
That tremble, or water when it sobs with heat
Kindled from under; and my tears fill my breast
And speck the fair dyed pillows round the king
With barren showers and salter than the sea,
Such dreams divide me dreaming; for long since
I dreamed that out of this my womb had sprung
Fire and a firebrand; this was ere my son,
Meleager, a goodly flower in fields of fight,
Felt the light touch him coming forth, and wailed
Childlike; but yet he was not; and in time
I bare him, and my heart was great; for yet
So royally was never strong man born,
Nor queen so nobly bore as noble a thing
As this my son was: such a birth God sent
And such a grace to bear it. Then came in
Three weaving women, and span each a thread,
Saying This for strength and That for luck, and one
Saying Till the brand upon the hearth burn down,
So long shall this man see good days and live.
And I with gathered raiment from the bed
Sprang, and drew forth the brand, and cast on it
Water, and trod the flame bare-foot, and crushed
With naked hand spark beaten out of spark
And blew against and quenched it; for I said,
These are the most high Fates that dwell with us,
And we find favour a little in their sight,
A little, and more we miss of, and much time
Foils us; howbeit they have pitied me, O son,
And thee most piteous, thee a tenderer thing
Than any flower of fleshly seed alive.
Wherefore I kissed and hid him with my hands,
And covered under arms and hair, and wept,
And feared to touch him with my tears, and laughed;
So light a thing was this man, grown so great

Men cast their heads back, seeing against the sun
Blaze the armed man carven on his shield, and hear
The laughter of little bells along the brace
Ring, as birds singing or flutes blown, and watch,
High up, the cloven shadow of either plume
Divide the bright light of the brass, and make
His helmet as a windy and wintering moon
Seen through blown cloud and plume-like drift, when ships
Drive, and men strive with all the sea, and oars
Break, and the beaks dip under, drinking death;
Yet was he then but a span long, and moaned
With inarticulate mouth inseparate words,
And with blind lips and fingers wrung my breast
Hard, and thrust out with foolish hands and feet,
Murmuring; but those grey women with bound hair
Who fright the gods frighted not him; he laughed
Seeing them, and pushed out hands to feel and haul
Distaff and thread, intangible; but they
Passed, and I hid the brand, and in my heart
Laughed likewise, having all my will of heaven.
But now I know not if to left or right
The gods have drawn us hither; for again
I dreamt, and saw the black brand burst on fire
As a branch bursts in flower, and saw the flame
Fade flower-wise, and Death came and with dry lips
Blew the charred ash into my breast; and Love
Trampled the ember and crushed it with swift feet.
This I have also at heart; that not for me,
Not for me only or son of mine, O girls,
The gods have wrought life, and desire of life,
Heart's love and heart's division; but for all
There shines one sun and one wind blows till night.
And when night comes the wind sinks and the sun,
And there is no light after, and no storm,
But sleep and much forgetfulness of things.
In such wise I gat knowledge of the gods
Years hence, and heard high sayings of one most wise,
Eurythemis my mother, who beheld
With eyes alive and spake with lips of these
As one on earth disfleshed and disallied
From breath or blood corruptible; such gifts
Time gave her, and an equal soul to these
And equal face to all things; thus she said.

But whatsoever intolerable or glad
The swift hours weave and unweave, I go hence
Full of mine own soul, perfect of myself,
Toward mine and me sufficient; and what chance
The gods cast lots for and shake out on us,
That shall we take, and that much bear withal.
And now, before these gather to the hunt,
I will go arm my son and bring him forth,
Lest love or some man's anger work him harm.

*CHORUS*

Before the beginning of years
   There came to the making of man
Time, with a gift of tears;
   Grief, with a glass that ran;
Pleasure, with pain for leaven;
   Summer, with flowers that fell;
Remembrance fallen from heaven,
   And madness risen from hell;
Strength without hands to smite;
   Love that endures for a breath:
Night, the shadow of light,
   And life, the shadow of death.

And the high gods took in hand
   Fire, and the falling of tears,
And a measure of sliding sand
   From under the feet of the years;
And froth and drift of the sea;
   And dust of the labouring earth;
And bodies of things to be
   In the houses of death and of birth;
And wrought with weeping and laughter,
   And fashioned with loathing and love,
With life before and after
   And death beneath and above,
For a day and a night and a morrow,
   That his strength might endure for a span
With travail and heavy sorrow,
   The holy spirit of man.

From the winds of the north and the south
   They gathered as unto strife;
They breathed upon his mouth,
   They filled his body with life;

Eyesight and speech they wrought
   For the veils of the soul therein,
A time for labour and thought,
   A time to serve and to sin;
They gave him light in his ways,
   And love, and a space for delight,
And beauty and length of days,
   And night, and sleep in the night.
His speech is a burning fire;
   With his lips he travaileth;
In his heart is a blind desire,
   In his eyes foreknowledge of death;
He weaves, and is clothed with derision;
   Sows, and he shall not reap;
His life is a watch or a vision
   Between a sleep and a sleep.

*MELEAGER*

O sweet new heaven and air without a star,
Fair day, be fair and welcome, as to men
With deeds to do and praise to pluck from thee.
Come forth a child, born with clear sound and light,
With laughter and swift limbs and prosperous looks;
That this great hunt with heroes for the hounds
May leave thee memorable and us well sped.

*ALTHÆA*

Son, first I praise thy prayer, then bid thee speed;
But the gods hear men's hands before their lips,
And heed beyond all crying and sacrifice
Light of things done and noise of labouring men.
But thou, being armed and perfect for the deed,
Abide; for like rain-flakes in a wind they grow,
The men thy fellows, and the choice of the world,
Bound to root out the tuskèd plague, and leave
Thanks and safe days and peace in Calydon.

*MELEAGER*

For the whole city and all the low-lying land
Flames, and the soft air sounds with them that come;
The gods give all these fruit of all their works.

*ALTHÆA*

Set thine eye thither and fix thy spirit and say
Whom there thou knowest; for sharp mixed shadow and wind
Blown up between the morning and the mist,

With steam of steeds and flash of bridle or wheel,
And fire, and parcels of the broken dawn,
And dust divided by hard light, and spears
That shine and shift as the edge of wild beasts' eyes,
Smite upon mine; so fiery their blind edge
Burns, and bright points break up and baffle day.

*MELEAGER*
The first, for many I know not, being far off,
Peleus the Larissæan, couched with whom
Sleeps the white sea-bred wife and silver-shod,
Fair as fled foam, a goddess; and their son
Most swift and splendid of men's children born,
Most like a god, full of the future fame.

*ALTHÆA*
Who are these shining like one sundered star?

*MELEAGER*
Thy sister's sons, a double flower of men.

*ALTHÆA*
O sweetest kin to me in all the world,
O twin-born blood of Leda, gracious heads
Like kindled lights in untempestuous heaven,
Fair flower-like stars on the iron foam of fight,
With what glad heart and kindliness of soul,
Even to the staining of both eyes with tears
And kindling of warm eyelids with desire,
A great way off I greet you, and rejoice
Seeing you so fair, and moulded like as gods.
Far off ye come, and least in years of these,
But lordliest, but worth love to look upon.

*MELEAGER*
Even such (for sailing hither I saw far hence,
And where Eurotas hollows his moist rock
Nigh Sparta with a strenuous-hearted stream)
Even such I saw their sisters; one swan-white,
The little Helen, and less fair than she
Fair Clytæmnestra, grave as pasturing fawns
Who feed and fear some arrow; but at whiles,
As one smitten with love or wrung with joy,
She laughs and lightens with her eyes, and then
Weeps; whereat Helen, having laughed, weeps too,
And the other chides her, and she being chid speaks nought,

But cheeks and lips and eyelids kisses her,
Laughing; so fare they, as in their bloomless bud
And full of unblown life, the blood of gods.

*ALTHÆA*
Sweet days befall them and good loves and lords,
And tender and temperate honours of the hearth,
Peace, and a perfect life and blameless bed.
But who shows next an eagle wrought in gold,
That flames and beats broad wings against the sun
And with void mouth gapes after emptier prey?

*MELEAGER*
Know by that sign the reign of Telamon
Between the fierce mouths of the encountering brine
On the strait reefs of twice-washed Salamis.

*ALTHÆA*
For like one great of hand he bears himself,
Vine-chapleted, with savours of the sea,
Glittering as wine and moving as a wave.
But who girt round there roughly follows him?

*MELEAGER*
Ancæus, great of hand, an iron bulk,
Two-edged for fight as the axe against his arm,
Who drives against the surge of stormy spears
Full-sailed; him Cepheus follows, his twin-born,
Chief name next his of all Arcadian men.

*ALTHÆA*
Praise be with men abroad; chaste lives with us,
Home-keeping days and household reverences.

*MELEAGER*
Next by the left unsandalled foot know thou
The sail and oar of this Ætolian land,
Thy brethren, Toxeus and the violent-souled
Plexippus, over-swift with hand and tongue;
For hands are fruitful, but the ignorant mouth
Blows and corrupts their work with barren breath.

*ALTHÆA*
Speech too bears fruit, being worthy; and air blows down
Things poisonous, and high-seated violences,
And with charmed words and songs have men put out
Wild evil, and the fire of tyrannies.

*MELEAGER*
Yea, all things have they, save the gods and love.

*ALTHÆA*
Love thou the law and cleave to things ordained.

*MELEAGER*
Law lives upon their lips whom these applaud.

*ALTHÆA*
How sayest thou these? what god applauds new things?

*MELEAGER*
Zeus, who hath fear and custom under foot.

*ALTHÆA*
But loves not laws thrown down and lives awry.

*MELEAGER*
Yet is not less himself than his own law.

*ALTHÆA*
Nor shifts and shuffles old things up and down.

*MELEAGER*
But what he will remoulds and discreates.

*ALTHÆA*
Much, but not this, that each thing live its life.

*MELEAGER*
Nor only live, but lighten and lift up higher.

*ALTHÆA*
Pride breaks itself, and too much gained is gone.

*MELEAGER*
Things gained are gone, but great things done endure.

*ALTHÆA*
Child, if a man serve law through all his life
And with his whole heart worship, him all gods
Praise; but who loves it only with his lips,
And not in heart and deed desiring it
Hides a perverse will with obsequious words,
Him heaven infatuates and his twin-born fate
Tracks, and gains on him, scenting sins far off,
And the swift hounds of violent death devour.
Be man at one with equal-minded gods,
So shall he prosper; not through laws torn up,

Violated rule and a new face of things.
A woman armed makes war upon herself,
Unwomanlike, and treads down use and wont
And the sweet common honour that she hath,
Love, and the cry of children, and the hand
Trothplight and mutual mouth of marriages.
This doth she, being unloved; whom if one love,
Not fire nor iron and the wide-mouthed wars
Are deadlier than her lips or braided hair.
For of the one comes poison, and a curse
Falls from the other and burns the lives of men.
But thou, son, be not filled with evil dreams,
Nor with desire of these things; for with time
Blind love burns out; but if one feed it full
Till some discolouring stain dyes all his life,
He shall keep nothing praiseworthy, nor die
The sweet wise death of old men honourable,
Who have lived out all the length of all their years
Blameless, and seen well-pleased the face of gods,
And without shame and without fear have wrought
Things memorable, and while their days held out
In sight of all men and the sun's great light
Have gat them glory and given of their own praise
To the earth that bare them and the day that bred,
Home friends and far-off hospitalities,
And filled with gracious and memorial fame
Lands loved of summer or washed by violent seas,
Towns populous and many unfooted ways,
And alien lips and native with their own.
But when white age and venerable death
Mow down the strength and life within their limbs,
Drain out the blood and darken their clear eyes,
Immortal honour is on them, having past
Through splendid life and death desirable
To the clear seat and remote throne of souls,
Lands indiscoverable in the unheard-of west,
Round which the strong stream of a sacred sea
Rolls without wind for ever, and the snow
There shows not her white wings and windy feet,
Nor thunder nor swift rain saith anything,
Nor the sun burns, but all things rest and thrive;
And these, filled full of days, divine and dead,
Sages and singers fiery from the god,

And such as loved their land and all things good
And, best beloved of best men, liberty,
Free lives and lips, free hands of men free-born,
And whatsoever on earth was honourable
And whosoever of all the ephemeral seed,
Live there a life no liker to the gods
But nearer than their life of terrene days.
Love thou such life and look for such a death.
But from the light and fiery dreams of love
Spring heavy sorrows and a sleepless life,
Visions not dreams, whose lids no charm shall close
Nor song assuage them waking; and swift death
Crushes with sterile feet the unripening ear,
Treads out the timeless vintage; whom do thou
Eschewing embrace the luck of this thy life,
Not without honour; and it shall bear to thee
Such fruit as men reap from spent hours and wear,
Few men, but happy; of whom be thou, O son,
Happiest, if thou submit thy soul to fate,
And set thine eyes and heart on hopes high-born
And divine deeds and abstinence divine.
So shalt thou be toward all men all thy days
As light and might communicable, and burn
From heaven among the stars above the hours,
And break not as a man breaks nor burn down:
For to whom other of all heroic names
Have the gods given his life in hand as thine?
And gloriously hast thou lived, and made thy life
To me that bare thee and to all men born
Thankworthy, a praise for ever; and hast won fame
When wild wars broke all round thy father's house,
And the mad people of windy mountain ways
Laid spears against us like a sea, and all
Ætolia thundered with Thessalian hoofs;
Yet these, as wind baffles the foam, and beats
Straight back the relaxed ripple, didst thou break
And loosen all their lances, till undone
And man from man they fell; for ye twain stood
God against god, Ares and Artemis,
And thou the mightier; wherefore she unleashed
A sharp-toothed curse thou too shalt overcome;
For in the greener blossom of thy life
Ere the full blade caught flower, and when time gave

Respite, thou didst not slacken soul nor sleep,
But with great hand and heart seek praise of men
Out of sharp straits and many a grievous thing,
Seeing the strange foam of undivided seas
On channels never sailed in, and by shores
Where the old winds cease not blowing, and all the night
Thunders, and day is no delight to men.

*CHORUS*

Meleager, a noble wisdom and fair words
The gods have given this woman; hear thou these.

*MELEAGER*

O mother, I am not fain to strive in speech
Nor set my mouth against thee, who art wise
Even as they say and full of sacred words.
But one thing I know surely, and cleave to this;
That though I be not subtle of wit as thou
Nor womanlike to weave sweet words, and melt
Mutable minds of wise men as with fire,
I too, doing justly and reverencing the gods,
Shall not want wit to see what things be right.
For whom they love and whom reject, being gods,
There is no man but seeth, and in good time
Submits himself, refraining all his heart.
And I too as thou sayest have seen great things;
Seen otherwhere, but chiefly when the sail
First caught between stretched ropes the roaring west,
And all our oars smote eastward, and the wind
First flung round faces of seafaring men
White splendid snow-flakes of the sundering foam,
And the first furrow in virginal green sea
Followed the plunging ploughshare of hewn pine,
And closed, as when deep sleep subdues man's breath
Lips close and heart subsides; and closing, shone
Sunlike with many a Nereid's hair, and moved
Round many a trembling mouth of doubtful gods,
Risen out of sunless and sonorous gulfs
Through waning water and into shallow light,
That watched us; and when flying the dove was snared
As with men's hands, but we shot after and sped
Clear through the irremeable Symplegades;
And chiefliest when hoar beach and herbless cliff
Stood out ahead from Colchis, and we heard

Clefts hoarse with wind, and saw through narrowing reefs
The lightning of the intolerable wave
Flash, and the white wet flame of breakers burn
Far under a kindling south-wind, as a lamp
Burns and bends all its blowing flame one way;
Wild heights untravelled of the wind, and vales
Cloven seaward by their violent streams, and white
With bitter flowers and bright salt scurf of brine;
Heard sweep their sharp swift gales, and bowing birdwise
Shriek with birds' voices, and with furious feet
Tread loose the long skirts of a storm; and saw
The whole white Euxine clash together and fall
Full-mouthed, and thunderous from a thousand throats:
Yet we drew thither and won the fleece and won
Medea, deadlier than the sea; but there
Seeing many a wonder and fearful things to men
I saw not one thing like this one seen here,
Most fair and fearful, feminine, a god,
Faultless; whom I that love not, being unlike,
Fear, and give honour, and choose from all the gods.

*OENEUS*

Lady, the daughter of Thestius, and thou, son,
Not ignorant of your strife nor light of wit,
Scared with vain dreams and fluttering like spent fire,
I come to judge between you, but a king
Full of past days and wise from years endured.
Nor thee I praise, who art fain to undo things done:
Nor thee, who art swift to esteem them overmuch.
For what the hours have given is given, and this
Changeless; howbeit these change, and in good time
Devise new things and good, not one thing still.
Us have they sent now at our need for help
Among men armed a woman, foreign born,
Virgin, not like the natural flower of things
That grows and bears and brings forth fruit and dies;
Unlovable, no light for a husband's house,
Espoused; a glory among unwedded girls,
And chosen of gods who reverence maidenhood.
These too we honour in honouring her; but thou,
Abstain thy feet from following, and thine eyes
From amorous touch; nor set toward hers thine heart,
Son, lest hate bear no deadlier fruit than love.

*ALTHÆA*

O king, thou art wise, but wisdom halts; and just,
But the gods love not justice more than fate,
And smite the righteous and the violent mouth,
And mix with insolent blood the reverent man's,
And bruise the holier as the lying lips.
Enough; for wise words fail me, and my heart
Takes fire and trembles flamewise, O my son,
O child, for thine head's sake; mine eyes wax thick,
Turning toward thee, so goodly a weaponed man,
So glorious; and for love of thine own eyes
They are darkened, and tears burn them, fierce as fire,
And my lips pause and my soul sinks with love.
But by thine hand, by thy sweet life and eyes,
By thy great heart and these clasped knees, O son,
I pray thee that thou slay me not with thee.
For there was never a mother woman-born
Loved her sons better; and never a queen of men
More perfect in her heart toward whom she loved.
For what lies light on many and they forget,
Small things and transitory as a wind o' the sea,
I forget never; I have seen thee all thine years
A man in arms, strong and a joy to men
Seeing thine head glitter and thine hand burn its way
Through a heavy and iron furrow of sundering spears;
But always also a flower of three suns old,
The small one thing that lying drew down my life
To lie with thee and feed thee; a child and weak,
Mine, a delight to no man, sweet to me.
Who then sought to thee? who gat help? who knew
If thou wert goodly? nay, no man at all.
Or what sea saw thee, or sounded with thine oar,
Child? or what strange land shone with war through thee?
But fair for me thou wert, O little life,
Fruitless, the fruit of mine own flesh, and blind,
More than much gold, ungrown, a foolish flower.
For silver nor bright snow nor feather of foam
Was whiter, and no gold yellower than thine hair,
O child, my child; and now thou art lordlier grown,
Not lovelier, nor a new thing in mine eyes,
I charge thee by thy soul and this my breast,
Fear thou the gods and me and thine own heart,
Lest all these turn against thee; for who knows

What wind upon what wave of altering time
Shall speak a storm and blow calamity?
And there is nothing stabile in the world
But the gods break it; yet not less, fair son,
If but one thing be stronger, if one endure,
Surely the bitter and the rooted love
That burns between us, going from me to thee,
Shall more endure than all things. What dost thou,
Following strange loves? why wilt thou kill mine heart?
Lo, I talk wild and windy words, and fall
From my clear wits, and seem of mine own self
Dethroned, dispraised, disseated; and my mind,
That was my crown, breaks, and mine heart is gone,
And I am naked of my soul, and stand
Ashamed, as a mean woman; take thou thought:
Live if thou wilt, and if thou wilt not, look,
The gods have given thee life to lose or keep,
Thou shalt not die as men die, but thine end
Fallen upon thee shall break me unaware.

*MELEAGER*

Queen, my whole heart is molten with thy tears,
And my limbs yearn with pity of thee, and love
Compels with grief mine eyes and labouring breath;
For what thou art I know thee, and this thy breast
And thy fair eyes I worship, and am bound
Toward thee in spirit and love thee in all my soul.
For there is nothing terribler to men
Than the sweet face of mothers, and the might.
But what shall be let be; for us the day
Once only lives a little, and is not found.
Time and the fruitful hour are more than we,
And these lay hold upon us; but thou, God,
Zeus, the sole steersman of the helm of things,
Father, be swift to see us, and as thou wilt
Help: or if adverse, as thou wilt, refrain.

*CHORUS*

We have seen thee, O Love, thou art fair; thou art goodly, O Love;
Thy wings make light in the air as the wings of a dove.
Thy feet are as winds that divide the stream of the sea;
Earth is thy covering to hide thee, the garment of thee.
Thou art swift and subtle and blind as a flame of fire;
Before thee the laughter, behind thee the tears of desire;

And twain go forth beside thee, a man with a maid;
Her eyes are the eyes of a bride whom delight makes afraid;
As the breath in the buds that stir is her bridal breath:
But Fate is the name of her; and his name is Death.

For an evil blossom was born
Of sea-foam and the frothing of blood,
Blood-red and bitter of fruit,
And the seed of it laughter and tears,
And the leaves of it madness and scorn;
A bitter flower from the bud,
Sprung of the sea without root,
Sprung without graft from the years.

The weft of the world was untorn
That is woven of the day on the night,
The hair of the hours was not white
Nor the raiment of time overworn,
When a wonder, a world's delight,
A perilous goddess was born;
And the waves of the sea as she came
Clove, and the foam at her feet,
Fawning, rejoiced to bring forth
A fleshly blossom, a flame
Filling the heavens with heat
To the cold white ends of the north.

And in air the clamorous birds,
And men upon earth that hear
Sweet articulate words
Sweetly divided apart,
And in shallow and channel and mere
The rapid and footless herds,
Rejoiced, being foolish of heart.

For all they said upon earth,
She is fair, she is white like a dove,
And the life of the world in her breath
Breathes, and is born at her birth;
For they knew thee for mother of love,
And knew thee not mother of death.

What hadst thou to do being born,
Mother, when winds were at ease,
As a flower of the springtime of corn,
A flower of the foam of the seas?

For bitter thou wast from thy birth,
  Aphrodite, a mother of strife;
For before thee some rest was on earth,
    A little respite from tears;
  A little pleasure of life;
For life was not then as thou art,
    But as one that waxeth in years
  Sweet-spoken, a fruitful wife;
    Earth had no thorn, and desire
No sting, neither death any dart;
  What hadst thou to do amongst these,
    Thou, clothed with a burning fire,
Thou, girt with sorrow of heart,
  Thou, sprung of the seed of the seas
As an ear from a seed of corn,
    As a brand plucked forth of a pyre,
As a ray shed forth of the morn,
  For division of soul and disease,
For a dart and a sting and a thorn?
What ailed thee then to be born?

Was there not evil enough,
  Mother, and anguish on earth
  Born with a man at his birth,
Wastes underfoot, and above
  Storm out of heaven, and dearth
Shaken down from the shining thereof,
    Wrecks from afar overseas
  And peril of shallow and firth,
    And tears that spring and increase
  In the barren places of mirth,
That thou, having wings as a dove,
  Being girt with desire for a girth,
    That thou must come after these,
That thou must lay on him love?

Thou shouldst not so have been born:
  But death should have risen with thee,
    Mother, and visible fear,
      Grief, and the wringing of hands,
And noise of many that mourn;
  The smitten bosom, the knee
    Bowed, and in each man's ear
      A cry as of perishing lands,

A moan as of people in prison,
A tumult of infinite griefs;
And thunder of storm on the sands,
And wailing of wives on the shore;
And under thee newly arisen
Loud shoals and shipwrecking reefs,
Fierce air and violent light;
Sail rent and sundering oar,
Darkness, and noises of night;
Clashing of streams in the sea,
Wave against wave as a sword,
Clamour of currents, and foam;
Rains making ruin on earth,
Winds that wax ravenous and roam
As wolves in a wolfish horde;
Fruits growing faint in the tree,
And blind things dead in their birth;
Famine, and blighting of corn,
When thy time was come to be born.

All these we know of; but thee
Who shall discern or declare?
In the uttermost ends of the sea
The light of thine eyelids and hair,
The light of thy bosom as fire
Between the wheel of the sun
And the flying flames of the air?
Wilt thou turn thee not yet nor have pity,
But abide with despair and desire
And the crying of armies undone,
Lamentation of one with another
And breaking of city by city;
The dividing of friend against friend,
The severing of brother and brother;
Wilt thou utterly bring to an end?
Have mercy, mother!

For against all men from of old
Thou hast set thine hand as a curse,
And cast out gods from their places.
These things are spoken of thee.
Strong kings and goodly with gold
Thou hast found out arrows to pierce,
And made their kingdoms and races
As dust and surf of the sea.

All these, overburdened with woes
And with length of their days waxen weak,
Thou slewest; and sentest moreover
Upon Tyro an evil thing,
Rent hair and a fetter and blows
Making bloody the flower of the cheek,
Though she lay by a god as a lover,
Though fair, and the seed of a king.
For of old, being full of thy fire,
She endured not longer to wear
On her bosom a saffron vest,
On her shoulder an ashwood quiver;
Being mixed and made one through desire
With Enipeus, and all her hair
Made moist with his mouth, and her breast
Filled full of the foam of the river.

*ATALANTA*

Sun, and clear light among green hills, and day
Late risen and long sought after, and you just gods
Whose hands divide anguish and recompense,
But first the sun's white sister, a maid in heaven,
On earth of all maids worshipped—hail, and hear,
And witness with me if not without sign sent,
Not without rule and reverence, I a maid
Hallowed, and huntress holy as whom I serve,
Here in your sight and eyeshot of these men
Stand, girt as they toward hunting, and my shafts
Drawn; wherefore all ye stand up on my side,
If I be pure and all ye righteous gods,
Lest one revile me, a woman, yet no wife,
That bear a spear for spindle, and this bow strung
For a web woven; and with pure lips salute
Heaven, and the face of all the gods, and dawn
Filling with maiden flames and maiden flowers
The starless fold o' the stars, and making sweet
The warm wan heights of the air, moon-trodden ways
And breathless gates and extreme hills of heaven.
Whom, having offered water and bloodless gifts,
Flowers, and a golden circlet of pure hair,
Next Artemis I bid be favourable
And make this day all golden, hers and ours,
Gracious and good and white to the unblamed end.
But thou, O well-beloved, of all my days

Bid it be fruitful, and a crown for all,
To bring forth leaves and bind round all my hair
With perfect chaplets woven for thine of thee.
For not without the word of thy chaste mouth,
For not without law given and clean command,
Across the white straits of the running sea
From Elis even to the Acheloïan horn,
I with clear winds came hither and gentle gods,
Far off my father's house, and left uncheered
Iasius, and uncheered the Arcadian hills
And all their green-haired waters, and all woods
Disconsolate, to hear no horn of mine
Blown, and behold no flash of swift white feet.

*MELEAGER*
For thy name's sake and awe toward thy chaste head,
O holiest Atalanta, no man dares
Praise thee, though fairer than whom all men praise,
And godlike for thy grace of hallowed hair
And holy habit of thine eyes, and feet
That make the blown foam neither swift nor white
Though the wind winnow and whirl it; yet we praise
Gods, found because of thee adorable
And for thy sake praiseworthiest from all men:
Thee therefore we praise also, thee as these,
Pure, and a light lit at the hands of gods.

*TOXEUS*
How long will ye whet spears with eloquence,
Fight, and kill beasts dry-handed with sweet words?
Cease, or talk still and slay thy boars at home.

*PLEXIPPUS*
Why, if she ride among us for a man,
Sit thou for her and spin; a man grown girl
Is worth a woman weaponed; sit thou here.

*MELEAGER*
Peace, and be wise; no gods love idle speech.

*PLEXIPPUS*
Nor any man a man's mouth woman-tongued.

*MELEAGER*
For my lips bite not sharper than mine hands.

*PLEXIPPUS*
Nay, both bite soft, but no whit softly mine.

*MELEAGER*
Keep thine hands clean; they have time enough to stain.

*PLEXIPPUS*
For thine shall rest and wax not red to-day.

*MELEAGER*
Have all thy will of words; talk out thine heart.

*ALTHÆA*
Refrain your lips, O brethren, and my son,
Lest words turn snakes and bite you uttering them.

*TOXEUS*
Except she give her blood before the gods,
What profit shall a maid be among men?

*PLEXIPPUS*
Let her come crowned and stretch her throat for a knife,
Bleat out her spirit and die, and so shall men
Through her too prosper and through prosperous gods,
But nowise through her living; shall she live
A flower-bud of the flower-bed, or sweet fruit
For kisses and the honey-making mouth,
And play the shield for strong men and the spear?
Then shall the heifer and her mate lock horns,
And the bride overbear the groom, and men
Gods; for no less division sunders these;
Since all things made are seasonable in time,
But if one alter unseasonable are all.
But thou, O Zeus, hear me that I may slay
This beast before thee and no man halve with me
Nor woman, lest these mock thee, though a god,
Who hast made men strong, and thou being wise be held
Foolish; for wise is that thing which endures.

*ATALANTA*
Men, and the chosen of all this people, and thou,
King, I beseech you a little bear with me.
For if my life be shameful that I live,
Let the gods witness and their wrath; but these
Cast no such word against me. Thou, O mine,
O holy, O happy goddess, if I sin
Changing the words of women and the works
For spears and strange men's faces, hast not thou
One shaft of all thy sudden seven that pierced
Seven through the bosom or shining throat or side,

All couched about one mother's loosening knees,
All holy born, engraffed of Tantalus?
But if toward any of you I am overbold
That take thus much upon me, let him think
How I, for all my forest holiness,
Fame, and this armed and iron maidenhood,
Pay thus much also; I shall have no man's love
For ever, and no face of children born
Or feeding lips upon me or fastening eyes
For ever, nor being dead shall kings my sons
Mourn me and bury, and tears on daughters' cheeks
Burn; but a cold and sacred life, but strange,
But far from dances and the back-blowing torch,
Far off from flowers or any bed of man,
Shall my life be for ever: me the snows
That face the first o' the morning, and cold hills
Full of the land-wind and sea-travelling storms
And many a wandering wing of noisy nights
That know the thunder and hear the thickening wolves—
Me the utmost pine and footless frost of woods
That talk with many winds and gods, the hours
Re-risen, and white divisions of the dawn,
Springs thousand-tongued with the intermitting reed
And streams that murmur of the mother snow—
Me these allure, and know me; but no man
Knows, and my goddess only. Lo now, see
If one of all you these things vex at all.
Would God that any of you had all the praise
And I no manner of memory when I die,
So might I show before her perfect eyes
Pure, whom I follow, a maiden to my death.
But for the rest let all have all they will;
For is it a grief to you that I have part,
Being woman merely, in your male might and deeds
Done by main strength? yet in my body is throned
As great a heart, and in my spirit, O men,
I have not less of godlike. Evil it were
That one a coward should mix with you, one hand
Fearful, one eye abase itself; and these
Well might ye hate and well revile, not me.
For not the difference of the several flesh
Being vile or noble or beautiful or base
Makes praiseworthy, but purer spirit and heart

Higher than these meaner mouths and limbs, that feed,
Rise, rest, and are and are not; and for me,
What should I say? but by the gods of the world
And this my maiden body, by all oaths
That bind the tongue of men and the evil will,
I am not mighty-minded, nor desire
Crowns, nor the spoil of slain things nor the fame;
Feed ye on these, eat and wax fat; cry out,
Laugh, having eaten, and leap without a lyre,
Sing, mix the wind with clamour, smite and shake
Sonorous timbrels and tumultuous hair,
And fill the dance up with tempestuous feet,
For I will none; but having prayed my prayers
And made thank-offering for prosperities,
I shall go hence and no man see me more.
What thing is this for you to shout me down,
What, for a man to grudge me this my life
As it were envious of all yours, and I
A thief of reputations? nay, for now,
If there be any highest in heaven, a god
Above all thrones and thunders of the gods
Throned, and the wheel of the world roll under him,
Judge he between me and all of you, and see
If I transgress at all: but ye, refrain
Transgressing hands and reinless mouths, and keep
Silence, lest by much foam of violent words
And proper poison of your lips ye die.

*OENEUS*

O flower of Tegea, maiden, fleetest foot
And holiest head of women, have good cheer
Of thy good words: but ye, depart with her
In peace and reverence, each with blameless eye
Following his fate; exalt your hands and hearts,
Strike, cease not, arrow on arrow and wound on wound,
And go with gods and with the gods return.

*CHORUS*

Who hath given man speech? or who hath set therein
A thorn for peril and a snare for sin?
For in the word his life is and his breath,
  And in the word his death,
That madness and the infatuate heart may breed
  From the word's womb the deed

And life bring one thing forth ere all pass by,
Even one thing which is ours yet cannot die—
Death. Hast thou seen him ever anywhere,
Time's twin-born brother, imperishable as he
Is perishable and plaintive, clothed with care
   And mutable as sand,
But death is strong and full of blood and fair
And perdurable and like a lord of land?
Nay, time thou seest not, death thou wilt not see
Till life's right hand be loosened from thine hand
   And thy life-days from thee.
For the gods very subtly fashion
   Madness with sadness upon earth:
Not knowing in any wise compassion,
   Nor holding pity of any worth;
And many things they have given and taken,
   And wrought and ruined many things;
The firm land have they loosed and shaken,
   And sealed the sea with all her springs;
They have wearied time with heavy burdens
   And vexed the lips of life with breath:
Set men to labour and given them guerdons,
   Death, and great darkness after death:
Put moans into the bridal measure
   And on the bridal wools a stain;
And circled pain about with pleasure,
   And girdled pleasure about with pain;
And strewed one marriage-bed with tears and fire
For extreme loathing and supreme desire.

What shall be done with all these tears of ours?
   Shall they make watersprings in the fair heaven
To bathe the brows of morning? or like flowers
Be shed and shine before the starriest hours,
   Or made the raiment of the weeping Seven?
Or rather, O our masters, shall they be
Food for the famine of the grievous sea,
   A great well-head of lamentation
Satiating the sad gods? or fall and flow
Among the years and seasons to and fro,
   And wash their feet with tribulation
And fill them full with grieving ere they go?
   Alas, our lords, and yet alas again,

Seeing all your iron heaven is gilt as gold
   But all we smite thereat in vain;
Smite the gates barred with groanings manifold,
   But all the floors are paven with our pain.
Yea, and with weariness of lips and eyes,
With breaking of the bosom, and with sighs,
   We labour, and are clad and fed with grief
And filled with days we would not fain behold
And nights we would not hear of; we wax old,
   All we wax old and wither like a leaf.
We are outcast, strayed between bright sun and moon;
   Our light and darkness are as leaves of flowers,
Black flowers and white, that perish; and the noon
   As midnight, and the night as daylight hours.
   A little fruit a little while is ours,
      And the worm finds it soon.

But up in heaven the high gods one by one
   Lay hands upon the draught that quickeneth,
Fulfilled with all tears shed and all things done,
   And stir with soft imperishable breath
   The bubbling bitterness of life and death,
And hold it to our lips and laugh; but they
Preserve their lips from tasting night or day,
   Lest they too change and sleep, the fates that spun,
The lips that made us and the hands that slay;
   Lest all these change, and heaven bow down to none,
Change and be subject to the secular sway
   And terrene revolution of the sun.
Therefore they thrust it from them, putting time away.

I would the wine of time, made sharp and sweet
   With multitudinous days and nights and tears
   And many mixing savours of strange years,
Were no more trodden of them under feet,
   Cast out and spilt about their holy places:
That life were given them as a fruit to eat
And death to drink as water; that the light
Might ebb, drawn backward from their eyes, and night
   Hide for one hour the imperishable faces.
That they might rise up sad in heaven, and know
Sorrow and sleep, one paler than young snow,
   One cold as blight of dew and ruinous rain;

Rise up and rest and suffer a little, and be
Awhile as all things born with us and we,
  And grieve as men, and like slain men be slain.

For now we know not of them; but one saith
  The gods are gracious, praising God; and one,
When hast thou seen? or hast thou felt his breath
  Touch, nor consume thine eyelids as the sun,
Nor fill thee to the lips with fiery death?
  None hath beheld him, none
Seen above other gods and shapes of things,
Swift without feet and flying without wings,
Intolerable, not clad with death or life,
  Insatiable, not known of night or day,
The lord of love and loathing and of strife
  Who gives a star and takes a sun away;
Who shapes the soul, and makes her a barren wife
  To the earthly body and grievous growth of clay;
Who turns the large limbs to a little flame
  And binds the great sea with a little sand;
Who makes desire, and slays desire with shame;
  Who shakes the heaven as ashes in his hand;
Who, seeing the light and shadow for the same,
  Bids day waste night as fire devours a brand,
Smites without sword, and scourges without rod;
  The supreme evil, God.
Yea, with thine hate, O God, thou hast covered us,
  One saith, and hidden our eyes away from sight,
And made us transitory and hazardous,
  Light things and slight;
Yet have men praised thee, saying, He hath made man thus,
  And he doeth right.
Thou hast kissed us, and hast smitten; thou hast laid
Upon us with thy left hand life, and said,
Live: and again thou hast said, Yield up your breath,
And with thy right hand laid upon us death.
Thou hast sent us sleep, and stricken sleep with dreams,
  Saying, Joy is not, but love of joy shall be;
Thou hast made sweet springs for all the pleasant streams,
  In the end thou hast made them bitter with the sea.
Thou hast fed one rose with dust of many men;
  Thou hast marred one face with fire of many tears;
Thou hast taken love, and given us sorrow again;

With pain thou hast filled us full to the eyes and ears.
Therefore because thou art strong, our father, and we
Feeble; and thou art against us, and thine hand
Constrains us in the shallows of the sea
And breaks us at the limits of the land;
Because thou hast bent thy lightnings as a bow,
And loosed the hours like arrows; and let fall
Sins and wild words and many a wingèd woe
And wars among us, and one end of all;
Because thou hast made the thunder, and thy feet
Are as a rushing water when the skies
Break, but thy face as an exceeding heat
And flames of fire the eyelids of thine eyes;
Because thou art over all who are over us;
Because thy name is life and our name death;
Because thou art cruel and men are piteous,
And our hands labour and thine hand scattereth;
Lo, with hearts rent and knees made tremulous,
Lo, with ephemeral lips and casual breath,
At least we witness of thee ere we die
That these things are not otherwise, but thus;
That each man in his heart sigheth, and saith,
That all men even as I,
All we are against thee, against thee, O God most high.

But ye, keep ye on earth
Your lips from over-speech,
Loud words and longing are so little worth;
And the end is hard to reach.
For silence after grievous things is good,
And reverence, and the fear that makes men whole,
And shame, and righteous governance of blood,
And lordship of the soul.
But from sharp words and wits men pluck no fruit,
And gathering thorns they shake the tree at root;
For words divide and rend;
But silence is most noble till the end.

*ALTHÆA*

I heard within the house a cry of news
And came forth eastward hither, where the dawn
Cheers first these warder gods that face the sun
And next our eyes unrisen; for unaware
Came clashes of swift hoofs and trampling feet

And through the windy pillared corridor
Light sharper than the frequent flames of day
That daily fill it from the fiery dawn;
Gleams, and a thunder of people that cried out,
And dust and hurrying horsemen; lo their chief,
That rode with OEneus rein by rein, returned.
What cheer, O herald of my lord the king?

*HERALD*
Lady, good cheer and great; the boar is slain.

*CHORUS*
Praised be all gods that look toward Calydon.

*ALTHÆA*
Good news and brief; but by whose happier hand?

*HERALD*
A maiden's and a prophet's and thy son's.

*ALTHÆA*
Well fare the spear that severed him and life.

*HERALD*
Thine own, and not an alien, hast thou blest.

*ALTHÆA*
Twice be thou too for my sake blest and his.

*HERALD*
At the king's word I rode afoam for thine.

*ALTHÆA*
Thou sayest he tarrieth till they bring the spoil?

*HERALD*
Hard by the quarry, where they breathe, O queen.

*ALTHÆA*
Speak thou their chance; but some bring flowers and crown
These gods and all the lintel, and shed wine,
Fetch sacrifice and slay; for heaven is good.

*HERALD*
Some furlongs northward where the brakes begin
West of that narrowing range of warrior hills
Whose brooks have bled with battle when thy son
Smote Acarnania, there all they made halt,
And with keen eye took note of spear and hound,

Royally ranked; Laertes island-born,
The young Gerenian Nestor, Panopeus,
And Cepheus and Ancæus, mightiest thewed,
Arcadians; next, and evil-eyed of these,
Arcadian Atalanta, with twain hounds
Lengthening the leash, and under nose and brow
Glittering with lipless tooth and fire-swift eye;
But from her white braced shoulder the plumed shafts
Rang, and the bow shone from her side; next her
Meleager, like a sun in spring that strikes
Branch into leaf and bloom into the world,
A glory among men meaner; Iphicles,
And following him that slew the biform bull
Pirithous, and divine Eurytion,
And, bride-bound to the gods, Æacides.
Then Telamon his brother, and Argive-born
The seer and sayer of visions and of truth,
Amphiaraus; and a four-fold strength,
Thine, even thy mother's and thy sister's sons.
And recent from the roar of foreign foam
Jason, and Dryas twin-begot with war,
A blossom of bright battle, sword and man
Shining; and Idas, and the keenest eye
Of Lynceus, and Admetus twice-espoused,
And Hippasus and Hyleus, great in heart.
These having halted bade blow horns, and rode
Through woods and waste lands cleft by stormy streams,
Past yew-trees and the heavy hair of pines,
And where the dew is thickest under oaks,
This way and that; but questing up and down
They saw no trail nor scented; and one said,
Plexippus, Help, or help not, Artemis,
And we will flay thy boarskin with male hands;
But saying, he ceased and said not that he would,
Seeing where the green ooze of a sun-struck marsh
Shook with a thousand reeds untunable,
And in their moist and multitudinous flower
Slept no soft sleep, with violent visions fed,
The blind bulk of the immeasurable beast.
And seeing, he shuddered with sharp lust of praise
Through all his limbs, and launched a double dart.
And missed; for much desire divided him,
Too hot of spirit and feebler than his will,

That his hand failed, though fervent; and the shaft,
Sundering the rushes, in a tamarisk stem
Shook, and stuck fast; then all abode save one,
The Arcadian Atalanta; from her side
Sprang her hounds, labouring at the leash, and slipped,
And plashed ear-deep with plunging feet; but she
Saying, Speed it as I send it for thy sake,
Goddess, drew bow and loosed; the sudden string
Rang, and sprang inward, and the waterish air
Hissed, and the moist plumes of the songless reeds
Moved as a wave which the wind moves no more.
But the boar heaved half out of ooze and slime
His tense flank trembling round the barbèd wound,
Hateful; and fiery with invasive eyes
And bristling with intolerable hair
Plunged, and the hounds clung, and green flowers and white
Reddened and broke all round them where they came.
And charging with sheer tusk he drove, and smote
Hyleus; and sharp death caught his sudden soul,
And violent sleep shed night upon his eyes.
Then Peleus, with strong strain of hand and heart,
Shot; but the sidelong arrow slid, and slew
His comrade born and loving countryman,
Under the left arm smitten, as he no less
Poised a like arrow; and bright blood brake afoam,
And falling, and weighed back by clamorous arms,
Sharp rang the dead limbs of Eurytion.
Then one shot happier, the Cadmean seer,
Amphiaraus; for his sacred shaft
Pierced the red circlet of one ravening eye
Beneath the brute brows of the sanguine boar,
Now bloodier from one slain; but he so galled
Sprang straight, and rearing cried no lesser cry
Than thunder and the roar of wintering streams
That mix their own foam with the yellower sea;
And as a tower that falls by fire in fight
With ruin of walls and all its archery,
And breaks the iron flower of war beneath,
Crushing charred limbs and molten arms of men;
So through crushed branches and the reddening brake
Clamoured and crashed the fervour of his feet,
And trampled, springing sideways from the tusk,

Too tardy a moving mould of heavy strength,
Ancæus; and as flakes of weak-winged snow
Break, all the hard thews of his heaving limbs
Broke, and rent flesh fell every way, and blood
Flew, and fierce fragments of no more a man.
Then all the heroes drew sharp breath, and gazed,
And smote not; but Meleager, but thy son,
Right in the wild way of the coming curse
Rock-rooted, fair with fierce and fastened lips,
Clear eyes, and springing muscle and shortening limb—
With chin aslant indrawn to a tightening throat,
Grave, and with gathered sinews, like a god,—
Aimed on the left side his well-handled spear
Grasped where the ash was knottiest hewn, and smote,
And with no missile wound, the monstrous boar
Right in the hairiest hollow of his hide
Under the last rib, sheer through bulk and bone,
Deep in; and deeply smitten, and to death,
The heavy horror with his hanging shafts
Leapt, and fell furiously, and from raging lips
Foamed out the latest wrath of all his life.
And all they praised the gods with mightier heart,
Zeus and all gods, but chiefliest Artemis,
Seeing; but Meleager bade whet knives and flay,
Strip and stretch out the splendour of the spoil;
And hot and horrid from the work all these
Sat, and drew breath and drank and made great cheer
And washed the hard sweat off their calmer brows.
For much sweet grass grew higher than grew the reed,
And good for slumber, and every holier herb,
Narcissus, and the low-lying melilote,
And all of goodliest blade and bloom that springs
Where, hid by heavier hyacinth, violet buds
Blossom and burn; and fire of yellower flowers
And light of crescent lilies, and such leaves
As fear the Faun's and know the Dryad's foot;
Olive and ivy and poplar dedicate,
And many a well-spring overwatched of these.
There now they rest; but me the king bade bear
Good tidings to rejoice this town and thee.
Wherefore be glad, and all ye give much thanks,
For fallen is all the trouble of Calydon.

*ALTHÆA*

Laud ye the gods; for this they have given is good,
And what shall be they hide until their time.
Much good and somewhat grievous hast thou said,
And either well; but let all sad things be,
Till all have made before the prosperous gods
Burnt-offering, and poured out the floral wine.
Look fair, O gods, and favourable; for we
Praise you with no false heart or flattering mouth,
Being merciful, but with pure souls and prayer.

*HERALD*

Thou hast prayed well; for whoso fears not these,
But once being prosperous waxes huge of heart,
Him shall some new thing unaware destroy.

CHORUS

O that I now, I too were
By deep wells and water-floods,
Streams of ancient hills, and where
All the wan green places bear
Blossoms cleaving to the sod,
Fruitless fruit, and grasses fair,
Or such darkest ivy-buds
As divide thy yellow hair,
Bacchus, and their leaves that nod
Round thy fawnskin brush the bare
Snow-soft shoulders of a god;
There the year is sweet, and there
Earth is full of secret springs,
And the fervent rose-cheeked hours,
Those that marry dawn and noon,
There are sunless, there look pale
In dim leaves and hidden air,
Pale as grass or latter flowers
Or the wild vine's wan wet rings
Full of dew beneath the moon,
And all day the nightingale
Sleeps, and all night sings;
There in cold remote recesses
That nor alien eyes assail,
Feet, nor imminence of wings,
Nor a wind nor any tune,
Thou, O queen and holiest,

Flower the whitest of all things,
With reluctant lengthening tresses
And with sudden splendid breast
Save of maidens unbeholden,
There art wont to enter, there
Thy divine swift limbs and golden
Maiden growth of unbound hair,
Bathed in waters white,
Shine, and many a maid's by thee
In moist woodland or the hilly
Flowerless brakes where wells abound
Out of all men's sight;
Or in lower pools that see
All their marges clothed all round
With the innumerable lily,
Whence the golden-girdled bee
Flits through flowering rush to fret
White or duskier violet,
Fair as those that in far years
With their buds left luminous
And their little leaves made wet,
From the warmer dew of tears,
Mother's tears in extreme need,
Hid the limbs of Iamus,
Of thy brother's seed;
For his heart was piteous
Toward him, even as thine heart now
Pitiful toward us;
Thine, O goddess, turning hither
A benignant blameless brow;
Seeing enough of evil done
And lives withered as leaves wither
In the blasting of the sun;
Seeing enough of hunters dead,
Ruin enough of all our year,
Herds and harvests slain and shed,
Herdsmen stricken many an one,
Fruits and flocks consumed together,
And great length of deadly days.
Yet with reverent lips and fear
Turn we toward thee, turn and praise
For this lightening of clear weather
And prosperities begun.

For not seldom, when all air
As bright water without breath
Shines, and when men fear not, fate
Without thunder unaware
Breaks, and brings down death.
Joy with grief ye great gods give,
Good with bad, and overbear
All the pride of us that live,
All the high estate,
As ye long since overbore,
As in old time long before,
Many a strong man and a great,
All that were.
But do thou, sweet, otherwise,
Having heed of all our prayer,
Taking note of all our sighs;
We beseech thee by thy light,
By thy bow, and thy sweet eyes,
And the kingdom of the night,
Be thou favourable and fair;
By thine arrows and thy might
And Orion overthrown;
By the maiden thy delight,
By the indissoluble zone
And the sacred hair.

*MESSENGER*

Maidens, if ye will sing now, shift your song,
Bow down, cry, wail for pity; is this a time
For singing? nay, for strewing of dust and ash,
Rent raiment, and for bruising of the breast.

*CHORUS*

What new thing wolf-like lurks behind thy words?
What snake's tongue in thy lips? what fire in the eyes?

*MESSENGER*

Bring me before the queen and I will speak.

*CHORUS*

Lo, she comes forth as from thank-offering made.

*MESSENGER*

A barren offering for a bitter gift.

*ALTHÆA*

What are these borne on branches, and the face
Covered? no mean men living, but now slain
Such honour have they, if any dwell with death.

*MESSENGER*

Queen, thy twain brethren and thy mother's sons.

*ALTHÆA*

Lay down your dead till I behold their blood
If it be mine indeed, and I will weep.

*MESSENGER*

Weep if thou wilt, for these men shall no more.

*ALTHÆA*

O brethren, O my father's sons, of me
Well loved and well reputed, I should weep
Tears dearer than the dear blood drawn from you
But that I know you not uncomforted,
Sleeping no shameful sleep, however slain,
For my son surely hath avenged you dead.

*MESSENGER*

Nay, should thine own seed slay himself, O queen?

*ALTHÆA*

Thy double word brings forth a double death.

*MESSENGER*

Know this then singly, by one hand they fell.

*ALTHÆA*

What mutterest thou with thine ambiguous mouth?

*MESSENGER*

Slain by thy son's hand; is that saying so hard?

*ALTHÆA*

Our time is come upon us: it is here.

*CHORUS*

O miserable, and spoiled at thine own hand.

*ALTHÆA*

Wert thou not called Meleager from this womb?

*CHORUS*

A grievous huntsman hath it bred to thee.

*ALTHÆA*
Wert thou born fire, and shalt thou not devour?

*CHORUS*
The fire thou madest, will it consume even thee?

*ALTHÆA*
My dreams are fallen upon me; burn thou too.

*CHORUS*
Not without God are visions born and die.

*ALTHÆA*
The gods are many about me; I am one.

*CHORUS*
She groans as men wrestling with heavier gods.

*ALTHÆA*
They rend me, they divide me, they destroy.

*CHORUS*
Or one labouring in travail of strange births.

*ALTHÆA*
They are strong, they are strong; I am broken, and these prevail.

*CHORUS*
The god is great against her; she will die.

*ALTHÆA*
Yea, but not now; for my heart too is great.
I would I were not here in sight of the sun.
But thou, speak all thou sawest, and I will die.

*MESSENGER*
O queen, for queenlike hast thou borne thyself,
A little word may hold so great mischance.
For in division of the sanguine spoil
These men thy brethren wrangling bade yield up
The boar's head and the horror of the hide
That this might stand a wonder in Calydon,
Hallowed; and some drew toward them; but thy son
With great hands grasping all that weight of hair
Cast down the dead heap clanging and collapsed
At female feet, saying This thy spoil not mine,
Maiden, thine own hand for thyself hath reaped,
And all this praise God gives thee: she thereat

Laughed, as when dawn touches the sacred night
The sky sees laugh and redden and divide
Dim lips and eyelids virgin of the sun,
Hers, and the warm slow breasts of morning heave,
Fruitful, and flushed with flame from lamp-lit hours,
And maiden undulation of clear hair
Colour the clouds; so laughed she from pure heart,
Lit with a low blush to the braided hair,
And rose-coloured and cold like very dawn,
Golden and godlike, chastely with chaste lips,
A faint grave laugh; and all they held their peace,
And she passed by them. Then one cried Lo now,
Shall not the Arcadian shoot out lips at us,
Saying all we were despoiled by this one girl?
And all they rode against her violently
And cast the fresh crown from her hair, and now
They had rent her spoil away, dishonouring her,
Save that Meleager, as a tame lion chafed,
Bore on them, broke them, and as fire cleaves wood
So clove and drove them, smitten in twain; but she
Smote not nor heaved up hand; and this man first,
Plexippus, crying out This for love's sake, sweet,
Drove at Meleager, who with spear straightening
Pierced his cheek through; then Toxeus made for him,
Dumb, but his spear spake; vain and violent words.
Fruitless; for him too stricken through both sides
The earth felt falling, and his horse's foam
Blanched thy son's face, his slayer; and these being slain,
None moved nor spake; but OEneus bade bear hence
These made of heaven infatuate in their deaths,
Foolish; for these would baffle fate, and fell.
And they passed on, and all men honoured her,
Being honourable, as one revered of heaven.

*ALTHÆA*

What say you, women? is all this not well done?

*CHORUS*

No man doth well but God hath part in him.

*ALTHÆA*

But no part here; for these my brethren born
Ye have no part in, these ye know not of
As I that was their sister, a sacrifice

Slain in their slaying. I would I had died for these;
For this man dead walked with me, child by child,
And made a weak staff for my feebler feet
With his own tender wrist and hand, and held
And led me softly and shewed me gold and steel
And shining shapes of mirror and bright crown
And all things fair; and threw light spears, and brought
Young hounds to huddle at my feet and thrust
Tame heads against my little maiden breasts
And please me with great eyes; and those days went
And these are bitter and I a barren queen
And sister miserable, a grievous thing
And mother of many curses; and she too,
My sister Leda, sitting overseas
With fair fruits round her, and her faultless lord,
Shall curse me, saying A sorrow and not a son,
Sister, thou barest, even a burning fire,
A brand consuming thine own soul and me.
But ye now, sons of Thestius, make good cheer,
For ye shall have such wood to funeral fire
As no king hath; and flame that once burnt down
Oil shall not quicken or breath relume or wine
Refresh again; much costlier than fine gold,
And more than many lives of wandering men.

*CHORUS*

O queen, thou hast yet with thee love-worthy things,
Thine husband, and the great strength of thy son.

*ALTHÆA*

Who shall get brothers for me while I live?
Who bear them? who bring forth in lieu of these?
Are not our fathers and our brethren one,
And no man like them? are not mine here slain?
Have we not hung together, he and I,
Flowerwise feeding as the feeding bees,
With mother-milk for honey? and this man too,
Dead, with my son's spear thrust between his sides,
Hath he not seen us, later born than he,
Laugh with lips filled, and laughed again for love?
There were no sons then in the world, nor spears,
Nor deadly births of women; but the gods
Allowed us, and our days were clear of these.

I would I had died unwedded, and brought forth
No swords to vex the world; for these that spake
Sweet words long since and loved me will not speak
Nor love nor look upon me; and all my life
I shall not hear nor see them living men.
But I too living, how shall I now live?
What life shall this be with my son, to know
What hath been and desire what will not be,
Look for dead eyes and listen for dead lips,
And kill mine own heart with remembering them,
And with those eyes that see their slayer alive
Weep, and wring hands that clasp him by the hand?
How shall I bear my dreams of them, to hear
False voices, feel the kisses of false mouths
And footless sound of perished feet, and then
Wake and hear only it may be their own hounds
Whine masterless in miserable sleep,
And see their boar-spears and their beds and seats
And all the gear and housings of their lives
And not the men? shall hounds and horses mourn,
Pine with strange eyes, and prick up hungry ears,
Famish and fail at heart for their dear lords,
And I not heed at all? and those blind things
Fall off from life for love's sake, and I live?
Surely some death is better than some life,
Better one death for him and these and me
For if the gods had slain them it may be
I had endured it; if they had fallen by war
Or by the nets and knives of privy death
And by hired hands while sleeping, this thing too
I had set my soul to suffer; or this hunt,
Had this despatched them under tusk or tooth
Torn, sanguine, trodden, broken; for all deaths
Or honourable or with facile feet avenged
And hands of swift gods following, all save this,
Are bearable; but not for their sweet land
Fighting, but not a sacrifice, lo these
Dead; for I had not then shed all mine heart
Out at mine eyes: then either with good speed,
Being just, I had slain their slayer atoningly,
Or strewn with flowers their fire and on their tombs
Hung crowns, and over them a song, and seen

Their praise outflame their ashes: for all men,
All maidens, had come thither, and from pure lips
Shed songs upon them, from heroic eyes
Tears; and their death had been a deathless life;
But now, by no man hired nor alien sword,
By their own kindred are they fallen, in peace,
After much peril, friendless among friends,
By hateful hands they loved; and how shall mine
Touch these returning red and not from war,
These fatal from the vintage of men's veins,
Dead men my brethren? how shall these wash off
No festal stains of undelightful wine,
How mix the blood, my blood on them, with me,
Holding mine hand? or how shall I say, son,
That am no sister? but by night and day
Shall we not sit and hate each other, and think
Things hate-worthy? not live with shamefast eyes,
Brow-beaten, treading soft with fearful feet,
Each unupbraided, each without rebuke
Convicted, and without a word reviled
Each of another? and I shall let thee live
And see thee strong and hear men for thy sake
Praise me, but these thou wouldest not let live
No man shall praise for ever? these shall lie
Dead, unbeloved, unholpen, all through thee?
Sweet were they toward me living, and mine heart
Desired them, but was then well satisfied,
That now is as men hungered; and these dead
I shall want always to the day I die.
For all things else and all men may renew;
Yea, son for son the gods may give and take,
But never a brother or sister any more.

*CHORUS*

Nay, for the son lies close about thine heart,
Full of thy milk, warm from thy womb, and drains
Life and the blood of life and all thy fruit,
Eats thee and drinks thee as who breaks bread and eats,
Treads wine and drinks, thyself, a sect of thee;
And if he feed not, shall not thy flesh faint?
Or drink not, are not thy lips dead for thirst?
This thing moves more than all things, even thy son,
That thou cleave to him; and he shall honour thee,

Thy womb that bare him and the breasts he knew,
Reverencing most for thy sake all his gods.

*ALTHÆA*

But these the gods too gave me, and these my son,
Not reverencing his gods nor mine own heart
Nor the old sweet years nor all venerable things,
But cruel, and in his ravin like a beast,
Hath taken away to slay them: yea, and she
She the strange woman, she the flower, the sword,
Red from spilt blood, a mortal flower to men,
Adorable, detestable—even she
Saw with strange eyes and with strange lips rejoiced,
Seeing these mine own slain of mine own, and me
Made miserable above all miseries made,
A grief among all women in the world,
A name to be washed out with all men's tears.

*CHORUS*

Strengthen thy spirit; is this not also a god,
Chance, and the wheel of all necessities?
Hard things have fallen upon us from harsh gods,
Whom lest worse hap rebuke we not for these.

*ALTHÆA*

My spirit is strong against itself, and I
For these things' sake cry out on mine own soul
That it endures outrage, and dolorous days,
And life, and this inexpiable impotence.
Weak am I, weak and shameful; my breath drawn
Shames me, and monstrous things and violent gods.
What shall atone? what heal me? what bring back
Strength to the foot, light to the face? what herb
Assuage me? what restore me? what release?
What strange thing eaten or drunken, O great gods,
Make me as you or as the beasts that feed,
Slay and divide and cherish their own hearts?
For these ye show us; and we less than these
Have not wherewith to live as all these things
Which all their lives fare after their own kind
As who doth well rejoicing; but we ill,
Weeping or laughing, we whom eyesight fails,
Knowledge and light of face and perfect heart,
And hands we lack, and wit; and all our days

Sin, and have hunger, and die infatuated.
For madness have ye given us and not health,
And sins whereof we know not; and for these
Death, and sudden destruction unaware.
What shall we say now? what thing comes of us?

*CHORUS*
Alas, for all this all men undergo.

*ALTHÆA*
Wherefore I will not that these twain, O gods,
Die as a dog dies, eaten of creeping things,
Abominable, a loathing; but though dead
Shall they have honour and such funereal flame
As strews men's ashes in their enemies' face
And blinds their eyes who hate them: lest men say,
"Lo how they lie, and living had great kin,
And none of these hath pity of them, and none
Regards them lying, and none is wrung at heart,
None moved in spirit for them, naked and slain,
Abhorred, abased, and no tears comfort them:"
And in the dark this grieve Eurythemis,
Hearing how these her sons come down to her
Unburied, unavenged, as kinless men,
And had a queen their sister. That were shame
Worse than this grief. Yet how to atone at all
I know not; seeing the love of my born son,
A new-made mother's new-born love, that grows
From the soft child to the strong man, now soft
Now strong as either, and still one sole same love,
Strives with me, no light thing to strive withal;
This love is deep, and natural to man's blood,
And ineffaceable with many tears.
Yet shall not these rebuke me though I die,
Nor she in that waste world with all her dead,
My mother, among the pale flocks fallen as leaves,
Folds of dead people, and alien from the sun;
Nor lack some bitter comfort, some poor praise,
Being queen, to have borne her daughter like a queen,
Righteous; and though mine own fire burn me too,
She shall have honour and these her sons, though dead.
But all the gods will, all they do, and we
Not all we would, yet somewhat; and one choice
We have, to live and do just deeds and die.

*CHORUS*
Terrible words she communes with, and turns
Swift fiery eyes in doubt against herself,
And murmurs as who talks in dreams with death.

*ALTHÆA*
For the unjust also dieth, and him all men
Hate, and himself abhors the unrighteousness,
And seeth his own dishonour intolerable.
But I being just, doing right upon myself,
Slay mine own soul, and no man born shames me.
For none constrains nor shall rebuke, being done,
What none compelled me doing; thus these things fare.
Ah, ah, that such things should so fare; ah me,
That I am found to do them and endure,
Chosen and constrained to choose, and bear myself
Mine own wound through mine own flesh to the heart
Violently stricken, a spoiler and a spoil,
A ruin ruinous, fallen on mine own son.
Ah, ah, for me too as for these; alas,
For that is done that shall be, and mine hand
Full of the deed, and full of blood mine eyes,
That shall see never nor touch anything
Save blood unstanched and fire unquenchable.

*CHORUS*
What wilt thou do? what ails thee? for the house
Shakes ruinously; wilt thou bring fire for it?

*ALTHÆA*
Fire in the roofs, and on the lintels fire.
Lo ye, who stand and weave, between the doors,
There; and blood drips from hand and thread, and stains
Threshold and raiment and me passing in
Flecked with the sudden sanguine drops of death.

*CHORUS*
Alas that time is stronger than strong men,
Fate than all gods: and these are fallen on us.

*ALTHÆA*
A little since and I was glad; and now
I never shall be glad or sad again.

*CHORUS*
Between two joys a grief grows unaware.

*ALTHÆA*
A little while and I shall laugh; and then
I shall weep never and laugh not any more.

*CHORUS*
What shall be said? for words are thorns to grief.
Withhold thyself a little and fear the gods.

*ALTHÆA*
Fear died when these were slain; and I am as dead,
And fear is of the living; these fear none.

*CHORUS*
Have pity upon all people for their sake.

*ALTHÆA*
It is done now; shall I put back my day?

*CHORUS*
An end is come, an end; this is of God.

*ALTHÆA*
I am fire, and burn myself; keep clear of fire.

*CHORUS*
The house is broken, is broken; it shall not stand.

*ALTHÆA*
Woe, woe for him that breaketh; and a rod
Smote it of old, and now the axe is here.

CHORUS

Not as with sundering of the earth
  Nor as with cleaving of the sea
Nor fierce foreshadowings of a birth
  Nor flying dreams of death to be
Nor loosening of the large world's girth
And quickening of the body of night,
  And sound of thunder in men's ears
And fire of lightning in men's sight,
  Fate, mother of desires and fears,
  Bore unto men the law of tears;
But sudden, an unfathered flame,
  And broken out of night, she shone,
She, without body, without name,
  In days forgotten and foregone;
And heaven rang round her as she came

Like smitten cymbals, and lay bare;
  Clouds and great stars, thunders and snows,
The blue sad fields and folds of air,
  The life that breathes, the life that grows,
  All wind, all fire, that burns or blows,
Even all these knew her: for she is great;
  The daughter of doom, the mother of death,
The sister of sorrow; a lifelong weight
  That no man's finger lighteneth,
Nor any god can lighten fate;
A landmark seen across the way
  Where one race treads as the other trod;
An evil sceptre, an evil stay,
  Wrought for a staff, wrought for a rod,
  The bitter jealousy of God.

  For death is deep as the sea,
    And fate as the waves thereof.
  Shall the waves take pity on thee
    Or the southwind offer thee love?
  Wilt thou take the night for thy day
  Or the darkness for light on thy way,
    Till thou say in thine heart Enough?
Behold, thou art over fair, thou art over wise;
The sweetness of spring in thine hair, and the light in thine eyes.
The light of the spring in thine eyes, and the sound in thine ears;
Yet thine heart shall wax heavy with sighs and thine eyelids with tears.
Wilt thou cover thine hair with gold, and with silver thy feet?
Hast thou taken the purple to fold thee, and made thy mouth sweet?
Behold, when thy face is made bare, he that loved thee shall hate;
Thy face shall be no more fair at the fall of thy fate.
For thy life shall fall as a leaf and be shed as the rain;
And the veil of thine head shall be grief; and the crown shall be pain.

*ALTHÆA*

Ho, ye that wail, and ye that sing, make way
Till I be come among you. Hide your tears,
Ye little weepers, and your laughing lips,
Ye laughers for a little; lo mine eyes
That outweep heaven at rainiest, and my mouth
That laughs as gods laugh at us. Fate's are we,
Yet fate is ours a breathing-space; yea, mine,
Fate is made mine for ever; he is my son,

My bedfellow, my brother. You strong gods,
Give place unto me; I am as any of you,
To give life and to take life. Thou, old earth,
That hast made man and unmade; thou whose mouth
Looks red from the eaten fruits of thine own womb;
Behold me with what lips upon what food
I feed and fill my body; even with flesh
Made of my body. Lo, the fire I lit
I burn with fire to quench it; yea, with flame
I burn up even the dust and ash thereof.

*CHORUS*
Woman, what fire is this thou burnest with?

*ALTHÆA*
Yea to the bone, yea to the blood and all.

*CHORUS*
For this thy face and hair are as one fire.

*ALTHÆA*
A tongue that licks and beats upon the dust.

*CHORUS*
And in thine eyes are hollow light and heat.

*ALTHÆA*
Of flame not fed with hand or frankincense.

*CHORUS*
I fear thee for the trembling of thine eyes.

*ALTHÆA*
Neither with love they tremble nor for fear.

*CHORUS*
And thy mouth shuddering like a shot bird.

*ALTHÆA*
Not as the bride's mouth when man kisses it.

*CHORUS*
Nay, but what thing is this thing thou hast done?

*ALTHÆA*
Look, I am silent, speak your eyes for me.

*CHORUS*
I see a faint fire lightening from the hall.

*ALTHÆA*
Gaze, stretch your eyes, strain till the lids drop off.

*CHORUS*
Flushed pillars down the flickering vestibule.

*ALTHÆA*
Stretch with your necks like birds: cry, chirp as they.

*CHORUS*
And a long brand that blackens: and white dust.

*ALTHÆA*
O children, what is this ye see? your eyes
Are blinder than night's face at fall of moon.
That is my son, my flesh, my fruit of life,
My travail, and the year's weight of my womb,
Meleager, a fire enkindled of mine hands
And of mine hands extinguished; this is he.

*CHORUS*
O gods, what word has flown out at thy mouth?

*ALTHÆA*
I did this and I say this and I die.

*CHORUS*
Death stands upon the doorway of thy lips,
And in thy mouth has death set up his house.

*ALTHÆA*
O death, a little, a little while, sweet death,
Until I see the brand burnt down and die.

*CHORUS*
She reels as any reed under the wind,
And cleaves unto the ground with staggering feet.

*ALTHÆA*
Girls, one thing will I say and hold my peace.
I that did this will weep not nor cry out,
Cry ye and weep: I will not call on gods,
Call ye on them; I will not pity man,
Shew ye your pity. I know not if I live;
Save that I feel the fire upon my face
And on my cheek the burning of a brand.
Yea the smoke bites me, yea I drink the steam

With nostril and with eyelid and with lip
Insatiate and intolerant; and mine hands
Burn, and fire feeds upon mine eyes; I reel
As one made drunk with living, whence he draws
Drunken delight; yet I, though mad for joy,
Loathe my long living and am waxen red
As with the shadow of shed blood; behold,
I am kindled with the flames that fade in him,
I am swollen with subsiding of his veins,
I am flooded with his ebbing; my lit eyes
Flame with the falling fire that leaves his lids
Bloodless; my cheek is luminous with blood
Because his face is ashen. Yet, O child,
Son, first-born, fairest—O sweet mouth, sweet eyes,
That drew my life out through my suckling breast,
That shone and clove mine heart through—O soft knees
Clinging, O tender treadings of soft feet,
Cheeks warm with little kissings—O child, child,
What have we made each other? Lo, I felt
Thy weight cleave to me, a burden of beauty, O son,
Thy cradled brows and loveliest loving lips,
The floral hair, the little lightening eyes,
And all thy goodly glory; with mine hands
Delicately I fed thee, with my tongue
Tenderly spake, saying, Verily in God's time,
For all the little likeness of thy limbs,
Son, I shall make thee a kingly man to fight,
A lordly leader; and hear before I die,
"She bore the goodliest sword of all the world."
Oh! oh! For all my life turns round on me;
I am severed from myself, my name is gone,
My name that was a healing, it is changed,
My name is a consuming. From this time,
Though mine eyes reach to the end of all these things,
My lips shall not unfasten till I die.

*SEMICHORUS*

She has filled with sighing the city,
  And the ways thereof with tears;
She arose, she girdled her sides,
She set her face as a bride's;
She wept, and she had no pity;
  Trembled, and felt no fears.

*SEMICHORUS*

Her eyes were clear as the sun,
Her brows were fresh as the day;
She girdled herself with gold,
Her robes were manifold;
But the days of her worship are done,
Her praise is taken away.

*SEMICHORUS*

For she set her hand to the fire,
With her mouth she kindled the same;
As the mouth of a flute-player,
So was the mouth of her;
With the might of her strong desire
She blew the breath of the flame.

*SEMICHORUS*

She set her hand to the wood,
She took the fire in her hand;
As one who is nigh to death,
She panted with strange breath;
She opened her lips unto blood,
She breathed and kindled the brand.

*SEMICHORUS*

As a wood-dove newly shot,
She sobbed and lifted her breast;
She sighed and covered her eyes,
Filling her lips with sighs;
She sighed, she withdrew herself not,
She refrained not, taking not rest;

*SEMICHORUS*

But as the wind which is drouth,
And as the air which is death,
As storm that severeth ships,
Her breath severing her lips,
The breath came forth of her mouth
And the fire came forth of her breath.

*SECOND MESSENGER*

Queen, and you maidens, there is come on us
A thing more deadly than the face of death;
Meleager the good lord is as one slain.

*SEMICHORUS*

Without sword, without sword is he stricken;
Slain, and slain without hand.

*SECOND MESSENGER*

For as keen ice divided of the sun
His limbs divide, and as thawed snow the flesh
Thaws from off all his body to the hair.

*SEMICHORUS*

He wastes as the embers quicken;
With the brand he fades as a brand.

*SECOND MESSENGER*

Even while they sang and all drew hither and he
Lifted both hands to crown the Arcadian's hair
And fix the looser leaves, both hands fell down.

*SEMICHORUS*

With rending of cheek and of hair
Lament ye, mourn for him, weep.

*SECOND MESSENGER*

Straightway the crown slid off and smote on earth,
First fallen; and he, grasping his own hair, groaned
And cast his raiment round his face and fell.

*SEMICHORUS*

Alas for visions that were,
And soothsayings spoken in sleep.

*SECOND MESSENGER*

But the king twitched his reins in and leapt down
And caught him, crying out twice "O child" and thrice,
So that men's eyelids thickened with their tears.

*SEMICHORUS*

Lament with a long lamentation,
Cry, for an end is at hand.

*SECOND MESSENGER*

O son, he said, son, lift thine eyes, draw breath,
Pity me; but Meleager with sharp lips
Gasped, and his face waxed like as sunburnt grass.

*SEMICHORUS*

Cry aloud, O thou kingdom, O nation,
O stricken, a ruinous land.

*SECOND MESSENGER*
Whereat king OEneus, straightening feeble knees,
With feeble hands heaved up a lessening weight,
And laid him sadly in strange hands, and wept.

*SEMICHORUS*
Thou art smitten, her lord, her desire,
Thy dear blood wasted as rain.

*SECOND MESSENGER*
And they with tears and rendings of the beard
Bear hither a breathing body, wept upon
And lightening at each footfall, sick to death.

*SEMICHORUS*
Thou madest thy sword as a fire,
With fire for a sword thou art slain.

*SECOND MESSENGER*
And lo, the feast turned funeral, and the crowns
Fallen; and the huntress and the hunter trapped;
And weeping and changed faces and veiled hair.

*MELEAGER*
Let your hands meet
Round the weight of my head;
Lift ye my feet
As the feet of the dead;
For the flesh of my body is molten, the limbs of it molten as lead.

*CHORUS*
O thy luminous face,
Thine imperious eyes!
O the grief, O the grace,
As of day when it dies!
Who is this bending over thee, lord, with tears and suppression of sighs?

*MELEAGER*
Is a bride so fair?
Is a maid so meek?
With unchapleted hair,
With unfilleted cheek,
Atalanta, the pure among women, whose name is as blessing to speak.

*ATALANTA*

I would that with feet
Unsandalled, unshod,
Overbold, overfleet,
I had swum not nor trod
From Arcadia to Calydon northward, a blast of the envy of God.

*MELEAGER*

Unto each man his fate;
Unto each as he saith
In whose fingers the weight
Of the world is as breath;
Yet I would that in clamour of battle mine hands had laid hold upon death.

*CHORUS*

Not with cleaving of shields
And their clash in thine ear,
When the lord of fought fields
Breaketh spearshaft from spear,
Thou art broken, our lord, thou art broken, with travail and labour and fear.

*MELEAGER*

Would God he had found me
Beneath fresh boughs!
Would God he had bound me
Unawares in mine house,
With light in mine eyes, and songs in my lips, and a crown on my brows!

*CHORUS*

Whence art thou sent from us?
Whither thy goal?
How art thou rent from us,
Thou that wert whole,
As with severing of eyelids and eyes, as with sundering of body and soul!

*MELEAGER*

My heart is within me
As an ash in the fire;
Whosoever hath seen me,
Without lute, without lyre,
Shall sing of me grievous things, even things that were ill to desire.

*CHORUS*

Who shall raise thee
  From the house of the dead?
Or what man praise thee
  That thy praise may be said?
Alas thy beauty! alas thy body! alas thine head!

*MELEAGER*

But thou, O mother,
  The dreamer of dreams,
Wilt thou bring forth another
  To feel the sun's beams
When I move among shadows a shadow, and wail by impassable streams?

*OENEUS*

What thing wilt thou leave me
  Now this thing is done?
A man wilt thou give me,
  A son for my son,
For the light of mine eyes, the desire of my life, the desirable one?

*CHORUS*

Thou wert glad above others,
  Yea, fair beyond word;
Thou wert glad among mothers;
  For each man that heard
Of thee, praise there was added unto thee, as wings to the feet of a bird.

*OENEUS*

Who shall give back
  Thy face of old years
With travail made black,
  Grown grey among fears,
Mother of sorrow, mother of cursing, mother of tears?

*MELEAGER*

Though thou art as fire
  Fed with fuel in vain,
My delight, my desire,
  Is more chaste than the rain,
More pure than the dewfall, more holy than stars are that live without stain.

*ATALANTA*

I would that as water
   My life's blood had thawn,
Or as winter's wan daughter
   Leaves lowland and lawn
Spring-stricken, or ever mine eyes had beheld thee made dark in thy dawn.

*CHORUS*

When thou dravest the men
   Of the chosen of Thrace,
None turned him again
   Nor endured he thy face
Clothed round with the blush of the battle, with light from a terrible place.

*OENEUS*

Thou shouldst die as he dies
   For whom none sheddeth tears;
Filling thine eyes
   And fulfilling thine ears
With the brilliance of battle, the bloom and the beauty, the splendour of spears.

*CHORUS*

In the ears of the world
   It is sung, it is told,
And the light thereof hurled
   And the noise thereof rolled
From the Acroceraunian snow to the ford of the fleece of gold.

*MELEAGER*

Would God ye could carry me
   Forth of all these;
Heap sand and bury me
   By the Chersonese
Where the thundering Bosphorus answers the thunder of Pontic seas.

*OENEUS*

Dost thou mock at our praise
   And the singing begun
And the men of strange days
   Praising my son
In the folds of the hills of home, high places of Calydon?

*MELEAGER*

For the dead man no home is;
Ah, better to be
What the flower of the foam is
In fields of the sea,
That the sea-waves might be as my raiment, the gulf-stream a garment for me.

*CHORUS*

Who shall seek thee and bring
And restore thee thy day,
When the dove dipt her wing
And the oars won their way
Where the narrowing Symplegades whitened the straits of Propontis with spray?

*MELEAGER*

Will ye crown me my tomb
Or exalt me my name,
Now my spirits consume,
Now my flesh is a flame?
Let the sea slake it once, and men speak of me sleeping to praise me or shame.

*CHORUS*

Turn back now, turn thee,
As who turns him to wake;
Though the life in thee burn thee,
Couldst thou bathe it and slake
Where the sea-ridge of Helle hangs heavier, and east upon west waters break?

*MELEAGER*

Would the winds blow me back
Or the waves hurl me home?
Ah, to touch in the track
Where the pine learnt to roam
Cold girdles and crowns of the sea-gods, cool blossoms of water and foam!

*CHORUS*

The gods may release
That they made fast;
Thy soul shall have ease
In thy limbs at the last;
But what shall they give thee for life, sweet life that is overpast?

*MELEAGER*

Not the life of men's veins,
Not of flesh that conceives;
But the grace that remains,
The fair beauty that cleaves
To the life of the rains in the grasses, the life of the dews on the leaves.

*CHORUS*

Thou wert helmsman and chief;
Wilt thou turn in an hour,
Thy limbs to the leaf,
Thy face to the flower,
Thy blood to the water, thy soul to the gods who divide and devour?

*MELEAGER*

The years are hungry,
They wail all their days;
The gods wax angry
And weary of praise;
And who shall bridle their lips? and who shall straiten their ways?

*CHORUS*

The gods guard over us
With sword and with rod;
Weaving shadow to cover us,
Heaping the sod,
That law may fulfil herself wholly, to darken man's face before God.

*MELEAGER*

O holy head of OEneus, lo thy son
Guiltless, yet red from alien guilt, yet foul
With kinship of contaminated lives,
Lo, for their blood I die; and mine own blood
For bloodshedding of mine is mixed therewith,
That death may not discern me from my kin.
Yet with clean heart I die and faultless hand,
Not shamefully; thou therefore of thy love
Salute me, and bid fare among the dead
Well, as the dead fare; for the best man dead
Fares sadly; nathless I now faring well
Pass without fear where nothing is to fear
Having thy love about me and thy goodwill,
O father, among dark places and men dead.

*OENEUS*

Child, I salute thee with sad heart and tears,
And bid thee comfort, being a perfect man
In fight, and honourable in the house of peace.
The gods give thee fair wage and dues of death,
And me brief days and ways to come at thee.

*MELEAGER*

Pray thou thy days be long before thy death,
And full of ease and kingdom; seeing in death
There is no comfort and none aftergrowth,
Nor shall one thence look up and see day's dawn
Nor light upon the land whither I go.
Live thou and take thy fill of days and die
When thy day comes; and make not much of death
Lest ere thy day thou reap an evil thing.
Thou too, the bitter mother and mother-plague
Of this my weary body—thou too, queen,
The source and end, the sower and the scythe,
The rain that ripens and the drought that slays,
The sand that swallows and the spring that feeds,
To make me and unmake me—thou, I say,
Althæa, since my father's ploughshare, drawn
Through fatal seedland of a female field,
Furrowed thy body, whence a wheaten ear
Strong from the sun and fragrant from the rains
I sprang and cleft the closure of thy womb,
Mother, I dying with unforgetful tongue
Hail thee as holy and worship thee as just
Who art unjust and unholy; and with my knees
Would worship, but thy fire and subtlety,
Dissundering them, devour me; for these limbs
Are as light dust and crumblings from mine urn
Before the fire has touched them; and my face
As a dead leaf or dead foot's mark on snow,
And all this body a broken barren tree
That was so strong, and all this flower of life
Disbranched and desecrated miserably,
And minished all that god-like muscle and might
And lesser than a man's: for all my veins
Fail me, and all mine ashen life burns down.
I would thou hadst let me live; but gods averse,
But fortune, and the fiery feet of change,

And time, these would not, these tread out my life,
These and not thou; me too thou hast loved, and I
Thee; but this death was mixed with all my life,
Mine end with my beginning: and this law,
This only, slays me, and not my mother at all.
And let no brother or sister grieve too sore,
Nor melt their hearts out on me with their tears,
Since extreme love and sorrowing overmuch
Vex the great gods, and overloving men
Slay and are slain for love's sake; and this house
Shall bear much better children; why should these
Weep? but in patience let them live their lives
And mine pass by forgotten: thou alone,
Mother, thou sole and only, thou not these,
Keep me in mind a little when I die
Because I was thy first-born; let thy soul
Pity me, pity even me gone hence and dead,
Though thou wert wroth, and though thou bear again
Much happier sons, and all men later born
Exceedingly excel me; yet do thou
Forget not, nor think shame; I was thy son.
Time was I did not shame thee; and time was
I thought to live and make thee honourable
With deeds as great as these men's; but they live,
These, and I die; and what thing should have been
Surely I know not; yet I charge thee, seeing
I am dead already, love me not the less,
Me, O my mother; I charge thee by these gods,
My father's, and that holier breast of thine,
By these that see me dying, and that which nursed,
Love me not less, thy first-born: though grief come,
Grief only, of me, and of all these great joy,
And shall come always to thee; for thou knowest,
O mother, O breasts that bare me, for ye know,
O sweet head of my mother, sacred eyes,
Ye know my soul albeit I sinned, ye know
Albeit I kneel not neither touch thy knees,
But with my lips I kneel, and with my heart
I fall about thy feet and worship thee.
And ye farewell now, all my friends; and ye,
Kinsmen, much younger and glorious more than I,
Sons of my mother's sister; and all farewell
That were in Colchis with me, and bare down

The waves and wars that met us: and though times
Change, and though now I be not anything,
Forget not me among you, what I did
In my good time; for even by all those days,
Those days and this, and your own living souls,
And by the light and luck of you that live,
And by this miserable spoil, and me
Dying, I beseech you, let my name not die.
But thou, dear, touch me with thy rose-like hands,
And fasten up mine eyelids with thy mouth,
A bitter kiss; and grasp me with thine arms,
Printing with heavy lips my light waste flesh,
Made light and thin by heavy-handed fate,
And with thine holy maiden eyes drop dew,
Drop tears for dew upon me who am dead,
Me who have loved thee; seeing without sin done
I am gone down to the empty weary house
Where no flesh is nor beauty nor swift eyes
Nor sound of mouth nor might of hands and feet.
But thou, dear, hide my body with thy veil,
And with thy raiment cover foot and head,
And stretch thyself upon me and touch hands
With hands and lips with lips: be pitiful
As thou art maiden perfect; let no man
Defile me to despise me, saying, This man
Died woman-wise, a woman's offering, slain
Through female fingers in his woof of life,
Dishonourable; for thou hast honoured me.
And now for God's sake kiss me once and twice
And let me go; for the night gathers me,
And in the night shall no man gather fruit.

*ATALANTA*

Hail thou: but I with heavy face and feet
Turn homeward and am gone out of thine eyes.

*CHORUS*

Who shall contend with his lords
  Or cross them or do them wrong?
Who shall bind them as with cords?
  Who shall tame them as with song?
Who shall smite them as with swords?
  For the hands of their kingdom are strong.

## FROM *POEMS AND BALLADS* (1866)

### A Ballad of Life

I found in dreams a place of wind and flowers,
   Full of sweet trees and colour of glad grass,
   In midst whereof there was
A lady clothed like summer with sweet hours.
Her beauty, fervent as a fiery moon,
   Made my blood burn and swoon
      Like a flame rained upon.
Sorrow had filled her shaken eyelids' blue,
And her mouth's sad red heavy rose all through
      Seemed sad with glad things gone.

She held a little cithern by the strings,
   Shaped heartwise, strung with subtle-coloured hair
   Of some dead lute-player
That in dead years had done delicious things.
The seven strings were named accordingly;
   The first string charity,
      The second tenderness,
The rest were pleasure, sorrow, sleep, and sin,
And loving-kindness, that is pity's kin
      And is most pitiless.

There were three men with her, each garmented
   With gold and shod with gold upon the feet;
   And with plucked ears of wheat
The first man's hair was wound upon his head:
His face was red, and his mouth curled and sad;
   All his gold garment had
      Pale stains of dust and rust.

A riven hood was pulled across his eyes;
The token of him being upon this wise
Made for a sign of Lust.

The next was Shame, with hollow heavy face
Coloured like green wood when flame kindles it.
He hath such feeble feet
They may not well endure in any place.
His face was full of grey old miseries,
And all his blood's increase
Was even increase of pain.
The last was Fear, that is akin to Death;
He is Shame's friend, and always as Shame saith
Fear answers him again.

My soul said in me; This is marvellous,
Seeing the air's face is not so delicate
Nor the sun's grace so great,
If sin and she be kin or amorous.
And seeing where maidens served her on their knees,
I bade one crave of these
To know the cause thereof.
Then Fear said: I am Pity that was dead.
And Shame said: I am Sorrow comforted.
And Lust said: I am Love.

Thereat her hands began a lute-playing
And her sweet mouth a song in a strange tongue;
And all the while she sung
There was no sound but long tears following
Long tears upon men's faces, waxen white
With extreme sad delight.
But those three following men
Became as men raised up among the dead;
Great glad mouths open and fair cheeks made red
With child's blood come again.

Then I said: Now assuredly I see
My lady is perfect, and transfigureth
All sin and sorrow and death,
Making them fair as her own eyelids be,
Or lips wherein my whole soul's life abides;
Or as her sweet white sides
And bosom carved to kiss.

Now therefore, if her pity further me,
Doubtless for her sake all my days shall be
As righteous as she is.

Forth, ballad, and take roses in both arms,
Even till the top rose touch thee in the throat
Where the least thornprick harms;
And girdled in thy golden singing-coat,
Come thou before my lady and say this;
Borgia, thy gold hair's colour burns in me,
Thy mouth makes beat my blood in feverish rhymes;
Therefore so many as these roses be,
Kiss me so many times.
Then it may be, seeing how sweet she
That she will stoop herself none otherwise
Than a blown vine-branch doth,
And kiss thee with soft laughter on thine eyes,
Ballad, and on thy mouth.

## Laus Veneris

Lors dit en plourant; Hélas trop malheureux homme et mauldict pescheur, oncques ne verrai-je clémence et miséricorde de Dieu. Ores m'en irai-je d'icy et me cacherai dedans le mont Horsel, en requérant de faveur et d'amoureuse merci ma doulce dame Vénus, car pour son amour serai-je bien à tout jamais damné en enfer. Voicy la fin de tous mes faicts d'armes et de toutes mes belles chansons. Hélas, trop belle estoyt la face de ma dame et ses yeulx, et en mauvais jour je vis ces chouses-là. Lors s'en alla tout en gémissant et se retourna chez elle, et là vescut tristement en grand amour près de sa dame. Puis après advint que le pape vit un jour esclater sur son baston force belles fleurs rouges et blanches et maints boutons de feuilles, et ainsi vit-il reverdir toute l'escorce. Ce dont il eut grande crainte et moult s'en esmut, et grande pitié lui prit de ce chevalier qui s'en estoyt départi sans espoir comme un homme misérable et damné. Doncques envoya force messaigers devers luy pour le ramener, disant qu'il aurait de Dieu grace et bonne absolution de son grand pesché d'amour. Mais oncques plus ne le virent; car toujours demeura ce pauvre chevalier auprès de Vénus la haulte et forte déesse ès flancs de la montagne amoureuse.

*Livre des grandes merveilles d'amour, escript en latin et en françoys par Maistre Antoine Gaget.* 1530.

## Laus Veneris

Asleep or waking is it? for her neck,
Kissed over close, wears yet a purple speck
  Wherein the pained blood falters and goes out;
Soft, and stung softly—fairer for a fleck.

But though my lips shut sucking on the place,
There is no vein at work upon her face;
  Her eyelids are so peaceable, no doubt
Deep sleep has warmed her blood through all its ways.

Lo, this is she that was the world's delight;
The old grey years were parcels of her might;
  The strewings of the ways wherein she trod
Were the twain seasons of the day and night.

Lo, she was thus when her clear limbs enticed
All lips that now grow sad with kissing Christ,
  Stained with blood fallen from the feet of God,
The feet and hands whereat our souls were priced.

Alas, Lord, surely thou art great and fair.
But lo her wonderfully woven hair!
  And thou didst heal us with thy piteous kiss;
But see now, Lord; her mouth is lovelier.

She is right fair; what hath she done to thee?
Nay, fair Lord Christ, lift up thine eyes and see;
  Had now thy mother such a lip—like this?
Thou knowest how sweet a thing it is to me.

Inside the Horsel here the air is hot;
Right little peace one hath for it, God wot;
  The scented dusty daylight burns the air,
And my heart chokes me till I hear it not.

Behold, my Venus, my soul's body, lies
With my love laid upon her garment-wise,
  Feeling my love in all her limbs and hair
And shed between her eyelids through her eyes.

She holds my heart in her sweet open hands
Hanging asleep; hard by her head there stands,
  Crowned with gilt thorns and clothed with flesh like fire,
Love, wan as foam blown up the salt burnt sands—

Hot as the brackish waifs of yellow spume
That shift and steam — loose clots of arid fume
  From the sea's panting mouth of dry desire;
There stands he, like one labouring at a loom.

The warp holds fast across; and every thread
That makes the woof up has dry specks of red;
  Always the shuttle cleaves clean through, and he
Weaves with the hair of many a ruined head.

Love is not glad nor sorry, as I deem;
Labouring he dreams, and labours in the dream,
  Till when the spool is finished, lo I see
His web, reeled off, curls and goes out like steam.

Night falls like fire; the heavy lights run low,
And as they drop, my blood and body so
  Shake as the flame shakes, full of days and hours
That sleep not neither weep they as they go.

Ah yet would God this flesh of mine might be
Where air might wash and long leaves cover me,
  Where tides of grass break into foam of flowers,
Or where the wind's feet shine along the sea.

Ah yet would God that stems and roots were bred
Out of my weary body and my head,
  That sleep were sealed upon me with a seal,
And I were as the least of all his dead.

Would God my blood were dew to feed the grass,
Mine ears made deaf and mine eyes blind as glass,
  My body broken as a turning wheel,
And my mouth stricken ere it saith Alas!

Ah God, that love were as a flower or flame,
That life were as the naming of a name,
  That death were not more pitiful than desire,
That these things were not one thing and the same!

Behold now, surely somewhere there is death:
For each man hath some space of years, he saith,
  A little space of time ere time expire,
A little day, a little way of breath.

And lo, between the sundawn and the sun,
His day's work and his night's work are undone;

And lo, between the nightfall and the light,
He is not, and none knoweth of such an one.

Ah God, that I were as all souls that be,
As any herb or leaf of any tree,
As men that toil through hours of labouring night,
As bones of men under the deep sharp sea.

Outside it must be winter among men;
For at the gold bars of the gates again
I heard all night and all the hours of it
The wind's wet wings and fingers drip with rain.

Knights gather, riding sharp for cold; I know
The ways and woods are strangled with the snow;
And with short song the maidens spin and sit
Until Christ's birthnight, lily-like, arow.

The scent and shadow shed about me make
The very soul in all my senses ache;
The hot hard night is fed upon my breath,
And sleep beholds me from afar awake.

Alas, but surely where the hills grow deep,
Or where the wild ways of the sea are steep,
Or in strange places somewhere there is death,
And on death's face the scattered hair of sleep.

There lover-like with lips and limbs that meet
They lie, they pluck sweet fruit of life and eat;
But me the hot and hungry days devour,
And in my mouth no fruit of theirs is sweet.

No fruit of theirs, but fruit of my desire,
For her love's sake whose lips through mine respire;
Her eyelids on her eyes like flower on flower,
Mine eyelids on mine eyes like fire on fire.

So lie we, not as sleep that lies by death,
With heavy kisses and with happy breath;
Not as man lies by woman, when the bride
Laughs low for love's sake and the words he saith.

For she lies, laughing low with love; she lies
And turns his kisses on her lips to sighs,
To sighing sound of lips unsatisfied,
And the sweet tears are tender with her eyes.

Ah, not as they, but as the souls that were
Slain in the old time, having found her fair;
   Who, sleeping with her lips upon their eyes,
Heard sudden serpents hiss across her hair.

Their blood runs round the roots of time like rain:
She casts them forth and gathers them again;
   With nerve and bone she weaves and multiplies
Exceeding pleasure out of extreme pain.

Her little chambers drip with flower-like red,
Her girdles, and the chaplets of her head,
   Her armlets and her anklets; with her feet
She tramples all that winepress of the dead.

Her gateways smoke with fume of flowers and fires,
With loves burnt out and unassuaged desires;
   Between her lips the steam of them is sweet,
The languor in her ears of many lyres.

Her beds are full of perfume and sad sound,
Her doors are made with music, and barred round
   With sighing and with laughter and with tears,
With tears whereby strong souls of men are bound.

There is the knight Adonis that was slain;
With flesh and blood she chains him for a chain;
   The body and the spirit in her ears
Cry, for her lips divide him vein by vein.

Yea, all she slayeth; yea, every man save me;
Me, love, thy lover that must cleave to thee
   Till the ending of the days and ways of earth,
The shaking of the sources of the sea.

Me, most forsaken of all souls that fell;
Me, satiated with things insatiable;
   Me, for whose sake the extreme hell makes mirth,
Yea, laughter kindles at the heart of hell.

Alas thy beauty! for thy mouth's sweet sake
My soul is bitter to me, my limbs quake
   As water, as the flesh of men that weep,
As their heart's vein whose heart goes nigh to break.

Ah God, that sleep with flower-sweet finger-tips
Would crush the fruit of death upon my lips;

Ah God, that death would tread the grapes of sleep
And wring their juice upon me as it drips.

There is no change of cheer for many days,
But change of chimes high up in the air, that sways
Rung by the running fingers of the wind;
And singing sorrows heard on hidden ways.

Day smiteth day in twain, night sundereth night,
And on mine eyes the dark sits as the light;
Yea, Lord, thou knowest I know not, having sinned,
If heaven be clean or unclean in thy sight.

Yea, as if earth were sprinkled over me,
Such chafed harsh earth as chokes a sandy sea,
Each pore doth yearn, and the dried blood thereof
Gasps by sick fits, my heart swims heavily,

There is a feverish famine in my veins;
Below her bosom, where a crushed grape stains
The white and blue, there my lips caught and clove
An hour since, and what mark of me remains?

I dare not always touch her, lest the kiss
Leave my lips charred. Yea, Lord, a little bliss,
Brief bitter bliss, one hath for a great sin;
Nathless thou knowest how sweet a thing it is.

Sin, is it sin whereby men's souls are thrust
Into the pit? yet had I a good trust
To save my soul before it slipped therein,
Trod under by the fire-shod feet of lust.

For if mine eyes fail and my soul takes breath,
I look between the iron sides of death
Into sad hell where all sweet love hath end,
All but the pain that never finisheth.

There are the naked faces of great kings,
The singing folk with all their lute-playings;
There when one cometh he shall have to friend
The grave that covets and the worm that clings.

There sit the knights that were so great of hand,
The ladies that were queens of fair green land,
Grown grey and black now, brought unto the dust,
Soiled, without raiment, clad about with sand.

There is one end for all of them; they sit
Naked and sad, they drink the dregs of it,
   Trodden as grapes in the wine-press of lust,
Trampled and trodden by the fiery feet.

I see the marvellous mouth whereby there fell
Cities and people whom the gods loved well,
   Yet for her sake on them the fire gat hold,
And for their sakes on her the fire of hell.

And softer than the Egyptian lote-leaf is,
The queen whose face was worth the world to kiss,
   Wearing at breast a suckling snake of gold;
And large pale lips of strong Semiramis,

Curled like a tiger's that curl back to feed;
Red only where the last kiss made them bleed;
   Her hair most thick with many a carven gem,
Deep in the mane, great-chested, like a steed.

Yea, with red sin the faces of them shine;
But in all these there was no sin like mine;
   No, not in all the strange great sins of them
That made the wine-press froth and foam with wine.

For I was of Christ's choosing, I God's knight,
No blinkard heathen stumbling for scant light;
   I can well see, for all the dusty days
Gone past, the clean great time of goodly fight.

I smell the breathing battle sharp with blows,
With shriek of shafts and snapping short of bows;
   The fair pure sword smites out in subtle ways,
Sounds and long lights are shed between the rows

Of beautiful mailed men; the edged light slips,
Most like a snake that takes short breath and dips
   Sharp from the beautifully bending head,
With all its gracious body lithe as lips

That curl in touching you; right in this wise
My sword doth, seeming fire in mine own eyes,
   Leaving all colours in them brown and red
And flecked with death; then the keen breaths like sighs,

The caught-up choked dry laughters following them,
When all the fighting face is grown a flame

For pleasure, and the pulse that stuns the ears,
And the heart's gladness of the goodly game.

Let me think yet a little; I do know
These things were sweet, but sweet such years ago,
Their savour is all turned now into tears;
Yea, ten years since, where the blue ripples blow,

The blue curled eddies of the blowing Rhine,
I felt the sharp wind shaking grass and vine
Touch my blood too, and sting me with delight
Through all this waste and weary body of mine

That never feels clear air; right gladly then
I rode alone, a great way off my men,
And heard the chiming bridle smite and smite,
And gave each rhyme thereof some rhyme again,

Till my song shifted to that iron one;
Seeing there rode up between me and the sun
Some certain of my foe's men, for his three
White wolves across their painted coats did run.

The first red-bearded, with square cheeks—alack,
I made my knave's blood turn his beard to black;
The slaying of him was a joy to see:
Perchance too, when at night he came not back,

Some woman fell a-weeping, whom this thief
Would beat when he had drunken; yet small grief
Hath any for the ridding of such knaves;
Yea, if one wept, I doubt her teen was brief.

This bitter love is sorrow in all lands,
Draining of eyelids, wringing of drenched hands,
Sighing of hearts and filling up of graves;
A sign across the head of the world he stands,

An one that hath a plague-mark on his brows;
Dust and spilt blood do track him to his house
Down under earth; sweet smells of lip and cheek,
Like a sweet snake's breath made more poisonous

With chewing of some perfumed deadly grass,
Are shed all round his passage if he pass,
And their quenched savour leaves the whole soul weak,
Sick with keen guessing whence the perfume was.

As one who hidden in deep sedge and reeds
Smells the rare scent made where a panther feeds,
  And tracking ever slotwise the warm smell
Is snapped upon by the sweet mouth and bleeds,

His head far down the hot sweet throat of her—
So one tracks love, whose breath is deadlier,
  And lo, one springe and you are fast in hell,
Fast as the gin's grip of a wayfarer.

I think now, as the heavy hours decease
One after one, and bitter thoughts increase
  One upon one, of all sweet finished things;
The breaking of the battle; the long peace

Wherein we sat clothed softly, each man's hair
Crowned with green leaves beneath white hoods of vair;
  The sounds of sharp spears at great tourneyings,
And noise of singing in the late sweet air.

I sang of love too, knowing nought thereof;
"Sweeter," I said, "the little laugh of love
  Than tears out of the eyes of Magdalen,
Or any fallen feather of the Dove.

"The broken little laugh that spoils a kiss,
The ache of purple pulses, and the bliss
  Of blinded eyelids that expand again—
Love draws them open with those lips of his,

"Lips that cling hard till the kissed face has grown
Of one same fire and colour with their own;
  Then ere one sleep, appeased with sacrifice,
Where his lips wounded, there his lips atone."

I sang these things long since and knew them not;
"Lo, here is love, or there is love, God wot,
  This man and that finds favour in his eyes,"
I said, "but I, what guerdon have I got?

"The dust of praise that is blown everywhere
In all men's faces with the common air;
  The bay-leaf that wants chafing to be sweet
Before they wind it in a singer's hair."

So that one dawn I rode forth sorrowing;
I had no hope but of some evil thing,

And so rode slowly past the windy wheat
And past the vineyard and the water-spring,

Up to the Horsel. A great elder-tree
Held back its heaps of flowers to let me see
The ripe tall grass, and one that walked therein,
Naked, with hair shed over to the knee.

She walked between the blossom and the grass;
I knew the beauty of her, what she was,
The beauty of her body and her sin,
And in my flesh the sin of hers, alas!

Alas! for sorrow is all the end of this.
O sad kissed mouth, how sorrowful it is!
O breast whereat some suckling sorrow clings,
Red with the bitter blossom of a kiss!

Ah, with blind lips I felt for you, and found
About my neck your hands and hair enwound,
The hands that stifle and the hair that stings,
I felt them fasten sharply without sound.

Yea, for my sin I had great store of bliss:
Rise up, make answer for me, let thy kiss
Seal my lips hard from speaking of my sin,
Lest one go mad to hear how sweet it is.

Yet I waxed faint with fume of barren bowers,
And murmuring of the heavy-headed hours;
And let the dove's beak fret and peck within
My lips in vain, and Love shed fruitless flowers.

So that God looked upon me when your hands
Were hot about me; yea, God brake my bands
To save my soul alive, and I came forth
Like a man blind and naked in strange lands

That hears men laugh and weep, and knows not whence
Nor wherefore, but is broken in his sense;
Howbeit I met folk riding from the north
Towards Rome, to purge them of their souls' offence,

And rode with them, and spake to none; the day
Stunned me like lights upon some wizard way,
And ate like fire mine eyes and mine eyesight;
So rode I, hearing all these chant and pray,

And marvelled; till before us rose and fell
White cursed hills, like outer skirts of hell
   Seen where men's eyes look through the day to night,
Like a jagged shell's lips, harsh, untunable,

Blown in between by devils' wrangling breath;
Nathless we won well past that hell and death,
   Down to the sweet land where all airs are good,
Even unto Rome where God's grace tarrieth.

Then came each man and worshipped at his knees
Who in the Lord God's likeness bears the keys
   To bind or loose, and called on Christ's shed blood,
And so the sweet-souled father gave him ease.

But when I came I fell down at his feet,
Saying, "Father, though the Lord's blood be right sweet,
   The spot it takes not off the panther's skin,
Nor shall an Ethiop's stain be bleached with it.

"Lo, I have sinned and have spat out at God,
Wherefore his hand is heavier and his rod
   More sharp because of mine exceeding sin,
And all his raiment redder than bright blood

"Before mine eyes; yea, for my sake I wot
The heat of hell is waxen seven times hot
   Through my great sin." Then spake he some sweet word,
Giving me cheer; which thing availed me not;

Yea, scarce I wist if such indeed were said;
For when I ceased—lo, as one newly dead
   Who hears a great cry out of hell, I heard
The crying of his voice across my head.

"Until this dry shred staff, that hath no whit
Of leaf nor bark, bear blossom and smell sweet,
   Seek thou not any mercy in God's sight,
For so long shalt thou be cast out from it."

Yea, what if dried-up stems wax red and green,
Shall that thing be which is not nor has been?
   Yea, what if sapless bark wax green and white,
Shall any good fruit grow upon my sin?

Nay, though sweet fruit were plucked of a dry tree,
And though men drew sweet waters of the sea,

There should not grow sweet leaves on this dead stem,
This waste wan body and shaken soul of me.

Yea, though God search it warily enough,
There is not one sound thing in all thereof;
Though he search all my veins through, searching them
He shall find nothing whole therein but love.

For I came home right heavy, with small cheer,
And lo my love, mine own soul's heart, more dear
Than mine own soul, more beautiful than God,
Who hath my being between the hands of her—

Fair still, but fair for no man saving me,
As when she came out of the naked sea
Making the foam as fire whereon she trod,
And as the inner flower of fire was she.

Yea, she laid hold upon me, and her mouth
Clove unto mine as soul to body doth,
And, laughing, made her lips luxurious;
Her hair had smells of all the sunburnt south,

Strange spice and flower, strange savour of crushed fruit,
And perfume the swart kings tread underfoot
For pleasure when their minds wax amorous,
Charred frankincense and grated sandal-root.

And I forgot fear and all weary things,
All ended prayers and perished thanksgivings,
Feeling her face with all her eager hair
Cleave to me, clinging as a fire that clings

To the body and to the raiment, burning them;
As after death I know that such-like flame
Shall cleave to me for ever; yea, what care,
Albeit I burn then, having felt the same?

Ah love, there is no better life than this;
To have known love, how bitter a thing it is,
And afterward be cast out of God's sight;
Yea, these that know not, shall they have such bliss

High up in barren heaven before his face
As we twain in the heavy-hearted place,
Remembering love and all the dead delight,
And all that time was sweet with for a space?

For till the thunder in the trumpet be,
Soul may divide from body, but not we
  One from another; I hold thee with my hand,
I let mine eyes have all their will of thee,

I seal myself upon thee with my might,
Abiding alway out of all men's sight
  Until God loosen over sea and land
The thunder of the trumpets of the night.

EXPLICIT LAUS VENERIS.

## The Triumph of Time

Before our lives divide for ever,
  While time is with us and hands are free,
(Time, swift to fasten and swift to sever
  Hand from hand, as we stand by the sea)
I will say no word that a man might say
Whose whole life's love goes down in a day;
For this could never have been; and never,
  Though the gods and the years relent, shall be.

Is it worth a tear, is it worth an hour,
  To think of things that are well outworn?
Of fruitless husk and fugitive flower,
  The dream foregone and the deed forborne?
Though joy be done with and grief be vain,
Time shall not sever us wholly in twain;
Earth is not spoilt for a single shower;
  But the rain has ruined the ungrown corn.

It will grow not again, this fruit of my heart,
  Smitten with sunbeams, ruined with rain.
The singing seasons divide and depart,
  Winter and summer depart in twain.
It will grow not again, it is ruined at root,
The bloodlike blossom, the dull red fruit;
Though the heart yet sickens, the lips yet smart,
  With sullen savour of poisonous pain.

I have given no man of my fruit to eat;
  I trod the grapes, I have drunken the wine.
Had you eaten and drunken and found it sweet,
  This wild new growth of the corn and vine,

This wine and bread without lees or leaven,
We had grown as gods, as the gods in heaven,
Souls fair to look upon, goodly to greet,
   One splendid spirit, your soul and mine.

In the change of years, in the coil of things,
   In the clamour and rumour of life to be,
We, drinking love at the furthest springs,
   Covered with love as a covering tree,
We had grown as gods, as the gods above,
Filled from the heart to the lips with love,
Held fast in his hands, clothed warm with his wings,
   O love, my love, had you loved but me!

We had stood as the sure stars stand, and moved
   As the moon moves, loving the world; and seen
Grief collapse as a thing disproved,
   Death consume as a thing unclean.
Twain halves of a perfect heart, made fast
Soul to soul while the years fell past;
Had you loved me once, as you have not loved;
   Had the chance been with us that has not been.

I have put my days and dreams out of mind,
   Days that are over, dreams that are done.
Though we seek life through, we shall surely find
   There is none of them clear to us now, not one.
But clear are these things; the grass and the sand,
Where, sure as the eyes reach, ever at hand,
With lips wide open and face burnt blind,
   The strong sea-daisies feast on the sun.

The low downs lean to the sea; the stream,
   One loose thin pulseless tremulous vein,
Rapid and vivid and dumb as a dream,
   Works downward, sick of the sun and the rain;
No wind is rough with the rank rare flowers;
The sweet sea, mother of loves and hours,
Shudders and shines as the grey winds gleam,
   Turning her smile to a fugitive pain.

Mother of loves that are swift to fade,
   Mother of mutable winds and hours.
A barren mother, a mother-maid,
   Cold and clean as her faint salt flowers.

I would we twain were even as she,
Lost in the night and the light of the sea,
Where faint sounds falter and wan beams wade,
   Break, and are broken, and shed into showers.

The loves and hours of the life of a man,
   They are swift and sad, being born of the sea.
Hours that rejoice and regret for a span,
   Born with a man's breath, mortal as he;
Loves that are lost ere they come to birth,
Weeds of the wave, without fruit upon earth.
I lose what I long for, save what I can,
   My love, my love, and no love for me!

It is not much that a man can save
   On the sands of life, in the straits of time,
Who swims in sight of the great third wave
   That never a swimmer shall cross or climb.
Some waif washed up with the strays and spars
That ebb-tide shows to the shore and the stars;
Weed from the water, grass from a grave,
   A broken blossom, a ruined rhyme.

There will no man do for your sake, I think,
   What I would have done for the least word said.
I had wrung life dry for your lips to drink,
   Broken it up for your daily bread:
Body for body and blood for blood,
As the flow of the full sea risen to flood
That yearns and trembles before it sink,
   I had given, and lain down for you, glad and dead.

Yea, hope at highest and all her fruit,
   And time at fullest and all his dower,
I had given you surely, and life to boot,
   Were we once made one for a single hour.
But now, you are twain, you are cloven apart,
Flesh of his flesh, but heart of my heart;
And deep in one is the bitter root,
   And sweet for one is the lifelong flower.

To have died if you cared I should die for you, clung
   To my life if you bade me, played my part
As it pleased you—these were the thoughts that stung,
   The dreams that smote with a keener dart

Than shafts of love or arrows of death;
These were but as fire is, dust, or breath,
Or poisonous foam on the tender tongue
  Of the little snakes that eat my heart.

I wish we were dead together to-day,
  Lost sight of, hidden away out of sight,
Clasped and clothed in the cloven clay,
  Out of the world's way, out of the light,
Out of the ages of worldly weather,
Forgotten of all men altogether,
As the world's first dead, taken wholly away,
  Made one with death, filled full of the night.

How we should slumber, how we should sleep,
  Far in the dark with the dreams and the dews!
And dreaming, grow to each other, and weep,
  Laugh low, live softly, murmur and muse;
Yea, and it may be, struck through by the dream,
Feel the dust quicken and quiver, and seem
Alive as of old to the lips, and leap
  Spirit to spirit as lovers use.

Sick dreams and sad of a dull delight;
  For what shall it profit when men are dead
To have dreamed, to have loved with the whole soul's might,
  To have looked for day when the day was fled?
Let come what will, there is one thing worth,
To have had fair love in the life upon earth:
To have held love safe till the day grew night,
  While skies had colour and lips were red.

Would I lose you now? would I take you then,
  If I lose you now that my heart has need?
And come what may after death to men,
  What thing worth this will the dead years breed?
Lose life, lose all; but at least I know,
O sweet life's love, having loved you so,
Had I reached you on earth, I should lose not again,
  In death nor life, nor in dream or deed.

Yea, I know this well: were you once sealed mine,
  Mine in the blood's beat, mine in the breath,
Mixed into me as honey in wine,
  Not time, that sayeth and gainsayeth,

Nor all strong things had severed us then;
Not wrath of gods, nor wisdom of men,
Nor all things earthly, nor all divine,
  Nor joy nor sorrow, nor life nor death.

I had grown pure as the dawn and the dew,
  You had grown strong as the sun or the sea.
But none shall triumph a whole life through:
  For death is one, and the fates are three.
At the door of life, by the gate of breath,
There are worse things waiting for men than death;
Death could not sever my soul and you,
  As these have severed your soul from me.

You have chosen and clung to the chance they sent you,
  Life sweet as perfume and pure as prayer.
But will it not one day in heaven repent you?
  Will they solace you wholly, the days that were?
Will you lift up your eyes between sadness and bliss,
Meet mine, and see where the great love is,
And tremble and turn and be changed? Content you;
  The gate is strait; I shall not be there.

But you, had you chosen, had you stretched hand,
  Had you seen good such a thing were done,
I too might have stood with the souls that stand
  In the sun's sight, clothed with the light of the sun;
But who now on earth need care how I live?
Have the high gods anything left to give,
Save dust and laurels and gold and sand?
  Which gifts are goodly; but I will none.

O all fair lovers about the world,
  There is none of you, none, that shall comfort me.
My thoughts are as dead things, wrecked and whirled
  Round and round in a gulf of the sea;
And still, through the sound and the straining stream,
Through the coil and chafe, they gleam in a dream,
The bright fine lips so cruelly curled,
  And strange swift eyes where the soul sits free.

Free, without pity, withheld from woe,
  Ignorant; fair as the eyes are fair.
Would I have you change now, change at a blow,
  Startled and stricken, awake and aware?

Yea, if I could, would I have you see
My very love of you filling me,
And know my soul to the quick, as I know
The likeness and look of your throat and hair?

I shall not change you. Nay, though I might,
Would I change my sweet one love with a word?
I had rather your hair should change in a night,
Clear now as the plume of a black bright bird;
Your face fail suddenly, cease, turn grey,
Die as a leaf that dies in a day.
I will keep my soul in a place out of sight,
Far off, where the pulse of it is not heard.

Far off it walks, in a bleak blown space,
Full of the sound of the sorrow of years.
I have woven a veil for the weeping face,
Whose lips have drunken the wine of tears;
I have found a way for the failing feet,
A place for slumber and sorrow to meet;
There is no rumour about the place,
Nor light, nor any that sees or hears.

I have hidden my soul out of sight, and said
"Let none take pity upon thee, none
Comfort thy crying: for lo, thou art dead,
Lie still now, safe out of sight of the sun.
Have I not built thee a grave, and wrought
Thy grave-clothes on thee of grievous thought,
With soft spun verses and tears unshed,
And sweet light visions of things undone?

"I have given thee garments and balm and myrrh,
And gold, and beautiful burial things.
But thou, be at peace now, make no stir;
Is not thy grave as a royal king's?
Fret not thyself though the end were sore;
Sleep, be patient, vex me no more.
Sleep; what hast thou to do with her?
The eyes that weep, with the mouth that sings?"

Where the dead red leaves of the years lie rotten,
The cold old crimes and the deeds thrown by,
The misconceived and the misbegotten,
I would find a sin to do ere I die,

Sure to dissolve and destroy me all through,
That would set you higher in heaven, serve you
And leave you happy, when clean forgotten,
As a dead man out of mind, am I.

Your lithe hands draw me, your face burns through me,
I am swift to follow you, keen to see;
But love lacks might to redeem or undo me;
As I have been, I know I shall surely be;
"What should such fellows as I do?" Nay,
My part were worse if I chose to play;
For the worst is this after all; if they knew me,
Not a soul upon earth would pity me.

And I play not for pity of these; but you,
If you saw with your soul what man am I,
You would praise me at least that my soul all through
Clove to you, loathing the lives that lie;
The souls and lips that are bought and sold,
The smiles of silver and kisses of gold,
The lapdog loves that whine as they chew,
The little lovers that curse and cry.

There are fairer women, I hear; that may be;
But I, that I love you and find you fair,
Who are more than fair in my eyes if they be,
Do the high gods know or the great gods care?
Though the swords in my heart for one were seven,
Would the iron hollow of doubtful heaven,
That knows not itself whether night-time or day be,
Reverberate words and a foolish prayer?

I will go back to the great sweet mother,
Mother and lover of men, the sea.
I will go down to her, I and none other,
Close with her, kiss her and mix her with me;
Cling to her, strive with her, hold her fast:
O fair white mother, in days long past
Born without sister, born without brother,
Set free my soul as thy soul is free.

O fair green-girdled mother of mine,
Sea, that art clothed with the sun and the rain,
Thy sweet hard kisses are strong like wine,
Thy large embraces are keen like pain.

Save me and hide me with all thy waves,
Find me one grave of thy thousand graves,
Those pure cold populous graves of thine
  Wrought without hand in a world without stain.

I shall sleep, and move with the moving ships,
  Change as the winds change, veer in the tide;
My lips will feast on the foam of thy lips,
  I shall rise with thy rising, with thee subside;
Sleep, and not know if she be, if she were,
Filled full with life to the eyes and hair,
As a rose is fulfilled to the roseleaf tips
  With splendid summer and perfume and pride.

This woven raiment of nights and days,
  Were it once cast off and unwound from me,
Naked and glad would I walk in thy ways,
  Alive and aware of thy ways and thee;
Clear of the whole world, hidden at home,
Clothed with the green and crowned with the foam,
A pulse of the life of thy straits and bays,
  A vein in the heart of the streams of the sea.

Fair mother, fed with the lives of men,
  Thou art subtle and cruel of heart, men say.
Thou hast taken, and shalt not render again;
  Thou art full of thy dead, and cold as they.
But death is the worst that comes of thee;
Thou art fed with our dead, O mother, O sea,
But when hast thou fed on our hearts? or when,
  Having given us love, hast thou taken away?

O tender-hearted, O perfect lover,
  Thy lips are bitter, and sweet thine heart.
The hopes that hurt and the dreams that hover,
  Shall they not vanish away and apart?
But thou, thou art sure, thou art older than earth;
Thou art strong for death and fruitful of birth;
Thy depths conceal and thy gulfs discover;
  From the first thou wert; in the end thou art.

And grief shall endure not for ever, I know.
  As things that are not shall these things be;
We shall live through seasons of sun and of snow,
  And none be grievous as this to me.

We shall hear, as one in a trance that hears,
The sound of time, the rhyme of the years;
Wrecked hope and passionate pain will grow
  As tender things of a spring-tide sea.

Sea-fruit that swings in the waves that hiss,
  Drowned gold and purple and royal rings.
And all time past, was it all for this?
  Times unforgotten, and treasures of things?
Swift years of liking and sweet long laughter,
That wist not well of the years thereafter
Till love woke, smitten at heart by a kiss,
  With lips that trembled and trailing wings?

There lived a singer in France of old
  By the tideless dolorous midland sea.
In a land of sand and ruin and gold
  There shone one woman, and none but she.
And finding life for her love's sake fail,
Being fain to see her, he bade set sail,
Touched land, and saw her as life grew cold,
  And praised God, seeing; and so died he.

Died, praising God for his gift and grace:
  For she bowed down to him weeping, and said
"Live;" and her tears were shed on his face
  Or ever the life in his face was shed.
The sharp tears fell through her hair, and stung
Once, and her close lips touched him and clung
Once, and grew one with his lips for a space;
  And so drew back, and the man was dead.

O brother, the gods were good to you.
  Sleep, and be glad while the world endures.
Be well content as the years wear through;
  Give thanks for life, and the loves and lures;
Give thanks for life, O brother, and death,
For the sweet last sound of her feet, her breath,
For gifts she gave you, gracious and few,
  Tears and kisses, that lady of yours.

Rest, and be glad of the gods; but I,
  How shall I praise them, or how take rest?
There is not room under all the sky
  For me that know not of worst or best,

Dream or desire of the days before,
Sweet things or bitterness, any more.
Love will not come to me now though I die,
  As love came close to you, breast to breast.

I shall never be friends again with roses;
  I shall loathe sweet tunes, where a note grown strong
Relents and recoils, and climbs and closes,
  As a wave of the sea turned back by song.
There are sounds where the soul's delight takes fire,
Face to face with its own desire;
A delight that rebels, a desire that reposes;
  I shall hate sweet music my whole life long.

The pulse of war and passion of wonder,
  The heavens that murmur, the sounds that shine,
The stars that sing and the loves that thunder,
  The music burning at heart like wine,
An armed archangel whose hands raise up
All senses mixed in the spirit's cup
Till flesh and spirit are molten in sunder—
  These things are over, and no more mine.

These were a part of the playing I heard
  Once, ere my love and my heart were at strife;
Love that sings and hath wings as a bird,
  Balm of the wound and heft of the knife.
Fairer than earth is the sea, and sleep
Than overwatching of eyes that weep,
Now time has done with his one sweet word,
  The wine and leaven of lovely life.

I shall go my ways, tread out my measure,
  Fill the days of my daily breath
With fugitive things not good to treasure,
  Do as the world doth, say as it saith;
But if we had loved each other—O sweet,
Had you felt, lying under the palms of your feet,
The heart of my heart, beating harder with pleasure
  To feel you tread it to dust and death—

Ah, had I not taken my life up and given
  All that life gives and the years let go,
The wine and honey, the balm and leaven,
  The dreams reared high and the hopes brought low?

Come life, come death, not a word be said;
Should I lose you living, and vex you dead?
I never shall tell you on earth; and in heaven,
  If I cry to you then, will you hear or know?

**Itylus**

Swallow, my sister, O sister swallow,
  How can thine heart be full of the spring?
    A thousand summers are over and dead.
What hast thou found in the spring to follow?
  What hast thou found in thine heart to sing?
    What wilt thou do when the summer is shed?

O swallow, sister, O fair swift swallow,
  Why wilt thou fly after spring to the south,
    The soft south whither thine heart is set?
Shall not the grief of the old time follow?
  Shall not the song thereof cleave to thy mouth?
    Hast thou forgotten ere I forget?

Sister, my sister, O fleet sweet swallow,
  Thy way is long to the sun and the south;
    But I, fulfilled of my heart's desire,
Shedding my song upon height, upon hollow,
  From tawny body and sweet small mouth
    Feed the heart of the night with fire.

I the nightingale all spring through,
  O swallow, sister, O changing swallow,
    All spring through till the spring be done,
Clothed with the light of the night on the dew,
  Sing, while the hours and the wild birds follow,
    Take flight and follow and find the sun.

Sister, my sister, O soft light swallow,
  Though all things feast in the spring's guest-chamber,
    How hast thou heart to be glad thereof yet?
For where thou fliest I shall not follow,
  Till life forget and death remember,
    Till thou remember and I forget.

Swallow, my sister, O singing swallow,
  I know not how thou hast heart to sing.
    Hast thou the heart? is it all past over?

Thy lord the summer is good to follow,
And fair the feet of thy lover the spring:
But what wilt thou say to the spring thy lover?

O swallow, sister, O fleeting swallow,
My heart in me is a molten ember
And over my head the waves have met.
But thou wouldst tarry or I would follow,
Could I forget or thou remember,
Couldst thou remember and I forget.

O sweet stray sister, O shifting swallow,
The heart's division divideth us.
Thy heart is light as a leaf of a tree;
But mine goes forth among sea-gulfs hollow
To the place of the slaying of Itylus,
The feast of Daulis, the Thracian sea.

O swallow, sister, O rapid swallow,
I pray thee sing not a little space.
Are not the roofs and the lintels wet?
The woven web that was plain to follow,
The small slain body, the flowerlike face,
Can I remember if thou forget?

O sister, sister, thy first-begotten!
The hands that cling and the feet that follow,
The voice of the child's blood crying yet
Who hath remembered me? who hath forgotten?
Thou hast forgotten, O summer swallow,
But the world shall end when I forget.

## Anactoria

τίνος αὖ τὺ πειθοῖ
μὰψ σαγηνεύσας φιλότατα;
SAPPHO.

My life is bitter with thy love; thine eyes
Blind me, thy tresses burn me, thy sharp sighs
Divide my flesh and spirit with soft sound,
And my blood strengthens, and my veins abound.
I pray thee sigh not, speak not, draw not breath;
Let life burn down, and dream it is not death.
I would the sea had hidden us, the fire

(Wilt thou fear that, and fear not my desire?)
Severed the bones that bleach, the flesh that cleaves,
And let our sifted ashes drop like leaves.
I feel thy blood against my blood: my pain
Pains thee, and lips bruise lips, and vein stings vein.
Let fruit be crushed on fruit, let flower on flower,
Breast kindle breast, and either burn one hour.
Why wilt thou follow lesser loves? are thine
Too weak to bear these hands and lips of mine?
I charge thee for my life's sake, O too sweet
To crush love with thy cruel faultless feet,
I charge thee keep thy lips from hers or his,
Sweetest, till theirs be sweeter than my kiss:
Lest I too lure, a swallow for a dove,
Erotion or Erinna to my love.
I would my love could kill thee; I am satiated
With seeing the live, and fain would have thee dead.
I would earth had thy body as fruit to eat,
And no mouth but some serpent's found thee sweet.
I would find grievous ways to have thee slain,
Intense device, and superflux of pain;
Vex thee with amorous agonies, and shake
Life at thy lips, and leave it there to ache;
Strain out thy soul with pangs too soft to kill,
Intolerable interludes, and infinite ill;
Relapse and reluctation of the breath,
Dumb tunes and shuddering semitones of death.
I am weary of all thy words and soft strange ways,
Of all love's fiery nights and all his days,
And all the broken kisses salt as brine
That shuddering lips make moist with waterish wine,
And eyes the bluer for all those hidden hours
That pleasure fills with tears and feeds from flowers,
Fierce at the heart with fire that half comes through,
But all the flowerlike white stained round with blue;
The fervent underlid, and that above
Lifted with laughter or abashed with love;
Thine amorous girdle, full of thee and fair,
And leavings of the lilies in thine hair.
Yea, all sweet words of thine and all thy ways,
And all the fruit of nights and flower of days,
And stinging lips wherein the hot sweet brine
That Love was born of burns and foams like wine,

And eyes insatiable of amorous hours,
Fervent as fire and delicate as flowers,
Coloured like night at heart, but cloven through
Like night with flame, dyed round like night with blue,
Clothed with deep eyelids under and above—
Yea, all thy beauty sickens me with love;
Thy girdle empty of thee and now not fair,
And ruinous lilies in thy languid hair.
Ah, take no thought for Love's sake; shall this be,
And she who loves thy lover not love thee?
Sweet soul, sweet mouth of all that laughs and lives,
Mine is she, very mine; and she forgives.
For I beheld in sleep the light that is
In her high place in Paphos, heard the kiss
Of body and soul that mix with eager tears
And laughter stinging through the eyes and ears;
Saw Love, as burning flame from crown to feet,
Imperishable, upon her storied seat;
Clear eyelids lifted toward the north and south,
A mind of many colours, and a mouth
Of many tunes and kisses; and she bowed,
With all her subtle face laughing aloud,
Bowed down upon me, saying, "Who doth thee wrong,
Sappho?" but thou—thy body is the song,
Thy mouth the music; thou art more than I,
Though my voice die not till the whole world die;
Though men that hear it madden; though love weep,
Though nature change, though shame be charmed to sleep.
Ah, wilt thou slay me lest I kiss thee dead?
Yet the queen laughed from her sweet heart and said:
"Even she that flies shall follow for thy sake,
And she shall give thee gifts that would not take,
Shall kiss that would not kiss thee" (yea, kiss me)
"When thou wouldst not"—when I would not kiss thee!
Ah, more to me than all men as thou art,
Shall not my songs assuage her at the heart?
Ah, sweet to me as life seems sweet to death,
Why should her wrath fill thee with fearful breath?
Nay, sweet, for is she God alone? hath she
Made earth and all the centuries of the sea,
Taught the sun ways to travel, woven most fine
The moonbeams, shed the starbeams forth as wine,
Bound with her myrtles, beaten with her rods,

The young men and the maidens and the gods?
Have we not lips to love with, eyes for tears,
And summer and flower of women and of years?
Stars for the foot of morning, and for noon
Sunlight, and exaltation of the moon;
Waters that answer waters, fields that wear
Lilies, and languor of the Lesbian air?
Beyond those flying feet of fluttered doves,
Are there not other gods for other loves?
Yea, though she scourge thee, sweetest, for my sake,
Blossom not thorns and flowers not blood should break.
Ah that my lips were tuneless lips, but pressed
To the bruised blossom of thy scourged white breast!
Ah that my mouth for Muses' milk were fed
On the sweet blood thy sweet small wounds had bled!
That with my tongue I felt them, and could taste
The faint flakes from thy bosom to the waist!
That I could drink thy veins as wine, and eat
Thy breasts like honey! that from face to feet
Thy body were abolished and consumed,
And in my flesh thy very flesh entombed!
Ah, ah, thy beauty! like a beast it bites,
Stings like an adder, like an arrow smites.
Ah sweet, and sweet again, and seven times sweet,
The paces and the pauses of thy feet!
Ah sweeter than all sleep or summer air
The fallen fillets fragrant from thine hair!
Yea, though their alien kisses do me wrong,
Sweeter thy lips than mine with all their song;
Thy shoulders whiter than a fleece of white,
And flower-sweet fingers, good to bruise or bite
As honeycomb of the inmost honey-cells,
With almond-shaped and roseleaf-coloured shells
And blood like purple blossom at the tips
Quivering; and pain made perfect in thy lips
For my sake when I hurt thee; O that I
Durst crush thee out of life with love, and die,
Die of thy pain and my delight, and be
Mixed with thy blood and molten into thee!
Would I not plague thee dying overmuch?
Would I not hurt thee perfectly? not touch
Thy pores of sense with torture, and make bright
Thine eyes with bloodlike tears and grievous light?

Strike pang from pang as note is struck from note,
Catch the sob's middle music in thy throat,
Take thy limbs living, and new-mould with these
A lyre of many faultless agonies?
Feed thee with fever and famine and fine drouth,
With perfect pangs convulse thy perfect mouth,
Make thy life shudder in thee and burn afresh,
And wring thy very spirit through the flesh?
Cruel? but love makes all that love him well
As wise as heaven and crueller than hell.
Me hath love made more bitter toward thee
Than death toward man; but were I made as he
Who hath made all things to break them one by one,
If my feet trod upon the stars and sun
And souls of men as his have alway trod,
God knows I might be crueller than God.
For who shall change with prayers or thanksgivings
The mystery of the cruelty of things?
Or say what God above all gods and years
With offering and blood-sacrifice of tears,
With lamentation from strange lands, from graves
Where the snake pastures, from scarred mouths of slaves,
From prison, and from plunging prows of ships
Through flamelike foam of the sea's closing lips—
With thwartings of strange signs, and wind-blown hair
Of comets, desolating the dim air,
When darkness is made fast with seals and bars,
And fierce reluctance of disastrous stars,
Eclipse, and sound of shaken hills, and wings
Darkening, and blind inexpiable things—
With sorrow of labouring moons, and altering light
And travail of the planets of the night,
And weeping of the weary Pleiads seven,
Feeds the mute melancholy lust of heaven?
Is not his incense bitterness, his meat
Murder? his hidden face and iron feet
Hath not man known, and felt them on their way
Threaten and trample all things and every day?
Hath he not sent us hunger? who hath cursed
Spirit and flesh with longing? filled with thirst
Their lips who cried unto him? who bade exceed
The fervid will, fall short the feeble deed,
Bade sink the spirit and the flesh aspire,

Pain animate the dust of dead desire,
And life yield up her flower to violent fate?
Him would I reach, him smite, him desecrate,
Pierce the cold lips of God with human breath,
And mix his immortality with death.
Why hath he made us? what had all we done
That we should live and loathe the sterile sun,
And with the moon wax paler as she wanes,
And pulse by pulse feel time grow through our veins?
Thee too the years shall cover; thou shalt be
As the rose born of one same blood with thee,
As a song sung, as a word said, and fall
Flower-wise, and be not any more at all,
Nor any memory of thee anywhere;
For never Muse has bound above thine hair
The high Pierian flower whose graft outgrows
All summer kinship of the mortal rose
And colour of deciduous days, nor shed
Reflex and flush of heaven about thine head,
Nor reddened brows made pale by floral grief
With splendid shadow from that lordlier leaf.
Yea, thou shalt be forgotten like spilt wine,
Except these kisses of my lips on thine
Brand them with immortality; but me—
Men shall not see bright fire nor hear the sea,
Nor mix their hearts with music, nor behold
Cast forth of heaven, with feet of awful gold
And plumeless wings that make the bright air blind,
Lightning, with thunder for a hound behind
Hunting through fields unfurrowed and unsown,
But in the light and laughter, in the moan
And music, and in grasp of lip and hand
And shudder of water that makes felt on land
The immeasurable tremor of all the sea,
Memories shall mix and metaphors of me.
Like me shall be the shuddering calm of night,
When all the winds of the world for pure delight
Close lips that quiver and fold up wings that ache;
When nightingales are louder for love's sake,
And leaves tremble like lute-strings or like fire;
Like me the one star swooning with desire
Even at the cold lips of the sleepless moon,
As I at thine; like me the waste white noon,

Burnt through with barren sunlight; and like me
The land-stream and the tide-stream in the sea.
I am sick with time as these with ebb and flow,
And by the yearning in my veins I know
The yearning sound of waters; and mine eyes
Burn as that beamless fire which fills the skies
With troubled stars and travailing things of flame;
And in my heart the grief consuming them
Labours, and in my veins the thirst of these,
And all the summer travail of the trees
And all the winter sickness; and the earth,
Filled full with deadly works of death and birth,
Sore spent with hungry lusts of birth and death,
Has pain like mine in her divided breath;
Her spring of leaves is barren, and her fruit
Ashes; her boughs are burdened, and her root
Fibrous and gnarled with poison; underneath
Serpents have gnawn it through with tortuous teeth
Made sharp upon the bones of all the dead,
And wild birds rend her branches overhead.
These, woven as raiment for his word and thought,
These hath God made, and me as these, and wrought
Song, and hath lit it at my lips; and me
Earth shall not gather though she feed on thee.
As a shed tear shalt thou be shed; but I—
Lo, earth may labour, men live long and die,
Years change and stars, and the high God devise
New things, and old things wane before his eyes
Who wields and wrecks them, being more strong than they—
But, having made me, me he shall not slay.
Nor slay nor satiate, like those herds of his
Who laugh and live a little, and their kiss
Contents them, and their loves are swift and sweet,
And sure death grasps and gains them with slow feet,
Love they or hate they, strive or bow their knees—
And all these end; he hath his will of these.
Yea, but albeit he slay me, hating me—
Albeit he hide me in the deep dear sea
And cover me with cool wan foam, and ease
This soul of mine as any soul of these,
And give me water and great sweet waves, and make
The very sea's name lordlier for my sake,
The whole sea sweeter—albeit I die indeed

And hide myself and sleep and no man heed,
Of me the high God hath not all his will.
Blossom of branches, and on each high hill
Clear air and wind, and under in clamorous vales
Fierce noises of the fiery nightingales,
Buds burning in the sudden spring like fire,
The wan washed sand and the waves' vain desire,
Sails seen like blown white flowers at sea, and words
That bring tears swiftest, and long notes of birds
Violently singing till the whole world sings—
I Sappho shall be one with all these things,
With all high things for ever; and my face
Seen once, my songs once heard in a strange place,
Cleave to men's lives, and waste the days thereof
With gladness and much sadness and long love.
Yea, they shall say, earth's womb has borne in vain
New things, and never this best thing again;
Borne days and men, borne fruits and wars and wine,
Seasons and songs, but no song more like mine.
And they shall know me as ye who have known me here,
Last year when I loved Atthis, and this year
When I love thee; and they shall praise me, and say
"She hath all time as all we have our day,
Shall she not live and have her will"—even I?
Yea, though thou diest, I say I shall not die.
For these shall give me of their souls, shall give
Life, and the days and loves wherewith I live,
Shall quicken me with loving, fill with breath,
Save me and serve me, strive for me with death.
Alas, that neither moon nor snow nor dew
Nor all cold things can purge me wholly through,
Assuage me nor allay me nor appease,
Till supreme sleep shall bring me bloodless ease;
Till time wax faint in all his periods;
Till fate undo the bondage of the gods,
And lay, to slake and satiate me all through,
Lotus and Lethe on my lips like dew,
And shed around and over and under me
Thick darkness and the insuperable sea.

**Hymn to Proserpine**
**(After the Proclamation in Rome of the Christian Faith)**

*Vicisti, Galilæe.*

I have lived long enough, having seen one thing, that love hath an end;
Goddess and maiden and queen, be near me now and befriend.
Thou art more than the day or the morrow, the seasons that laugh or
that weep;
For these give joy and sorrow; but thou, Proserpina, sleep.
Sweet is the treading of wine, and sweet the feet of the dove;
But a goodlier gift is thine than foam of the grapes or love.
Yea, is not even Apollo, with hair and harpstring of gold,
A bitter God to follow, a beautiful God to behold?
I am sick of singing: the bays burn deep and chafe: I am fain
To rest a little from praise and grievous pleasure and pain.
For the Gods we know not of, who give us our daily breath,
We know they are cruel as love or life, and lovely as death.
O Gods dethroned and deceased, cast forth, wiped out in a day!
From your wrath is the world released, redeemed from your chains,
men say.
New Gods are crowned in the city; their flowers have broken your rods;
They are merciful, clothed with pity, the young compassionate Gods.
But for me their new device is barren, the days are bare;
Things long past over suffice, and men forgotten that were.
Time and the Gods are at strife; ye dwell in the midst thereof,
Draining a little life from the barren breasts of love.
I say to you, cease, take rest; yea, I say to you all, be at peace,
Till the bitter milk of her breast and the barren bosom shall cease.
Wilt thou yet take all, Galilean? but these thou shalt not take,
The laurel, the palms and the paean, the breasts of the nymphs in the brake;
Breasts more soft than a dove's, that tremble with tenderer breath;
And all the wings of the Loves, and all the joy before death;
All the feet of the hours that sound as a single lyre,
Dropped and deep in the flowers, with strings that flicker like fire.
More than these wilt thou give, things fairer than all these things?
Nay, for a little we live, and life hath mutable wings.
A little while and we die; shall life not thrive as it may?
For no man under the sky lives twice, outliving his day.
And grief is a grievous thing, and a man hath enough of his tears:
Why should he labour, and bring fresh grief to blacken his years?
Thou hast conquered, O pale Galilean; the world has grown grey from
thy breath;

We have drunken of things Lethean, and fed on the fullness of death.
Laurel is green for a season, and love is sweet for a day;
But love grows bitter with treason, and laurel outlives not May.
Sleep, shall we sleep after all? for the world is not sweet in the end;
For the old faiths loosen and fall, the new years ruin and rend.
Fate is a sea without shore, and the soul is a rock that abides;
But her ears are vexed with the roar and her face with the foam of the tides.
O lips that the live blood faints in, the leavings of racks and rods!
O ghastly glories of saints, dead limbs of gibbeted Gods!
Though all men abase them before you in spirit, and all knees bend,
I kneel not neither adore you, but standing, look to the end.
All delicate days and pleasant, all spirits and sorrows are cast
Far out with the foam of the present that sweeps to the surf of the past:
Where beyond the extreme sea-wall, and between the remote sea-gates,
Waste water washes, and tall ships founder, and deep death waits:
Where, mighty with deepening sides, clad about with the seas as with wings,
And impelled of invisible tides, and fulfilled of unspeakable things,
White-eyed and poisonous-finned, shark-toothed and serpentine-curled,
Rolls, under the whitening wind of the future, the wave of the world.
The depths stand naked in sunder behind it, the storms flee away;
In the hollow before it the thunder is taken and snared as a prey;
In its sides is the north-wind bound; and its salt is of all men's tears;
With light of ruin, and sound of changes, and pulse of years:
With travail of day after day, and with trouble of hour upon hour;
And bitter as blood is the spray; and the crests are as fangs that devour:
And its vapour and storm of its steam as the sighing of spirits to be;
And its noise as the noise in a dream; and its depth as the roots of the sea:
And the height of its heads as the height of the utmost stars of the air:
And the ends of the earth at the might thereof tremble, and time is made bare.
Will ye bridle the deep sea with reins, will ye chasten the high sea with rods?
Will ye take her to chain her with chains, who is older than all ye Gods?
All ye as a wind shall go by, as a fire shall ye pass and be past;
Ye are Gods, and behold, ye shall die, and the waves be upon you at last.

In the darkness of time, in the deeps of the years, in the changes of things,
Ye shall sleep as a slain man sleeps, and the world shall forget you for kings.
Though the feet of thine high priests tread where thy lords and our forefathers trod,
Though these that were Gods are dead, and thou being dead art a God,
Though before thee the throned Cytherean be fallen, and hidden her head,
Yet thy kingdom shall pass, Galilean, thy dead shall go down to thee dead.
Of the maiden thy mother men sing as a goddess with grace clad around;
Thou art throned where another was king; where another was queen she is crowned.
Yea, once we had sight of another: but now she is queen, say these.
Not as thine, not as thine was our mother, a blossom of flowering seas,
Clothed round with the world's desire as with raiment, and fair as the foam,
And fleeter than kindled fire, and a goddess, and mother of Rome.
For thine came pale and a maiden, and sister to sorrow; but ours,
Her deep hair heavily laden with odour and colour of flowers,
White rose of the rose-white water, a silver splendour, a flame,
Bent down unto us that besought her, and earth grew sweet with her name.
For thine came weeping, a slave among slaves, and rejected; but she
Came flushed from the full-flushed wave, and imperial, her foot on the sea.
And the wonderful waters knew her, the winds and the viewless ways,
And the roses grew rosier, and bluer the sea-blue stream of the bays.
Ye are fallen, our lords, by what token? we wist that ye should not fall.
Ye were all so fair that are broken; and one more fair than ye all.
But I turn to her still, having seen she shall surely abide in the end;
Goddess and maiden and queen, be near me now and befriend.
O daughter of earth, of my mother, her crown and blossom of birth,
I am also, I also, thy brother; I go as I came unto earth.
In the night where thine eyes are as moons are in heaven, the night where thou art,
Where the silence is more than all tunes, where sleep overflows from the heart,
Where the poppies are sweet as the rose in our world, and the red rose is white,

And the wind falls faint as it blows with the fume of the flowers of the night,
And the murmur of spirits that sleep in the shadow of Gods from afar
Grows dim in thine ears and deep as the deep dim soul of a star,
In the sweet low light of thy face, under heavens untrod by the sun,
Let my soul with their souls find place, and forget what is done and undone.
Thou art more than the Gods who number the days of our temporal breath;
For these give labour and slumber; but thou, Proserpina, death.
Therefore now at thy feet I abide for a season in silence. I know
I shall die as my fathers died, and sleep as they sleep; even so.
For the glass of the years is brittle wherein we gaze for a span;
A little soul for a little bears up this corpse which is man.*
So long I endure, no longer; and laugh not again, neither weep.
For there is no God found stronger than death; and death is a sleep.

*ψυχάριον εἶ βαστάζον νεκρόν. EPICTETUS

## Hermaphroditus

I

Lift up thy lips, turn round, look back for love,
Blind love that comes by night and casts out rest;
Of all things tired thy lips look weariest,
Save the long smile that they are wearied of.
Ah sweet, albeit no love be sweet enough,
Choose of two loves and cleave unto the best;
Two loves at either blossom of thy breast
Strive until one be under and one above.
Their breath is fire upon the amorous air,
Fire in thine eyes and where thy lips suspire:
And whosoever hath seen thee, being so fair,
Two things turn all his life and blood to fire;
A strong desire begot on great despair,
A great despair cast out by strong desire.

II

Where between sleep and life some brief space is,
With love like gold bound round about the head,
Sex to sweet sex with lips and limbs is wed,
Turning the fruitful feud of hers and his

To the waste wedlock of a sterile kiss;
  Yet from them something like as fire is shed
  That shall not be assuaged till death be dead,
Though neither life nor sleep can find out this.
Love made himself of flesh that perisheth
  A pleasure-house for all the loves his kin;
But on the one side sat a man like death,
  And on the other a woman sat like sin.
So with veiled eyes and sobs between his breath
  Love turned himself and would not enter in.

III

Love, is it love or sleep or shadow or light
  That lies between thine eyelids and thine eyes?
  Like a flower laid upon a flower it lies,
Or like the night's dew laid upon the night.
Love stands upon thy left hand and thy right,
  Yet by no sunset and by no moonrise
  Shall make thee man and ease a woman's sighs,
Or make thee woman for a man's delight.
To what strange end hath some strange god made fair
  The double blossom of two fruitless flowers?
Hid love in all the folds of all thy hair,
  Fed thee on summers, watered thee with showers,
Given all the gold that all the seasons wear
  To thee that art a thing of barren hours?

IV

Yea, love, I see; it is not love but fear.
  Nay, sweet, it is not fear but love, I know;
  Or wherefore should thy body's blossom blow
So sweetly, or thine eyelids leave so clear
Thy gracious eyes that never made a tear—
  Though for their love our tears like blood should flow,
  Though love and life and death should come and go,
So dreadful, so desirable, so dear?
Yea, sweet, I know; I saw in what swift wise
  Beneath the woman's and the water's kiss
  Thy moist limbs melted into Salmacis,
And the large light turned tender in thine eyes,
And all thy boy's breath softened into sighs;
  But Love being blind, how should he know of this?

*Au Musée du Louvre, Mars* 1863.

## Anima Anceps

Till death have broken
Sweet life's love-token,
Till all be spoken
   That shall be said,
What dost thou praying,
O soul, and playing
With song and saying,
   Things flown and fled?
For this we know not—
That fresh springs flow not
And fresh griefs grow not
   When men are dead;
When strange years cover
Lover and lover,
And joys are over
   And tears are shed.

If one day's sorrow
Mar the day's morrow—
If man's life borrow
   And man's death pay—
If souls once taken,
If lives once shaken,
Arise, awaken,
   By night, by day—
Why with strong crying
And years of sighing,
Living and dying,
   Fast ye and pray?
For all your weeping,
Waking and sleeping,
Death comes to reaping
   And takes away.

Though time rend after
Roof-tree from rafter,
A little laughter
   Is much more worth
Than thus to measure
The hour, the treasure,
The pain, the pleasure,
   The death, the birth;

Grief, when days alter,
Like joy shall falter;
Song-book and psalter,
   Mourning and mirth.
Live like the swallow;
Seek not to follow
Where earth is hollow
   Under the earth.

## A Match

If love were what the rose is,
   And I were like the leaf,
Our lives would grow together
In sad or singing weather,
Blown fields or flowerful closes,
   Green pleasure or grey grief;
If love were what the rose is,
   And I were like the leaf.

If I were what the words are,
   And love were like the tune,
With double sound and single
Delight our lips would mingle,
With kisses glad as birds are
   That get sweet rain at noon;
If I were what the words are,
   And love were like the tune.

If you were life, my darling,
   And I your love were death,
We'd shine and snow together
Ere March made sweet the weather
With daffodil and starling
   And hours of fruitful breath;
If you were life, my darling,
   And I your love were death.

If you were thrall to sorrow,
   And I were page to joy,
We'd play for lives and seasons
With loving looks and treasons
And tears of night and morrow

And laughs of maid and boy;
If you were thrall to sorrow,
And I were page to joy.

If you were April's lady,
And I were lord in May,
We'd throw with leaves for hours
And draw for days with flowers,
Till day like night were shady
And night were bright like day;
If you were April's lady,
And I were lord in May.

If you were queen of pleasure,
And I were king of pain,
We'd hunt down love together,
Pluck out his flying-feather,
And teach his feet a measure,
And find his mouth a rein;
If you were queen of pleasure,
And I were king of pain.

## Faustine

*Ave Faustina Imperatrix, morituri te salutant.*

Lean back, and get some minutes' peace;
Let your head lean
Back to the shoulder with its fleece
Of locks, Faustine.

The shapely silver shoulder stoops,
Weighed over clean
With state of splendid hair that droops
Each side, Faustine.

Let me go over your good gifts
That crown you queen;
A queen whose kingdom ebbs and shifts
Each week, Faustine.

Bright heavy brows well gathered up:
White gloss and sheen;
Carved lips that make my lips a cup
To drink, Faustine,

Wine and rank poison, milk and blood,
  Being mixed therein
Since first the devil threw dice with God
  For you, Faustine.

Your naked new-born soul, their stake,
  Stood blind between;
God said "let him that wins her take
  And keep Faustine."

But this time Satan throve, no doubt;
  Long since, I ween,
God's part in you was battered out;
  Long since, Faustine.

The die rang sideways as it fell,
  Rang cracked and thin,
Like a man's laughter heard in hell
  Far down, Faustine,

A shadow of laughter like a sigh,
  Dead sorrow's kin;
So rang, thrown down, the devil's die
  That won Faustine.

A suckling of his breed you were,
  One hard to wean;
But God, who lost you, left you fair,
  We see, Faustine.

You have the face that suits a woman
  For her soul's screen —
The sort of beauty that's called human
  In hell, Faustine.

You could do all things but be good
  Or chaste of mien;
And that you would not if you could,
  We know, Faustine.

Even he who cast seven devils out
  Of Magdalene
Could hardly do as much, I doubt,
  For you, Faustine.

Did Satan make you to spite God?
  Or did God mean

To scourge with scorpions for a rod
  Our sins, Faustine?

I know what queen at first you were,
  As though I had seen
Red gold and black imperious hair
  Twice crown Faustine.

As if your fed sarcophagus
  Spared flesh and skin,
You come back face to face with us,
  The same Faustine.

She loved the games men played with death,
  Where death must win;
As though the slain man's blood and breath
  Revived Faustine.

Nets caught the pike, pikes tore the net;
  Lithe limbs and lean
From drained-out pores dripped thick red sweat
  To soothe Faustine.

She drank the steaming drift and dust
  Blown off the scene;
Blood could not ease the bitter lust
  That galled Faustine.

All round the foul fat furrows reeked,
  Where blood sank in;
The circus splashed and seethed and shrieked
  All round Faustine.

But these are gone now: years entomb
  The dust and din;
Yea, even the bath's fierce reek and fume
  That slew Faustine.

Was life worth living then? and now
  Is life worth sin?
Where are the imperial years? and how
  Are you Faustine?

Your soul forgot her joys, forgot
  Her times of teen;
Yea, this life likewise will you not
  Forget, Faustine?

For in the time we know not of
   Did fate begin
Weaving the web of days that wove
   Your doom, Faustine.

The threads were wet with wine, and all
   Were smooth to spin;
They wove you like a Bacchanal,
   The first Faustine.

And Bacchus cast your mates and you
   Wild grapes to glean;
Your flower-like lips were dashed with dew
   From his, Faustine.

Your drenched loose hands were stretched to hold
   The vine's wet green,
Long ere they coined in Roman gold
   Your face, Faustine.

Then after change of soaring feather
   And winnowing fin,
You woke in weeks of feverish weather,
   A new Faustine.

A star upon your birthday burned,
   Whose fierce serene
Red pulseless planet never yearned
   In heaven, Faustine.

Stray breaths of Sapphic song that blew
   Through Mitylene
Shook the fierce quivering blood in you
   By night, Faustine.

The shameless nameless love that makes
   Hell's iron gin
Shut on you like a trap that breaks
   The soul, Faustine.

And when your veins were void and dead,
   What ghosts unclean
Swarmed round the straitened barren bed
   That hid Faustine?

What sterile growths of sexless root
   Or epicene?

What flower of kisses without fruit
  Of love, Faustine?

What adders came to shed their coats?
  What coiled obscene
Small serpents with soft stretching throats
  Caressed Faustine?

But the time came of famished hours,
  Maimed loves and mean,
This ghastly thin-faced time of ours,
  To spoil Faustine.

You seem a thing that hinges hold,
  A love-machine
With clockwork joints of supple gold—
  No more, Faustine.

Not godless, for you serve one God,
  The Lampsacene,
Who metes the gardens with his rod;
  Your lord, Faustine.

If one should love you with real love
  (Such things have been,
Things your fair face knows nothing of,
  It seems, Faustine);

That clear hair heavily bound back,
  The lights wherein
Shift from dead blue to burnt-up black;
  Your throat, Faustine,

Strong, heavy, throwing out the face
  And hard bright chin
And shameful scornful lips that grace
  Their shame, Faustine,

Curled lips, long since half kissed away,
  Still sweet and keen;
You'd give him—poison shall we say?
  Or what, Faustine?

## Stage Love

When the game began between them for a jest,
He played king and she played queen to match the best;

Laughter soft as tears, and tears that turned to laughter,
These were things she sought for years and sorrowed after.

Pleasure with dry lips, and pain that walks by night;
All the sting and all the stain of long delight;
These were things she knew not of, that knew not of her,
When she played at half a love with half a lover.

Time was chorus, gave them cues to laugh or cry;
They would kill, befool, amuse him, let him die;
Set him webs to weave to-day and break to-morrow,
Till he died for good in play, and rose in sorrow.

What the years mean; how time dies and is not slain;
How love grows and laughs and cries and wanes again;
These were things she came to know, and take their measure,
When the play was played out so for one man's pleasure.

## The Leper

Nothing is better, I well think,
  Than love; the hidden well-water
Is not so delicate to drink:
  This was well seen of me and her.

I served her in a royal house;
  I served her wine and curious meat.
For will to kiss between her brows,
  I had no heart to sleep or eat.

Mere scorn God knows she had of me,
  A poor scribe, nowise great or fair,
Who plucked his clerk's hood back to see
  Her curled-up lips and amorous hair.

I vex my head with thinking this.
  Yea, though God always hated me,
And hates me now that I can kiss
  Her eyes, plait up her hair to see

How she then wore it on the brows,
  Yet am I glad to have her dead
Here in this wretched wattled house
  Where I can kiss her eyes and head.

Nothing is better, I well know,
  Than love; no amber in cold sea

Or gathered berries under snow:
That is well seen of her and me.

Three thoughts I make my pleasure of:
First I take heart and think of this:
That knight's gold hair she chose to love,
His mouth she had such will to kiss.

Then I remember that sundawn
I brought him by a privy way
Out at her lattice, and thereon
What gracious words she found to say.

(Cold rushes for such little feet—
Both feet could lie into my hand.
A marvel was it of my sweet
Her upright body could so stand.)

"Sweet friend, God give you thank and grace;
Now am I clean and whole of shame,
Nor shall men burn me in the face
For my sweet fault that scandals them."

I tell you over word by word.
She, sitting edgewise on her bed,
Holding her feet, said thus. The third,
A sweeter thing than these, I said.

God, that makes time and ruins it
And alters not, abiding God,
Changed with disease her body sweet,
The body of love wherein she abode.

Love is more sweet and comelier
Than a dove's throat strained out to sing.
All they spat out and cursed at her
And cast her forth for a base thing.

They cursed her, seeing how God had wrought
This curse to plague her, a curse of his.
Fools were they surely, seeing not
How sweeter than all sweet she is.

He that had held her by the hair,
With kissing lips blinding her eyes,
Felt her bright bosom, strained and bare,
Sigh under him, with short mad cries

Out of her throat and sobbing mouth
  And body broken up with love,
With sweet hot tears his lips were loth
  Her own should taste the savour of,

Yea, he inside whose grasp all night
  Her fervent body leapt or lay,
Stained with sharp kisses red and white,
  Found her a plague to spurn away.

I hid her in this wattled house,
  I served her water and poor bread.
For joy to kiss between her brows
  Time upon time I was nigh dead.

Bread failed; we got but well-water
  And gathered grass with dropping seed.
I had such joy of kissing her,
  I had small care to sleep or feed.

Sometimes when service made me glad
  The sharp tears leapt between my lids,
Falling on her, such joy I had
  To do the service God forbids.

"I pray you let me be at peace,
  Get hence, make room for me to die."
She said that: her poor lip would cease,
  Put up to mine, and turn to cry.

I said, "Bethink yourself how love
  Fared in us twain, what either did;
Shall I unclothe my soul thereof?
  That I should do this, God forbid."

Yea, though God hateth us, he knows
  That hardly in a little thing
Love faileth of the work it does
  Till it grow ripe for gathering.

Six months, and now my sweet is dead
  A trouble takes me; I know not
If all were done well, all well said,
  No word or tender deed forgot.

Too sweet, for the least part in her,
  To have shed life out by fragments; yet,

Could the close mouth catch breath and stir,
   I might see something I forget.

Six months, and I sit still and hold
   In two cold palms her cold two feet.
Her hair, half grey half ruined gold,
   Thrills me and burns me in kissing it.

Love bites and stings me through, to see
   Her keen face made of sunken bones.
Her worn-off eyelids madden me,
   That were shot through with purple once.

She said, "Be good with me; I grow
   So tired for shame's sake, I shall die
If you say nothing:" even so.
   And she is dead now, and shame put by.

Yea, and the scorn she had of me
   In the old time, doubtless vexed her then.
I never should have kissed her. See
   What fools God's anger makes of men!

She might have loved me a little too,
   Had I been humbler for her sake.
But that new shame could make love new
   She saw not—yet her shame did make.

I took too much upon my love,
   Having for such mean service done
Her beauty and all the ways thereof,
   Her face and all the sweet thereon.

Yea, all this while I tended her,
   I know the old love held fast his part:
I know the old scorn waxed heavier,
   Mixed with sad wonder, in her heart.

It may be all my love went wrong—
   A scribe's work writ awry and blurred,
Scrawled after the blind evensong—
   Spoilt music with no perfect word.

But surely I would fain have done
   All things the best I could. Perchance
Because I failed, came short of one,
   She kept at heart that other man's.

I am grown blind with all these things:
   It may be now she hath in sight
Some better knowledge; still there clings
   The old question. Will not God do right?

En ce temps-là estoyt dans ce pays grand nombre de ladres et de meseaulx, ce dont le roy eut grand desplaisir, veu que Dieu dust en estre moult griefvement courroucé. Ores il advint qu'une noble damoyselle appelée Yolande de Sallières estant atteincte et touste guastée de ce vilain mal, tous ses amys et ses parens ayant devant leurs yeux la paour de Dieu la firent issir fors de leurs maisons et oncques ne voulurent recepvoir ni reconforter chose mauldicte de Dieu et à tous les hommes puante et abhominable. Ceste dame avoyt esté moult belle et gracieuse de formes, et de son corps elle estoyt large et de vie lascive. Pourtant nul des amans qui l'avoyent souventesfois accollée et baisée moult tendrement ne voulust plus héberger si laide femme et si détestable pescheresse. Ung seul clerc qui feut premièrement son lacquays et son entremetteur en matière d'amour la reçut chez luy et la récéla dans une petite cabane. Là mourut la meschinette de grande misère et de male mort: et après elle décéda ledist clerc qui pour grand amour l'avoyt six mois durant soignée, lavée, habillée et deshabillée tous les jours de ses mains propres. Mesme dist-on que ce meschant homme et mauldict clerc se remémourant de la grande beauté passée et guastée de ceste femme se délectoyt maintesfois à la baiser sur sa bouche orde et lépreuse et l'accoller doulcement de ses mains amoureuses. Aussy est-il mort de ceste mesme maladie abhominable. Cecy advint près Fontainebellant en Gastinois. Et quand ouyt le roy Philippe ceste adventure moult en estoyt esmerveillé.

*Grandes Chroniques de France,* 1505.

## Before the Mirror
## (Verses Written Under a Picture)
## Inscribed to J. A. Whistler

I

White rose in red rose-garden
   Is not so white;
Snowdrops that plead for pardon
   And pine for fright
Because the hard East blows
Over their maiden rows
   Grow not as this face grows from pale to bright.

Behind the veil, forbidden,
  Shut up from sight,
Love, is there sorrow hidden,
  Is there delight?
Is joy thy dower or grief,
White rose of weary leaf,
  Late rose whose life is brief, whose loves are light?

Soft snows that hard winds harden
  Till each flake bite
Fill all the flowerless garden
  Whose flowers took flight
Long since when summer ceased,
And men rose up from feast,
  And warm west wind grew east, and warm day night.

II

"Come snow, come wind or thunder
  High up in air,
I watch my face, and wonder
  At my bright hair;
Nought else exalts or grieves
The rose at heart, that heaves
  With love of her own leaves and lips that pair.

"She knows not loves that kissed her
  She knows not where.
Art thou the ghost, my sister,
  White sister there,
Am I the ghost, who knows?
My hand, a fallen rose,
  Lies snow-white on white snows, and takes no care.

"I cannot see what pleasures
  Or what pains were;
What pale new loves and treasures
  New years will bear;
What beam will fall, what shower,
What grief or joy for dower;
  But one thing knows the flower; the flower is fair."

III

Glad, but not flushed with gladness,
  Since joys go by;
Sad, but not bent with sadness,

Since sorrows die;
Deep in the gleaming glass
She sees all past things pass,
And all sweet life that was lie down and lie.

There glowing ghosts of flowers
Draw down, draw nigh;
And wings of swift spent hours
Take flight and fly;
She sees by formless gleams,
She hears across cold streams,
Dead mouths of many dreams that sing and sigh.

Face fallen and white throat lifted,
With sleepless eye
She sees old loves that drifted,
She knew not why,
Old loves and faded fears
Float down a stream that hears
The flowing of all men's tears beneath the sky.

## Dolores
## (Notre-Dame des Sept Douleurs)

Cold eyelids that hide like a jewel
Hard eyes that grow soft for an hour;
The heavy white limbs, and the cruel
Red mouth like a venomous flower;
When these are gone by with their glories,
What shall rest of thee then, what remain,
O mystic and sombre Dolores,
Our Lady of Pain?

Seven sorrows the priests give their Virgin;
But thy sins, which are seventy times seven,
Seven ages would fail thee to purge in,
And then they would haunt thee in heaven:
Fierce midnights and famishing morrows,
And the loves that complete and control
All the joys of the flesh, all the sorrows
That wear out the soul.

O garment not golden but gilded,
O garden where all men may dwell,

O tower not of ivory, but builded
By hands that reach heaven from hell;
O mystical rose of the mire,
O house not of gold but of gain,
O house of unquenchable fire,
Our Lady of Pain!

O lips full of lust and of laughter,
Curled snakes that are fed from my breast,
Bite hard, lest remembrance come after
And press with new lips where you pressed.
For my heart too springs up at the pressure,
Mine eyelids too moisten and burn;
Ah, feed me and fill me with pleasure,
Ere pain come in turn.

In yesterday's reach and to-morrow's,
Out of sight though they lie of to-day,
There have been and there yet shall be sorrows
That smite not and bite not in play.
The life and the love thou despisest,
These hurt us indeed, and in vain,
O wise among women, and wisest,
Our Lady of Pain.

Who gave thee thy wisdom? what stories
That stung thee, what visions that smote?
Wert thou pure and a maiden, Dolores,
When desire took thee first by the throat?
What bud was the shell of a blossom
That all men may smell to and pluck?
What milk fed thee first at what bosom?
What sins gave thee suck?

We shift and bedeck and bedrape us,
Thou art noble and nude and antique;
Libitina thy mother, Priapus
Thy father, a Tuscan and Greek.
We play with light loves in the portal,
And wince and relent and refrain;
Loves die, and we know thee immortal,
Our Lady of Pain.

Fruits fail and love dies and time ranges;
Thou art fed with perpetual breath,

And alive after infinite changes,
   And fresh from the kisses of death;
Of languors rekindled and rallied,
   Of barren delights and unclean,
Things monstrous and fruitless, a pallid
   And poisonous queen.

Could you hurt me, sweet lips, though I hurt you?
   Men touch them, and change in a trice
The lilies and languors of virtue
   For the raptures and roses of vice;
Those lie where thy foot on the floor is,
   These crown and caress thee and chain,
O splendid and sterile Dolores,
   Our Lady of Pain.

There are sins it may be to discover,
   There are deeds it may be to delight.
What new work wilt thou find for thy lover,
   What new passions for daytime or night?
What spells that they know not a word of
   Whose lives are as leaves overblown?
What tortures undreamt of, unheard of,
   Unwritten, unknown?

Ah beautiful passionate body
   That never has ached with a heart!
On thy mouth though the kisses are bloody,
   Though they sting till it shudder and smart,
More kind than the love we adore is,
   They hurt not the heart or the brain,
O bitter and tender Dolores,
   Our Lady of Pain.

As our kisses relax and redouble,
   From the lips and the foam and the fangs
Shall no new sin be born for men's trouble,
   No dream of impossible pangs?
With the sweet of the sins of old ages
   Wilt thou satiate thy soul as of yore?
Too sweet is the rind, say the sages,
   Too bitter the core.

Hast thou told all thy secrets the last time,
   And bared all thy beauties to one?

Ah, where shall we go then for pastime,
If the worst that can be has been done?
But sweet as the rind was the core is;
We are fain of thee still, we are fain,
O sanguine and subtle Dolores,
Our Lady of Pain.

By the hunger of change and emotion,
By the thirst of unbearable things,
By despair, the twin-born of devotion,
By the pleasure that winces and stings,
The delight that consumes the desire,
The desire that outruns the delight,
By the cruelty deaf as a fire
And blind as the night,

By the ravenous teeth that have smitten
Through the kisses that blossom and bud,
By the lips intertwisted and bitten
Till the foam has a savour of blood,
By the pulse as it rises and falters,
By the hands as they slacken and strain,
I adjure thee, respond from thine altars,
Our Lady of Pain.

Wilt thou smile as a woman disdaining
The light fire in the veins of a boy?
But he comes to thee sad, without feigning,
Who has wearied of sorrow and joy;
Less careful of labour and glory
Than the elders whose hair has uncurled:
And young, but with fancies as hoary
And grey as the world.

I have passed from the outermost portal
To the shrine where a sin is a prayer;
What care though the service be mortal?
O our Lady of Torture, what care?
All thine the last wine that I pour is,
The last in the chalice we drain,
O fierce and luxurious Dolores,
Our Lady of Pain.

All thine the new wine of desire,
The fruit of four lips as they clung

Till the hair and the eyelids took fire,
  The foam of a serpentine tongue,
The froth of the serpents of pleasure,
  More salt than the foam of the sea,
Now felt as a flame, now at leisure
  As wine shed for me.

Ah thy people, thy children, thy chosen,
  Marked cross from the womb and perverse!
They have found out the secret to cozen
  The gods that constrain us and curse;
They alone, they are wise, and none other;
  Give me place, even me, in their train,
O my sister, my spouse, and my mother,
  Our Lady of Pain.

For the crown of our life as it closes
  Is darkness, the fruit thereof dust;
No thorns go as deep as a rose's,
  And love is more cruel than lust.
Time turns the old days to derision,
  Our loves into corpses or wives;
And marriage and death and division
  Make barren our lives.

And pale from the past we draw nigh thee,
  And satiate with comfortless hours;
And we know thee, how all men belie thee,
  And we gather the fruit of thy flowers;
The passion that slays and recovers,
  The pangs and the kisses that rain
On the lips and the limbs of thy lovers,
  Our Lady of Pain.

The desire of thy furious embraces
  Is more than the wisdom of years,
On the blossom though blood lie in traces,
  Though the foliage be sodden with tears.
For the lords in whose keeping the door is
  That opens on all who draw breath
Gave the cypress to love, my Dolores,
  The myrtle to death.

And they laughed, changing hands in the measure,
  And they mixed and made peace after strife;

Pain melted in tears, and was pleasure;
  Death tingled with blood, and was life.
Like lovers they melted and tingled,
  In the dusk of thine innermost fane;
In the darkness they murmured and mingled,
  Our Lady of Pain.

In a twilight where virtues are vices,
  In thy chapels, unknown of the sun,
To a tune that enthralls and entices,
  They were wed, and the twain were as one.
For the tune from thine altar hath sounded
  Since God bade the world's work begin,
And the fume of thine incense abounded,
  To sweeten the sin.

Love listens, and paler than ashes,
  Through his curls as the crown on them slips,
Lifts languid wet eyelids and lashes,
  And laughs with insatiable lips.
Thou shalt hush him with heavy caresses,
  With music that scares the profane;
Thou shalt darken his eyes with thy tresses,
  Our Lady of Pain.

Thou shalt blind his bright eyes though he wrestle,
  Thou shalt chain his light limbs though he strive;
In his lips all thy serpents shall nestle,
  In his hands all thy cruelties thrive.
In the daytime thy voice shall go through him,
  In his dreams he shall feel thee and ache;
Thou shalt kindle by night and subdue him
  Asleep and awake.

Thou shalt touch and make redder his roses
  With juice not of fruit nor of bud;
When the sense in the spirit reposes,
  Thou shalt quicken the soul through the blood.
Thine, thine the one grace we implore is,
  Who would live and not languish or feign,
O sleepless and deadly Dolores,
  Our Lady of Pain.

Dost thou dream, in a respite of slumber,
  In a lull of the fires of thy life,

Of the days without name, without number,
  When thy will stung the world into strife;
When, a goddess, the pulse of thy passion
  Smote kings as they revelled in Rome;
And they hailed thee re-risen, O Thalassian,
  Foam-white, from the foam?

When thy lips had such lovers to flatter;
  When the city lay red from thy rods,
And thine hands were as arrows to scatter
  The children of change and their gods;
When the blood of thy foemen made fervent
  A sand never moist from the main,
As one smote them, their lord and thy servant,
  Our Lady of Pain.

On sands by the storm never shaken,
  Nor wet from the washing of tides;
Nor by foam of the waves overtaken,
  Nor winds that the thunder bestrides;
But red from the print of thy paces,
  Made smooth for the world and its lords,
Ringed round with a flame of fair faces,
  And splendid with swords.

There the gladiator, pale for thy pleasure,
  Drew bitter and perilous breath;
There torments laid hold on the treasure
  Of limbs too delicious for death;
When thy gardens were lit with live torches;
  When the world was a steed for thy rein;
When the nations lay prone in thy porches,
  Our Lady of Pain.

When, with flame all around him aspirant,
  Stood flushed, as a harp-player stands,
The implacable beautiful tyrant,
  Rose-crowned, having death in his hands;
And a sound as the sound of loud water
  Smote far through the flight of the fires,
And mixed with the lightning of slaughter
  A thunder of lyres.

Dost thou dream of what was and no more is,
  The old kingdoms of earth and the kings?

Dost thou hunger for these things, Dolores,
   For these, in a world of new things?
But thy bosom no fasts could emaciate,
   No hunger compel to complain
Those lips that no bloodshed could satiate,
   Our Lady of Pain.

As of old when the world's heart was lighter,
   Through thy garments the grace of thee glows,
The white wealth of thy body made whiter
   By the blushes of amorous blows,
And seamed with sharp lips and fierce fingers,
   And branded by kisses that bruise;
When all shall be gone that now lingers,
   Ah, what shall we lose?

Thou wert fair in the fearless old fashion,
   And thy limbs are as melodies yet,
And move to the music of passion
   With lithe and lascivious regret.
What ailed us, O gods, to desert you
   For creeds that refuse and restrain?
Come down and redeem us from virtue,
   Our Lady of Pain.

All shrines that were Vestal are flameless,
   But the flame has not fallen from this;
Though obscure be the god, and though nameless
   The eyes and the hair that we kiss;
Low fires that love sits by and forges
   Fresh heads for his arrows and thine;
Hair loosened and soiled in mid orgies
   With kisses and wine.

Thy skin changes country and colour,
   And shrivels or swells to a snake's.
Let it brighten and bloat and grow duller,
   We know it, the flames and the flakes,
Red brands on it smitten and bitten,
   Round skies where a star is a stain,
And the leaves with thy litanies written,
   Our Lady of Pain.

On thy bosom though many a kiss be,
   There are none such as knew it of old.

Was it Alciphron once or Arisbe,
Male ringlets or feminine gold,
That thy lips met with under the statue,
Whence a look shot out sharp after thieves
From the eyes of the garden-god at you
Across the fig-leaves?

Then still, through dry seasons and moister,
One god had a wreath to his shrine;
Then love was the pearl of his oyster,*
And Venus rose red out of wine.
We have all done amiss, choosing rather
Such loves as the wise gods disdain;
Intercede for us thou with thy father,
Our Lady of Pain.

In spring he had crowns of his garden,
Red corn in the heat of the year,
Then hoary green olives that harden
When the grape-blossom freezes with fear;
And milk-budded myrtles with Venus
And vine-leaves with Bacchus he trod;
And ye said, "We have seen, he hath seen us,
A visible God."

What broke off the garlands that girt you?
What sundered you spirit and clay?
Weak sins yet alive are as virtue
To the strength of the sins of that day.
For dried is the blood of thy lover,
Ipsithilla, contracted the vein;
Cry aloud, "Will he rise and recover,
Our Lady of Pain?"

Cry aloud; for the old world is broken:
Cry out; for the Phrygian is priest,
And rears not the bountiful token
And spreads not the fatherly feast.
From the midmost of Ida, from shady
Recesses that murmur at morn,
They have brought and baptized her, Our Lady,
A goddess new-born.

*_Nam te præcipuè in suis urbibus colit ora_
_Hellespontia, cæteris ostreosior oris._
CATULL. i.

And the chaplets of old are above us,
And the oyster-bed teems out of reach;
Old poets outsing and outlove us,
And Catullus makes mouths at our speech.
Who shall kiss, in thy father's own city,
With such lips as he sang with, again?
Intercede for us all of thy pity,
Our Lady of Pain.

Out of Dindymus heavily laden
Her lions draw bound and unfed
A mother, a mortal, a maiden,
A queen over death and the dead.
She is cold, and her habit is lowly,
Her temple of branches and sods;
Most fruitful and virginal, holy,
A mother of gods.

She hath wasted with fire thine high places,
She hath hidden and marred and made sad
The fair limbs of the Loves, the fair faces
Of gods that were goodly and glad.
She slays, and her hands are not bloody;
She moves as a moon in the wane,
White-robed, and thy raiment is ruddy,
Our Lady of Pain.

They shall pass and their places be taken,
The gods and the priests that are pure.
They shall pass, and shalt thou not be shaken?
They shall perish, and shalt thou endure?
Death laughs, breathing close and relentless
In the nostrils and eyelids of lust,
With a pinch in his fingers of scentless
And delicate dust.

But the worm shall revive thee with kisses;
Thou shalt change and transmute as a god,
As the rod to a serpent that hisses,
As the serpent again to a rod.
Thy life shall not cease though thou doff it;
Thou shalt live until evil be slain,
And good shall die first, said thy prophet,
Our Lady of Pain.

Did he lie? did he laugh? does he know it,
  Now he lies out of reach, out of breath,
Thy prophet, thy preacher, thy poet,
  Sin's child by incestuous Death?
Did he find out in fire at his waking,
  Or discern as his eyelids lost light,
When the bands of the body were breaking
  And all came in sight?

Who has known all the evil before us,
  Or the tyrannous secrets of time?
Though we match not the dead men that bore us
  At a song, at a kiss, at a crime—
Though the heathen outface and outlive us,
  And our lives and our longings are twain—
Ah, forgive us our virtues, forgive us,
  Our Lady of Pain.

Who are we that embalm and embrace thee
  With spices and savours of song?
What is time, that his children should face thee?
  What am I, that my lips do thee wrong?
I could hurt thee—but pain would delight thee;
  Or caress thee—but love would repel;
And the lovers whose lips would excite thee
  Are serpents in hell.

Who now shall content thee as they did,
  Thy lovers, when temples were built
And the hair of the sacrifice braided
  And the blood of the sacrifice spilt,
In Lampsacus fervent with faces,
  In Aphaca red from thy reign,
Who embraced thee with awful embraces,
  Our Lady of Pain?

Where are they, Cotytto or Venus,
  Astarte or Ashtaroth, where?
Do their hands as we touch come between us?
  Is the breath of them hot in thy hair?
From their lips have thy lips taken fever,
  With the blood of their bodies grown red?
Hast thou left upon earth a believer
  If these men are dead?

They were purple of raiment and golden,
   Filled full of thee, fiery with wine,
Thy lovers, in haunts unbeholden,
   In marvellous chambers of thine.
They are fled, and their footprints escape us,
   Who appraise thee, adore, and abstain,
O daughter of Death and Priapus,
   Our Lady of Pain.

What ails us to fear overmeasure,
   To praise thee with timorous breath,
O mistress and mother of pleasure,
   The one thing as certain as death?
We shall change as the things that we cherish,
   Shall fade as they faded before,
As foam upon water shall perish,
   As sand upon shore.

We shall know what the darkness discovers,
   If the grave-pit be shallow or deep;
And our fathers of old, and our lovers,
   We shall know if they sleep not or sleep.
We shall see whether hell be not heaven,
   Find out whether tares be not grain,
And the joys of thee seventy times seven,
   Our Lady of Pain.

### The Garden of Proserpine

Here, where the world is quiet;
   Here, where all trouble seems
Dead winds' and spent waves' riot
   In doubtful dreams of dreams;
I watch the green field growing
For reaping folk and sowing,
For harvest-time and mowing,
   A sleepy world of streams.

I am tired of tears and laughter,
   And men that laugh and weep;
Of what may come hereafter
   For men that sow to reap:

I am weary of days and hours,
Blown buds of barren flowers,
Desires and dreams and powers
   And everything but sleep.

Here life has death for neighbour,
   And far from eye or ear
Wan waves and wet winds labour,
   Weak ships and spirits steer;
They drive adrift, and whither
They wot not who make thither;
But no such winds blow hither,
   And no such things grow here.

No growth of moor or coppice,
   No heather-flower or vine,
But bloomless buds of poppies,
   Green grapes of Proserpine,
Pale beds of blowing rushes
Where no leaf blooms or blushes
Save this whereout she crushes
   For dead men deadly wine.

Pale, without name or number,
   In fruitless fields of corn,
They bow themselves and slumber
   All night till light is born;
And like a soul belated,
In hell and heaven unmated,
By cloud and mist abated
   Comes out of darkness morn.

Though one were strong as seven,
   He too with death shall dwell,
Nor wake with wings in heaven,
   Nor weep for pains in hell;
Though one were fair as roses,
His beauty clouds and closes;
And well though love reposes,
   In the end it is not well.

Pale, beyond porch and portal,
   Crowned with calm leaves, she stands
Who gathers all things mortal
   With cold immortal hands;

Her languid lips are sweeter
Than love's who fears to greet her
To men that mix and meet her
   From many times and lands.

She waits for each and other,
   She waits for all men born;
Forgets the earth her mother,
   The life of fruits and corn;
And spring and seed and swallow
Take wing for her and follow
Where summer song rings hollow
   And flowers are put to scorn.

There go the loves that wither,
   The old loves with wearier wings;
And all dead years draw thither,
   And all disastrous things;
Dead dreams of days forsaken,
Blind buds that snows have shaken,
Wild leaves that winds have taken,
   Red strays of ruined springs.

We are not sure of sorrow,
   And joy was never sure;
To-day will die to-morrow;
   Time stoops to no man's lure;
And love, grown faint and fretful,
With lips but half regretful
Sighs, and with eyes forgetful
   Weeps that no loves endure.

From too much love of living,
   From hope and fear set free,
We thank with brief thanksgiving
   Whatever gods may be
That no life lives for ever;
That dead men rise up never;
That even the weariest river
   Winds somewhere safe to sea.

Then star nor sun shall waken,
   Nor any change of light:
Nor sound of waters shaken,
   Nor any sound or sight:

Nor wintry leaves nor vernal,
Nor days nor things diurnal;
Only the sleep eternal
In an eternal night.

## Hendecasyllabics

In the month of the long decline of roses
I, beholding the summer dead before me,
Set my face to the sea and journeyed silent,
Gazing eagerly where above the sea-mark
Flame as fierce as the fervid eyes of lions
Half divided the eyelids of the sunset;
Till I heard as it were a noise of waters
Moving tremulous under feet of angels
Multitudinous, out of all the heavens;
Knew the fluttering wind, the fluttered foliage,
Shaken fitfully, full of sound and shadow;
And saw, trodden upon by noiseless angels,
Long mysterious reaches fed with moonlight,
Sweet sad straits in a soft subsiding channel,
Blown about by the lips of winds I knew not,
Winds not born in the north nor any quarter,
Winds not warm with the south nor any sunshine;
Heard between them a voice of exultation,
"Lo, the summer is dead, the sun is faded,
Even like as a leaf the year is withered,
All the fruits of the day from all her branches
Gathered, neither is any left to gather.
All the flowers are dead, the tender blossoms,
All are taken away; the season wasted,
Like an ember among the fallen ashes.
Now with light of the winter days, with moonlight,
Light of snow, and the bitter light of hoarfrost,
We bring flowers that fade not after autumn,
Pale white chaplets and crowns of latter seasons,
Fair false leaves (but the summer leaves were falser),
Woven under the eyes of stars and planets
When low light was upon the windy reaches
Where the flower of foam was blown, a lily
Dropt among the sonorous fruitless furrows
And green fields of the sea that make no pasture:

Since the winter begins, the weeping winter,
All whose flowers are tears, and round his temples
Iron blossom of frost is bound for ever."

## Sapphics

All the night sleep came not upon my eyelids,
Shed not dew, nor shook nor unclosed a feather,
Yet with lips shut close and with eyes of iron
   Stood and beheld me.

Then to me so lying awake a vision
Came without sleep over the seas and touched me,
Softly touched mine eyelids and lips; and I too,
   Full of the vision,

Saw the white implacable Aphrodite,
Saw the hair unbound and the feet unsandalled
Shine as fire of sunset on western waters;
   Saw the reluctant

Feet, the straining plumes of the doves that drew her,
Looking always, looking with necks reverted,
Back to Lesbos, back to the hills whereunder
   Shone Mitylene;

Heard the flying feet of the Loves behind her
Make a sudden thunder upon the waters,
As the thunder flung from the strong unclosing
   Wings of a great wind.

So the goddess fled from her place, with awful
Sound of feet and thunder of wings around her;
While behind a clamour of singing women
   Severed the twilight.

Ah the singing, ah the delight, the passion!
All the Loves wept, listening; sick with anguish,
Stood the crowned nine Muses about Apollo;
   Fear was upon them,

While the tenth sang wonderful things they knew not.
Ah the tenth, the Lesbian! the nine were silent,
None endured the sound of her song for weeping;
   Laurel by laurel,

Faded all their crowns; but about her forehead,
Round her woven tresses and ashen temples
White as dead snow, paler than grass in summer,
  Ravaged with kisses,

Shone a light of fire as a crown for ever.
Yea, almost the implacable Aphrodite
Paused, and almost wept; such a song was that song.
  Yea, by her name too

Called her, saying, "Turn to me, O my Sappho;"
Yet she turned her face from the Loves, she saw not
Tears for laughter darken immortal eyelids,
  Heard not about her

Fearful fitful wings of the doves departing,
Saw not how the bosom of Aphrodite
Shook with weeping, saw not her shaken raiment,
  Saw not her hands wrung;

Saw the Lesbians kissing across their smitten
Lutes with lips more sweet than the sound of lute-strings,
Mouth to mouth and hand upon hand, her chosen,
  Fairer than all men;

Only saw the beautiful lips and fingers,
Full of songs and kisses and little whispers,
Full of music; only beheld among them
  Soar, as a bird soars

Newly fledged, her visible song, a marvel,
Made of perfect sound and exceeding passion,
Sweetly shapen, terrible, full of thunders,
  Clothed with the wind's wings.

Then rejoiced she, laughing with love, and scattered
Roses, awful roses of holy blossom;
Then the Loves thronged sadly with hidden faces
  Round Aphrodite,

Then the Muses, stricken at heart, were silent;
Yea, the gods waxed pale; such a song was that song.
All reluctant, all with a fresh repulsion,
  Fled from before her.

All withdrew long since, and the land was barren,
Full of fruitless women and music only.

Now perchance, when winds are assuaged at sunset,
   Lulled at the dewfall,

By the grey sea-side, unassuaged, unheard of,
Unbeloved, unseen in the ebb of twilight,
Ghosts of outcast women return lamenting,
   Purged not in Lethe,

Clothed about with flame and with tears, and singing
Songs that move the heart of the shaken heaven,
Songs that break the heart of the earth with pity,
   Hearing, to hear them.

### Dedication
### 1865

The sea gives her shells to the shingle,
   The earth gives her streams to the sea;
They are many, but my gift is single,
   My verses, the firstfruits of me.
Let the wind take the green and the grey leaf,
   Cast forth without fruit upon air;
Take rose-leaf and vine-leaf and bay-leaf
   Blown loose from the hair.

The night shakes them round me in legions,
   Dawn drives them before her like dreams;
Time sheds them like snows on strange regions,
   Swept shoreward on infinite streams;
Leaves pallid and sombre and ruddy,
   Dead fruits of the fugitive years;
Some stained as with wine and made bloody,
   And some as with tears.

Some scattered in seven years' traces,
   As they fell from the boy that was then;
Long left among idle green places,
   Or gathered but now among men;
On seas full of wonder and peril,
   Blown white round the capes of the north;
Or in islands where myrtles are sterile
   And loves bring not forth.

O daughters of dreams and of stories
   That life is not wearied of yet,

Faustine, Fragoletta, Dolores,
  Félise and Yolande and Juliette,
Shall I find you not still, shall I miss you,
  When sleep, that is true or that seems,
Comes back to me hopeless to kiss you,
  O daughters of dreams?

They are past as a slumber that passes,
  As the dew of a dawn of old time;
More frail than the shadows on glasses,
  More fleet than a wave or a rhyme.
As the waves after ebb drawing seaward,
  When their hollows are full of the night,
So the birds that flew singing to me-ward
  Recede out of sight.

The songs of dead seasons, that wander
  On wings of articulate words;
Lost leaves that the shore-wind may squander,
  Light flocks of untameable birds;
Some sang to me dreaming in class-time
  And truant in hand as in tongue;
For the youngest were born of boy's pastime,
  The eldest are young.

Is there shelter while life in them lingers,
  Is there hearing for songs that recede,
Tunes touched from a harp with man's fingers
  Or blown with boy's mouth in a reed?
Is there place in the land of your labour,
  Is there room in your world of delight,
Where change has not sorrow for neighbour
  And day has not night?

In their wings though the sea-wind yet quivers,
  Will you spare not a space for them there
Made green with the running of rivers
  And gracious with temperate air;
In the fields and the turreted cities,
  That cover from sunshine and rain
Fair passions and bountiful pities
  And loves without stain?

In a land of clear colours and stories,
  In a region of shadowless hours,
Where earth has a garment of glories

And a murmur of musical flowers;
In woods where the spring half uncovers
The flush of her amorous face,
By the waters that listen for lovers,
For these is there place?

For the song-birds of sorrow, that muffle
Their music as clouds do their fire:
For the storm-birds of passion, that ruffle
Wild wings in a wind of desire;
In the stream of the storm as it settles
Blown seaward, borne far from the sun,
Shaken loose on the darkness like petals
Dropt one after one?

Though the world of your hands be more gracious
And lovelier in lordship of things
Clothed round by sweet art with the spacious
Warm heaven of her imminent wings,
Let them enter, unfledged and nigh fainting,
For the love of old loves and lost times;
And receive in your palace of painting
This revel of rhymes.

Though the seasons of man full of losses
Make empty the years full of youth,
If but one thing be constant in crosses,
Change lays not her hand upon truth;
Hopes die, and their tombs are for token
That the grief as the joy of them ends
Ere time that breaks all men has broken
The faith between friends.

Though the many lights dwindle to one light,
There is help if the heaven has one;
Though the skies be discrowned of the sunlight
And the earth dispossessed of the sun,
They have moonlight and sleep for repayment,
When, refreshed as a bride and set free,
With stars and sea-winds in her raiment,
Night sinks on the sea.

## FROM *SONGS BEFORE SUNRISE* (1871)

### Prelude

Between the green bud and the red
Youth sat and sang by Time, and shed
   From eyes and tresses flowers and tears,
   From heart and spirit hopes and fears,
Upon the hollow stream whose bed
   Is channelled by the foamless years;
And with the white the gold-haired head
   Mixed running locks, and in Time's ears
Youth's dreams hung singing, and Time's truth
Was half not harsh in the ears of Youth.

Between the bud and the blown flower
Youth talked with joy and grief an hour,
   With footless joy and wingless grief
   And twin-born faith and disbelief
Who share the seasons to devour;
   And long ere these made up their sheaf
Felt the winds round him shake and shower
   The rose-red and the blood-red leaf,
Delight whose germ grew never grain,
And passion dyed in its own pain.

Then he stood up, and trod to dust
Fear and desire, mistrust and trust,
   And dreams of bitter sleep and sweet,
   And bound for sandals on his feet
Knowledge and patience of what must
   And what things may be, in the heat
And cold of years that rot and rust
   And alter; and his spirit's meat

Was freedom, and his staff was wrought
Of strength, and his cloak woven of thought.

For what has he whose will sees clear
To do with doubt and faith and fear,
  Swift hopes and slow despondencies?
  His heart is equal with the sea's
And with the sea-wind's, and his ear
  Is level to the speech of these,
And his soul communes and takes cheer
  With the actual earth's equalities,
Air, light, and night, hills, winds, and streams,
And seeks not strength from strengthless dreams.

His soul is even with the sun
Whose spirit and whose eye are one,
  Who seeks not stars by day, nor light
  And heavy heat of day by night.
Him can no God cast down, whom none
  Can lift in hope beyond the height
Of fate and nature and things done
  By the calm rule of might and right
That bids men be and bear and do,
And die beneath blind skies or blue.

To him the lights of even and morn
Speak no vain things of love or scorn,
  Fancies and passions miscreate
  By man in things dispassionate.
Nor holds he fellowship forlorn
  With souls that pray and hope and hate,
And doubt they had better not been born,
  And fain would lure or scare off fate
And charm their doomsman from their doom
And make fear dig its own false tomb.

He builds not half of doubts and half
Of dreams his own soul's cenotaph,
  Whence hopes and fears with helpless eyes,
  Wrapt loose in cast-off cerecloths, rise
And dance and wring their hands and laugh,
  And weep thin tears and sigh light sighs,
And without living lips would quaff
  The living spring in man that lies,
And drain his soul of faith and strength
It might have lived on a life's length.

He hath given himself and hath not sold
To God for heaven or man for gold,
   Or grief for comfort that it gives,
   Or joy for grief's restoratives.
He hath given himself to time, whose fold
   Shuts in the mortal flock that lives
On its plain pasture's heat and cold
   And the equal year's alternatives.
Earth, heaven, and time, death, life, and he,
Endure while they shall be to be.

"Yet between death and life are hours
To flush with love and hide in flowers;
   What profit save in these?" men cry:
   "Ah, see, between soft earth and sky,
What only good things here are ours!"
   They say, "what better wouldst thou try,
What sweeter sing of? or what powers
   Serve, that will give thee ere thou die
More joy to sing and be less sad,
More heart to play and grow more glad?"

Play then and sing; we too have played,
We likewise, in that subtle shade.
   We too have twisted through our hair
   Such tendrils as the wild Loves wear,
And heard what mirth the Mænads made,
   Till the wind blew our garlands bare
And left their roses disarrayed,
   And smote the summer with strange air,
And disengirdled and discrowned
The limbs and locks that vine-wreaths bound.

We too have tracked by star-proof trees
The tempest of the Thyiades
   Scare the loud night on hills that hid
   The blood-feasts of the Bassarid,
Heard their song's iron cadences
   Fright the wolf hungering from the kid,
Outroar the lion-throated seas,
   Outchide the north-wind if it chid,
And hush the torrent-tongued ravines
With thunders of their tambourines.

But the fierce flute whose notes acclaim
Dim goddesses of fiery fame,

Cymbal and clamorous kettledrum,
Timbrels and tabrets, all are dumb
That turned the high chill air to flame;
The singing tongues of fire are numb
That called on Cotys by her name
Edonian, till they felt her come
And maddened, and her mystic face
Lightened along the streams of Thrace.

For Pleasure slumberless and pale,
And Passion with rejected veil,
Pass, and the tempest-footed throng
Of hours that follow them with song
Till their feet flag and voices fail,
And lips that were so loud so long
Learn silence, or a wearier wail;
So keen is change, and time so strong,
To weave the robes of life and rend
And weave again till life have end.

But weak is change, but strengthless time,
To take the light from heaven, or climb
The hills of heaven with wasting feet.
Songs they can stop that earth found meet,
But the stars keep their ageless rhyme;
Flowers they can slay that spring thought sweet,
But the stars keep their spring sublime;
Passions and pleasures can defeat,
Actions and agonies control,
And life and death, but not the soul.

Because man's soul is man's God still,
What wind soever waft his will
Across the waves of day and night
To port or shipwreck, left or right,
By shores and shoals of good and ill;
And still its flame at mainmast height
Through the rent air that foam-flakes fill
Sustains the indomitable light
Whence only man hath strength to steer
Or helm to handle without fear.

Save his own soul's light overhead,
None leads him, and none ever led,

Across birth's hidden harbour-bar,
Past youth where shoreward shallows are,
Through age that drives on toward the red
Vast void of sunset hailed from far,
To the equal waters of the dead;
Save his own soul he hath no star,
And sinks, except his own soul guide,
Helmless in middle turn of tide.

No blast of air or fire of sun
Puts out the light whereby we run
With girded loins our lamplit race,
And each from each takes heart of grace
And spirit till his turn be done,
And light of face from each man's face
In whom the light of trust is one;
Since only souls that keep their place
By their own light, and watch things roll,
And stand, have light for any soul.

A little time we gain from time
To set our seasons in some chime,
For harsh or sweet or loud or low,
With seasons played out long ago
And souls that in their time and prime
Took part with summer or with snow,
Lived abject lives out or sublime,
And had their chance of seed to sow
For service or disservice done
To those days dead and this their son.

A little time that we may fill
Or with such good works or such ill
As loose the bonds or make them strong
Wherein all manhood suffers wrong.
By rose-hung river and light-foot rill
There are who rest not; who think long
Till they discern as from a hill
At the sun's hour of morning song,
Known of souls only, and those souls free,
The sacred spaces of the sea.

## Hertha

I am that which began;
Out of me the years roll;
Out of me God and man;
I am equal and whole;
God changes, and man, and the form of them bodily; I am the soul.

Before ever land was,
Before ever the sea,
Or soft hair of the grass,
Or fair limbs of the tree,
Or the flesh-coloured fruit of my branches, I was, and thy soul was in me.

First life on my sources
First drifted and swam;
Out of me are the forces
That save it or damn;
Out of me man and woman, and wild-beast and bird; before God was, I am.

Beside or above me
Nought is there to go;
Love or unlove me,
Unknow me or know,
I am that which unloves me and loves; I am stricken, and I am the blow.

I the mark that is missed
And the arrows that miss,
I the mouth that is kissed
And the breath in the kiss,
The search, and the sought, and the seeker, the soul and the body that is.

I am that thing which blesses
My spirit elate;
That which caresses
With hands uncreate
My limbs unbegotten that measure the length of the measure of fate.

But what thing dost thou now,
Looking Godward, to cry
"I am I, thou art thou,
I am low, thou art high"?
I am thou, whom thou seekest to find him; find thou but thyself, thou art I.

I the grain and the furrow,
The plough-cloven clod
And the ploughshare drawn thorough,
The germ and the sod,
The deed and the doer, the seed and the sower, the dust which is God.

Hast thou known how I fashioned thee,
Child, underground?
Fire that impassioned thee,
Iron that bound,
Dim changes of water, what thing of all these hast thou known of or found?

Canst thou say in thine heart
Thou hast seen with thine eyes
With what cunning of art
Thou wast wrought in what wise,
By what force of what stuff thou wast shapen, and shown on my breast to the skies?

Who hath given, who hath sold it thee,
Knowledge of me?
Hath the wilderness told it thee?
Hast thou learnt of the sea?
Hast thou communed in spirit with night? have the winds taken counsel with thee?

Have I set such a star
To show light on thy brow
That thou sawest from afar
What I show to thee now?
Have ye spoken as brethren together, the sun and the mountains and thou?

What is here, dost thou know it?
What was, hast thou known?
Prophet nor poet
Nor tripod nor throne
Nor spirit nor flesh can make answer, but only thy mother alone.

Mother, not maker,
Born, and not made;
Though her children forsake her,
Allured or afraid,
Praying prayers to the God of their fashion, she stirs not for all that have prayed.

A creed is a rod,
And a crown is of night;
But this thing is God,
To be man with thy might,
To grow straight in the strength of thy spirit, and live out thy life as the light.

I am in thee to save thee,
As my soul in thee saith;
Give thou as I gave thee,
Thy life-blood and breath,
Green leaves of thy labour, white flowers of thy thought, and red fruit of thy death.

Be the ways of thy giving
As mine were to thee;
The free life of thy living,
Be the gift of it free;
Not as servant to lord, nor as master to slave, shalt thou give thee to me.

O children of banishment,
Souls overcast,
Were the lights ye see vanish meant
Alway to last,
Ye would know not the sun overshining the shadows and stars overpast.

I that saw where ye trod
The dim paths of the night
Set the shadow called God
In your skies to give light;
But the morning of manhood is risen, and the shadow-less soul is in sight.

The tree many-rooted
That swells to the sky
With frondage red-fruited,
The life-tree am I;
In the buds of your lives is the sap of my leaves: ye shall live and not die.

But the Gods of your fashion
That take and that give,
In their pity and passion
That scourge and forgive,
They are worms that are bred in the bark that falls off; they shall die and not live.

My own blood is what stanches
The wounds in my bark;
Stars caught in my branches
Make day of the dark,
And are worshipped as suns till the sunrise shall tread out their fires as a spark.

Where dead ages hide under
The live roots of the tree,
In my darkness the thunder
Makes utterance of me;
In the clash of my boughs with each other ye hear the waves sound of the sea.

That noise is of Time,
As his feathers are spread
And his feet set to climb
Through the boughs overhead,
And my foliage rings round him and rustles, and branches are bent with his tread.

The storm-winds of ages
Blow through me and cease,
The war-wind that rages,
The spring-wind of peace,
Ere the breath of them roughen my tresses, ere one of my blossoms increase.

All sounds of all changes,
All shadows and lights
On the world's mountain-ranges
And stream-riven heights,
Whose tongue is the wind's tongue and language of storm-clouds on earth-shaking nights;

All forms of all faces,
All works of all hands
In unsearchable places
Of time-stricken lands,
All death and all life, and all reigns and all ruins, drop through me as sands.

Though sore be my burden
And more than ye know,
And my growth have no guerdon
But only to grow,
Yet I fail not of growing for lightnings above me or deathworms below.

These too have their part in me,
As I too in these;
Such fire is at heart in me,
Such sap is this tree's,
Which hath in it all sounds and all secrets of infinite lands and of seas.

In the spring-coloured hours
When my mind was as May's,
There brake forth of me flowers
By centuries of days,
Strong blossoms with perfume of manhood, shot out from my spirit as rays.

And the sound of them springing
And smell of their shoots
Were as warmth and sweet singing
And strength to my roots;
And the lives of my children made perfect with freedom of soul were my fruits.

I bid you but be;
I have need not of prayer;
I have need of you free
As your mouths of mine air;
That my heart may be greater within me, beholding the fruits of me fair.

More fair than strange fruit is
Of faiths ye espouse;
In me only the root is
That blooms in your boughs;
Behold now your God that ye made you, to feed him with faith of your vows.

In the darkening and whitening
Abysses adored,
With dayspring and lightning
For lamp and for sword,
God thunders in heaven, and his angels are red with the wrath of the Lord.

O my sons, O too dutiful
Toward Gods not of me,
Was not I enough beautiful?
Was it hard to be free?
For behold, I am with you, am in you and of you; look forth now and see.

Lo, winged with world's wonders,
   With miracles shod,
With the fires of his thunders
   For raiment and rod,
God trembles in heaven, and his angels are white with the terror
   of God.

For his twilight is come on him,
   His anguish is here;
And his spirits gaze dumb on him,
   Grown grey from his fear;
And his hour taketh hold on him stricken, the last of his infinite year.

Thought made him and breaks him,
   Truth slays and forgives;
But to you, as time takes him,
   This new thing it gives,
Even love, the beloved Republic, that feeds upon freedom and lives.

For truth only is living,
   Truth only is whole,
And the love of his giving
   Man's polestar and pole;
Man, pulse of my centre, and fruit of my body, and seed of my soul.

One birth of my bosom;
   One beam of mine eye;
One topmost blossom
   That scales the sky;
Man, equal and one with me, man that is made of me, man that is I.

## Before a Crucifix

Here, down between the dusty trees,
   At this lank edge of haggard wood,
Women with labour-loosened knees,
   With gaunt backs bowed by servitude,
Stop, shift their loads, and pray, and fare
Forth with souls easier for the prayer.

The suns have branded black, the rains
   Striped grey this piteous God of theirs;
The face is full of prayers and pains,
   To which they bring their pains and prayers;
Lean limbs that shew the labouring bones,
And ghastly mouth that gapes and groans.

God of this grievous people, wrought
After the likeness of their race,
By faces like thine own besought,
Thine own blind helpless eyeless face,
I too, that have nor tongue nor knee
For prayer, I have a word to thee.

It was for this then, that thy speech
Was blown about the world in flame
And men's souls shot up out of reach
Of fear or lust or thwarting shame—
That thy faith over souls should pass
As sea-winds burning the grey grass?

It was for this, that prayers like these
Should spend themselves about thy feet,
And with hard overlaboured knees
Kneeling, these slaves of men should beat
Bosoms too lean to suckle sons
And fruitless as their orisons?

It was for this, that men should make
Thy name a fetter on men's necks,
Poor men's made poorer for thy sake,
And women's withered out of sex?
It was for this, that slaves should be,
Thy word was passed to set men free?

The nineteenth wave of the ages rolls
Now deathward since thy death and birth.
Hast thou fed full men's starved-out souls?
Hast thou brought freedom upon earth?
Or are there less oppressions done
In this wild world under the sun?

Nay, if indeed thou be not dead,
Before thy terrene shrine be shaken,
Look down, turn usward, bow thine head;
O thou that wast of God forsaken,
Look on thine household here, and see
These that have not forsaken thee.

Thy faith is fire upon their lips,
Thy kingdom golden in their hands;
They scourge us with thy words for whips,
They brand us with thy words for brands;

The thirst that made thy dry throat shrink
To their moist mouths commends the drink.

The toothèd thorns that bit thy brows
  Lighten the weight of gold on theirs;
Thy nakedness enrobes thy spouse
  With the soft sanguine stuff she wears
Whose old limbs use for ointment yet
Thine agony and bloody sweat.

The blinding buffets on thine head
  On their crowned heads confirm the crown;
Thy scourging dyes their raiment red,
  And with thy bands they fasten down
For burial in the blood-bought field
The nations by thy stripes unhealed.

With iron for thy linen bands
  And unclean cloths for winding-sheet
They bind the people's nail-pierced hands,
  They hide the people's nail-pierced feet;
And what man or what angel known
Shall roll back the sepulchral stone?

But these have not the rich man's grave
  To sleep in when their pain is done.
These were not fit for God to save.
  As naked hell-fire is the sun
In their eyes living, and when dead
These have not where to lay their head.

They have no tomb to dig, and hide;
  Earth is not theirs, that they should sleep.
On all these tombless crucified
  No lovers' eyes have time to weep.
So still, for all man's tears and creeds,
The sacred body hangs and bleeds.

Through the left hand a nail is driven,
  Faith, and another through the right,
Forged in the fires of hell and heaven,
  Fear that puts out the eye of light:
And the feet soiled and scarred and pale
Are pierced with falsehood for a nail.

And priests against the mouth divine
  Push their sponge full of poison yet

And bitter blood for myrrh and wine,
   And on the same reed is it set
Wherewith before they buffeted
The people's disanointed head.

O sacred head, O desecrate,
   O labour-wounded feet and hands,
O blood poured forth in pledge to fate
   Of nameless lives in divers lands,
O slain and spent and sacrificed
People, the grey-grown speechless Christ!

Is there a gospel in the red
   Old witness of thy wide-mouthed wounds?
From thy blind stricken tongueless head
   What desolate evangel sounds
A hopeless note of hope deferred?
What word, if there be any word?

O son of man, beneath man's feet
   Cast down, O common face of man
Whereon all blows and buffets meet,
   O royal, O republican
Face of the people bruised and dumb
And longing till thy kingdom come!

The soldiers and the high priests part
   Thy vesture: all thy days are priced,
And all the nights that eat thine heart.
   And that one seamless coat of Christ,
The freedom of the natural soul,
They cast their lots for to keep whole.

No fragment of it save the name
   They leave thee for a crown of scorns
Wherewith to mock thy naked shame
   And forehead bitten through with thorns
And, marked with sanguine sweat and tears,
The stripes of eighteen hundred years.

And we seek yet if God or man
   Can loosen thee as Lazarus,
Bid thee rise up republican
   And save thyself and all of us;
But no disciple's tongue can say
When thou shalt take our sins away.

And mouldering now and hoar with moss
   Between us and the sunlight swings
The phantom of a Christless cross
   Shadowing the sheltered heads of kings
And making with its moving shade
The souls of harmless men afraid.

It creaks and rocks to left and right
   Consumed of rottenness and rust,
Worm-eaten of the worms of night,
   Dead as their spirits who put trust,
Round its base muttering as they sit,
In the time-cankered name of it.

Thou, in the day that breaks thy prison,
   People, though these men take thy name,
And hail and hymn thee rearisen,
   Who made songs erewhile of thy shame,
Give thou not ear; for these are they
Whose good day was thine evil day.

Set not thine hand unto their cross.
   Give not thy soul up sacrificed.
Change not the gold of faith for dross
   Of Christian creeds that spit on Christ.
Let not thy tree of freedom be
Regrafted from that rotting tree.

This dead God here against my face
   Hath help for no man; who hath seen
The good works of it, or such grace
   As thy grace in it, Nazarene,
As that from thy live lips which ran
For man's sake, O thou son of man?

The tree of faith ingraffed by priests
   Puts its foul foliage out above thee,
And round it feed man-eating beasts
   Because of whom we dare not love thee;
Though hearts reach back and memories ache,
We cannot praise thee for their sake.

O hidden face of man, whereover
   The years have woven a viewless veil,
If thou wast verily man's lover,
   What did thy love or blood avail?

Thy blood the priests make poison of,
And in gold shekels coin thy love.

So when our souls look back to thee
  They sicken, seeing against thy side,
Too foul to speak of or to see,
  The leprous likeness of a bride,
Whose kissing lips through his lips grown
Leave their God rotten to the bone.

When we would see thee man, and know
  What heart thou hadst toward men indeed,
Lo, thy blood-blackened altars; lo,
  The lips of priests that pray and feed
While their own hell's worm curls and licks
The poison of the crucifix.

Thou bad'st let children come to thee;
  What children now but curses come?
What manhood in that God can be
  Who sees their worship, and is dumb?
No soul that lived, loved, wrought, and died,
Is this their carrion crucified.

Nay, if their God and thou be one,
  If thou and this thing be the same,
Thou shouldst not look upon the sun;
  The sun grows haggard at thy name.
Come down, be done with, cease, give o'er;
Hide thyself, strive not, be no more.

## Genesis

In the outer world that was before this earth,
  That was before all shape or space was born,
Before the blind first hour of time had birth,
  Before night knew the moonlight or the morn;

Yea, before any world had any light,
  Or anything called God or man drew breath,
Slowly the strong sides of the heaving night
  Moved, and brought forth the strength of life and death.

And the sad shapeless horror increate
  That was all things and one thing, without fruit,

Limit, or law; where love was none, nor hate,
  Where no leaf came to blossom from no root;

The very darkness that time knew not of,
  Nor God laid hand on, nor was man found there,
Ceased, and was cloven in several shapes; above
  Light, and night under, and fire, earth, water, and air.

Sunbeams and starbeams, and all coloured things,
  All forms and all similitudes began;
And death, the shadow cast by life's wide wings,
  And God, the shade cast by the soul of man.

Then between shadow and substance, night and light,
  Then between birth and death, and deeds and days,
The illimitable embrace and the amorous fight
  That of itself begets, bears, rears, and slays,

The immortal war of mortal things, that is
  Labour and life and growth and good and ill,
The mild antiphonies that melt and kiss,
  The violent symphonies that meet and kill,

All nature of all things began to be.
  But chiefliest in the spirit (beast or man,
Planet of heaven or blossom of earth or sea)
  The divine contraries of life began.

For the great labour of growth, being many, is one;
  One thing the white death and the ruddy birth;
The invisible air and the all-beholden sun,
  And barren water and many-childed earth.

And these things are made manifest in men
  From the beginning forth unto this day:
Time writes and life records them, and again
  Death seals them lest the record pass away.

For if death were not, then should growth not be,
  Change, nor the life of good nor evil things;
Nor were there night at all nor light to see,
  Nor water of sweet nor water of bitter springs.

For in each man and each year that is born
  Are sown the twin seeds of the strong twin powers;
The white seed of the fruitful helpful morn,
  The black seed of the barren hurtful hours.

And he that of the black seed eateth fruit,
  To him the savour as honey shall be sweet;
And he in whom the white seed hath struck root,
  He shall have sorrow and trouble and tears for meat.

And him whose lips the sweet fruit hath made red
  In the end men loathe and make his name a rod;
And him whose mouth on the unsweet fruit hath fed
  In the end men follow and know for very God.

And of these twain, the black seed and the white,
  All things come forth, endured of men and done;
And still the day is great with child of night,
  And still the black night labours with the sun.

And each man and each year that lives on earth
  Turns hither or thither, and hence or thence is fed;
And as a man before was from his birth,
  So shall a man be after among the dead.

## FROM *SONGS OF TWO NATIONS* (1876)

### Locusta

Come close and see her and hearken. This is she.
  Stop the ways fast against the stench that nips
  Your nostril as it nears her. Lo, the lips
That between prayer and prayer find time to be
Poisonous, the hands holding a cup and key,
  Key of deep hell, cup whence blood reeks and drips;
  The loose lewd limbs, the reeling hingeless hips,
The scurf that is not skin but leprosy.
This haggard harlot grey of face and green
With the old hand's cunning mixes her new priest
The cup she mixed her Nero, stirred and spiced.
She lisps of Mary and Jesus Nazarene
With a tongue tuned, and head that bends to the east,
Praying. There are who say she is bride of Christ.

## FROM *POEMS AND BALLADS, SECOND SERIES* (1878)

### A Forsaken Garden

In a coign of the cliff between lowland and highland,
   At the sea-down's edge between windward and lee,
Walled round with rocks as an inland island,
   The ghost of a garden fronts the sea.
A girdle of brushwood and thorn encloses
   The steep square slope of the blossomless bed
Where the weeds that grew green from the graves of its roses
      Now lie dead.

The fields fall southward, abrupt and broken,
   To the low last edge of the long lone land.
If a step should sound or a word be spoken,
   Would a ghost not rise at the strange guest's hand?
So long have the grey bare walks lain guestless,
   Through branches and briars if a man make way,
He shall find no life but the sea-wind's, restless
   Night and day.

The dense hard passage is blind and stifled
   That crawls by a track none turn to climb
To the strait waste place that the years have rifled
   Of all but the thorns that are touched not of time.
The thorns he spares when the rose is taken;
   The rocks are left when he wastes the plain.
The wind that wanders, the weeds wind-shaken,
      These remain.

Not a flower to be pressed of the foot that falls not;
   As the heart of a dead man the seed-plots are dry;
From the thicket of thorns whence the nightingale calls not,
   Could she call, there were never a rose to reply.

Over the meadows that blossom and wither
  Rings but the note of a sea-bird's song;
Only the sun and the rain come hither
    All year long.

The sun burns sere and the rain dishevels
  One gaunt bleak blossom of scentless breath.
Only the wind here hovers and revels
  In a round where life seems barren as death.
Here there was laughing of old, there was weeping,
  Haply, of lovers none ever will know,
Whose eyes went seaward a hundred sleeping
    Years ago.

Heart handfast in heart as they stood, "Look thither,"
  Did he whisper? "look forth from the flowers to the sea;
For the foam-flowers endure when the rose-blossoms wither,
  And men that love lightly may die — but we?"
And the same wind sang and the same waves whitened,
  And or ever the garden's last petals were shed,
In the lips that had whispered, the eyes that had lightened,
  Love was dead.

Or they loved their life through, and then went whither?
  And were one to the end — but what end who knows?
Love deep as the sea as a rose must wither,
  As the rose-red seaweed that mocks the rose.
Shall the dead take thought for the dead to love them?
  What love was ever as deep as a grave?
They are loveless now as the grass above them
    Or the wave.

All are at one now, roses and lovers,
  Not known of the cliffs and the fields and the sea.
Not a breath of the time that has been hovers
  In the air now soft with a summer to be.
Not a breath shall there sweeten the seasons hereafter
  Of the flowers or the lovers that laugh now or weep,
When as they that are free now of weeping and laughter
  We shall sleep.

Here death may deal not again for ever;
  Here change may come not till all change end.
From the graves they have made they shall rise up never,
  Who have left nought living to ravage and rend.

Earth, stones, and thorns of the wild ground growing,
   While the sun and the rain live, these shall be;
Till a last wind's breath upon all these blowing
   Roll the sea.

Till the slow sea rise and the sheer cliff crumble,
   Till terrace and meadow the deep gulfs drink,
Till the strength of the waves of the high tides humble
   The fields that lessen, the rocks that shrink,
Here now in his triumph where all things falter,
   Stretched out on the spoils that his own hand spread,
As a god self-slain on his own strange altar,
   Death lies dead.

**Sestina**

I saw my soul at rest upon a day
   As a bird sleeping in the nest of night,
Among soft leaves that give the starlight way
   To touch its wings but not its eyes with light;
So that it knew as one in visions may,
   And knew not as men waking, of delight.

This was the measure of my soul's delight;
   It had no power of joy to fly by day,
Nor part in the large lordship of the light;
   But in a secret moon-beholden way
Had all its will of dreams and pleasant night,
   And all the love and life that sleepers may.

But such life's triumph as men waking may
   It might not have to feed its faint delight
Between the stars by night and sun by day,
   Shut up with green leaves and a little light;
Because its way was as a lost star's way,
   A world's not wholly known of day or night.

All loves and dreams and sounds and gleams of night
   Made it all music that such minstrels may,
And all they had they gave it of delight;
   But in the full face of the fire of day
What place shall be for any starry light,
   What part of heaven in all the wide sun's way?

Yet the soul woke not, sleeping by the way,
   Watched as a nursling of the large-eyed night,
And sought no strength nor knowledge of the day,
   Nor closer touch conclusive of delight,
Nor mightier joy nor truer than dreamers may,
   Nor more of song than they, nor more of light.

For who sleeps once and sees the secret light
   Whereby sleep shows the soul a fairer way
Between the rise and rest of day and night,
   Shall care no more to fare as all men may,
But be his place of pain or of delight,
   There shall he dwell, beholding night as day.

Song, have thy day and take thy fill of light
   Before the night be fallen across thy way;
Sing while he may, man hath no long delight.

**The Complaint of Lisa**
*(Double Sestina)*
**Decameron, x. 7**

There is no woman living that draws breath
So sad as I, though all things sadden her.
There is not one upon life's weariest way
Who is weary as I am weary of all but death.
Toward whom I look as looks the sunflower
All day with all his whole soul toward the sun;
While in the sun's sight I make moan all day,
And all night on my sleepless maiden bed
Weep and call out on death, O Love, and thee,
That thou or he would take me to the dead,
And know not what thing evil I have done
That life should lay such heavy hand on me.

Alas, Love, what is this thou wouldst with me?
What honour shalt thou have to quench my breath,
Or what shall my heart broken profit thee?
O Love, O great god Love, what have I done,
That thou shouldst hunger so after my death?
My heart is harmless as my life's first day:
Seek out some false fair woman, and plague her
Till her tears even as my tears fill her bed:

I am the least flower in thy flowery way,
But till my time be come that I be dead
Let me live out my flower-time in the sun
Though my leaves shut before the sunflower.

O Love, Love, Love, the kingly sunflower!
Shall he the sun hath looked on look on me,
That live down here in shade, out of the sun,
Here living in the sorrow and shadow of death?
Shall he that feeds his heart full of the day
Care to give mine eyes light, or my lips breath?
Because she loves him shall my lord love her
Who is as a worm in my lord's kingly way?
I shall not see him or know him alive or dead;
But thou, I know thee, O Love, and pray to thee
That in brief while my brief life-days be done,
And the worm quickly make my marriage-bed.

For underground there is no sleepless bed:
But here since I beheld my sunflower
These eyes have slept not, seeing all night and day
His sunlike eyes, and face fronting the sun.
Wherefore if anywhere be any death,
I would fain find and fold him fast to me,
That I may sleep with the world's eldest dead,
With her that died seven centuries since, and her
That went last night down the night-wandering way.
For this is sleep indeed, when labour is done,
Without love, without dreams, and without breath,
And without thought, O name unnamed! of thee.

Ah, but, forgetting all things, shall I thee?
Wilt thou not be as now about my bed
There underground as here before the sun?
Shall not thy vision vex me alive and dead,
Thy moving vision without form or breath?
I read long since the bitter tale of her
Who read the tale of Launcelot on a day,
And died, and had no quiet after death,
But was moved ever along a weary way,
Lost with her love in the underworld; ah me,
O my king, O my lordly sunflower,
Would God to me too such a thing were done!

But if such sweet and bitter things be done,
Then, flying from life, I shall not fly from thee.

For in that living world without a sun
Thy vision will lay hold upon me dead,
And meet and mock me, and mar my peace in death.
Yet if being wroth God had such pity on her,
Who was a sinner and foolish in her day,
That even in hell they twain should breathe one breath,
Why should he not in some wise pity me?
So if I sleep not in my soft strait bed
I may look up and see my sunflower
As he the sun, in some divine strange way.

O poor my heart, well knowest thou in what way
This sore sweet evil unto us was done.
For on a holy and a heavy day
I was arisen out of my still small bed
To see the knights tilt, and one said to me
"The king," and seeing him, somewhat stopped my breath,
And if the girl spake more, I heard not her,
For only I saw what I shall see when dead,
A kingly flower of knights, a sunflower,
That shone against the sunlight like the sun,
And like a fire, O heart, consuming thee,
The fire of love that lights the pyre of death.

Howbeit I shall not die an evil death
Who have loved in such a sad and sinless way,
That this my love, lord, was no shame to thee.
So when mine eyes are shut against the sun,
O my soul's sun, O the world's sunflower,
Thou nor no man will quite despise me dead.
And dying I pray with all my low last breath
That thy whole life may be as was that day,
That feast-day that made trothplight death and me,
Giving the world light of thy great deeds done;
And that fair face brightening thy bridal bed,
That God be good as God hath been to her.

That all things goodly and glad remain with her,
All things that make glad life and goodly death;
That as a bee sucks from a sunflower
Honey, when summer draws delighted breath,
Her soul may drink of thy soul in like way,
And love make life a fruitful marriage-bed
Where day may bring forth fruits of joy to day
And night to night till days and nights be dead.

And as she gives light of her love to thee,
Give thou to her the old glory of days long done;
And either give some heat or light to me,
To warm me where I sleep without the sun.

O sunflower made drunken with the sun,
O knight whose lady's heart draws thine to her,
Great king, glad lover, I have a word to thee.
There is a weed lives out of the sun's way,
Hid from the heat deep in the meadow's bed,
That swoons and whitens at the wind's least breath,
A flower star-shaped, that all a summer day
Will gaze her soul out on the sunflower
For very love till twilight finds her dead.
But the great sunflower heeds not her poor death,
Knows not when all her loving life is done;
And so much knows my lord the king of me.

Aye, all day long he has no eye for me;
With golden eye following the golden sun
From rose-coloured to purple-pillowed bed,
From birthplace to the flame-lit place of death,
From eastern end to western of his way.
So mine eye follows thee, my sunflower,
So the white star-flower turns and yearns to thee,
The sick weak weed, not well alive or dead,
Trod underfoot if any pass by her,
Pale, without colour of summer or summer breath
In the shrunk shuddering petals, that have done
No work but love, and die before the day.

But thou, to-day, to-morrow, and every day,
Be glad and great, O love whose love slays me.
Thy fervent flower made fruitful from the sun
Shall drop its golden seed in the world's way,
That all men thereof nourished shall praise thee
For grain and flower and fruit of works well done;
Till thy shed seed, O shining sunflower,
Bring forth such growth of the world's garden-bed
As like the sun shall outlive age and death.
And yet I would thine heart had heed of her
Who loves thee alive; but not till she be dead.
Come, Love, then, quickly, and take her utmost breath.

Song, speak for me who am dumb as are the dead;
From my sad bed of tears I send forth thee,

To fly all day from sun's birth to sun's death
Down the sun's way after the flying sun,
For love of her that gave thee wings and breath,
Ere day be done, to seek the sunflower.

## Ave atque Vale

IN MEMORY OF CHARLES BAUDELAIRE

*Nous devrions pourtant lui porter quelques fleurs;*
*Les morts, les pauvres morts, ont de grandes douleurs,*
*Et quand Octobre souffle, émondeur des vieux arbres,*
*Son vent mélancolique à l'entour de leurs marbres,*
*Certe, ils doivent trouver les vivants bien ingrats.*
*Les Fleurs du Mal.*

I

Shall I strew on thee rose or rue or laurel,
  Brother, on this that was the veil of thee?
  Or quiet sea-flower moulded by the sea,
Or simplest growth of meadow-sweet or sorrel,
  Such as the summer-sleepy Dryads weave,
  Waked up by snow-soft sudden rains at eve?
Or wilt thou rather, as on earth before,
  Half-faded fiery blossoms, pale with heat
  And full of bitter summer, but more sweet
To thee than gleanings of a northern shore
  Trod by no tropic feet?

II

For always thee the fervid languid glories
  Allured of heavier suns in mightier skies;
  Thine ears knew all the wandering watery sighs
Where the sea sobs round Lesbian promontories,
  The barren kiss of piteous wave to wave
  That knows not where is that Leucadian grave
Which hides too deep the supreme head of song.
  Ah, salt and sterile as her kisses were,
  The wild sea winds her and the green gulfs bear
Hither and thither, and vex and work her wrong,
  Blind gods that cannot spare.

III

Thou sawest, in thine old singing season, brother,
  Secrets and sorrows unbeheld of us:

Fierce loves, and lovely leaf-buds poisonous,
Bare to thy subtler eye, but for none other
Blowing by night in some unbreathed-in clime;
The hidden harvest of luxurious time,
Sin without shape, and pleasure without speech;
And where strange dreams in a tumultuous sleep
Make the shut eyes of stricken spirits weep;
And with each face thou sawest the shadow on each,
Seeing as men sow men reap.

VI

O sleepless heart and sombre soul unsleeping,
That were athirst for sleep and no more life
And no more love, for peace and no more strife!
Now the dim gods of death have in their keeping
Spirit and body and all the springs of song,
Is it well now where love can do no wrong,
Where stingless pleasure has no foam or fang
Behind the unopening closure of her lips?
Is it not well where soul from body slips
And flesh from bone divides without a pang
As dew from flower-bell drips?

V

It is enough; the end and the beginning
Are one thing to thee, who art past the end.
O hand unclasped of unbeholden friend,
For thee no fruits to pluck, no palms for winning,
No triumph and no labour and no lust,
Only dead yew-leaves and a little dust.
O quiet eyes wherein the light saith nought,
Whereto the day is dumb, nor any night
With obscure finger silences your sight,
Nor in your speech the sudden soul speaks thought,
Sleep, and have sleep for light.

VI

Now all strange hours and all strange loves are over,
Dreams and desires and sombre songs and sweet,
Hast thou found place at the great knees and feet
Of some pale Titan-woman like a lover,
Such as thy vision here solicited,
Under the shadow of her fair vast head,
The deep division of prodigious breasts,

The solemn slope of mighty limbs asleep,
The weight of awful tresses that still keep
The savour and shade of old-world pine-forests
Where the wet hill-winds weep?

VII

Hast thou found any likeness for thy vision?
O gardener of strange flowers, what bud, what bloom,
Hast thou found sown, what gathered in the gloom?
What of despair, of rapture, of derision,
What of life is there, what of ill or good?
Are the fruits grey like dust or bright like blood?
Does the dim ground grow any seed of ours,
The faint fields quicken any terrene root,
In low lands where the sun and moon are mute
And all the stars keep silence? Are there flowers
At all, or any fruit?

VIII

Alas, but though my flying song flies after,
O sweet strange elder singer, thy more fleet
Singing, and footprints of thy fleeter feet,
Some dim derision of mysterious laughter
From the blind tongueless warders of the dead,
Some gainless glimpse of Proserpine's veiled head,
Some little sound of unregarded tears
Wept by effaced unprofitable eyes,
And from pale mouths some cadence of dead sighs—
These only, these the hearkening spirit hears,
Sees only such things rise.

IX

Thou art far too far for wings of words to follow,
Far too far off for thought or any prayer.
What ails us with thee, who art wind and air?
What ails us gazing where all seen is hollow?
Yet with some fancy, yet with some desire,
Dreams pursue death as winds a flying fire,
Our dreams pursue our dead and do not find.
Still, and more swift than they, the thin flame flies,
The low light fails us in elusive skies,
Still the foiled earnest ear is deaf, and blind
Are still the eluded eyes.

X

Not thee, O never thee, in all time's changes,
  Not thee, but this the sound of thy sad soul,
  The shadow of thy swift spirit, this shut scroll
I lay my hand on, and not death estranges
  My spirit from communion of thy song—
  These memories and these melodies that throng
Veiled porches of a Muse funereal—
  These I salute, these touch, these clasp and fold
  As though a hand were in my hand to hold,
Or through mine ears a mourning musical
  Of many mourners rolled.

XI

I among these, I also, in such station
  As when the pyre was charred, and piled the sods,
  And offering to the dead made, and their gods,
The old mourners had, standing to make libation,
  I stand, and to the gods and to the dead
  Do reverence without prayer or praise, and shed
Offering to these unknown, the gods of gloom,
  And what of honey and spice my seedlands bear,
  And what I may of fruits in this chilled air,
And lay, Orestes-like, across the tomb
  A curl of severed hair.

XII

But by no hand nor any treason stricken,
  Not like the low-lying head of Him, the King,
  The flame that made of Troy a ruinous thing,
Thou liest, and on this dust no tears could quicken
  There fall no tears like theirs that all men hear
  Fall tear by sweet imperishable tear
Down the opening leaves of holy poets' pages.
  Thee not Orestes, not Electra mourns;
  But bending us-ward with memorial urns
The most high Muses that fulfil all ages
  Weep, and our God's heart yearns.

XIII

For, sparing of his sacred strength, not often
  Among us darkling here the lord of light
  Makes manifest his music and his might
In hearts that open and in lips that soften
  With the soft flame and heat of songs that shine.

Thy lips indeed he touched with bitter wine,
And nourished them indeed with bitter bread;
Yet surely from his hand thy soul's food came,
The fire that scarred thy spirit at his flame
Was lighted, and thine hungering heart he fed
Who feeds our hearts with fame.

XIV

Therefore he too now at thy soul's sunsetting,
God of all suns and songs, he too bends down
To mix his laurel with thy cypress crown,
And save thy dust from blame and from forgetting.
Therefore he too, seeing all thou wert and art,
Compassionate, with sad and sacred heart,
Mourns thee of many his children the last dead,
And hallows with strange tears and alien sighs
Thine unmelodious mouth and sunless eyes,
And over thine irrevocable head
Sheds light from the under skies.

XV

And one weeps with him in the ways Lethean,
And stains with tears her changing bosom chill:
That obscure Venus of the hollow hill,
That thing transformed which was the Cytherean,
With lips that lost their Grecian laugh divine
Long since, and face no more called Erycine;
A ghost, a bitter and luxurious god.
Thee also with fair flesh and singing spell
Did she, a sad and second prey, compel
Into the footless places once more trod,
And shadows hot from hell.

XVI

And now no sacred staff shall break in blossom,
No choral salutation lure to light
A spirit sick with perfume and sweet night
And love's tired eyes and hands and barren bosom.
There is no help for these things; none to mend
And none to mar; not all our songs, O friend,
Will make death clear or make life durable.
Howbeit with rose and ivy and wild vine
And with wild notes about this dust of thine
At least I fill the place where white dreams dwell
And wreathe an unseen shrine.

XVII

Sleep; and if life was bitter to thee, pardon,
   If sweet, give thanks; thou hast no more to live;
   And to give thanks is good, and to forgive.
Out of the mystic and the mournful garden
   Where all day through thine hands in barren braid
   Wove the sick flowers of secrecy and shade,
Green buds of sorrow and sin, and remnants grey,
   Sweet-smelling, pale with poison, sanguine-hearted,
   Passions that sprang from sleep and thoughts that started,
Shall death not bring us all as thee one day
   Among the days departed?

XVIII

For thee, O now a silent soul, my brother,
   Take at my hands this garland, and farewell.
   Thin is the leaf, and chill the wintry smell,
And chill the solemn earth, a fatal mother,
   With sadder than the Niobean womb,
   And in the hollow of her breasts a tomb.
Content thee, howsoe'er, whose days are done;
   There lies not any troublous thing before,
   Nor sight nor sound to war against thee more,
For whom all winds are quiet as the sun,
   All waters as the shore.

## Sonnet (with a Copy of *Mademoiselle de Maupin*)

This is the golden book of spirit and sense,
   The holy writ of beauty; he that wrought
   Made it with dreams and faultless words and thought
That seeks and finds and loses in the dense
Dim air of life that beauty's excellence
   Wherewith love makes one hour of life distraught
   And all hours after follow and find not aught.
Here is that height of all love's eminence
Where man may breathe but for a breathing-space
   And feel his soul burn as an altar-fire
   To the unknown God of unachieved desire,
And from the middle mystery of the place
   Watch lights that break, hear sounds as of a quire,
But see not twice unveiled the veiled God's face.

## A Ballad of Dreamland

I hid my heart in a nest of roses,
Out of the sun's way, hidden apart;
In a softer bed than the soft white snow's is,
Under the roses I hid my heart.
Why would it sleep not? why should it start,
When never a leaf of the rose-tree stirred?
What made sleep flutter his wings and part?
Only the song of a secret bird.

Lie still, I said, for the wind's wing closes,
And mild leaves muffle the keen sun's dart;
Lie still, for the wind on the warm sea dozes,
And the wind is unquieter yet than thou art.
Does a thought in thee still as a thorn's wound smart?
Does the fang still fret thee of hope deferred?
What bids the lids of thy sleep dispart?
Only the song of a secret bird.

The green land's name that a charm encloses,
It never was writ in the traveller's chart,
And sweet on its trees as the fruit that grows is,
It never was sold in the merchant's mart.
The swallows of dreams through its dim fields dart,
And sleep's are the tunes in its tree-tops heard;
No hound's note wakens the wildwood hart,
Only the song of a secret bird.

ENVOI

In the world of dreams I have chosen my part,
To sleep for a season and hear no word
Of true love's truth or of light love's art,
Only the song of a secret bird.

## A Ballad of François Villon
## Prince of All Ballad-Makers

Bird of the bitter bright grey golden morn
Scarce risen upon the dusk of dolorous years,
First of us all and sweetest singer born
Whose far shrill note the world of new men hears
Cleave the cold shuddering shade as twilight clears;

When song new-born put off the old world's attire
And felt its tune on her changed lips expire,
Writ foremost on the roll of them that came
Fresh girt for service of the latter lyre,
Villon, our sad bad glad mad brother's name!

Alas the joy, the sorrow, and the scorn,
That clothed thy life with hopes and sins and fears,
And gave thee stones for bread and tares for corn
And plume-plucked gaol-birds for thy starveling peers
Till death clipt close their flight with shameful shears;
Till shifts came short and loves were hard to hire,
When lilt of song nor twitch of twangling wire
Could buy thee bread or kisses; when light fame
Spurned like a ball and haled through brake and briar,
Villon, our sad bad glad mad brother's name!

Poor splendid wings so frayed and soiled and torn!
Poor kind wild eyes so dashed with light quick tears!
Poor perfect voice, most blithe when most forlorn,
That rings athwart the sea whence no man steers
Like joy-bells crossed with death-bells in our ears!
What far delight has cooled the fierce desire
That like some ravenous bird was strong to tire
On that frail flesh and soul consumed with flame,
But left more sweet than roses to respire,
Villon, our sad bad glad mad brother's name?

ENVOI
Prince of sweet songs made out of tears and fire,
A harlot was thy nurse, a God thy sire;
Shame soiled thy song, and song assoiled thy shame.
But from thy feet now death has washed the mire,
Love reads out first at head of all our quire,
Villon, our sad bad glad mad brother's name.

### A Vision of Spring in Winter

O tender time that love thinks long to see,
Sweet foot of spring that with her footfall sows
Late snowlike flowery leavings of the snows,
Be not too long irresolute to be;
O mother-month, where have they hidden thee?
Out of the pale time of the flowerless rose

I reach my heart out toward the springtime lands,
  I stretch my spirit forth to the fair hours,
  The purplest of the prime;
I lean my soul down over them, with hands
  Made wide to take the ghostly growths of flowers;
  I send my love back to the lovely time.

II

Where has the greenwood hid thy gracious head?
  Veiled with what visions while the grey world grieves,
  Or muffled with what shadows of green leaves,
What warm intangible green shadows spread
To sweeten the sweet twilight for thy bed?
  What sleep enchants thee? what delight deceives?
Where the deep dreamlike dew before the dawn
  Feels not the fingers of the sunlight yet
    Its silver web unweave,
Thy footless ghost on some unfooted lawn
  Whose air the unrisen sunbeams fear to fret
    Lives a ghost's life of daylong dawn and eve.

III

Sunrise it sees not, neither set of star,
  Large nightfall, nor imperial plenilune,
  Nor strong sweet shape of the full-breasted noon;
But where the silver-sandalled shadows are,
Too soft for arrows of the sun to mar,
  Moves with the mild gait of an ungrown moon:
Hard overhead the half-lit crescent swims,
  The tender-coloured night draws hardly breath,
    The light is listening;
They watch the dawn of slender-shapen limbs,
  Virginal, born again of doubtful death,
    Chill foster-father of the weanling spring.

IV

As sweet desire of day before the day,
  As dreams of love before the true love born,
  From the outer edge of winter overworn
The ghost arisen of May before the May
Takes through dim air her unawakened way,
  The gracious ghost of morning risen ere morn.
With little unblown breasts and child-eyed looks
  Following, the very maid, the girl-child spring,
    Lifts windward her bright brows,

Dips her light feet in warm and moving brooks,
And kindles with her own mouth's colouring
The fearful firstlings of the plumeless boughs.

V

I seek thee sleeping, and awhile I see,
Fair face that art not, how thy maiden breath
Shall put at last the deadly days to death
And fill the fields and fire the woods with thee
And seaward hollows where my feet would be
When heaven shall hear the word that April saith
To change the cold heart of the weary time,
To stir and soften all the time to tears,
Tears joyfuller than mirth;
As even to May's clear height the young days climb
With feet not swifter than those fair first years
Whose flowers revive not with thy flowers on earth.

VI

I would not bid thee, though I might, give back
One good thing youth has given and borne away;
I crave not any comfort of the day
That is not, nor on time's retrodden track
Would turn to meet the white-robed hours or black
That long since left me on their mortal way;
Nor light nor love that has been, nor the breath
That comes with morning from the sun to be
And sets light hope on fire;
No fruit, no flower thought once too fair for death,
No flower nor hour once fallen from life's green tree,
No leaf once plucked or once fulfilled desire.

VII

The morning song beneath the stars that fled
With twilight through the moonless mountain air,
While youth with burning lips and wreathless hair
Sang toward the sun that was to crown his head,
Rising; the hopes that triumphed and fell dead,
The sweet swift eyes and songs of hours that were;
These may'st thou not give back for ever; these,
As at the sea's heart all her wrecks lie waste,
Lie deeper than the sea;
But flowers thou may'st, and winds, and hours of ease,
And all its April to the world thou may'st
Give back, and half my April back to me.

## Translation from the French of Villon
## The Complaint of the Fair Armouress

I

Meseemeth I heard cry and groan
   That sweet who was the armourer's maid;
For her young years she made sore moan,
   And right upon this wise she said;
   "Ah fierce old age with foul bald head,
To spoil fair things thou art over fain;
   Who holdeth me? who? would God I were dead!
Would God I were well dead and slain!

II

"Lo, thou hast broken the sweet yoke
   That my high beauty held above
All priests and clerks and merchant-folk;
   There was not one but for my love
   Would give me gold and gold enough,
Though sorrow his very heart had riven,
   To win from me such wage thereof
As now no thief would take if given.

III

"I was right chary of the same,
   God wot it was my great folly,
For love of one sly knave of them,
   Good store of that same sweet had he;
   For all my subtle wiles, perdie,
God wot I loved him well enow;
   Right evilly he handled me,
But he loved well my gold, I trow.

IV

"Though I gat bruises green and black,
   I loved him never the less a jot;
Though he bound burdens on my back,
   If he said 'Kiss me and heed it not'
   Right little pain I felt, God wot,
When that foul thief's mouth, found so sweet,
   Kissed me—Much good thereof I got!
I keep the sin and the shame of it.

V

"And he died thirty year agone.
   I am old now, no sweet thing to see;

By God, though, when I think thereon,
And of that good glad time, woe's me,
And stare upon my changed body
Stark naked, that has been so sweet,
Lean, wizen, like a small dry tree,
I am nigh mad with the pain of it.

VI

"Where is my faultless forehead's white,
The lifted eyebrows, soft gold hair,
Eyes wide apart and keen of sight,
With subtle skill in the amorous air;
The straight nose, great nor small, but fair,
The small carved ears of shapeliest growth,
Chin dimpling, colour good to wear,
And sweet red splendid kissing mouth?

VII

"The shapely slender shoulders small,
Long arms, hands wrought in glorious wise,
Round little breasts, the hips withal
High, full of flesh, not scant of size,
Fit for all amorous masteries;
The large loins, and the flower that was
Planted above my strong round thighs
In a small garden of soft grass.

VIII

"A writhled forehead, hair gone grey,
Fallen eyebrows, eyes gone blind and red,
Their laughs and looks all fled away,
Yea, all that smote men's hearts are fled;
The bowed nose, fallen from goodlihead;
Foul flapping ears like water-flags;
Peaked chin, and cheeks all waste and dead,
And lips that are two skinny rags:

IX

"Thus endeth all the beauty of us.
The arms made short, the hands made lean,
The shoulders bowed and ruinous,
The breasts, alack! all fallen in;
The flanks too, like the breasts, grown thin;
As for the sweet place, out on it!
For the lank thighs, no thighs but skin,
They are specked with spots like sausage-meat.

X

"So we make moan for the old sweet days,
  Poor old light women, two or three
Squatting above the straw-fire's blaze,
  The bosom crushed against the knee,
  Like faggots on a heap we be,
Round fires soon lit, soon quenched and done;
  And we were once so sweet, even we!
Thus fareth many and many an one."

## FROM *SONGS OF THE SPRINGTIDES* (1880)

### On the Cliffs

*ἱμερόφωνος ὑηδὼν.*
*Sappho.*

Between the moondawn and the sundown here
The twilight hangs half starless; half the sea
Still quivers as for love or pain or fear
Or pleasure mightier than these all may be
A man's live heart might beat
Wherein a God's with mortal blood should meet
And fill its pulse too full to bear the strain
With fear or love or pleasure's twin-born, pain.
Fiercely the gaunt woods to the grim soil cling
That bears for all fair fruits
Wan wild sparse flowers of windy and wintry spring
Between the tortive serpent-shapen roots
Wherethrough their dim growth hardly strikes and shoots
And shews one gracious thing
Hardly, to speak for summer one sweet word
Of summer's self scarce heard.
But higher the steep green sterile fields, thick-set
With flowerless hawthorn even to the upward verge
Whence the woods gathering watch new cliffs emerge
Higher than their highest of crowns that sea-winds fret,
Hold fast, for all that night or wind can say,
Some pale pure colour yet,
Too dim for green and luminous for grey.
Between the climbing inland cliffs above
And these beneath that breast and break the bay,
A barren peace too soft for hate or love
Broods on an hour too dim for night or day.

O wind, O wingless wind that walk'st the sea,
Weak wind, wing-broken, wearier wind than we,
Who are yet not spirit-broken, maimed like thee,
Who wail not in our inward night as thou
In the outer darkness now,
What word has the old sea given thee for mine ear
From thy faint lips to hear?
For some word would she send me, knowing not how.

Nay, what far other word
Than ever of her was spoken, or of me
Or all my winged white kinsfolk of the sea
Between fresh wave and wave was ever heard,
Cleaves the clear dark enwinding tree with tree
Too close for stars to separate and to see
Enmeshed in multitudinous unity?
What voice of what strong God hath stormed and stirred
The fortressed rock of silence, rent apart
Even to the core Night's all-maternal heart?
What voice of God grown heavenlier in a bird,
Made keener of edge to smite
Than lightning—yea, thou knowest, O mother Night,
Keen as that cry from thy strange children sent
Wherewith the Athenian judgment-shrine was rent,
For wrath that all their wrath was vainly spent,
Their wrath for wrong made right
By justice in her own divine despite
That bade pass forth unblamed
The sinless matricide and unashamed?
Yea, what new cry is this, what note more bright
Than their song's wing of words was dark of flight,
What word is this thou hast heard,
Thine and not thine or theirs, O Night, what word
More keen than lightning and more sweet than light?
As all men's hearts grew godlike in one bird
And all those hearts cried on thee, crying with might,
Hear us, O mother Night.

Dumb is the mouth of darkness as of death:
Light, sound and life are one
In the eyes and lips of dawn that draw the sun
To hear what first child's word with glimmering breath
Their weak wan weanling child the twilight saith;
But night makes answer none.

God, if thou be God, — bird, if bird thou be, —
Do thou then answer me.
For but one word, what wind soever blow,
Is blown up usward ever from the sea.
In fruitless years of youth dead long ago
And deep beneath their own dead leaves and snow
Buried, I heard with bitter heart and sere
The same sea's word unchangeable, nor knew
But that mine own life-days were changeless too
And sharp and salt with unshed tear on tear
And cold and fierce and barren; and my soul,
Sickening, swam weakly with bated breath
In a deep sea like death,
And felt the wind buffet her face with brine
Hard, and harsh thought on thought in long bleak roll
Blown by keen gusts of memory sad as thine
Heap the weight up of pain, and break, and leave
Strength scarce enough to grieve
In the sick heavy spirit, unmanned with strife
Of waves that beat at the tired lips of life.

Nay, sad may be man's memory, sad may be
The dream he weaves him as for shadow of thee,
But scarce one breathing-space, one heartbeat long,
Wilt thou take shadow of sadness on thy song.
Not thou, being more than man or man's desire,
Being bird and God in one,
With throat of gold and spirit of the sun;
The sun whom all our souls and songs call sire,
Whose godhead gave thee, chosen of all our quire,
Thee only of all that serve, of all that sing
Before our sire and king,
Borne up some space on time's world-wandering wing,
This gift, this doom, to bear till time's wing tire —
Life everlasting of eternal life.

Thee only of all; yet can no memory say
How many a night and day
My heart has been as thy heart, and my life
As thy life is, a sleepless hidden thing,
Full of the thirst and hunger of winter and spring,
That seeks its food not in such love or strife
As fill men's hearts with passionate hours and rest.
From no loved lips and on no loving breast

Have I sought ever for such gifts as bring
Comfort, to stay the secret soul with sleep.
The joys, the loves, the labours, whence men reap
Rathe fruit of hopes and fears,
I have made not mine; the best of all my days
Have been as those fair fruitless summer strays,
Those water-waifs that but the sea-wind steers,
Flakes of glad foam or flowers on footless ways
That take the wind in season and the sun,
And when the wind wills is their season done.

For all my days as all thy days from birth
My heart as thy heart was in me as thee,
Fire; and not all the fountains of the sea
Have waves enough to quench it, nor on earth
Is fuel enough to feed,
While day sows night and night sows day for seed.

We were not marked for sorrow, thou nor I,
For joy nor sorrow, sister, were we made,
To take delight and grief to live and die,
Assuaged by pleasures or by pains affrayed
That melt men's hearts and alter; we retain
A memory mastering pleasure and all pain,
A spirit within the sense of ear and eye,
A soul behind the soul, that seeks and sings
And makes our life move only with its wings
And feed but from its lips, that in return
Feed of our hearts wherein the old fires that burn
Have strength not to consume
Nor glory enough to exalt us past our doom.

*Ah, ah, the doom* (thou knowest whence rang that wail)
*Of the shrill nightingale!*
(From whose wild lips, thou knowest, that wail was thrown)
*For round about her have the great gods cast*
*A wing-borne body, and clothed her close and fast*
*With a sweet life that hath no part in moan.*
*But me, for me* (how hadst thou heart to hear?)
*Remains a sundering with the two-edged spear.*

*Ah, for her doom!* so cried in presage then
The bodeful bondslave of the king of men,
And might not win her will.
Too close the entangling dragnet woven of crime,

The snare of ill new-born of elder ill,
The curse of new time for an elder time,
Had caught, and held her yet,
Enmeshed intolerably in the intolerant net,
Who thought with craft to mock the God most high,
And win by wiles his crown of prophecy
From the Sun's hand sublime,
As God were man, to spare or to forget.

But thou, — the gods have given thee and forgiven thee
More than our master gave
That strange-eyed spirit-wounded strange-tongued slave
There questing houndlike where the roofs red-wet
Reeked as a wet red grave.
Life everlasting has their strange grace given thee,
Even hers whom thou wast wont to sing and serve
With eyes, but not with song, too swift to swerve;
Yet might not even thine eyes estranged estrange her,
Who seeing thee too, but inly, burn and bleed
Like that pale princess-priest of Priam's seed,
For stranger service gave thee guerdon stranger;
If this indeed be guerdon, this indeed
Her mercy, this thy meed —
That thou, being more than all we born, being higher
Than all heads crowned of him that only gives
The light whereby man lives,
The bay that bids man moved of God's desire
Lay hand on lute or lyre,
Set lip to trumpet or deflowered green reed —
If this were given thee for a grace indeed,
That thou, being first of all these, thou alone
Shouldst have the grace to die not, but to live
And lose nor change one pulse of song, one tone
Of all that were thy lady's and thine own,
Thy lady's whom thou criedst on to forgive,
Thou, priest and sacrifice on the altar-stone
Where none may worship not of all that live,
Love's priestess, errant on dark ways diverse;
If this were grace indeed for Love to give,
If this indeed were blessing and no curse.

Love's priestess, mad with pain and joy of song,
Song's priestess, mad with joy and pain of love,
Name above all names that are lights above,

We have loved, praised, pitied, crowned and done thee wrong,
O thou past praise and pity; thou the sole
Utterly deathless, perfect only and whole
Immortal, body and soul.
For over all whom time hath overpast
The shadow of sleep inexorable is cast,
The implacable sweet shadow of perfect sleep
That gives not back what life gives death to keep;
Yea, all that lived and loved and sang and sinned
Are all borne down death's cold sweet soundless wind
That blows all night and knows not whom its breath,
Darkling, may touch to death:
But one that wind hath touched and changed not,—one
Whose body and soul are parcel of the sun;
One that earth's fire could burn not, nor the sea
Quench; nor might human doom take hold on thee;
All praise, all pity, all dreams have done thee wrong,
All love, with eyes love-blinded from above;
Song's priestess, mad with joy and pain of love,
Love's priestess, mad with pain and joy of song.

Hast thou none other answer then for me
Than the air may have of thee,
Or the earth's warm woodlands girdling with green girth
Thy secret sleepless burning life on earth,
Or even the sea that once, being woman crowned
And girt with fire and glory of anguish round,
Thou wert so fain to seek to, fain to crave
If she would hear thee and save
And give thee comfort of thy great green grave?
Because I have known thee always who thou art,
Thou knowest, have known thee to thy heart's own heart,
Nor ever have given light ear to storied song
That did thy sweet name sweet unwitting wrong,
Nor ever have called thee nor would call for shame,
Thou knowest, but inly by thine only name,
Sappho—because I have known thee and loved, hast thou
None other answer now?
As brother and sister were we, child and bird,
Since thy first Lesbian word
Flamed on me, and I knew not whence I knew
This was the song that struck my whole soul through,
Pierced my keen spirit of sense with edge more keen,

Even when I knew not, — even ere sooth was seen, —
When thou wast but the tawny sweet winged thing
Whose cry was but of spring.

And yet even so thine ear should hear me — yea,
Hear me this nightfall by this northland bay,
Even for their sake whose loud good word I had,
Singing of thee in the all-beloved clime
Once, where the windy wine of spring makes mad
Our sisters of Majano, who kept time
Clear to my choral rhyme.
Yet was the song acclaimed of these aloud
Whose praise had made mute humbleness misproud,
The song with answering song applauded thus,
But of that Daulian dream of Itylus.
So but for love's love haply was it — nay,
How else? — that even their song took my song's part,
For love of love and sweetness of sweet heart,
Or god-given glorious madness of mid May
And heat of heart and hunger and thirst to sing,
Full of the new wine of the wind of spring.

Or if this were not, and it be not sin
To hold myself in spirit of thy sweet kin,
In heart and spirit of song;
If this my great love do thy grace no wrong,
Thy grace that gave me grace to dwell therein;
If thy gods thus be my gods, and their will
Made my song part of thy song — even such part
As man's hath of God's heart —
And my life like as thy life to fulfil;
What have our gods then given us? Ah, to thee,
Sister, much more, much happier than to me,
Much happier things they have given, and more of grace
Than falls to man's light race;
For lighter are we, all our love and pain
Lighter than thine, who knowest of time or place
Thus much, that place nor time
Can heal or hurt or lull or change again
The singing soul that makes his soul sublime
Who hears the far fall of its fire-fledged rhyme
Fill darkness as with bright and burning rain
Till all the live gloom inly glows, and light
Seems with the sound to cleave the core of night.

The singing soul that moves thee, and that moved
When thou wast woman, and their songs divine
Who mixed for Grecian mouths heaven's lyric wine
Fell dumb, fell down reproved
Before one sovereign Lesbian song of thine.
That soul, though love and life had fain held fast,
Wind-winged with fiery music, rose and past
Through the indrawn hollow of earth and heaven and hell,
As through some strait sea-shell
The wide sea's immemorial song, — the sea
That sings and breathes in strange men's ears of thee
How in her barren bride-bed, void and vast,
Even thy soul sang itself to sleep at last.

To sleep? Ah, then, what song is this, that here
Makes all the night one ear,
One ear fulfilled and mad with music, one
Heart kindling as the heart of heaven, to hear
A song more fiery than the awakening sun
Sings, when his song sets fire
To the air and clouds that build the dead night's pyre?
*O thou of divers-coloured mind, O thou*
*Deathless, God's daughter subtle-souled* — lo, now,
Now too the song above all songs, in flight
Higher than the day-star's height,
And sweet as sound the moving wings of night!
*Thou of the divers-coloured seat* — behold,
Her very song of old! —
*O deathless, O God's daughter subtle-souled!*
That same cry through this boskage overhead
Rings round reiterated,
Palpitates as the last palpitated,
The last that panted through her lips and died
Not down this grey north sea's half sapped cliff-side
That crumbles toward the coastline, year by year
More near the sands and near;
The last loud lyric fiery cry she cried,
Heard once on heights Leucadian, — heard not here.

Not here; for this that fires our northland night,
This is the song that made
Love fearful, even the heart of love afraid,
With the great anguish of its great delight.
No swan-song, no far-fluttering half-drawn breath,

No word that love of love's sweet nature saith,
No dirge that lulls the narrowing lids of death,
No healing hymn of peace-prevented strife, —
This is her song of life.

*I love thee*, — hark, one tenderer note than all —
*Atthis, of old time, once* — one low long fall,
Sighing — one long low lovely loveless call,
Dying — one pause in song so flamelike fast —
*Atthis, long since in old time overpast* —
One soft first pause and last.
One, — then the old rage of rapture's fieriest rain
Storms all the music-maddened night again.

*Child of God, close craftswoman, I beseech thee,*
*Bid not ache nor agony break nor master,*
*Lady, my spirit* —
O thou her mistress, might her cry not reach thee?
Our Lady of all men's loves, could Love go past her,
Pass, and not hear it?

She hears not as she heard not; hears not me,
O treble-natured mystery, — how should she
Hear, or give ear? — who heard and heard not thee;
Heard, and went past, and heard not; but all time
Hears all that all the ravin of his years
Hath cast not wholly out of all men's ears
And dulled to death with deep dense funeral chime
Of their reiterate rhyme.
And now of all songs uttering all her praise,
All hers who had thy praise and did thee wrong,
Abides one song yet of her lyric days,
Thine only, this thy song.

O soul triune, woman and god and bird,
Man, man at least has heard.
All ages call thee conqueror, and thy cry
The mightiest as the least beneath the sky
Whose heart was ever set to song, or stirred
With wind of mounting music blown more high
Than wildest wing may fly,
Hath heard or hears, — even Æschylus as I.
But when thy name was woman, and thy word
Human, — then haply, surely then meseems
This thy bird's note was heard on earth of none,

Of none save only in dreams.
In all the world then surely was but one
Song; as in heaven at highest one sceptred sun
Regent, on earth here surely without fail
One only, one imperious nightingale.
Dumb was the field, the woodland mute, the lawn
Silent; the hill was tongueless as the vale
Even when the last fair waif of cloud that felt
Its heart beneath the colouring moonrays melt,
At high midnoon of midnight half withdrawn,
Bared all the sudden deep divine moondawn.
Then, unsaluted by her twin-born tune,
That latter timeless morning of the moon
Rose past its hour of moonrise; clouds gave way
To the old reconquering ray,
But no song answering made it more than day;
No cry of song by night
Shot fire into the cloud-constraining light.
One only, one Æolian island heard
Thrill, but through no bird's throat,
In one strange manlike maiden's godlike note,
The song of all these as a single bird.
Till the sea's portal was as funeral gate
For that sole singer in all time's ageless date
Singled and signed for so triumphal fate,
All nightingales but one in all the world
All her sweet life were silent; only then,
When her life's wing of womanhood was furled,
Their cry, this cry of thine was heard again,
As of me now, of any born of men.
Through sleepless clear spring nights filled full of thee,
Rekindled here, thy ruling song has thrilled
The deep dark air and subtle tender sea
And breathless hearts with one bright sound fulfilled.
Or at midnoon to me
Swimming, and birds about my happier head
Skimming, one smooth soft way by water and air,
To these my bright born brethren and to me
Hath not the clear wind borne or seemed to bear
A song wherein all earth and heaven and sea
Were molten in one music made of thee
To enforce us, O our sister of the shore,
Look once in heart back landward and adore?

For songless were we sea-mews, yet had we
More joy than all things joyful of thee — more,
Haply, than all things happiest; nay, save thee,
In thy strong rapture of imperious joy
Too high for heart of sea-borne bird or boy,
What living things were happiest if not we?
But knowing not love nor change nor wrath nor wrong,
No more we knew of song.

Song, and the secrets of it, and their might,
What blessings curse it and what curses bless,
I know them since my spirit had first in sight,
Clear as thy song's words or the live sun's light,
The small dark body's Lesbian loveliness
That held the fire eternal; eye and ear
Were as a god's to see, a god's to hear,
Through all his hours of daily and nightly chime,
The sundering of the two-edged spear of time:
The spear that pierces even the sevenfold shields
Of mightiest Memory, mother of all songs made,
And wastes all songs as roseleaves kissed and frayed
As here the harvest of the foam-flowered fields;
But thine the spear may waste not that he wields
Since first the God whose soul is man's live breath,
The sun whose face hath our sun's face for shade,
Put all the light of life and love and death
Too strong for life, but not for love too strong,
Where pain makes peace with pleasure in thy song,
And in thine heart, where love and song make strife,
Fire everlasting of eternal life.

## FROM *STUDIES IN SONG* (1880)

### By the North Sea

I

A land that is lonelier than ruin;
  A sea that is stranger than death:
Far fields that a rose never blew in,
  Wan waste where the winds lack breath;
Waste endless and boundless and flowerless
  But of marsh-blossoms fruitless as free:
Where earth lies exhausted, as powerless
    To strive with the sea.

Far flickers the flight of the swallows,
  Far flutters the weft of the grass
Spun dense over desolate hollows
  More pale than the clouds as they pass:
Thick woven as the weft of a witch is
  Round the heart of a thrall that hath sinned,
Whose youth and the wrecks of its riches
    Are waifs on the wind.

The pastures are herdless and sheepless,
  No pasture or shelter for herds:
The wind is relentless and sleepless,
  And restless and songless the birds;
Their cries from afar fall breathless,
  Their wings are as lightnings that flee;
For the land has two lords that are deathless:
  Death's self, and the sea.

These twain, as a king with his fellow,
  Hold converse of desolate speech:

And her waters are haggard and yellow
   And crass with the scurf of the beach:
And his garments are grey as the hoary
   Wan sky where the day lies dim;
And his power is to her, and his glory,
      As hers unto him.

In the pride of his power she rejoices,
   In her glory he glows and is glad:
In her darkness the sound of his voice is,
   With his breath she dilates and is mad:
"If thou slay me, O death, and outlive me,
   Yet thy love hath fulfilled me of thee."
"Shall I give thee not back if thou give me,
   O sister, O sea?"

And year upon year dawns living,
   And age upon age drops dead:
And his hand is not weary of giving,
   And the thirst of her heart is not fed:
And the hunger that moans in her passion,
   And the rage in her hunger that roars,
As a wolf's that the winter lays lash on,
      Still calls and implores.

Her walls have no granite for girder,
   No fortalice fronting her stands:
But reefs the bloodguiltiest of murder
   Are less than the banks of her sands:
These number their slain by the thousand;
   For the ship hath no surety to be,
When the bank is abreast of her bows and
      Aflush with the sea.

No surety to stand, and no shelter
   To dawn out of darkness but one,
Out of waters that hurtle and welter
   No succour to dawn with the sun,
But a rest from the wind as it passes,
   Where, hardly redeemed from the waves,
Lie thick as the blades of the grasses
   The dead in their graves.

A multitude noteless of numbers,
   As wild weeds cast on an heap:

And sounder than sleep are their slumbers,
  And softer than song is their sleep;
And sweeter than all things and stranger
  The sense, if perchance it may be,
That the wind is divested of danger
    And scatheless the sea.

That the roar of the banks they breasted
  Is hurtless as bellowing of herds,
And the strength of his wings that invested
  The wind, as the strength of a bird's;
As the sea-mew's might or the swallow's
  That cry to him back if he cries,
As over the graves and their hollows
    Days darken and rise.

As the souls of the dead men disburdened
  And clean of the sins that they sinned,
With a lovelier than man's life guerdoned
  And delight as a wave's in the wind,
And delight as the wind's in the billow,
  Birds pass, and deride with their glee
The flesh that has dust for its pillow
  As wrecks have the sea.

When the ways of the sun wax dimmer,
  Wings flash through the dusk like beams;
As the clouds in the lit sky glimmer,
  The bird in the graveyard gleams;
As the cloud at its wing's edge whitens
  When the clarions of sunrise are heard,
The graves that the bird's note brightens
  Grow bright for the bird.

As the waves of the numberless waters
  That the wind cannot number who guides
Are the sons of the shore and the daughters
  Here lulled by the chime of the tides:
And here in the press of them standing
  We know not if these or if we
Live truliest, or anchored to landing
  Or drifted to sea.

In the valley he named of decision
  No denser were multitudes met

When the soul of the seer in her vision
   Saw nations for doom of them set;
Saw darkness in dawn, and the splendour
   Of judgment, the sword and the rod;
But the doom here of death is more tender
   And gentler the god.

And gentler the wind from the dreary
   Sea-banks by the waves overlapped,
Being weary, speaks peace to the weary
   From slopes that the tide-stream hath sapped;
And sweeter than all that we call so
   The seal of their slumber shall be
Till the graves that embosom them also
   Be sapped of the sea.

II

For the heart of the waters is cruel,
   And the kisses are dire of their lips,
And their waves are as fire is to fuel
   To the strength of the sea-faring ships,
Though the sea's eye gleam as a jewel
   To the sun's eye back as he dips.

Though the sun's eye flash to the sea's
   Live light of delight and of laughter,
And her lips breathe back to the breeze
   The kiss that the wind's lips waft her
From the sun that subsides, and sees
   No gleam of the storm's dawn after.

And the wastes of the wild sea-marches
   Where the borderers are matched in their might—
Bleak fens that the sun's weight parches,
   Dense waves that reject his light—
Change under the change-coloured arches
   Of changeless morning and night.

The waves are as ranks enrolled
   Too close for the storm to sever:
The fens lie naked and cold,
   But their heart fails utterly never:
The lists are set from of old,
   And the warfare endureth for ever.

III

Miles, and miles, and miles of desolation!
  Leagues on leagues on leagues without a change!
Sign or token of some eldest nation
  Here would make the strange land not so strange.
Time-forgotten, yea since time's creation,
  Seem these borders where the sea-birds range.

Slowly, gladly, full of peace and wonder
  Grows his heart who journeys here alone.
Earth and all its thoughts of earth sink under
  Deep as deep in water sinks a stone.
Hardly knows it if the rollers thunder,
  Hardly whence the lonely wind is blown.

Tall the plumage of the rush-flower tosses,
  Sharp and soft in many a curve and line
Gleam and glow the sea-coloured marsh-mosses
  Salt and splendid from the circling brine.
Streak on streak of glimmering seashine crosses
  All the land sea-saturate as with wine.

Far, and far between, in divers orders,
  Clear grey steeples cleave the low grey sky;
Fast and firm as time-unshaken warders,
  Hearts made sure by faith, by hope made high.
These alone in all the wild sea-borders
  Fear no blast of days and nights that die.

All the land is like as one man's face is,
  Pale and troubled still with change of cares.
Doubt and death pervade her clouded spaces:
  Strength and length of life and peace are theirs;
Theirs alone amid these weary places,
  Seeing not how the wild world frets and fares.

Firm and fast where all is cloud that changes
  Cloud-clogged sunlight, cloud by sunlight thinned,
Stern and sweet, above the sand-hill ranges
  Watch the towers and tombs of men that sinned
Once, now calm as earth whose only change is
  Wind, and light, and wind, and cloud, and wind.

Out and in and out the sharp straits wander,
  In and out and in the wild way strives,

Starred and paved and lined with flowers that squander
Gold as golden as the gold of hives,
Salt and moist and multiform: but yonder
See, what sign of life or death survives?

Seen then only when the songs of olden
Harps were young whose echoes yet endure,
Hymned of Homer when his years were golden,
Known of only when the world was pure,
Here is Hades, manifest, beholden,
Surely, surely here, if aught be sure!

Where the border-line was crossed, that, sundering
Death from life, keeps weariness from rest,
None can tell, who fares here forward wondering;
None may doubt but here might end his quest.
Here life's lightning joys and woes once thundering
Sea-like round him cease like storm suppressed.

Here the wise wave-wandering steadfast-hearted
Guest of many a lord of many a land
Saw the shape or shade of years departed,
Saw the semblance risen and hard at hand,
Saw the mother long from love's reach parted,
Anticleia, like a statue stand.

Statue? nay, nor tissued image woven
Fair on hangings in his father's hall;
Nay, too fast her faith of heart was proven,
Far too firm her loveliest love of all;
Love wherethrough the loving heart was cloven,
Love that hears not when the loud Fates call.

Love that lives and stands up re-created
Then when life has ebbed and anguish fled;
Love more strong than death or all things fated,
Child's and mother's, lit by love and led;
Love that found what life so long awaited
Here, when life came down among the dead.

Here, where never came alive another,
Came her son across the sundering tide
Crossed before by many a warrior brother
Once that warred on Ilion at his side;
Here spread forth vain hands to clasp the mother
Dead, that sorrowing for his love's sake died.

Parted, though by narrowest of divisions,
   Clasp he might not, only might implore,
Sundered yet by bitterest of derisions,
   Son, and mother from the son she bore—
Here? But all dispeopled here of visions
   Lies, forlorn of shadows even, the shore.

All too sweet such men's Hellenic speech is,
   All too fain they lived of light to see,
Once to see the darkness of these beaches,
   Once to sing this Hades found of me
Ghostless, all its gulfs and creeks and reaches,
   Sky, and shore, and cloud, and waste, and sea.

IV

But aloft and afront of me faring
   Far forward as folk in a dream
That strive, between doubting and daring,
   Right on till the goal for them gleam,
Full forth till their goal on them lighten,
   The harbour where fain they would be,
What headlands there darken and brighten?
      What change in the sea?

What houses and woodlands that nestle
   Safe inland to lee of the hill
As it slopes from the headlands that wrestle
   And succumb to the strong sea's will?
Truce is not, nor respite, nor pity,
   For the battle is waged not of hands
Where over the grave of a city
      The ghost of it stands.

Where the wings of the sea-wind slacken,
   Green lawns to the landward thrive,
Fields brighten and pine-woods blacken,
   And the heat in their heart is alive;
They blossom and warble and murmur,
   For the sense of their spirit is free:
But harder to shoreward and firmer
      The grasp of the sea.

Like ashes the low cliffs crumble,
   The banks drop down into dust,
The heights of the hills are made humble,

As a reed's is the strength of their trust:
As a city's that armies environ,
The strength of their stay is of sand:
But the grasp of the sea is as iron,
Laid hard on the land.

A land that is thirstier than ruin;
A sea that is hungrier than death;
Heaped hills that a tree never grew in;
Wide sands where the wave draws breath;
All solace is here for the spirit
That ever for ever may be
For the soul of thy son to inherit,
My mother, my sea.

O delight of the headlands and beaches!
O desire of the wind on the wold,
More glad than a man's when it reaches
That end which it sought from of old
And the palm of possession is dreary
To the sense that in search of it sinned;
But nor satisfied ever nor weary
Is ever the wind.

The delight that he takes but in living
Is more than of all things that live:
For the world that has all things for giving
Has nothing so goodly to give:
But more than delight his desire is,
For the goal where his pinions would be
Is immortal as air or as fire is,
Immense as the sea.

Though hence come the moan that he borrows
From darkness and depth of the night,
Though hence be the spring of his sorrows,
Hence too is the joy of his might;
The delight that his doom is for ever
To seek and desire and rejoice,
And the sense that eternity never
Shall silence his voice.

That satiety never may stifle
Nor weariness ever estrange
Nor time be so strong as to rifle
Nor change be so great as to change

His gift that renews in the giving,
   The joy that exalts him to be
Alone of all elements living
      The lord of the sea.

What is fire, that its flame should consume her?
   More fierce than all fires are her waves:
What is earth, that its gulfs should entomb her?
   More deep are her own than their graves.
Life shrinks from his pinions that cover
   The darkness by thunders bedinned:
But she knows him, her lord and her lover
      The godhead of wind.

For a season his wings are about her,
   His breath on her lips for a space;
Such rapture he wins not without her
   In the width of his worldwide race.
Though the forests bow down, and the mountains
   Wax dark, and the tribes of them flee,
His delight is more deep in the fountains
      And springs of the sea.

There are those too of mortals that love him,
   There are souls that desire and require,
Be the glories of midnight above him
   Or beneath him the daysprings of fire:
And their hearts are as harps that approve him
   And praise him as chords of a lyre
That were fain with their music to move him
      To meet their desire

To descend through the darkness to grace them,
   Till darkness were lovelier than light:
To encompass and grasp and embrace them,
   Till their weakness were one with his might:
With the strength of his wings to caress them,
   With the blast of his breath to set free;
With the mouths of his thunders to bless them
      For sons of the sea.

For these have the toil and the guerdon
   That the wind has eternally: these
Have part in the boon and the burden
   Of the sleepless unsatisfied breeze,
That finds not, but seeking rejoices

That possession can work him no wrong:
And the voice at the heart of their voice is
The sense of his song.

For the wind's is their doom and their blessing;
To desire, and have always above
A possession beyond their possessing,
A love beyond reach of their love.
Green earth has her sons and her daughters,
And these have their guerdons; but we
Are the wind's and the sun's and the water's,
Elect of the sea.

V

For the sea too seeks and rejoices,
Gains and loses and gains,
And the joy of her heart's own choice is
As ours, and as ours are her pains:
As the thoughts of our hearts are her voices,
And as hers is the pulse of our veins.

Her fields that know not of dearth
Nor lie for their fruit's sake fallow
Laugh large in the depth of their mirth:
But inshore here in the shallow,
Embroiled with encumbrance of earth,
Their skirts are turbid and yellow.

The grime of her greed is upon her,
The sign of her deed is her soil;
As the earth's is her own dishonour,
And corruption the crown of her toil:
She hath spoiled and devoured, and her honour
Is this, to be shamed by her spoil.

But afar where pollution is none,
Nor ensign of strife nor endeavour,
Where her heart and the sun's are one,
And the soil of her sin comes never,
She is pure as the wind and the sun,
And her sweetness endureth for ever.

VI

Death, and change, and darkness everlasting,
Deaf, that hears not what the daystar saith,

Blind, past all remembrance and forecasting,
   Dead, past memory that it once drew breath;
These, above the washing tides and wasting,
   Reign, and rule this land of utter death.

Change of change, darkness of darkness, hidden,
   Very death of very death, begun
When none knows, — the knowledge is forbidden —
   Self-begotten, self-proceeding, one,
Born, not made — abhorred, unchained, unchidden,
   Night stands here defiant of the sun.

Change of change, and death of death begotten,
   Darkness born of darkness, one and three,
Ghostly godhead of a world forgotten,
   Crowned with heaven, enthroned on land and sea,
Here, where earth with dead men's bones is rotten,
   God of Time, thy likeness worships thee.

Lo, thy likeness of thy desolation,
   Shape and figure of thy might, O Lord,
Formless form, incarnate miscreation,
   Served of all things living and abhorred;
Earth herself is here thine incarnation,
   Time, of all things born on earth adored.

All that worship thee are fearful of thee;
   No man may not worship thee for fear:
Prayers nor curses prove not nor disprove thee,
   Move nor change thee with our change of cheer:
All at last, though all abhorred thee, love thee,
   God, the sceptre of whose throne is here.

Here thy throne and sceptre of thy station,
   Here the palace paven for thy feet;
Here thy sign from nation unto nation
   Passed as watchword for thy guards to greet,
Guards that go before thine exaltation,
   Ages, clothed with bitter years and sweet.

Here, where sharp the sea-bird shrills his ditty,
   Flickering flame-wise through the clear live calm,
Rose triumphal, crowning all a city,
   Roofs exalted once with prayer and psalm,
Built of holy hands for holy pity,
   Frank and fruitful as a sheltering palm.

Church and hospice wrought in faultless fashion,
Hall and chancel bounteous and sublime,
Wide and sweet and glorious as compassion,
Filled and thrilled with force of choral chime,
Filled with spirit of prayer and thrilled with passion,
Hailed a God more merciful than Time.

Ah, less mighty, less than Time prevailing,
Shrunk, expelled, made nothing at his nod,
Less than clouds across the sea-line sailing,
Lies he, stricken by his master's rod.
"Where is man?" the cloister murmurs wailing;
Back the mute shrine thunders — "Where is God?"

Here is all the end of all his glory —
Dust, and grass, and barren silent stones.
Dead, like him, one hollow tower and hoary
Naked in the sea-wind stands and moans,
Filled and thrilled with its perpetual story:
Here, where earth is dense with dead men's bones.

Low and loud and long, a voice for ever,
Sounds the wind's clear story like a song.
Tomb from tomb the waves devouring sever,
Dust from dust as years relapse along;
Graves where men made sure to rest, and never
Lie dismantled by the seasons' wrong.

Now displaced, devoured and desecrated,
Now by Time's hands darkly disinterred,
These poor dead that sleeping here awaited
Long the archangel's re-creating word,
Closed about with roofs and walls high-gated
Till the blast of judgment should be heard,

Naked, shamed, cast out of consecration,
Corpse and coffin, yea the very graves,
Scoffed at, scattered, shaken from their station,
Spurned and scourged of wind and sea like slaves,
Desolate beyond man's desolation,
Shrink and sink into the waste of waves.

Tombs, with bare white piteous bones protruded,
Shroudless, down the loose collapsing banks,
Crumble, from their constant place detruded,
That the sea devours and gives not thanks.

Graves where hope and prayer and sorrow brooded
  Gape and slide and perish, ranks on ranks.

Rows on rows and line by line they crumble,
  They that thought for all time through to be.
Scarce a stone whereon a child might stumble
  Breaks the grim field paced alone of me.
Earth, and man, and all their gods wax humble
  Here, where Time brings pasture to the sea.

VII

But afar on the headland exalted,
  But beyond in the curl of the bay,
From the depth of his dome deep-vaulted
  Our father is lord of the day.
Our father and lord that we follow,
  For deathless and ageless is he;
And his robe is the whole sky's hollow,
    His sandal the sea.

Where the horn of the headland is sharper,
  And her green floor glitters with fire,
The sea has the sun for a harper,
  The sun has the sea for a lyre.
The waves are a pavement of amber,
  By the feet of the sea-winds trod
To receive in a god's presence-chamber
    Our father, the God.

Time, haggard and changeful and hoary,
  Is master and God of the land:
But the air is fulfilled of the glory
  That is shed from our lord's right hand.
O father of all of us ever,
  All glory be only to thee
From heaven, that is void of thee never,
    And earth, and the sea.

O Sun, whereof all is beholden,
  Behold now the shadow of this death,
This place of the sepulchres, olden
  And emptied and vain as a breath.
The bloom of the bountiful heather
  Laughs broadly beyond in thy light
As dawn, with her glories to gather,
    At darkness and night.

Though the Gods of the night lie rotten
  And their honour be taken away
And the noise of their names forgotten,
  Thou, Lord, art God of the day.
Thou art father and saviour and spirit,
  O Sun, of the soul that is free
And hath grace of thy grace to inherit
    Thine earth and thy sea.

The hills and the sands and the beaches,
  The waters adrift and afar,
The banks and the creeks and the reaches,
  How glad of thee all these are!
The flowers, overflowing, overcrowded,
  Are drunk with the mad wind's mirth:
The delight of thy coming unclouded
    Makes music of earth.

I, last least voice of her voices,
  Give thanks that were mute in me long
To the soul in my soul that rejoices
  For the song that is over my song.
Time gives what he gains for the giving
  Or takes for his tribute of me;
My dreams to the wind everliving,
    My song to the sea.

## FROM *HEPTALOGIA* (1880)

### The Higher Pantheism in a Nutshell

One, who is not, we see: but one, whom we see not, is:
Surely this is not that: but that is assuredly this.

What, and wherefore, and whence? for under is over and under:
If thunder could be without lightning, lightning could be without thunder.

Doubt is faith in the main: but faith, on the whole, is doubt:
We cannot believe by proof: but could we believe without?

Why, and whither, and how? for barley and rye are not clover:
Neither are straight lines curves: yet over is under and over.

Two and two may be four: but four and four are not eight:
Fate and God may be twain: but God is the same thing as fate.

Ask a man what he thinks, and get from a man what he feels:
God, once caught in the fact, shows you a fair pair of heels.

Body and spirit are twins: God only knows which is which:
The soul squats down in the flesh, like a tinker drunk in a ditch.

More is the whole than a part: but half is more than the whole:
Clearly, the soul is the body: but is not the body the soul?

One and two are not one: but one and nothing is two:
Truth can hardly be false, if falsehood cannot be true.

Once the mastodon was: pterodactyls were common as cocks:
Then the mammoth was God: now is He a prize ox.

Parallels all things are: yet many of these are askew:
You are certainly I: but certainly I am not you.

Springs the rock from the plain, shoots the stream from the rock:
Cocks exist for the hen: but hens exist for the cock.

God, whom we see not, is: and God, who is not, we see:
Fiddle, we know, is diddle: and diddle, we take it, is dee.

### Sonnet for a Picture

That nose is out of drawing. With a gasp,
She pants upon the passionate lips that ache
With the red drain of her own mouth, and make
A monochord of colour. Like an asp,
One lithe lock wriggles in his rutilant grasp.
Her bosom is an oven of myrrh, to bake
Love's white warm shewbread to a browner cake.
The lock his fingers clench has burst its hasp.
The legs are absolutely abominable.
Ah! what keen overgust of wild-eyed woes
Flags in that bosom, flushes in that nose?
Nay! Death sets riddles for desire to spell,
Responsive. What red hem earth's passion sews,
But may be ravenously unripped in hell?

### Nephelidia

From the depth of the dreamy decline of the dawn through a notable nimbus of nebulous noonshine,
Pallid and pink as the palm of the flag-flower that flickers with fear of the flies as they float,
Are they looks of our lovers that lustrously lean from a marvel of mystic miraculous moonshine,
These that we feel in the blood of our blushes that thicken and threaten with throbs through the throat?
Thicken and thrill as a theatre thronged at appeal of an actor's appalled agitation,
Fainter with fear of the fires of the future than pale with the promise of pride in the past;
Flushed with the famishing fullness of fever that reddens with radiance of rathe recreation,
Gaunt as the ghastliest of glimpses that gleam through the gloom of the gloaming when ghosts go aghast?
Nay, for the nick of the tick of the time is a tremulous touch on the temples of terror,
Strained as the sinews yet strenuous with strife of the dead who is dumb as the dust-heaps of death:

Surely no soul is it, sweet as the spasm of erotic emotional exquisite error,
Bathed in the balms of beatified bliss, beatific itself by beatitude's breath.
Surely no spirit or sense of a soul that was soft to the spirit and soul of our senses
Sweetens the stress of suspiring suspicion that sobs in the semblance and sound of a sigh;
Only this oracle opens Olympian, in mystical moods and triangular tenses—
"Life is the lust of a lamp for the light that is dark till the dawn of the day when we die."
Mild is the mirk and monotonous music of memory, melodiously mute as it may be,
While the hope in the heart of a hero is bruised by the breach of men's rapiers, resigned to the rod;
Made meek as a mother whose bosom-beats bound with the bliss-bringing bulk of a balm-breathing baby,
As they grope through the grave-yard of creeds, under skies growing green at a groan for the grimness of God.
Blank is the book of his bounty beholden of old, and its binding is blacker than bluer:
Out of blue into black is the scheme of the skies, and their dews are the wine of the bloodshed of things;
Till the darkling desire of delight shall be free as a fawn that is freed from the fangs that pursue her,
Till the heart-beats of hell shall be hushed by a hymn from the hunt that has harried the kennel of kings.

## TRISTRAM OF LYONESSE

Spring speaks again, and all our woods are stirred,
  And all our wide glad wastes aflower around,
  That twice have heard keen April's clarion sound
Since here we first together saw and heard
Spring's light reverberate and reiterate word
  Shine forth and speak in season. Life stands crowned
  Here with the best one thing it ever found,
As of my soul's best birthdays dawns the third.

There is a friend that as the wise man saith
  Cleaves closer than a brother: nor to me
    Hath time not shown, through days like waves at strife,
This truth more sure than all things else but death,
  This pearl most perfect found in all the sea
    That washes toward your feet these waifs of life.

THE PINES: *April* 1882

### PRELUDE

### TRISTRAM AND ISEULT

Love, that is first and last of all things made,
The light that has the living world for shade,
The spirit that for temporal veil has on
The souls of all men woven in unison,
One fiery raiment with all lives inwrought
And lights of sunny and starry deed and thought,
And alway through new act and passion new
Shines the divine same body and beauty through,
The body spiritual of fire and light
That is to worldly noon as noon to night;
Love, that is flesh upon the spirit of man
And spirit within the flesh whence breath began;
Love, that keeps all the choir of lives in chime;
Love, that is blood within the veins of time;

That wrought the whole world without stroke of hand,
Shaping the breadth of sea, the length of land,
And with the pulse and motion of his breath
Through the great heart of the earth strikes life and death,
The sweet twain chords that make the sweet tune live
Through day and night of things alternative,
Through silence and through sound of stress and strife,
And ebb and flow of dying death and life;
Love, that sounds loud or light in all men's ears,
Whence all men's eyes take fire from sparks of tears,
That binds on all men's feet or chains or wings;
Love, that is root and fruit of terrene things;
Love, that the whole world's waters shall not drown,
The whole world's fiery forces not burn down;
Love, that what time his own hands guard his head
The whole world's wrath and strength shall not strike dead;
Love, that if once his own hands make his grave
The whole world's pity and sorrow shall not save;
Love, that for very life shall not be sold,
Nor bought nor bound with iron nor with gold;
So strong that heaven, could love bid heaven farewell,
Would turn to fruitless and unflowering hell;
So sweet that hell, to hell could love be given,
Would turn to splendid and sonorous heaven;
Love that is fire within thee and light above,
And lives by grace of nothing but of love;
Through many and lovely thoughts and much desire
Led these twain to the life of tears and fire;
Through many and lovely days and much delight
Led these twain to the lifeless life of night.
  Yea, but what then? albeit all this were thus,
And soul smote soul and left it ruinous,
And love led love as eyeless men lead men,
Through chance by chance to deathward—Ah, what then?
Hath love not likewise led them further yet,
Out through the years where memories rise and set,
Some large as suns, some moon-like warm and pale,
Some starry-sighted, some through clouds that sail
Seen as red flame through spectral float of fume,
Each with the blush of its own special bloom
On the fair face of its own coloured light,
Distinguishable in all the host of night,
Divisible from all the radiant rest
And separable in splendour? Hath the best

Light of love's all, of all that burn and move,
A better heaven than heaven is? Hath not love
Made for all these their sweet particular air
To shine in, their own beams and names to bear,
Their ways to wander and their wards to keep,
Till story and song and glory and all things sleep?
Hath he not plucked from death of lovers dead
Their musical soft memories, and kept red
The rose of their remembrance in men's eyes,
The sunsets of their stories in his skies,
The blush of their dead blood in lips that speak
Of their dead lives, and in the listener's cheek
That trembles with the kindling pity lit
In gracious hearts for some sweet fever-fit,
A fiery pity enkindled of pure thought
By tales that make their honey out of nought,
The faithless faith that lives without belief
Its light life through, the griefless ghost of grief?
Yea, as warm night refashions the sere blood
In storm-struck petal or in sun-struck bud,
With tender hours and tempering dew to cure
The hunger and thirst of day's distemperature
And ravin of the dry discolouring hours,
Hath he not bid relume their flameless flowers
With summer fire and heat of lamping song,
And bid the short-lived things, long dead, live long,
And thought remake their wan funereal fames,
And the sweet shining signs of women's names
That mark the months out and the weeks anew
He moves in changeless change of seasons through
To fill the days up of his dateless year
Flame from Queen Helen to Queen Guenevere?
For first of all the sphery signs whereby
Love severs light from darkness, and most high,
In the white front of January there glows
The rose-red sign of Helen like a rose:
And gold-eyed as the shore-flower shelterless
Whereon the sharp-breathed sea blows bitterness,
A storm-star that the seafarers of love
Strain their wind-wearied eyes for glimpses of,
Shoots keen through February's grey frost and damp
The lamplike star of Hero for a lamp;
The star that Marlowe sang into our skies

With mouth of gold, and morning in his eyes;
And in clear March across the rough blue sea
The signal sapphire of Alcyone
Makes bright the blown brows of the wind-foot year;
And shining like a sunbeam-smitten tear
Full ere it fall, the fair next sign in sight
Burns opal-wise with April-coloured light
When air is quick with song and rain and flame,
My birth-month star that in love's heaven hath name
Iseult, a light of blossom and beam and shower,
My singing sign that makes the song-tree flower;
Next like a pale and burning pearl beyond
The rose-white sphere of flower-named Rosamond
Signs the sweet head of Maytime; and for June
Flares like an angered and storm-reddening moon
Her signal sphere, whose Carthaginian pyre
Shadowed her traitor's flying sail with fire;
Next, glittering as the wine-bright jacinth-stone,
A star south-risen that first to music shone,
The keen girl-star of golden Juliet bears
Light northward to the month whose forehead wears
Her name for flower upon it, and his trees
Mix their deep English song with Veronese;
And like an awful sovereign chrysolite
Burning, the supreme fire that blinds the night,
The hot gold head of Venus kissed by Mars,
A sun-flower among small sphered flowers of stars,
The light of Cleopatra fills and burns
The hollow of heaven whence ardent August yearns;
And fixed and shining as the sister-shed
Sweet tears for Phaethon disorbed and dead,
The pale bright autumn's amber-coloured sphere,
That through September sees the saddening year
As love sees change through sorrow, hath to name
Francesca's; and the star that watches flame
The embers of the harvest overgone
Is Thisbe's, slain of love in Babylon,
Set in the golden girdle of sweet signs
A blood-bright ruby; last save one light shines
An eastern wonder of sphery chrysopras,
The star that made men mad, Angelica's;
And latest named and lordliest, with a sound
Of swords and harps in heaven that ring it round,

Last love-light and last love-song of the year's,
Gleams like a glorious emerald Guenevere's.
These are the signs wherethrough the year sees move,
Full of the sun, the sun-god which is love,
A fiery body blood-red from the heart
Outward, with fire-white wings made wide apart,
That close not and unclose not, but upright
Steered without wind by their own light and might
Sweep through the flameless fire of air that rings
From heaven to heaven with thunder of wheels and wings
And antiphones of motion-moulded rhyme
Through spaces out of space and timeless time.
   So shine above dead chance and conquered change
The spherèd signs, and leave without their range
Doubt and desire, and hope with fear for wife,
Pale pains, and pleasures long worn out of life.
Yea, even the shadows of them spiritless,
Through the dim door of sleep that seem to press,
Forms without form, a piteous people and blind,
Men and no men, whose lamentable kind
The shadow of death and shadow of life compel
Through semblances of heaven and false-faced hell,
Through dreams of light and dreams of darkness tost
On waves innavigable, are these so lost?
Shapes that wax pale and shift in swift strange wise,
Void faces with unspeculative eyes,
Dim things that gaze and glare, dead mouths that move,
Featureless heads discrowned of hate and love,
Mockeries and masks of motion and mute breath,
Leavings of life, the superflux of death—
If these things and no more than these things be
Left when man ends or changes, who can see?
Or who can say with what more subtle sense
Their subtler natures taste in air less dense
A life less thick and palpable than ours,
Warmed with faint fires and sweetened with dead flowers
And measured by low music? how time fares
In that wan time-forgotten world of theirs,
Their pale poor world too deep for sun or star
To live in, where the eyes of Helen are,
And hers who made as God's own eyes to shine
The eyes that met them of the Florentine,
Wherein the godhead thence transfigured lit

All time for all men with the shadow of it?
Ah, and these too felt on them as God's grace
The pity and glory of this man's breathing face;
For these too, these my lovers, these my twain,
Saw Dante, saw God visible by pain,
With lips that thundered and with feet that trod
Before men's eyes incognisable God;
Saw love and wrath and light and night and fire
Live with one life and at one mouth respire,
And in one golden sound their whole soul heard
Sounding, one sweet immitigable word.
   They have the night, who had like us the day;
We, whom day binds, shall have the night as they.
We, from the fetters of the light unbound,
Healed of our wound of living, shall sleep sound.
All gifts but one the jealous God may keep
From our soul's longing, one he cannot — sleep.
This, though he grudge all other grace to prayer,
This grace his closed hand cannot choose but spare.
This, though his ear be sealed to all that live,
Be it lightly given or lothly, God must give.
We, as the men whose name on earth is none,
We too shall surely pass out of the sun;
Out of the sound and eyeless light of things,
Wide as the stretch of life's time-wandering wings,
Wide as the naked world and shadowless,
And long-lived as the world's own weariness.
Us too, when all the fires of time are cold,
The heights shall hide us and the depths shall hold.
Us too, when all the tears of time are dry,
The night shall lighten from her tearless eye.
Blind is the day and eyeless all its light,
But the large unbewildered eye of night
Hath sense and speculation; and the sheer
Limitless length of lifeless life and clear,
The timeless space wherein the brief worlds move
Clothed with light life and fruitful with light love,
With hopes that threaten, and with fears that cease,
Past fear and hope, hath in it only peace.
   Yet of these lives inlaid with hopes and fears,
Spun fine as fire and jewelled thick with tears,
These lives made out of loves that long since were,
Lives wrought as ours of earth and burning air,

Fugitive flame, and water of secret springs,
And clothed with joys and sorrows as with wings,
Some yet are good, if aught be good, to save
Some while from washing wreck and wrecking wave.
Was such not theirs, the twain I take, and give
Out of my life to make their dead life live
Some days of mine, and blow my living breath
Between dead lips forgotten even of death?
So many and many of old have given my twain
Love and live song and honey-hearted pain,
Whose root is sweetness and whose fruit is sweet,
So many and with such joy have tracked their feet,
What should I do to follow? yet I too,
I have the heart to follow, many or few
Be the feet gone before me; for the way,
Rose-red with remnant roses of the day
Westward, and eastward white with stars that break,
Between the green and foam is fair to take
For any sail the sea-wind steers for me
From morning into morning, sea to sea.

## I

## THE SAILING OF THE SWALLOW

About the middle music of the spring
Came from the castled shore of Ireland's king
A fair ship stoutly sailing, eastward bound
And south by Wales and all its wonders round
To the loud rocks and ringing reaches home
That take the wild wrath of the Cornish foam,
Past Lyonesse unswallowed of the tides
And high Carlion that now the steep sea hides
To the wind-hollowed heights and gusty bays
Of sheer Tintagel, fair with famous days.
Above the stem a gilded swallow shone,
Wrought with straight wings and eyes of glittering stone
As flying sunward oversea, to bear
Green summer with it through the singing air.
And on the deck between the rowers at dawn,
As the bright sail with brightening wind was drawn,
Sat with full face against the strengthening light
Iseult, more fair than foam or dawn was white.

Her gaze was glad past love's own singing of,
And her face lovely past desire of love.
Past thought and speech her maiden motions were,
And a more golden sunrise was her hair.
The very veil of her bright flesh was made
As of light woven and moonbeam-coloured shade
More fine than moonbeams; white her eyelids shone
As snow sun-stricken that endures the sun,
And through their curled and coloured clouds of deep
Luminous lashes thick as dreams in sleep
Shone as the sea's depth swallowing up the sky's
The springs of unimaginable eyes.
As the wave's subtler emerald is pierced through
With the utmost heaven's inextricable blue,
And both are woven and molten in one sleight
Of amorous colour and implicated light
Under the golden guard and gaze of noon,
So glowed their awless amorous plenilune,
Azure and gold and ardent grey, made strange
With fiery difference and deep interchange
Inexplicable of glories multiform;
Now as the sullen sapphire swells toward storm
Foamless, their bitter beauty grew acold,
And now afire with ardour of fine gold.
Her flower-soft lips were meek and passionate,
For love upon them like a shadow sate
Patient, a foreseen vision of sweet things,
A dream with eyes fast shut and plumeless wings
That knew not what man's love or life should be,
Nor had it sight nor heart to hope or see
What thing should come, but childlike satisfied
Watched out its virgin vigil in soft pride
And unkissed expectation; and the glad
Clear cheeks and throat and tender temples had
Such maiden heat as if a rose's blood
Beat in the live heart of a lily-bud.
Between the small round breasts a white way led
Heavenward, and from slight foot to slender head
The whole fair body flower-like swayed and shone
Moving, and what her light hand leant upon
Grew blossom-scented: her warm arms began
To round and ripen for delight of man
That they should clasp and circle: her fresh hands,

Like regent lilies of reflowering lands
Whose vassal firstlings, crown and star and plume,
Bow down to the empire of that sovereign bloom,
Shone sceptreless, and from her face there went
A silent light as of a God content;
Save when, more swift and keen than love or shame,
Some flash of blood, light as the laugh of flame,
Broke it with sudden beam and shining speech,
As dream by dream shot through her eyes, and each
Outshone the last that lightened, and not one
Showed her such things as should be borne and done.
Though hard against her shone the sunlike face
That in all change and wreck of time and place
Should be the star of her sweet living soul.
Nor had love made it as his written scroll
For evil will and good to read in yet;
But smooth and mighty, without scar or fret,
Fresh and high-lifted was the helmless brow
As the oak-tree flower that tops the topmost bough,
Ere it drop off before the perfect leaf;
And nothing save his name he had of grief,
The name his mother, dying as he was born,
Made out of sorrow in very sorrow's scorn,
And set it on him smiling in her sight,
Tristram; who now, clothed with sweet youth and might,
As a glad witness wore that bitter name,
The second symbol of the world for fame.
Famous and full of fortune was his youth
Ere the beard's bloom had left his cheek unsmooth,
And in his face a lordship of strong joy
And height of heart no chance could curb or cloy
Lightened, and all that warmed them at his eyes
Loved them as larks that kindle as they rise
Toward light they turn to music love the blue strong skies.
So like the morning through the morning moved
Tristram, a light to look on and be loved.
Song sprang between his lips and hands, and shone
Singing, and strengthened and sank down thereon
As a bird settles to the second flight,
Then from beneath his harping hands with might
Leapt, and made way and had its fill and died,
And all whose hearts were fed upon it sighed
Silent, and in them all the fire of tears

Burned as wine drunken not with lips but ears.
And gazing on his fervent hands that made
The might of music all their souls obeyed
With trembling strong subservience of delight,
Full many a maid that had him once in sight
Thought in the secret rapture of her heart
In how dark onset had these hands borne part
How oft, and were so young and sweet of skill;
And those red lips whereon the song burned still,
What words and cries of battle had they flung
Athwart the swing and shriek of swords, so young;
And eyes as glad as summer, what strange youth
Fed them so full of happy heart and truth,
That had seen sway from side to sundering side
The steel flow of that terrible springtide
That the moon rules not, but the fire and light
Of men's hearts mixed in the mid mirth of fight.
Therefore the joy and love of him they had
Made thought more amorous in them and more glad
For his fame's sake remembered, and his youth
Gave his fame flowerlike fragrance and soft growth
As of a rose requickening, when he stood
Fair in their eye, a flower of faultless blood.
And that sad queen to whom his life was death,
A rose plucked forth of summer in mid breath,
A star fall'n out of season in mid throe
Of that life's joy that makes the star's life glow,
Made their love sadder toward him and more strong.
And in mid change of time and fight and song
Chance cast him westward on the low sweet strand
Where songs are sung of the old green Irish land,
And the sky loves it, and the sea loves best,
And as a bird is taken to man's breast
The sweet-souled land where sorrow sweetest sings
Is wrapt round with them as with hands and wings
And taken to the sea's heart as a flower.
There in the luck and light of his good hour
Came to the king's court like a noteless man
Tristram, and while some half a season ran
Abode before him harping in his hall,
And taught sweet craft of new things musical
To the dear maiden mouth and innocent hands
That for his sake are famous in all lands.

Yet was not love between them, for their fate
Lay wrapt in its appointed hour at wait,
And had no flower to show yet, and no sting.
But once being vexed with some past wound the king
Bade give him comfort of sweet baths, and then
Should Iseult watch him as his handmaiden,
For his more honour in men's sight, and ease
The hurts he had with holy remedies
Made by her mother's magic in strange hours
Out of live roots and life-compelling flowers.
And finding by the wound's shape in his side
This was the knight by whom their strength had died
And all their might in one man overthrown
Had left their shame in sight of all men shown,
She would have slain him swordless with his sword;
Yet seemed he to her so great and fair a lord
She heaved up hand and smote not; then said he,
Laughing—'What comfort shall this dead man be,
Damsel? what hurt is for my blood to heal?
But set your hand not near the toothèd steel
Lest the fang strike it.'—'Yea, the fang,' she said,
'Should it not sting the very serpent dead
That stung mine uncle? for his slayer art thou,
And half my mother's heart is bloodless now
Through thee, that mad'st the veins of all her kin
Bleed in his wounds whose veins through thee ran thin.'
Yet thought she how their hot chief's violent heart
Had flung the fierce word forth upon their part
Which bade to battle the best knight that stood
On Arthur's, and so dying of his wild mood
Had set upon his conqueror's flesh the seal
Of his mishallowed and anointed steel,
Whereof the venom and enchanted might
Made the sign burn here branded in her sight.
These things she stood recasting, and her soul
Subsiding till its wound of wrath were whole
Grew smooth again, as thought still softening stole
Through all its tempered passion; nor might hate
Keep high the fire against him lit of late;
But softly from his smiling sight she passed.
And peace thereafter made between them fast
Made peace between two kingdoms, when he went

Home with hands reconciled and heart content,
To bring fair truce 'twixt Cornwall's wild bright strand
And the long wrangling wars of that loud land.
And when full peace was struck betwixt them twain
Forth must he fare by those green straits again,
And bring back Iseult for a plighted bride
And set to reign at Mark his uncle's side.
So now with feast made and all triumphs done
They sailed between the moonfall and the sun
Under the spent stars eastward; but the queen
Out of wise heart and subtle love had seen
Such things as might be, dark as in a glass,
And lest some doom of these should come to pass
Bethought her with her secret soul alone
To work some charm for marriage unison
And strike the heart of Iseult to her lord
With power compulsive more than stroke of sword.
Therefore with marvellous herbs and spells she wrought
To win the very wonder of her thought,
And brewed it with her secret hands and blest
And drew and gave out of her secret breast
To one her chosen and Iseult's handmaiden,
Brangwain, and bade her hide from sight of men
This marvel covered in a golden cup,
So covering in her heart the counsel up
As in the gold the wondrous wine lay close;
And when the last shout with the last cup rose
About the bride and bridegroom bound to bed,
Then should this one word of her will be said
To her new-married maiden child, that she
Should drink with Mark this draught in unity,
And no lip touch it for her sake but theirs:
For with long love and consecrating prayers
The wine was hallowed for their mouths to pledge;
And if a drop fell from the beaker's edge
That drop should Iseult hold as dear as blood
Shed from her mother's heart to do her good.
And having drunk they twain should be one heart
Who were one flesh till fleshly death should part—
Death, who parts all. So Brangwain swore, and kept
The hid thing by her while she waked or slept.
And now they sat to see the sun again

Whose light of eye had looked on no such twain
Since Galahault in the rose-time of the year
Brought Launcelot first to sight of Guenevere.
   And Tristram caught her changing eyes and said:
"As this day raises daylight from the dead
Might not this face the life of a dead man?"
   And Iseult, gazing where the sea was wan
Out of the sun's way, said: "I pray you not
Praise me, but tell me there in Camelot,
Saving the queen, who hath most name of fair?
I would I were a man and dwelling there,
That I might win me better praise than yours,
Even such as you have; for your praise endures,
That with great deeds ye wring from mouths of men,
But ours—for shame, where is it? Tell me then,
Since woman may not wear a better here,
Who of this praise hath most save Guenevere?"
   And Tristram, lightening with a laugh held in—
"Surely a little praise is this to win,
A poor praise and a little! but of these
Hapless, whom love serves only with bowed knees,
Of such poor women fairer face hath none
That lifts her eyes alive against the sun
Than Arthur's sister, whom the north seas call
Mistress of isles; so yet majestical
Above the crowns on younger heads she moves,
Outlightening with her eyes our late-born loves."
   "Ah," said Iseult, "is she more tall than I?
Look, I am tall;" and struck the mast hard by,
With utmost upward reach of her bright hand;
"And look, fair lord, now, when I rise and stand,
How high with feet unlifted I can touch
Standing straight up; could this queen do thus much?
Nay, over tall she must be then, like me;
Less fair than lesser women. May this be,
That still she stands the second stateliest there,
So more than many so much younger fair,
She, born when yet the king your lord was not,
And has the third knight after Launcelot
And after you to serve her? nay, sir, then
God made her for a godlike sign to men."
   "Ay," Tristram answered, "for a sign, a sign—
Would God it were not! for no planets shine

With half such fearful forecast of men's fate
As a fair face so more unfortunate."
Then with a smile that lit not on her brows
But moved upon her red mouth tremulous
Light as a sea-bird's motion oversea,
"Yea," quoth Iseult, "the happier hap for me,
With no such face to bring men no such fate.
Yet her might all we women born too late
Praise for good hap, who so enskied above
Not more in age excels us than man's love."
There came a glooming light on Tristram's face
Answering: "God keep you better in his grace
Than to sit down beside her in men's sight.
For if men be not blind whom God gives light
And lie not in whose lips he bids truth live,
Great grief shall she be given, and greater give.
For Merlin witnessed of her years ago
That she should work woe and should suffer woe
Beyond the race of women: and in truth
Her face, a spell that knows nor age nor youth,
Like youth being soft, and subtler-eyed than age,
With lips that mock the doom her eyes presage,
Hath on it such a light of cloud and fire,
With charm and change of keen or dim desire,
And over all a fearless look of fear
Hung like a veil across its changing cheer,
Made up of fierce foreknowledge and sharp scorn,
That it were better she had not been born.
For not love's self can help a face which hath
Such insubmissive anguish of wan wrath,
Blind prescience and self-contemptuous hate
Of her own soul and heavy-footed fate,
Writ broad upon its beauty: none the less
Its fire of bright and burning bitterness
Takes with as quick a flame the sense of men
As any sunbeam, nor is quenched again
With any drop of dewfall; yea, I think
No herb of force or blood-compelling drink
Would heal a heart that ever it made hot.
Ay, and men too that greatly love her not,
Seeing the great love of her and Lamoracke,
Make no great marvel, nor look strangely back
When with his gaze about her she goes by

Pale as a breathless and star-quickening sky
Between moonrise and sunset, and moves out
Clothed with the passion of his eyes about
As night with all her stars, yet night is black;
And she, clothed warm with love of Lamoracke,
Girt with his worship as with girdling gold,
Seems all at heart anhungered and acold,
Seems sad at heart and loveless of the light,
As night, star-clothed or naked, is but night."
   And with her sweet eyes sunken, and the mirth
Dead in their look as earth lies dead in earth
That reigned on earth and triumphed, Iseult said:
"Is it her shame of something done and dead
Or fear of something to be born and done
That so in her soul's eye puts out the sun?"
   And Tristram answered: "Surely, as I think,
This gives her soul such bitterness to drink,
The sin born blind, the sightless sin unknown,
Wrought when the summer in her blood was blown
But scarce aflower, and spring first flushed her will
With bloom of dreams no fruitage should fulfil,
When out of vision and desire was wrought
The sudden sin that from the living thought
Leaps a live deed and dies not: then there came
On that blind sin swift eyesight like a flame
Touching the dark to death, and made her mad
With helpless knowledge that too late forbade
What was before the bidding: and she knew
How sore a life dead love should lead her through
To what sure end how fearful; and though yet
Nor with her blood nor tears her way be wet
And she look bravely with set face on fate,
Yet she knows well the serpent hour at wait
Somewhere to sting and spare not; ay, and he,
Arthur" —
                    "The king," quoth Iseult suddenly,
"Doth the king too live so in sight of fear?
They say sin touches not a man so near
As shame a woman; yet he too should be
Part of the penance, being more deep than she
Set in the sin."
                    "Nay," Tristram said, "for thus
It fell by wicked hap and hazardous,

That wittingly he sinned no more than youth
May sin and be assoiled of God and truth,
Repenting; since in his first year of reign
As he stood splendid with his foemen slain
And light of new-blown battles, flushed and hot
With hope and life, came greeting from King Lot
Out of his wind-worn islands oversea,
And homage to my king and fealty
Of those north seas wherein the strange shapes swim,
As from his man; and Arthur greeted him
As his good lord and courteously, and bade
To his high feast; who coming with him had
This Queen Morgause of Orkney, his fair wife,
In the green middle Maytime of her life,
And scarce in April was our king's as then,
And goodliest was he of all flowering men,
And of what graft as yet himself knew not;
But cold as rains in autumn was King Lot
And grey-grown out of season: so there sprang
Swift love between them, and all spring through sang
Light in their joyous hearing; for none knew
The bitter bond of blood between them two,
Twain fathers but one mother, till too late
The sacred mouth of Merlin set forth fate
And brake the secret seal on Arthur's birth,
And showed his ruin and his rule on earth
Inextricable, and light on lives to be.
For surely, though time slay us, yet shall we
Have such high name and lordship of good days
As shall sustain us living, and men's praise
Shall burn a beacon lit above us dead.
And of the king how shall not this be said
When any of us from any mouth has praise,
That such were men in only this king's days,
In Arthur's? yea, come shine or shade, no less
His name shall be one name with knightliness,
His fame one light with sunlight. Yet in sooth
His age shall bear the burdens of his youth
And bleed from his own bloodshed; for indeed
Blind to him blind his sister brought forth seed,
And of the child between them shall be born
Destruction: so shall God not suffer scorn,
Nor in men's souls and lives his law lie dead."

And as one moved and marvelling Iseult said:
"Great pity it is and strange it seems to me
God could not do them so much right as we,
Who slay not men for witless evil done;
And these the noblest under God's glad sun
For sin they knew not he that knew shall slay,
And smite blind men for stumbling in fair day.
What good is it to God that such should die?
Shall the sun's light grow sunnier in the sky
Because their light of spirit is clean put out?"
And sighing, she looked from wave to cloud about,
And even with that the full-grown feet of day
Sprang upright on the quivering water-way,
And his face burned against her meeting face
Most like a lover's thrilled with great love's grace
Whose glance takes fire and gives; the quick sea shone
And shivered like spread wings of angels blown
By the sun's breath before him; and a low
Sweet gale shook all the foam-flowers of thin snow
As into rainfall of sea-roses shed
Leaf by wild leaf on that green garden-bed
Which tempests till and sea-winds turn and plough:
For rosy and fiery round the running prow
Fluttered the flakes and feathers of the spray,
And bloomed like blossoms cast by God away
To waste on the ardent water; swift the moon
Withered to westward as a face in swoon
Death-stricken by glad tidings: and the height
Throbbed and the centre quivered with delight
And the depth quailed with passion as of love,
Till like the heart of some new-mated dove
Air, light, and wave seemed full of burning rest,
With motion as of one God's beating breast.
And her heart sprang in Iseult, and she drew
With all her spirit and life the sunrise through,
And through her lips the keen triumphant air
Sea-scented, sweeter than land-roses were,
And through her eyes the whole rejoicing east
Sun-satisfied, and all the heaven at feast
Spread for the morning; and the imperious mirth
Of wind and light that moved upon the earth,
Making the spring, and all the fruitful might
And strong regeneration of delight

That swells the seedling leaf and sapling man,
Since the first life in the first world began
To burn and burgeon through void limbs and veins,
And the first love with sharp sweet procreant pains
To pierce and bring forth roses; yea, she felt
Through her own soul the sovereign morning melt,
And all the sacred passion of the sun;
And as the young clouds flamed and were undone
About him coming, touched and burnt away
In rosy ruin and yellow spoil of day,
The sweet veil of her body and corporal sense
Felt the dawn also cleave it, and incense
With light from inward and with effluent heat
The kindling soul through fleshly hands and feet.
And as the august great blossom of the dawn
Burst, and the full sun scarce from sea withdrawn
Seemed on the fiery water a flower afloat,
So as a fire the mighty morning smote
Throughout her, and incensed with the influent hour
Her whole soul's one great mystical red flower
Burst, and the bud of her sweet spirit broke
Rose-fashion, and the strong spring at a stroke
Thrilled, and was cloven, and from the full sheath came
The whole rose of the woman red as flame:
And all her Mayday blood as from a swoon
Flushed, and May rose up in her and was June.
So for a space her heart as heavenward burned:
Then with half summer in her eyes she turned,
And on her lips was April yet, and smiled,
As though the spirit and sense unreconciled
Shrank laughing back, and would not ere its hour
Let life put forth the irrevocable flower.
  And the soft speech between them grew again
With questionings and records of what men
Rose mightiest, and what names for love or fight
Shone starriest overhead of queen or knight.
There Tristram spake of many a noble thing,
High feast and storm of tournay round the king,
Strange quest by perilous lands of marsh and brake
And circling woods branch-knotted like a snake
And places pale with sins that they had seen,
Where was no life of red fruit or of green
But all was as a dead face wan and dun;

And bowers of evil builders whence the sun
Turns silent, and the moon holds hardly light
Above them through the sick and star-crossed night;
And of their hands through whom such holds lay waste,
And all their strengths dishevelled and defaced
Fell ruinous, and were not from north to south:
And of the might of Merlin's ancient mouth,
The son of no man's loins, begot by doom
In speechless sleep out of a spotless womb;
For sleeping among graves where none had rest
And ominous houses of dead bones unblest
Among the grey grass rough as old rent hair
And wicked herbage whitening like despair
And blown upon with blasts of dolorous breath
From gaunt rare gaps and hollow doors of death,
A maid unspotted, senseless of the spell,
Felt not about her breathe some thing of hell
Whose child and hers was Merlin; and to him
Great light from God gave sight of all things dim
And wisdom of all wondrous things, to say
What root should bear what fruit of night or day,
And sovereign speech and counsel higher than man;
Wherefore his youth like age was wise and wan,
And his age sorrowful and fain to sleep;
Yet should sleep never, neither laugh nor weep,
Till in some depth of deep sweet land or sea
The heavenly hands of holier Nimue,
That was the nurse of Launcelot, and most sweet
Of all that move with magical soft feet
Among us, being of lovelier blood and breath,
Should shut him in with sleep as kind as death:
For she could pass between the quick and dead:
And of her love toward Pelleas, for whose head
Love-wounded and world-wearied she had won
A place beyond all pain in Avalon;
And of the fire that wasted afterward
The loveless eyes and bosom of Ettarde,
In whose false love his faultless heart had burned;
And now being rapt from her, her lost heart yearned
To seek him, and passed hungering out of life:
And after all the thunder-hours of strife
That roared between King Claudas and King Ban
How Nimue's mighty nursling waxed to man,

And how from his first field such grace he got
That all men's hearts bowed down to Launcelot,
And how the high prince Galahault held him dear
And led him even to love of Guenevere
And to that kiss which made break forth as fire
The laugh that was the flower of his desire,
The laugh that lightened at her lips for bliss
To win from Love so great a lover's kiss:
And of the toil of Balen all his days
To reap but thorns for fruit and tears for praise,
Whose hap was evil as his heart was good,
And all his works and ways by wold and wood
Led through much pain to one last labouring day
When blood for tears washed grief with life away:
And of the kin of Arthur, and their might;
The misborn head of Mordred, sad as night,
With cold waste cheeks and eyes as keen as pain,
And the close angry lips of Agravaine;
And gracious Gawain, scattering words as flowers,
The kindliest head of worldly paramours;
And the fair hand of Gareth, found in fight
Strong as a sea-beast's tushes and as white;
And of the king's self, glorious yet and glad
For all the toil and doubt of doom he had,
Clothed with men's loves and full of kingly days.
  Then Iseult said: "Let each knight have his praise
And each good man good witness of his worth;
But when men laud the second name on earth,
Whom would they praise to have no worldly peer
Save him whose love makes glorious Guenevere?"
  "Nay," Tristram said, "such man as he is none."
  "What," said she, "there is none such under sun
Of all the large earth's living? yet I deemed
Men spake of one—but maybe men that dreamed,
Fools and tongue-stricken, witless, babbler's breed—
That for all high things was his peer indeed
Save this one highest, to be so loved and love."
  And Tristram: "Little wit had these thereof;
For there is none such in the world as this."
  "Ay, upon land," quoth Iseult, "none such is,
I doubt not, nor where fighting folk may be;
But were there none such between sky and sea,
The world's whole worth were poorer than I wist."

And Tristram took her flower-white hand and kissed,
Laughing; and through his fair face as in shame
The light blood lightened. "Hear they no such name?"
She said; and he, "If there be such a word,
I wot the queen's poor harper hath not heard."
Then, as the fuller-feathered hours grew long,
He holp to speed their warm slow feet with song.

"Love, is it morning risen or night deceased
That makes the mirth of this triumphant east?
  Is it bliss given or bitterness put by
That makes most glad men's hearts at love's high feast?
  Grief smiles, joy weeps, that day should live and die.

"Is it with soul's thirst or with body's drouth
That summer yearns out sunward to the south,
  With all the flowers that when thy birth drew nigh
Were molten in one rose to make thy mouth?
  O love, what care though day should live and die?

"Is the sun glad of all the love on earth,
The spirit and sense and work of things and worth?
  Is the moon sad because the month must fly
And bring her death that can but bring back birth?
  For all these things as day must live and die.

"Love, is it day that makes thee thy delight
Or thou that seest day made out of thy light?
  Love, as the sun and sea are thou and I,
Sea without sun dark, sun without sea bright;
  The sun is one though day should live and die.

"O which is elder, night or light, who knows?
And life or love, which first of these twain grows?
  For life is born of love to wail and cry,
And love is born of life to heal his woes,
  And light of night, that day should live and die.

"O sun of heaven above the worldly sea,
O very love, what light is this of thee!
  My sea of soul is deep as thou art high,
But all thy light is shed through all of me,
  As love's through love, while day shall live and die.

"Nay," said Iseult, "your song is hard to read."
"Ay?" said he: "or too light a song to heed,

Too slight to follow, it may be? Who shall sing
Of love but as a churl before a king
If by love's worth men rate his worthiness?
Yet as the poor churl's worth to sing is less,
Surely the more shall be the great king's grace
To show for churlish love a kindlier face."
"No churl," she said, "but one in soothsayer's wise
Who tells but truths that help no more than lies.
I have heard men sing of love a simpler way
Than these wrought riddles made of night and day,
Like jewelled reins whereon the rhyme-bells hang."
And Tristram smiled and changed his song and sang.

"The breath between my lips of lips not mine,
Like spirit in sense that makes pure sense divine,
Is as life in them from the living sky
That entering fills my heart with blood of thine
And thee with me, while day shall live and die.

"Thy soul is shed into me with thy breath,
And in my heart each heartbeat of thee saith
How in thy life the lifesprings of me lie,
Even one life to be gathered of one death
In me and thee, though day may live and die.

"Ah, who knows now if in my veins it be
My blood that feels life sweet, or blood of thee,
And this thine eyesight kindled in mine eye
That shows me in thy flesh the soul of me,
For thine made mine, while day may live and die?

"Ah, who knows yet if one be twain or one,
And sunlight separable again from sun,
And I from thee with all my lifesprings dry,
And thou from me with all thine heartbeats done,
Dead separate souls while day shall live and die?

"I see my soul within thine eyes, and hear
My spirit in all thy pulses thrill with fear,
And in my lips the passion of thee sigh,
And music of me made in mine own ear;
Am I not thou while day shall live and die?

"Art thou not I as I thy love am thou?
So let all things pass from us; we are now,
For all that was and will be, who knows why?
And all that is and is not, who knows how?
Who knows? God knows why day should live and die."

And Iseult mused and spake no word, but sought
Through all the hushed ways of her tongueless thought
What face or covered likeness of a face
In what veiled hour or dream-determined place
She seeing might take for love's face, and believe
This was the spirit to whom all spirits cleave.
For that sweet wonder of the twain made one
And each one twain, incorporate sun with sun,
Star with star molten, soul with soul imbued,
And all the soul's works, all their multitude,
Made one thought and one vision and one song,
Love—this thing, this, laid hand on her so strong
She could not choose but yearn till she should see.
So went she musing down her thoughts; but he,
Sweet-hearted as a bird that takes the sun
With clear strong eyes and feels the glad god run
Bright through his blood and wide rejoicing wings,
And opens all himself to heaven and sings,
Made her mind light and full of noble mirth
With words and songs the gladdest grown on earth,
Till she was blithe and high of heart as he.
So swam the Swallow through the springing sea.

And while they sat at speech as at a feast,
Came a light wind fast hardening forth of the east
And blackening till its might had marred the skies;
And the sea thrilled as with heart-sundering sighs
One after one drawn, with each breath it drew,
And the green hardened into iron blue,
And the soft light went out of all its face.
Then Tristram girt him for an oarsman's place
And took his oar and smote, and toiled with might
In the east wind's full face and the strong sea's spite
Labouring; and all the rowers rowed hard, but he
More mightily than any wearier three.
And Iseult watched him rowing with sinless eyes
That loved him but in holy girlish wise
For noble joy in his fair manliness
And trust and tender wonder; none the less
She thought if God had given her grace to be
Man, and make war on danger of earth and sea,
Even such a man she would be; for his stroke
Was mightiest as the mightier water broke,
And in sheer measure like strong music drave

Clean through the wet weight of the wallowing wave;
And as a tune before a great king played
For triumph was the tune their strong strokes made,
And sped the ship through with smooth strife of oars
Over the mid sea's grey foam-paven floors,
For all the loud breach of the waves at will.
So for an hour they fought the storm out still,
And the shorn foam spun from the blades, and high
The keel sprang from the wave-ridge, and the sky
Glared at them for a breath's space through the rain;
Then the bows with a sharp shock plunged again
Down, and the sea clashed on them, and so rose
The bright stem like one panting from swift blows,
And as a swimmer's joyous beaten head
Rears itself laughing, so in that sharp stead
The light ship lifted her long quivering bows
As might the man his buffeted strong brows
Out of the wave-breach; for with one stroke yet
Went all men's oars together, strongly set
As to loud music, and with hearts uplift
They smote their strong way through the drench and drift:
Till the keen hour had chafed itself to death
And the east wind fell fitfully, breath by breath,
Tired; and across the thin and slackening rain
Sprang the face southward of the sun again.
Then all they rested and were eased at heart;
And Iseult rose up where she sat apart,
And with her sweet soul deepening her deep eyes
Cast the furs from her and subtle embroideries
That wrapped her from the storming rain and spray,
And shining like all April in one day,
Hair, face, and throat dashed with the straying showers,
She stood the first of all the whole world's flowers,
And laughed on Tristram with her eyes, and said,
"I too have heart then, I was not afraid."
And answering some light courteous word of grace
He saw her clear face lighten on his face
Unwittingly, with unenamoured eyes,
For the last time. A live man in such wise
Looks in the deadly face of his fixed hour
And laughs with lips wherein he hath no power
To keep the life yet some five minutes' space.
So Tristram looked on Iseult face to face

And knew not, and she knew not. The last time—
The last that should be told in any rhyme
Heard anywhere on mouths of singing men
That ever should sing praise of them again;
The last hour of their hurtless hearts at rest,
The last that peace should touch them, breast to breast,
The last that sorrow far from them should sit,
This last was with them, and they knew not it.
For Tristram being athirst with toil now spake,
Saying, "Iseult, for all dear love's labour's sake
Give me to drink, and give me for a pledge
The touch of four lips on the beaker's edge."
And Iseult sought and would not wake Brangwain
Who slept as one half dead with fear and pain,
Being tender-natured; so with hushed light feet
Went Iseult round her, with soft looks and sweet
Pitying her pain; so sweet a spirited thing
She was, and daughter of a kindly king.
And spying what strange bright secret charge was kept
Fast in that maid's white bosom while she slept,
She sought and drew the gold cup forth and smiled
Marvelling, with such light wonder as a child
That hears of glad sad life in magic lands;
And bare it back to Tristram with pure hands
Holding the love-draught that should be for flame
To burn out of them fear and faith and shame,
And lighten all their life up in men's sight,
And make them sad for ever. Then the knight
Bowed toward her and craved whence had she this strange thing
That might be spoil of some dim Asian king,
By starlight stolen from some waste place of sands,
And a maid bore it here in harmless hands.
And Iseult, laughing—"Other lords that be
Feast, and their men feast after them; but we,
Our men must keep the best wine back to feast
Till they be full and we of all men least
Feed after them and fain to fare so well:
So with mine handmaid and your squire it fell
That hid this bright thing from us in a wile:"
And with light lips yet full of their swift smile,
And hands that wist not though they dug a grave,
Undid the hasps of gold, and drank, and gave,
And he drank after, a deep glad kingly draught:

And all their life changed in them, for they quaffed
Death; if it be death so to drink, and fare
As men who change and are what these twain were.
And shuddering with eyes full of fear and fire
And heart-stung with a serpentine desire
He turned and saw the terror in her eyes
That yearned upon him shining in such wise
As a star midway in the midnight fixed.
   Their Galahault was the cup, and she that mixed;
Nor other hand there needed, nor sweet speech
To lure their lips together; each on each
Hung with strange eyes and hovered as a bird
Wounded, and each mouth trembled for a word;
Their heads neared, and their hands were drawn in one,
And they saw dark, though still the unsunken sun
Far through fine rain shot fire into the south;
And their four lips became one burning mouth.

## II

## THE QUEEN'S PLEASANCE

Out of the night arose the second day,
And saw the ship's bows break the shoreward spray.
As the sun's boat of gold and fire began
To sail the sea of heaven unsailed of man,
And the soft waves of sacred air to break
Round the prow launched into the morning's lake,
They saw the sign of their sea-travel done.
   Ah, was not something seen of yester-sun,
When the sweet light that lightened all the skies
Saw nothing fairer than one maiden's eyes,
That whatsoever in all time's years may be
To-day's sun nor to-morrow's sun shall see?
Not while she lives, not when she comes to die,
Shall she look sunward with that sinless eye.
   Yet fairer now than song may show them stand
Tristram and Iseult, hand in amorous hand,
Soul-satisfied, their eyes made great and bright
With all the love of all the livelong night;
With all its hours yet singing in their ears
No mortal music made of thoughts and tears,
But such a song, past conscience of man's thought,

As hearing he grows god and knows it not.
Nought else they saw nor heard but what the night
Had left for seal upon their sense and sight,
Sound of past pulses beating, fire of amorous light.
Enough, and overmuch, and never yet
Enough, though love still hungering feed and fret,
To fill the cup of night which dawn must overset.
For still their eyes were dimmer than with tears
And dizzier from diviner sounds their ears
Than though from choral thunders of the quiring spheres.
They heard not how the landward waters rang,
Nor saw where high into the morning sprang,
Riven from the shore and bastioned with the sea,
Toward summits where the north wind's nest might be,
A wave-walled palace with its eastern gate
Full of the sunrise now and wide at wait,
And on the mighty-moulded stairs that clomb
Sheer from the fierce lip of the lapping foam
The knights of Mark that stood before the wall.
So with loud joy and storm of festival
They brought the bride in up the towery way
That rose against the rising front of day,
Stair based on stair, between the rocks unhewn,
To those strange halls wherethrough the tidal tune
Rang loud or lower from soft or strengthening sea,
Tower shouldering tower, to windward and to lee,
With change of floors and stories, flight on flight,
That clomb and curled up to the crowning height
Whence men might see wide east and west in one
And on one sea waned moon and mounting sun.
And severed from the sea-rock's base, where stand
Some worn walls yet they saw the broken strand,
The beachless cliff that in the sheer sea dips,
The sleepless shore inexorable to ships,
And the straight causeway's bare gaunt spine between
The sea-spanned walls and naked mainland's green.
  On the mid stairs, between the light and dark,
Before the main tower's portal stood King Mark,
Crowned: and his face was as the face of one
Long time athirst and hungering for the sun
In barren thrall of bitter bonds, who now
Thinks here to feel its blessing on his brow.
A swart lean man, but kinglike, still of guise,

With black streaked beard and cold unquiet eyes,
Close-mouthed, gaunt-cheeked, wan as a morning moon,
Though hardly time on his worn hair had strewn
The thin first ashes from a sparing hand:
Yet little fire there burnt upon the brand,
And way-worn seemed he with life's wayfaring.
So between shade and sunlight stood the king,
And his face changed nor yearned not toward his bride;
But fixed between mild hope and patient pride
Abode what gift of rare or lesser worth
This day might bring to all his days on earth.
But at the glory of her when she came
His heart endured not: very fear and shame
Smote him, to take her by the hand and kiss,
Till both were molten in the burning bliss,
And with a thin flame flushing his cold face
He led her silent to the bridal place.
There were they wed and hallowed of the priest;
And all the loud time of the marriage feast
One thought within three hearts was as a fire,
Where craft and faith took counsel with desire.
For when the feast had made a glorious end
They gave the new queen for her maids to tend
At dawn of bride-night, and thereafter bring
With marriage music to the bridegroom king.
Then by device of craft between them laid
To him went Brangwain delicately, and prayed
That this thing even for love's sake might not be,
But without sound or light or eye to see
She might come in to bride-bed: and he laughed,
As one that wist not well of wise love's craft,
And bade all bridal things be as she would.
Yet of his gentleness he gat not good;
For clothed and covered with the nuptial dark
Soft like a bride came Brangwain to King Mark,
And to the queen came Tristram; and the night
Fled, and ere danger of detective light
From the king sleeping Brangwain slid away,
And where had lain her handmaid Iseult lay.
And the king waking saw beside his head
That face yet passion-coloured, amorous red
From lips not his, and all that strange hair shed
Across the tissued pillows, fold on fold,

Innumerable, incomparable, all gold,
To fire men's eyes with wonder, and with love
Men's hearts; so shone its flowering crown above
The brows enwound with that imperial wreath,
And framed with fragrant radiance round the face beneath.
  And the king marvelled, seeing with sudden start
Her very glory, and said out of his heart;
"What have I done of good for God to bless
That all this he should give me, tress on tress,
All this great wealth and wondrous? Was it this
That in mine arms I had all night to kiss,
And mix with me this beauty? this that seems
More fair than heaven doth in some tired saint's dreams,
Being part of that same heaven? yea, more, for he,
Though loved of God so, yet but seems to see,
But to me sinful such great grace is given
That in mine hands I hold this part of heaven,
Not to mine eyes lent merely. Doth God make
Such things so godlike for man's mortal sake?
Have I not sinned, that in this fleshly life
Have made of her a mere man's very wife?"
  So the king mused and murmured; and she heard
The faint sound trembling of each breathless word,
And laughed into the covering of her hair.
  And many a day for many a month as fair
Slid over them like music; and as bright
Burned with love's offerings many a secret night.
And many a dawn to many a fiery noon
Blew prelude, when the horn's heart-kindling tune
Lit the live woods with sovereign sound of mirth
Before the mightiest huntsman hailed on earth
Lord of its lordliest pleasure, where he rode
Hard by her rein whose peerless presence glowed
Not as that white queen's of the virgin hunt
Once, whose crown-crescent braves the night-wind's brunt,
But with the sun for frontlet of a queenlier front.
For where the flashing of her face was turned
As lightning was the fiery light that burned
From eyes and brows enkindled more with speed
And rapture of the rushing of her steed
Than once with only beauty; and her mouth
Was as a rose athirst that pants for drouth
Even while it laughs for pleasure of desire,

And all her heart was as a leaping fire.
Yet once more joy they took of woodland ways
Than came of all those flushed and fiery days
When the loud air was mad with life and sound,
Through many a dense green mile, of horn and hound
Before the king's hunt going along the wind,
And ere the timely leaves were changed or thinned,
Even in mid maze of summer. For the knight
Forth was once ridden toward some frontier fight
Against the lewd folk of the Christless lands
That warred with wild and intermittent hands
Against the king's north border; and there came
A knight unchristened yet of unknown name,
Swart Palamede, upon a secret quest,
To high Tintagel, and abode as guest
In likeness of a minstrel with the king.
Nor was there man could sound so sweet a string,
Save Tristram only, of all held best on earth.
And one loud eve, being full of wine and mirth,
Ere sunset left the walls and waters dark,
To that strange minstrel strongly swore King Mark,
By all that makes a knight's faith firm and strong,
That he for guerdon of his harp and song
Might crave and have his liking. Straight there came
Up the swart cheek a flash of swarthier flame,
And the deep eyes fulfilled of glittering night
Laughed out in lightnings of triumphant light
As the grim harper spake: "O king, I crave
No gift of man that king may give to slave,
But this thy crowned queen only, this thy wife,
Whom yet unseen I loved, and set my life
On this poor chance to compass, even as here,
Being fairer famed than all save Guenevere."
Then as the noise of seaward storm that mocks
With roaring laughter from reverberate rocks
The cry from ships near shipwreck, harsh and high
Rose all the wrath and wonder in one cry
Through all the long roof's hollow depth and length
That hearts of strong men kindled in their strength
May speak in laughter lion-like, and cease,
Being wearied: only two men held their peace
And each glared hard on other: but King Mark
Spake first of these: "Man, though thy craft be dark

And thy mind evil that begat this thing,
Yet stands the word once plighted of a king
Fast: and albeit less evil it were for me
To give my life up than my wife, or be
A landless man crowned only with a curse,
Yet this in God's and all men's sight were worse,
To live soul-shamed, a man of broken troth,
Abhorred of men as I abhor mine oath
Which yet I may forswear not." And he bowed
His head, and wept: and all men wept aloud,
Save one, that heard him weeping: but the queen
Wept not: and statelier yet than eyes had seen
That ever looked upon her queenly state
She rose, and in her eyes her heart was great
And full of wrath seen manifest and scorn
More strong than anguish to go thence forlorn
Of all men's comfort and her natural right.
And they went forth into the dawn of night.
Long by wild ways and clouded light they rode,
Silent; and fear less keen at heart abode
With Iseult than with Palamede: for awe
Constrained him, and the might of love's high law,
That can make lewd men loyal; and his heart
Yearned on her, if perchance with amorous art
And soothfast skill of very love he might
For courtesy find favour in her sight
And comfort of her mercies: for he wist
More grace might come of that sweet mouth unkissed
Than joy for violence done it, that should make
His name abhorred for shame's disloyal sake.
And in the stormy starlight clouds were thinned
And thickened by short gusts of changing wind
That panted like a sick man's fitful breath:
And like a moan of lions hurt to death
Came the sea's hollow noise along the night.
But ere its gloom from aught but foam had light
They halted, being aweary: and the knight
As reverently forbore her where she lay
As one that watched his sister's sleep till day.
Nor durst he kiss or touch her hand or hair
For love and shamefast pity, seeing how fair
She slept, and fenceless from the fitful air.
And shame at heart stung nigh to death desire,

But grief at heart burned in him like a fire
For hers and his own sorrowing sake, that had
Such grace for guerdon as makes glad men sad,
To have their will and want it. And the day
Sprang: and afar along the wild waste way
They heard the pulse and press of hurrying horse-hoofs play:
And like the rushing of a ravenous flame
Whose wings make tempest of the darkness, came
Upon them headlong as in thunder borne
Forth of the darkness of the labouring morn
Tristram: and up forthright upon his steed
Leapt, as one blithe of battle, Palamede,
And mightily with shock of horse and man
They lashed together: and fair that fight began
As fair came up that sunrise: to and fro,
With knees nigh staggered and stout heads bent low
From each quick shock of spears on either side,
Reeled the strong steeds heavily, haggard-eyed
And heartened high with passion of their pride
As sheer the stout spears shocked again, and flew
Sharp-splintering: then, his sword as each knight drew,
They flashed and foined full royally, so long
That but to see so fair a strife and strong
A man might well have given out of his life
One year's void space forlorn of love or strife.
As when a bright north-easter, great of heart,
Scattering the strengths of squadrons, hurls apart
Ship from ship labouring violently, in such toil
As earns but ruin—with even so strong recoil
Back were the steeds hurled from the spear-shock, fain
And foiled of triumph: then with tightened rein
And stroke of spur, inveterate, either knight
Bore in again upon his foe with might,
Heart-hungry for the hot-mouthed feast of fight
And all athirst of mastery: but full soon
The jarring notes of that tempestuous tune
Fell, and its mighty music made of hands
Contending, clamorous through the loud waste lands,
Broke at once off; and shattered from his steed
Fell, as a mainmast ruining, Palamede,
Stunned: and those lovers left him where he lay,
And lightly through green lawns they rode away.
There was a bower beyond man's eye more fair

Than ever summer dews and sunniest air
Fed full with rest and radiance till the boughs
Had wrought a roof as for a holier house
Than aught save love might breathe in; fairer far
Than keeps the sweet light back of moon and star
From high kings' chambers: there might love and sleep
Divide for joy the darkling hours, and keep
With amorous alternation of sweet strife
The soft and secret ways of death and life
Made smooth for pleasure's feet to rest and run
Even from the moondawn to the kindling sun,
Made bright for passion's feet to run and rest
Between the midnight's and the morning's breast,
Where hardly though her happy head lie down
It may forget the hour that wove its crown;
Where hardly though her joyous limbs be laid
They may forget the mirth that midnight made.
And thither, ere sweet night had slain sweet day,
Iseult and Tristram took their wandering way,
And rested, and refreshed their hearts with cheer
In hunters' fashion of the woods; and here
More sweet it seemed, while this might be, to dwell
And take of all world's weariness farewell
Than reign of all world's lordship queen and king.
Nor here would time for three moons' changes bring
Sorrow nor thought of sorrow; but sweet earth
Fostered them like her babes of eldest birth,
Reared warm in pathless woods and cherished well.
And the sun sprang above the sea and fell,
And the stars rose and sank upon the sea;
And outlaw-like, in forest wise and free,
The rising and the setting of their lights
Found those twain dwelling all those days and nights.
And under change of sun and star and moon
Flourished and fell the chaplets woven of June,
And fair through fervours of the deepening sky
Panted and passed the hours that lit July,
And each day blessed them out of heaven above,
And each night crowned them with the crown of love.
Nor till the might of August overhead
Weighed on the world was yet one roseleaf shed
Of all their joy's warm coronal, nor aught
Touched them in passing ever with a thought

That ever this might end on any day
Or any night not love them where they lay;
But like a babbling tale of barren breath
Seemed all report and rumour held of death,
And a false bruit the legend tear-impearled
That such a thing as change was in the world.
And each bright song upon his lips that came,
Mocking the powers of change and death by name,
Blasphemed their bitter godhead, and defied
Time, though clothed round with ruin as kings with pride,
To blot the glad life out of love: and she
Drank lightly deep of his philosophy
In that warm wine of amorous words which is
Sweet with all truths of all philosophies.
For well he wist all subtle ways of song,
And in his soul the secret eye was strong
That burns in meditation, till bright words
Break flamelike forth as notes from fledgeling birds
That feel the soul speak through them of the spring.
So fared they night and day as queen and king
Crowned of a kingdom wide as day and night.
Nor ever cloudlet swept or swam in sight
Across the darkling depths of their delight
Whose stars no skill might number, nor man's art
Sound the deep stories of its heavenly heart.
Till, even for wonder that such life should live,
Desires and dreams of what death's self might give
Would touch with tears and laughter and wild speech
The lips and eyes of passion, fain to reach,
Beyond all bourne of time or trembling sense,
The verge of love's last possible eminence.
Out of the heaven that storm nor shadow mars,
Deep from the starry depth beyond the stars,
A yearning ardour without scope or name
Fell on them, and the bright night's breath of flame
Shot fire into their kisses; and like fire
The lit dews lightened on the leaves, as higher
Night's heart beat on toward midnight. Far and fain
Somewhiles the soft rush of rejoicing rain
Solaced the darkness, and from steep to steep
Of heaven they saw the sweet sheet lightning leap
And laugh its heart out in a thousand smiles,
When the clear sea for miles on glimmering miles

Burned as though dawn were strewn abroad astray,
Or, showering out of heaven, all heaven's array
Had paven instead the waters: fain and far
Somewhiles the burning love of star for star
Spake words that love might wellnigh seem to hear
In such deep hours as turn delight to fear
Sweet as delight's self ever. So they lay
Tranced once, nor watched along the fiery bay
The shine of summer darkness palpitate and play.
She had nor sight nor voice; her swooning eyes
Knew not if night or light were in the skies;
Across her beauty sheer the moondawn shed
Its light as on a thing as white and dead;
Only with stress of soft fierce hands she prest
Between the throbbing blossoms of her breast
His ardent face, and through his hair her breath
Went quivering as when life is hard on death;
And with strong trembling fingers she strained fast
His head into her bosom; till at last,
Satiate with sweetness of that burning bed,
His eyes afire with tears, he raised his head
And laughed into her lips; and all his heart
Filled hers; then face from face fell, and apart
Each hung on each with panting lips, and felt
Sense into sense and spirit in spirit melt.
"Hast thou no sword? I would not live till day;
O love, this night and we must pass away,
It must die soon, and let not us die late."
"Take then my sword and slay me; nay, but wait
Till day be risen; what, wouldst thou think to die
Before the light take hold upon the sky?"
"Yea, love; for how shall we have twice, being twain,
This very night of love's most rapturous reign?
Live thou and have thy day, and year by year
Be great, but what shall I be? Slay me here;
Let me die not when love lies dead, but now
Strike through my heart: nay, sweet, what heart hast thou?
Is it so much I ask thee, and spend my breath
In asking? nay, thou knowest it is but death.
Hadst thou true heart to love me, thou wouldst give
This: but for hate's sake thou wilt let me live."
Here he caught up her lips with his, and made
The wild prayer silent in her heart that prayed,

And strained her to him till all her faint breath sank
And her bright light limbs palpitated and shrank
And rose and fluctuated as flowers in rain
That bends them and they tremble and rise again
And heave and straighten and quiver all through with bliss
And turn afresh their mouths up for a kiss,
Amorous, athirst of that sweet influent love;
So, hungering towards his hovering lips above,
Her red-rose mouth yearned silent, and her eyes
Closed, and flashed after, as through June's darkest skies
The divine heartbeats of the deep live light
Make open and shut the gates of the outer night.
   Long lay they still, subdued with love, nor knew
If cloud or light changed colour as it grew,
If star or moon beheld them; if above
The heaven of night waxed fiery with their love,
Or earth beneath were moved at heart and root
To burn as they, to burn and bring forth fruit
Unseasonable for love's sake; if tall trees
Bowed, and close flowers yearned open, and the breeze
Failed and fell silent as a flame that fails:
And all that hour unheard the nightingales
Clamoured, and all the woodland soul was stirred,
And depth and height were one great song unheard,
As though the world caught music and took fire
From the instant heart alone of their desire.
   So sped their night of nights between them: so,
For all fears past and shadows, shine and snow,
That one pure hour all-golden where they lay
Made their life perfect and their darkness day.
And warmer waved its harvest yet to reap,
Till in the lovely fight of love and sleep
At length had sleep the mastery; and the dark
Was lit with soft live gleams they might not mark,
Fleet butterflies, each like a dead flower's ghost,
White, blue, and sere leaf-coloured; but the most
White as the sparkle of snow-flowers in the sun
Ere with his breath they lie at noon undone
Whose kiss devours their tender beauty, and leaves
But raindrops on the grass and sere thin leaves
That were engraven with traceries of the snow
Flowerwise ere any flower of earth's would blow;
So swift they sprang and sank, so sweet and light

They swam the deep dim breathless air of night.
Now on her rose-white amorous breast half bare,
Now on her slumberous love-dishevelled hair,
The white wings lit and vanished, and afresh
Lit soft as snow lights on her snow-soft flesh,
On hand or throat or shoulder; and she stirred
Sleeping, and spake some tremulous bright word,
And laughed upon some dream too sweet for truth,
Yet not so sweet as very love and youth
That there had charmed her eyes to sleep at last.
Nor woke they till the perfect night was past,
And the soft sea thrilled with blind hope of light.
But ere the dusk had well the sun in sight
He turned and kissed her eyes awake and said,
Seeing earth and water neither quick nor dead
And twilight hungering toward the day to be,
"As the dawn loves the sunlight I love thee."
And even as rays with cloudlets in the skies
Confused in brief love's bright contentious wise,
Sleep strove with sense rekindling in her eyes;
And as the flush of birth scarce overcame
The pale pure pearl of unborn light with flame
Soft as may touch the rose's heart with shame
To break not all reluctant out of bud,
Stole up her sleeping cheek her waking blood;
And with the lovely laugh of love that takes
The whole soul prisoner ere the whole sense wakes,
Her lips for love's sake bade love's will be done.
And all the sea lay subject to the sun.

## III

## TRISTRAM IN BRITTANY

"'As the dawn loves the sunlight I love thee;'
As men that shall be swallowed of the sea
Love the sea's lovely beauty; as the night
That wanes before it loves the young sweet light,
And dies of loving; as the worn-out noon
Loves twilight, and as twilight loves the moon
That on its grave a silver seal shall set—
We have loved and slain each other, and love yet.
Slain; for we live not surely, being in twain:

In her I lived, and in me she is slain,
Who loved me that I brought her to her doom,
Who loved her that her love might be my tomb.
As all the streams on earth and all fresh springs
And sweetest waters, every brook that sings,
Each fountain where the young year dips its wings
First, and the first-fledged branches of it wave,
Even with one heart's love seek one bitter grave.
From hills that first see bared the morning's breast
And heights the sun last yearns to from the west,
All tend but toward the sea, all born most high
Strive downward, passing all things joyous by,
Seek to it and cast their lives in it and die.
So strive all lives for death which all lives win;
So sought her soul to my soul, and therein
Was poured and perished: O my love, and mine
Sought to thee and died of thee and died as thine.
As the dawn loves the sunlight that must cease
Ere dawn again may rise and pass in peace;
Must die that she being dead may live again,
To be by his new rising nearly slain.
So rolls the great wheel of the great world round,
And no change in it and no fault is found,
And no true life of perdurable breath,
And surely no irrevocable death.
Day after day night comes that day may break,
And day comes back for night's reiterate sake.
Each into each dies, each of each is born:
Day past is night, shall night past not be morn?
Out of this moonless and faint-hearted night
That love yet lives in, shall there not be light?
Light strong as love, that love may live in yet?
Alas, but how shall foolish hope forget
How all these loving things that kill and die
Meet not but for a breath's space and pass by?
Night is kissed once of dawn and dies, and day
But touches twilight and is rapt away.
So may my love and her love meet once more,
And meeting be divided as of yore.
Yea, surely as the day-star loves the sun
And when he hath risen is utterly undone,
So is my love of her and hers of me—

And its most sweetness bitter as the sea.
Would God yet dawn might see the sun and die!"
  Three years had looked on earth and passed it by
Since Tristram looked on Iseult, when he stood
So communing with dreams of evil and good,
And let all sad thoughts through his spirit sweep
As leaves through air or tears through eyes that weep
Or snowflakes through dark weather: and his soul,
That had seen all those sightless seasons roll
One after one, wave over weary wave,
Was in him as a corpse is in its grave.
Yet, for his heart was mighty, and his might
Through all the world as a great sound and light,
The mood was rare upon him; save that here
In the low sundawn of the lightening year
With all last year's toil and its triumph done
He could not choose but yearn for that set sun
Which at this season saw the firstborn kiss
That made his lady's mouth one fire with his.
Yet his great heart being greater than his grief
Kept all the summer of his strength in leaf
And all the rose of his sweet spirit in flower;
Still his soul fed upon the sovereign hour
That had been or that should be; and once more
He looked through drifted sea and drifting shore
That crumbled in the wave-breach, and again
Spake sad and deep within himself: "What pain
Should make a man's soul wholly break and die,
Sapped as weak sand by water? How shall I
Be less than all less things are that endure
And strive and yield when time is? Nay, full sure
All these and we are parts of one same end;
And if through fire or water we twain tend
To that sure life where both must be made one,
If one we be, what matter? Thou, O sun,
The face of God, if God thou be not—nay,
What but God should I think thee, what should say,
Seeing thee rerisen, but very God?—should I,
I fool, rebuke thee sovereign in thy sky,
The clouds dead round thee and the air alive,
The winds that lighten and the waves that strive
Toward this shore as to that beneath thy breath,
Because in me my thoughts bear all towards death?

O sun, that when we are dead wilt rise as bright,
Air deepening up toward heaven, and nameless light,
And heaven immeasurable, and faint clouds blown
Between us and the lowest aerial zone
And each least skirt of their imperial state—
Forgive us that we held ourselves so great!
What should I do to curse you? I indeed
Am a thing meaner than this least wild weed
That my foot bruises and I know not—yet
Would not be mean enough for worms to fret
Before their time and mine was.
"Ah, and ye
Light washing weeds, blind waifs of dull blind sea,
Do ye so thirst and hunger and aspire,
Are ye so moved with such long strong desire
In the ebb and flow of your sad life, and strive
Still toward some end ye shall not see alive—
But at high noon ye know it by light and heat
Some half-hour, till ye feel the fresh tide beat
Up round you, and at night's most bitter noon
The ripples leave you naked to the moon?
And this dim dusty heather that I tread,
These half-born blossoms, born at once and dead,
Sere brown as funeral cloths, and purple as pall,
What if some life and grief be in them all?
"Ay, what of these? but, O strong sun! O sea!
I bid not you, divine things! comfort me,
I stand not up to match you in your sight—
Who hath said ye have mercy toward us, ye who have might?
And though ye had mercy, I think I would not pray
That ye should change your counsel or your way
To make our life less bitter: if such power
Be given the stars on one deciduous hour,
And such might be in planets to destroy
Grief and rebuild, and break and build up joy,
What man would stretch forth hand on them to make
Fate mutable, God foolish, for his sake?
For if in life or death be aught of trust,
And if some unseen just God or unjust
Put soul into the body of natural things
And in time's pauseless feet and worldwide wings
Some spirit of impulse and some sense of will
That steers them through the seas of good and ill

To some incognizable and actual end,
Be it just or unjust, foe to man or friend,
How should we make the stable spirit to swerve,
How teach the strong soul of the world to serve,
The imperious will in time and sense in space
That gives man life turn back to give man place —
The conscious law lose conscience of its way,
The rule and reason fail from night and day,
The streams flow back toward whence the springs began,
That less of thirst might sear the lips of man?
Let that which is be, and sure strengths stand sure,
And evil or good and death or life endure,
Not alterable and rootless, but indeed
A very stem born of a very seed
That brings forth fruit in season: how should this
Die that was sown, and that not be which is,
And the old fruit change that came of the ancient root,
And he that planted bid it not bear fruit,
And he that watered smite his vine with drouth
Because its grapes are bitter in our mouth,
And he that kindled quench the sun with night
Because its beams are fire against our sight,
And he that tuned untune the sounding spheres
Because their song is thunder in our ears?
How should the skies change and the stars, and time
Break the large concord of the years that chime,
Answering, as wave to wave beneath the moon
That draws them shoreward, mar the whole tide's tune
For the instant foam's sake on one turning wave —
For man's sake that is grass upon a grave?
How should the law that knows not soon or late,
For whom no time nor space is — how should fate,
That is not good nor evil, wise nor mad,
Nor just nor unjust, neither glad nor sad —
How should the one thing that hath being, the one
That moves not as the stars move or the sun
Or any shadow or shape that lives or dies
In likeness of dead earth or living skies,
But its own darkness and its proper light
Clothe it with other names than day or night,
And its own soul of strength and spirit of breath
Feed it with other powers than life or death —
How should it turn from its great way to give

Man that must die a clearer space to live?
Why should the waters of the sea be cleft,
The hills be molten to his right and left,
That he from deep to deep might pass dry-shod,
Or look between the viewless heights on God?
Hath he such eyes as, when the shadows flee,
The sun looks out with to salute the sea?
Is his hand bounteous as the morning's hand?
Or where the night stands hath he feet to stand?
Will the storm cry not when he bids it cease?
Is it his voice that saith to the east wind, Peace?
Is his breath mightier than the west wind's breath?
Doth his heart know the things of life and death?
Can his face bring forth sunshine and give rain,
Or his weak will that dies and lives again
Make one thing certain or bind one thing fast,
That as he willed it shall be at the last?
How should the storms of heaven and kindled lights
And all the depths of things and topless heights
And air and earth and fire and water change
Their likeness, and the natural world grow strange,
And all the limits of their life undone
Lose count of time and conscience of the sun,
And that fall under which was fixed above,
That man might have a larger hour for love?"
　So musing with close lips and lifted eyes
That smiled with self-contempt to live so wise,
With silent heart so hungry now so long,
So late grown clear, so miserably made strong,
About the wolds a banished man he went,
The brown wolds bare and sad as banishment,
By wastes of fruitless flowerage, and grey downs
That felt the sea-wind shake their wild-flower crowns
As though fierce hands would pluck from some grey head
The spoils of majesty despised and dead,
And fill with crying and comfortless strange sound
Their hollow sides and heights of herbless ground.
Yet as he went fresh courage on him came,
Till dawn rose too within him as a flame;
The heart of the ancient hills and his were one;
The winds took counsel with him, and the sun
Spake comfort; in his ears the shout of birds
Was as the sound of clear sweet-spirited words,

The noise of streams as laughter from above
Of the old wild lands, and as a cry of love
Spring's trumpet-blast blown over moor and lea:
The skies were red as love is, and the sea
Was as the floor of heaven for love to tread.
So went he as with light about his head,
And in the joyous travail of the year
Grew April-hearted; since nor grief nor fear
Can master so a young man's blood so long
That it shall move not to the mounting song
Of that sweet hour when earth replumes her wings
And with fair face and heart set heavenward sings
As an awakened angel unaware
That feels his sleep fall from him, and his hair
By some new breath of wind and music stirred,
Till like the sole song of one heavenly bird
Sounds all the singing of the host of heaven,
And all the glories of the sovereign Seven
Are as one face of one incorporate light.
And as that host of singers in God's sight
Might draw toward one that slumbered, and arouse
The lips requickened and rekindling brows,
So seemed the earthly host of all things born
In sight of spring and eyeshot of the morn,
All births of land or waifs of wind and sea,
To draw toward him that sorrowed, and set free
From presage and remembrance of all pains
The life that leapt and lightened in his veins.
So with no sense abashed nor sunless look,
But with exalted eyes and heart, he took
His part of sun or storm-wind, and was glad,
For all things lost, of these good things he had.
   And the spring loved him surely, being from birth
One made out of the better part of earth,
A man born as at sunrise; one that saw
Not without reverence and sweet sense of awe
But wholly without fear of fitful breath
The face of life watched by the face of death;
And living took his fill of rest and strife,
Of love and change, and fruit and seed of life,
And when his time to live in light was done
With unbent head would pass out of the sun:
A spirit as morning, fair and clear and strong,

Whose thought and work were as one harp and song
Heard through the world as in a strange king's hall
Some great guest's voice that sings of festival.
So seemed all things to love him, and his heart
In all their joy of life to take such part,
That with the live earth and the living sea
He was as one that communed mutually
With naked heart to heart of friend to friend:
And the star deepening at the sunset's end,
And the moon fallen before the gate of day
As one sore wearied with vain length of way,
And the winds wandering, and the streams and skies,
As faces of his fellows in his eyes.
Nor lacked there love where he was evermore
Of man and woman, friend of sea or shore,
Not measurable with weight of graven gold,
Free as the sun's gift of the world to hold
Given each day back to man's reconquering sight
That loses but its lordship for a night.
And now that after many a season spent
In barren ways and works of banishment,
Toil of strange fights and many a fruitless field,
Ventures of quest and vigils under shield,
He came back to the strait of sundering sea
That parts green Cornwall from grey Brittany,
Where dwelt the high king's daughter of the lands,
Iseult, named alway from her fair white hands,
She looked on him and loved him; but being young
Made shamefastness a seal upon her tongue,
And on her heart, that none might hear its cry,
Set the sweet signet of humility.
Yet when he came a stranger in her sight,
A banished man and weary, no such knight
As when the Swallow dipped her bows in foam
Steered singing that imperial Iseult home,
This maiden with her sinless sixteen years
Full of sweet thoughts and hopes that played at fears
Cast her eyes on him but in courteous wise,
And lo, the man's face burned upon her eyes
As though she had turned them on the naked sun:
And through her limbs she felt sweet passion run
As fire that flowed down from her face, and beat
Soft through stirred veins on even to her hands and feet

As all her body were one heart on flame,
Athrob with love and wonder and sweet shame.
And when he spake there sounded in her ears
As 'twere a song out of the graves of years
Heard, and again forgotten, and again
Remembered with a rapturous pulse of pain.
But as the maiden mountain snow sublime
Takes the first sense of April's trembling time
Soft on a brow that burns not though it blush
To feel the sunrise hardly half aflush,
So took her soul the sense of change, nor thought
That more than maiden love was more than nought.
Her eyes went hardly after him, her cheek
Grew scarce a goodlier flower to hear him speak,
Her bright mouth no more trembled than a rose
May for the least wind's breathless sake that blows
Too soft to sue save for a sister's kiss,
And if she sighed in sleep she knew not this.
Yet in her heart hovered the thoughts of things
Past, that with lighter or with heavier wings
Beat round about her memory, till it burned
With grief that brightened and with hope that yearned,
Seeing him so great and sad, nor knowing what fate
Had bowed and crowned a head so sad and great.
Nor might she guess but little, first or last,
Though all her heart so hung upon his past,
Of what so bowed him for what sorrow's sake:
For scarce of aught at any time he spake
That from his own land oversea had sent
His lordly life to barren banishment.
Yet still or soft or keen remembrance clung
Close round her of the least word from his tongue
That fell by chance of courtesy, to greet
With grace of tender thanks her pity, sweet
As running streams to men's way-wearied feet.
And when between strange words her name would fall,
Suddenly straightway to that lure's recall
Back would his heart bound as the falconer's bird,
And tremble and bow down before the word.
"Iseult" — and all the cloudlike world grew flame,
And all his heart flashed lightning at her name;
"Iseult" — and all the wan waste weary skies
Shone as his queen's own love-enkindled eyes.

And seeing the bright blood in his face leap up
As red wine mantling in a royal cup
To hear the sudden sweetness of the sound
Ring, but ere well his heart had time to bound
His cheek would change, and grief bow down his head,
"Haply," the girl's heart, though she spake not, said,
"This name of mine was worn of one long dead,
Some sister that he loved:" and therewithal
Would pity bring her heart more deep in thrall.
But once, when winds about the world made mirth,
And March held revel hard on April's birth
Till air and sea were jubilant as earth,
Delight and doubt in sense and soul began,
And yearning of the maiden toward the man,
Harping on high before her: for his word
Was fire that kindled in her heart that heard,
And alway through the rhymes reverberate came
The virginal soft burden of her name.
And ere the full song failed upon her ear
Joy strove within her till it cast out fear,
And all her heart was as his harp, and rang
Swift music, made of hope whose birthnote sprang
Bright in the blood that kindled as he sang.

"Stars know not how we call them, nor may flowers
Know by what happy name the hovering hours
  Baptize their new-born heads with dew and flame:
And Love, adored of all time as of ours,
  Iseult, knew nought for ages of his name.

"With many tongues men called on him, but he
Wist not which word of all might worthiest be
  To sound for ever in his ear the same,
Till heart of man might hear and soul might see,
  Iseult, the radiance ringing from thy name.

"By many names men called him, as the night
By many a name calls many a starry light,
  Her several sovereigns of dividual fame;
But day by one name only calls aright,
  Iseult, the sun that bids men praise his name.

"In many a name of man his name soared high
And song shone round it soaring, till the sky
  Rang rapture, and the world's fast-founded frame

Trembled with sense of triumph, even as I,
   Iseult, with sense of worship at thy name.

"In many a name of woman smiled his power
Incarnate, as all summer in a flower,
   Till winter bring forgetfulness or shame:
But thine, the keystone of his topless tower,
   Iseult, is one with Love's own lordliest name.

"Iseult my love, Iseult my queen twice crowned,
In thee my death, in thee my life lies bound:
   Names are there yet that all men's hearts acclaim,
But Love's own heart rings answer to the sound,
   Iseult, that bids it bow before thy name."

There ceased his voice yearning upon the word,
Struck with strong passion dumb: but she that heard
Quailed to the heart, and trembled ere her eyes
Durst let the loving light within them rise,
And yearn on his for answer: yet at last,
Albeit not all her fear was overpast,
Hope, kindling even the frost of fear apace
With sweet fleet bloom and breath of gradual grace,
Flushed in the changing roses of her face.
And ere the strife took truce of white with red,
Or joy for soft shame's sake durst lift up head,
Something she would and would not fain have said,
And wist not what the fluttering word would be,
But rose and reached forth to him her hand: and he,
Heart-stricken, bowed his head and dropped his knee,
And on her fragrant hand his lips were fire;
And their two hearts were as one trembling lyre
Touched by the keen wind's kiss with brief desire
And music shuddering at its own delight.
So dawned the moonrise of their marriage night.

## IV

## THE MAIDEN MARRIAGE

Spring watched her last moon burn and fade with May
While the days deepened toward a bridal day.
And on her snowbright hand the ring was set
While in the maiden's ear the song's word yet
Hovered, that hailed as love's own queen by name

Iseult: and in her heart the word was flame;
A pulse of light, a breath of tender fire,
Too dear for doubt, too driftless for desire.
Between her father's hand and brother's led
From hall to shrine, from shrine to marriage-bed,
She saw not how by hap at home-coming
Fell from her new lord's hand a royal ring,
Whereon he looked, and felt the pulse astart
Speak passion in his faith-forsaken heart.
For this was given him of the hand wherein
That heart's pledge lay for ever: so the sin
That should be done if truly he should take
This maid to wife for strange love's faithless sake
Struck all his mounting spirit abashed, and fear
Fell cold for shame's sake on his changing cheer.
Yea, shame's own fire that burned upon his brow
To bear the brand there of a broken vow
Was frozen again for very fear thereof
That wrung his heart with keener pangs than love.
And all things rose upon him, all things past
Ere last they parted, cloven in twain at last,
Iseult from Tristram, Tristram from the queen;
And how men found them in the wild woods green
Sleeping, but sundered by the sword between,
Dividing breast from amorous breast a span,
But scarce in heart the woman from the man
As far as hope from joy or sleep from truth,
And Mark that saw them held for sacred sooth
These were no fleshly lovers, by that sign
That severed them, still slumbering; so divine
He deemed it: how at waking they beheld
The king's folk round the king, and uncompelled
Were fain to follow and fare among them home
Back to the towers washed round with rolling foam
And storied halls wherethrough sea-music rang:
And how report thereafter swelled and sprang,
A full-mouthed serpent, hissing in men's ears
Word of their loves: and one of all his peers
That most he trusted, being his kinsman born,
A man base-moulded for the stamp of scorn,
Whose heart with hate was keen and cold and dark,
Gave note by midnight whisper to King Mark
Where he might take them sleeping; how ere day

Had seen the grim next morning all away
Fast bound they brought him down a weary way
With forty knights about him, and their chief
That traitor who for trust had given him grief,
To the old hoar chapel, like a strait stone tomb
Sheer on the sea-rocks, there to take his doom:
How, seeing he needs must die, he bade them yet
Bethink them if they durst for shame forget
What deeds for Cornwall had he done, and wrought
For all their sake what rescue, when he fought
Against the fierce foul Irish foe that came
To take of them for tribute in their shame
Three hundred heads of children; whom in fight
His hand redeeming slew Moraunt the knight
That none durst lift his eyes against, not one
Had heart but he, who now had help of none,
To take the battle; whence great shame it were
To knighthood, yea, foul shame on all men there,
To see him die so shamefully: nor durst
One man look up, nor one make answer first,
Save even the very traitor, who defied
And would have slain him naked in his pride,
But he, that saw the sword plucked forth to slay,
Looked on his hands, and wrenched their bonds away,
Haling those twain that he went bound between
Suddenly to him, and kindling in his mien
Shone lion-fashion forth with eyes alight,
And lion-wise leapt on that kinsman knight
And wrung forth of his felon hands with might
The sword that should have slain him weaponless,
And smote him sheer down: then came all the press
All raging in upon him; but he wrought
So well for his deliverance as they fought
That ten strong knights rejoicingly he slew,
And took no wound, nor wearied: then the crew
Waxed greater, and their cry on him; but he
Had won the chapel now above the sea
That chafed right under: then the heart in him
Sprang, seeing the low cliff clear to leap, and swim
Right out by the old blithe way the sea-mew takes
Across the bounding billow-belt that breaks
For ever, but the loud bright chain it makes
To bind the bridal bosom of the land

Time shall unlink not ever, till his hand
Fall by its own last blow dead: thence again
Might he win forth into the green great main
Far on beyond, and there yield up his breath
At least, with God's will, by no shameful death,
Or haply save himself, and come anew
Some long day later, ere sweet life were through.
And as the sea-gull hovers high, and turns
With eyes wherein the keen heart glittering yearns
Down toward the sweet green sea whereon the broad noon burns,
And suddenly, soul-stricken with delight,
Drops, and the glad wave gladdens, and the light
Sees wing and wave confuse their fluttering white,
So Tristram one brief breathing-space apart
Hung, and gazed down; then with exulting heart
Plunged: and the fleet foam round a joyous head
Flashed, that shot under, and ere a shaft had sped
Rose again radiant, a rejoicing star,
And high along the water-ways afar
Triumphed: and all they deemed he needs must die;
But Gouvernayle his squire, that watched hard by,
Sought where perchance a man might win ashore,
Striving, with strong limbs labouring long and sore,
And there abode an hour: till as from fight
Crowned with hard conquest won by mastering might,
Hardly, but happier for the imperious toil,
Swam the knight in forth of the close waves' coil,
Sea-satiate, bruised with buffets of the brine,
Laughing, and flushed as one afire with wine:
All this came hard upon him in a breath;
And how he marvelled in his heart that death
Should be no bitterer than it seemed to be
There, in the strenuous impulse of the sea
Borne as to battle deathward: and at last
How all his after seasons overpast
Had brought him darkling to this dark sweet hour,
Where his foot faltered nigh the bridal bower.
And harder seemed the passage now to pass,
Though smoother-seeming than the still sea's glass,
More fit for very manhood's heart to fear,
Than all straits past of peril. Hardly here
Might aught of all things hearten him save one,
Faith: and as men's eyes quail before the sun

So quailed his heart before the star whose light
Put out the torches of his bridal night,
So quailed and shrank with sense of faith's keen star
That burned as fire beheld by night afar
Deep in the darkness of his dreams; for all
The bride-house now seemed hung with heavier pall
Than clothes the house of mourning. Yet at last,
Soul-sick with trembling at the heart, he passed
Into the sweet light of the maiden bower
Where lay the lonely lily-featured flower
That, lying within his hand to gather, yet
Might not be gathered of it. Fierce regret
And bitter loyalty strove hard at strife
With amorous pity toward the tender wife
That wife indeed might never be, to wear
The very crown of wedlock; never bear
Children, to watch and worship her white hair
When time should change, with hand more soft than snow,
The fashion of its glory; never know
The loveliness of laughing love that lives
On little lips of children: all that gives
Glory and grace and reverence and delight
To wedded woman by her bridal right,
All praise and pride that flowers too fair to fall,
Love that should give had stripped her of them all
And left her bare for ever. So his thought
Consumed him, as a fire within that wrought
Visibly, ravening till its wrath were spent:
So pale he stood, so bowed and passion-rent,
Before the blithe-faced bride-folk, ere he went
Within the chamber, heavy-eyed: and there
Gleamed the white hands and glowed the glimmering hair
That might but move his memory more of one more fair,
More fair than all this beauty: but in sooth
So fair she too shone in her flower of youth
That scarcely might man's heart hold fast its truth,
Though strong, who gazed upon her: for her eyes
Were emerald-soft as evening-coloured skies,
And a smile in them like the light therein
Slept, or shone out in joy that knew not sin,
Clear as a child's own laughter: and her mouth,
Albeit no rose full-hearted from the south
And passion-coloured for the perfect kiss

That signs the soul for love and stamps it his,
Was soft and bright as any bud new-blown;
And through her cheek the gentler lifebloom shone
Of mild wild roses nigh the northward sea.
So in her bride-bed lay the bride: and he
Drew nigh, and all the high sad heart in him
Yearned on her, seeing the twilight meek and dim
Through all the soft alcove tremblingly lit
With hovering silver, as a heart in it
Beating, that burned from one deep lamp above,
Fainter than fire of torches, as the love
Within him fainter than a bridegroom's fire,
No marriage-torch red with the heart's desire,
But silver-soft, a flameless light that glowed
Starlike along night's dark and starry road
Wherein his soul was traveller. And he sighed,
Seeing, and with eyes set sadly toward his bride
Laid him down by her, and spake not: but within
His heart spake, saying how sore should be the sin
To break toward her, that of all womankind
Was faithfullest, faith plighted, or unbind
The bond first linked between them when they drank
The love-draught: and his quick blood sprang and sank,
Remembering in the pulse of all his veins
That red swift rapture, all its fiery pains
And all its fierier pleasures: and he spake
Aloud, one burning word for love's keen sake—
"Iseult;" and full of love and lovelier fear
A virgin voice gave answer—"I am here."
And a pang rent his heart at root: but still,
For spirit and flesh were vassals to his will,
Strong faith held mastery on them: and the breath
Felt on his face did not his will to death,
Nor glance nor lute-like voice nor flower-soft touch
Might so prevail upon it overmuch
That constancy might less prevail than they,
For all he looked and loved her as she lay
Smiling; and soft as bird alights on bough
He kissed her maiden mouth and blameless brow,
Once, and again his heart within him sighed:
But all his young blood's yearning toward his bride,
How hard soe'er it held his life awake
For passion, and sweet nature's unforbidden sake,

And will that strove unwillingly with will it might not break,
Fell silent as a wind abashed, whose breath
Dies out of heaven, suddenly done to death,
When in between them on the dumb dusk air
Floated the bright shade of a face more fair
Than hers that hard beside him shrank and smiled
And wist of all no more than might a child.
So had she all her heart's will, all she would,
For love's sake that sufficed her, glad and good,
All night safe sleeping in her maidenhood.

## V

## ISEULT AT TINTAGEL

But that same night in Cornwall oversea
Couched at Queen Iseult's hand, against her knee,
With keen kind eyes that read her whole heart's pain
Fast at wide watch lay Tristram's hound Hodain,
The goodliest and the mightiest born on earth,
That many a forest day of fiery mirth
Had plied his craft before them; and the queen
Cherished him, even for those dim years between,
More than of old in those bright months far flown
When ere a blast of Tristram's horn was blown
Each morning as the woods rekindled, ere
Day gat full empire of the glimmering air,
Delight of dawn would quicken him, and fire
Spring and pant in his breath with bright desire
To be among the dewy ways on quest:
But now perforce at restless-hearted rest
He chafed through days more barren than the sand,
Soothed hardly but soothed only with her hand,
Though fain to fawn thereon and follow, still
With all his heart and all his loving will
Desiring one divided from his sight,
For whose lost sake dawn was as dawn of night
And noon as night's noon in his eyes was dark.
But in the halls far under sat King Mark,
Feasting, and full of cheer, with heart uplift,
As on the night that harper gat his gift:
And music revelled on the fitful air,
And songs came floated up the festal stair,

And muffled roar of wassail, where the king
Took heart from wine-cups and the quiring string
Till all his cold thin veins rejoiced and ran
Strong as with lifeblood of a kinglier man.
But the queen shut from sound her wearied ears,
Shut her sad eyes from sense of aught save tears,
And wrung her hair with soft fierce hands, and prayed:
"O God, God born of woman, of a maid,
Christ, once in flesh of thine own fashion clad;
O very love, so glad in heaven and sad
On earth for earth's sake alway; since thou art
Pure only, I only impure of spirit and heart,
Since thou for sin's sake and the bitter doom
Didst as a veil put on a virgin's womb,
I that am none, and cannot hear or see
Or shadow or likeness or a sound of thee
Far off, albeit with man's own speech and face
Thou shine yet and thou speak yet, showing forth grace—
Ah me! grace only shed on souls that are
Lit and led forth of shadow by thy star—
Alas! to these men only grace, to these,
Lord, whom thy love draws Godward, to thy knees—
I, can I draw thee me-ward, can I seek,
Who love thee not, to love me? seeing how weak,
Lord, all this little love I bear thee is,
And how much is my strong love more than this,
My love that I love man with, that I bear
Him sinning through me sinning? wilt thou care,
God, for this love, if love be any, alas,
In me to give thee, though long since there was,
How long, when I too, Lord, was clean, even I,
That now am unclean till the day I die—
Haply by burning, harlot-fashion, made
A horror in all hearts of wife and maid,
Hateful, not knowing if ever in these mine eyes
Shone any light of thine in any wise
Or this were love at all that I bore thee?"
And the night spake, and thundered on the sea,
Ravening aloud for ruin of lives: and all
The bastions of the main cliff's northward wall
Rang response out from all their deepening length,
As the east wind girded up his godlike strength
And hurled in hard against that high-towered hold

The fleeces of the flock that knows no fold,
The rent white shreds of shattering storm: but she
Heard not nor heeded wind or storming sea,
Knew not if night were mild or mad with wind.
"Yea, though deep lips and tender hair be thinned,
Though cheek wither, brow fade, and bosom wane,
Shall I change also from this heart again
To maidenhood of heart and holiness?
Shall I more love thee, Lord, or love him less—
Ah miserable! though spirit and heart be rent,
Shall I repent, Lord God? shall I repent?
Nay, though thou slay me! for herein I am blest,
That as I loved him yet I love him best—
More than mine own soul or thy love or thee,
Though thy love save and my love save not me.
Blest am I beyond women even herein,
That beyond all born women is my sin,
And perfect my transgression: that above
All offerings of all others is my love,
Who have chosen it only, and put away for this
Thee, and my soul's hope, Saviour, of the kiss
Wherewith thy lips make welcome all thine own
When in them life and death are overthrown;
The sinless lips that seal the death of sin,
The kiss wherewith their dumb lips touched begin
Singing in heaven.
"Where we shall never, love,
Never stand up nor sing! for God above
Knows us, how too much more than God to me
Thy sweet love is, my poor love is to thee!
Dear, dost thou see now, dost thou hear to-night,
Sleeping, my waste wild speech, my face worn white,
—Speech once heard soft by thee, face once kissed red!—
In such a dream as when men see their dead
And know not if they know if dead these be?
Ah love, are thy days my days, and to thee
Are all nights like as my nights? does the sun
Grieve thee? art thou soul-sick till day be done,
And weary till day rises? is thine heart
Full of dead things as mine is? Nay, thou art
Man, with man's strength and praise and pride of life,
No bondwoman, no queen, no loveless wife

That would be shamed albeit she had not sinned."
And swordlike was the sound of the iron wind,
And as a breaking battle was the sea.
"Nay, Lord, I pray thee let him love not me,
Love me not any more, nor like me die,
And be no more than such a thing as I.
Turn his heart from me, lest my love too lose
Thee as I lose thee, and his fair soul refuse
For my sake thy fair heaven, and as I fell
Fall, and be mixed with my soul and with hell.
Let me die rather, and only; let me be
Hated of him so he be loved of thee,
Lord: for I would not have him with me there
Out of thy light and love in the unlit air,
Out of thy sight in the unseen hell where I
Go gladly, going alone, so thou on high
Lift up his soul and love him—Ah, Lord, Lord,
Shalt thou love as I love him? she that poured
From the alabaster broken at thy feet
An ointment very precious, not so sweet
As that poured likewise forth before thee then
From the rehallowed heart of Magdalen,
From a heart broken, yearning like the dove,
An ointment very precious which is love—
Couldst thou being holy and God, and sinful she,
Love her indeed as surely she loved thee?
Nay, but if not, then as we sinners can
Let us love still in the old sad wise of man.
For with less love than my love, having had
Mine, though God love him he shall not be glad.
And with such love as my love, I wot well,
He shall not lie disconsolate in hell:
Sad only as souls for utter love's sake be
Here, and a little sad, perchance, for me—
Me happy, me more glad than God above,
In the utmost hell whose fires consume not love!
For in the waste ways emptied of the sun
He would say—'Dear, thy place is void, and one
Weeps among angels for thee, with his face
Veiled, saying, O sister, how thy chosen place
Stands desolate, that God made fair for thee!
Is heaven not sweeter, and we thy brethren, we
Fairer than love on earth and life in hell?'

And I — with me were all things then not well?
Should I not answer — 'O love, be well content;
Look on me, and behold if I repent.'
This were more to me than an angel's wings.
Yea, many men pray God for many things,
But I pray that this only thing may be."
   And as a full field charging was the sea,
And as the cry of slain men was the wind.
   "Yea, since I surely loved him, and he sinned
Surely, though not as my sin his be black,
God, give him to me — God, God, give him back!
For now how should we live in twain or die?
I am he indeed, thou knowest, and he is I.
Not man and woman several as we were,
But one thing with one life and death to bear.
How should one love his own soul overmuch?
And time is long since last I felt the touch,
The sweet touch of my lover, hand and breath,
In such delight as puts delight to death,
Burn my soul through, till spirit and soul and sense,
In the sharp grasp of the hour, with violence
Died, and again through pangs of violent birth
Lived, and laughed out with refluent might of mirth;
Laughed each on other and shuddered into one,
As a cloud shuddering dies into the sun.
Ah, sense is that or spirit, soul or flesh,
That only love lulls or awakes afresh?
Ah, sweet is that or bitter, evil or good,
That very love allays not as he would?
Nay, truth is this or vanity, that gives
No love assurance when love dies or lives?
This that my spirit is wrung withal, and yet
No surelier knows if haply thine forget,
Thou that my spirit is wrung for, nor can say
Love is not in thee dead as yesterday?
Dost thou feel, thou, this heartbeat whence my heart
Would send thee word what life is mine apart,
And know by keen response what life is thine?
Dost thou not hear one cry of all of mine?
O Tristram's heart, have I no part in thee?"
   And all her soul was as the breaking sea,
And all her heart anhungered as the wind.
   "Dost thou repent thee of the sin we sinned?

Dost thou repent thee of the days and nights
That kindled and that quenched for us their lights,
The months that feasted us with all their hours,
The ways that breathed of us in all their flowers,
The dells that sang of us with all their doves?
Dost thou repent thee of the wildwood loves?
Is thine heart changed, and hallowed? art thou grown
God's, and not mine? Yet, though my heart make moan,
Fain would my soul give thanks for thine, if thou
Be saved—yea, fain praise God, and knows not how.
How should it know thanksgiving? nay, or learn
Aught of the love wherewith thine own should burn,
God's, that should cast out as an evil thing
Mine? yea, what hand of prayer have I to cling,
What heart to prophesy, what spirit of sight
To strain insensual eyes toward increate light,
Who look but back on life wherein I sinned?"
  And all their past came wailing in the wind,
And all their future thundered in the sea.
  "But if my soul might touch the time to be,
If hand might handle now or eye behold
My life and death ordained me from of old,
Life palpable, compact of blood and breath,
Visible, present, naked, very death,
Should I desire to know before the day
These that I know not, nor is man that may?
For haply, seeing, my heart would break for fear,
And my soul timeless cast its load off here,
Its load of life too bitter, love too sweet,
And fall down shamed and naked at thy feet,
God, who wouldst take no pity of it, nor give
One hour back, one of all its hours to live
Clothed with my mortal body, that once more,
Once, on this reach of barren beaten shore,
This stormy strand of life, ere sail were set,
Had haply felt love's arms about it yet—
Yea, ere death's bark put off to seaward, might
With many a grief have bought me one delight
That then should know me never. Ah, what years
Would I endure not, filled up full with tears,
Bitter like blood and dark as dread of death,
To win one amorous hour of mingling breath,
One fire-eyed hour and sunnier than the sun,

For all these nights and days like nights but one?
One hour of heaven born once, a stormless birth,
For all these windy weary hours of earth?
One, but one hour from birth of joy to death,
For all these hungering hours of feverish breath?
And I should lose this, having died and sinned."
  And as man's anguish clamouring cried the wind,
And as God's anger answering rang the sea.
  "And yet what life — Lord God, what life for me
Has thy strong wrath made ready? Dost thou think
How lips whose thirst hath only tears to drink
Grow grey for grief untimely? Dost thou know,
O happy God, how men wax weary of woe —
Yea, for their wrong's sake that thine hand hath done
Come even to hate thy semblance in the sun?
Turn back from dawn and noon and all thy light
To make their souls one with the soul of night?
Christ, if thou hear yet or have eyes to see,
Thou that hadst pity, and hast no pity on me,
Know'st thou no more, as in this life's sharp span,
What pain thou hadst on earth, what pain hath man?
Hast thou no care, that all we suffer yet?
What help is ours of thee if thou forget?
What profit have we though thy blood were given,
If we that sin bleed and be not forgiven?
Not love but hate, thou bitter God and strange,
Whose heart as man's heart hath grown cold with change,
Not love but hate thou showest us that have sinned."
  And like a world's cry shuddering was the wind,
And like a God's voice threatening was the sea.
  O "Nay, Lord, for thou wast gracious; nay, in thee
No change can come with time or varying fate,
No tongue bid thine be less compassionate,
No sterner eye rebuke for mercy thine,
No sin put out thy pity — no, not mine.
Thou knowest us, Lord, thou knowest us, all we are,
He, and the soul that hath his soul for star:
Thou knowest as I know, Lord, how much more worth
Than all souls clad and clasped about with earth,
But most of all, God, how much more than I,
Is this man's soul that surely shall not die.
What righteousness, what judgment, Lord most high,
Were this, to bend a brow of doom as grim

As threats me, me the adulterous wife, on him?
There lies none other nightly by his side:
He hath not sought, he shall not seek a bride.
Far as God sunders earth from heaven above,
So far was my love born beneath his love.
I loved him as the sea-wind loves the sea,
To rend and ruin it only and waste: but he,
As the sea loves a sea-bird loved he me,
To foster and uphold my tired life's wing,
And bounteously beneath me spread forth spring,
A springtide space whereon to float or fly,
A world of happy water, whence the sky
Glowed goodlier, lightening from so glad a glass,
Than with its own light only. Now, alas!
Cloud hath come down and clothed it round with storm,
And gusts and fits of eddying winds deform
The feature of its glory. Yet be thou,
God, merciful: nay, show but justice now,
And let the sin in him that scarce was his
Stand expiated with exile: and be this
The price for him, the atonement this, that I
With all the sin upon me live, and die
With all thy wrath on me that most have sinned."
   And like man's heart relenting sighed the wind,
And as God's wrath subsiding sank the sea.
   "But if such grace be possible — if it be
Not sin more strange than all sins past, and worse
Evil, that cries upon thee for a curse,
To pray such prayers from such a heart, do thou
Hear, and make wide thine hearing toward me now;
Let not my soul and his for ever dwell
Sundered: though doom keep always heaven and hell
Irreconcilable, infinitely apart,
Keep not in twain for ever heart and heart
That once, albeit by not thy law, were one;
Let this be not thy will, that this be done.
Let all else, all thou wilt of evil, be,
But no doom, none, dividing him and me."
   By this was heaven stirred eastward, and there came
Up the rough ripple a labouring light like flame;
And dawn, sore trembling still and grey with fear,
Looked hardly forth, a face of heavier cheer
Than one which grief or dread yet half enshrouds,

Wild-eyed and wan, across the cleaving clouds.
And Iseult, worn with watch long held on pain,
Turned, and her eye lit on the hound Hodain,
And all her heart went out in tears: and he
Laid his kind head along her bended knee,
Till round his neck her arms went hard, and all
The night past from her as a chain might fall:
But yet the heart within her, half undone,
Wailed, and was loth to let her see the sun.
  And ere full day brought heaven and earth to flower,
Far thence, a maiden in a marriage bower,
That moment, hard by Tristram, oversea,
Woke with glad eyes Iseult of Brittany.

## VI

## JOYOUS GARD

A little time, O Love, a little light,
A little hour for ease before the night.
Sweet Love, that art so bitter; foolish Love,
Whom wise men know for wiser, and thy dove
More subtle than the serpent; for thy sake
These pray thee for a little beam to break,
A little grace to help them, lest men think
Thy servants have but hours like tears to drink.
O Love, a little comfort, lest they fear
To serve as these have served thee who stand here.
  For these are thine, thy servants these, that stand
Here nigh the limit of the wild north land,
At margin of the grey great eastern sea,
Dense-islanded with peaks and reefs, that see
No life but of the fleet wings fair and free
Which cleave the mist and sunlight all day long
With sleepless flight and cries more glad than song.
Strange ways of life have led them hither, here
To win fleet respite from desire and fear
With armistice from sorrow; strange and sweet
Ways trodden by forlorn and casual feet
Till kindlier chance woke toward them kindly will
In happier hearts of lovers, and their ill
Found rest, as healing surely might it not,
By gift and kingly grace of Launcelot

At gracious bidding given of Guenevere.
For in the trembling twilight of this year
Ere April sprang from hope to certitude
Two hearts of friends fast linked had fallen at feud
As they rode forth on hawking, by the sign
Which gave his new bride's brother Ganhardine
To know the truth of Tristram's dealing, how
Faith kept of him against his marriage vow
Kept virginal his bride-bed night and morn;
Whereat, as wroth his blood should suffer scorn,
Came Ganhardine to Tristram, saying, "Behold,
We have loved thee, and for love we have shown of old
Scorn hast thou shown us: wherefore is thy bride
Not thine indeed, a stranger at thy side,
Contemned? what evil hath she done, to be
Mocked with mouth-marriage and despised of thee,
Shamed, set at nought, rejected?" But there came
On Tristram's brow and eye the shadow and flame
Confused of wrath and wonder, ere he spake,
Saying, "Hath she bid thee for thy sister's sake
Plead with me, who believed of her in heart
More nobly than to deem such piteous part
Should find so fair a player? or whence hast thou
Of us this knowledge?" "Nay," said he, "but now,
Riding beneath these whitethorns overhead,
There fell a flower into her girdlestead
Which laughing she shook out, and smiling said—
'Lo, what large leave the wind hath given this stray,
To lie more near my heart than till this day
Aught ever since my mother lulled me lay
Or even my lord came ever;' whence I wot
We are all thy scorn, a race regarded not
Nor held as worth communion of thine own,
Except in her be found some fault alone
To blemish our alliance." Then replied
Tristram, "Nor blame nor scorn may touch my bride,
Albeit unknown of love she live, and be
Worth a man worthier than her love thought me.
Faith only, faith withheld me, faith forbade
The blameless grace wherewith love's grace makes glad
All lives linked else in wedlock; not that less
I loved the sweet light of her loveliness,

But that my love toward faith was more: and thou,
Albeit thine heart be keen against me now,
Couldst thou behold my very lady, then
No more of thee than of all other men
Should this my faith be held a faithless fault."
And ere that day their hawking came to halt,
Being sore of him entreated for a sign,
He sware to bring his brother Ganhardine
To sight of that strange Iseult: and thereon
Forth soon for Cornwall are these brethren gone,
Even to that royal pleasance where the hunt
Rang ever of old with Tristram's horn in front
Blithe as the queen's horse bounded at his side:
And first of all her dames forth pranced in pride
That day before them, with a ringing rein
All golden-glad, the king's false bride Brangwain,
The queen's true handmaid ever: and on her
Glancing, "Be called for all time truth-teller,
O Tristram, of all true men's tongues alive,"
Quoth Ganhardine; "for may my soul so thrive
As yet mine eye drank never sight like this."
"Ay?" Tristram said, "and she thou look'st on is
So great in grace of goodliness, that thou
Hast less thought left of wrath against me now,
Seeing but my lady's handmaid? Nay, behold;
See'st thou no light more golden than of gold
Shine where she moves in midst of all, above
All, past all price or praise or prayer of love?
Lo, this is she." But as one mazed with wine
Stood, stunned in spirit and stricken, Ganhardine,
And gazed out hard against them: and his heart
As with a sword was cloven, and rent apart
As with strong fangs of fire; and scarce he spake,
Saying how his life for even a handmaid's sake
Was made a flame within him. And the knight
Bade him, being known of none that stood in sight,
Bear to Brangwain his ring, that she unseen
Might give in token privily to the queen
And send swift word where under moon or sun
They twain might yet be no more twain but one.
And that same night, under the stars that rolled
Over their warm deep wildwood nights of old
Whose hours for grains of sand shed sparks of fire,
Such way was made anew for their desire

By secret wile of sickness feigned, to keep
The king far off her vigils or her sleep,
That in the queen's pavilion midway set
By glimmering moondawn were those lovers met,
And Ganhardine of Brangwain gat him grace.
And in some passionate soft interspace
Between two swells of passion, when their lips
Breathed, and made room for such brief speech as slips
From tongues athirst with draughts of amorous wine
That leaves them thirstier than the salt sea's brine,
Was counsel taken how to fly, and where
Find covert from the wild world's ravening air
That hunts with storm the feet of nights and days
Through strange thwart lines of life and flowerless ways.
Then said Iseult: "Lo, now the chance is here
Foreshown me late by word of Guenevere,
To give me comfort of thy rumoured wrong,
My traitor Tristram, when report was strong
Of me forsaken and thine heart estranged:
Nor should her sweet soul toward me yet be changed
Nor all her love lie barren, if mine hand
Crave harvest of it from the flowering land.
See therefore if this counsel please thee not,
That we take horse in haste for Camelot
And seek that friendship of her plighted troth
Which love shall be full fain to lend, nor loth
Shall my love be to take it." So next night
The multitudinous stars laughed round their flight,
Fulfilling far with laughter made of light
The encircling deeps of heaven: and in brief space
At Camelot their long love gat them grace
Of those fair twain whose heads men's praise impearled
As love's two lordliest lovers in the world:
And thence as guests for harbourage past they forth
To win this noblest hold of all the north.
Far by wild ways and many days they rode,
Till clear across June's kingliest sunset glowed
The great round girth of goodly wall that showed
Where for one clear sweet season's length should be
Their place of strength to rest in, fain and free,
By the utmost margin of the loud lone sea.
　And now, O Love, what comfort? God most high,
Whose life is as a flower's to live and die,
Whose light is everlasting: Lord, whose breath

Speaks music through the deathless lips of death
Whereto time's heart rings answer: Bard, whom time
Hears, and is vanquished with a wandering rhyme
That once thy lips made fragrant: Seer, whose sooth
Joy knows not well, but sorrow knows for truth,
Being priestess of thy soothsayings: Love, what grace
Shall these twain find at last before thy face?
This many a year they have served thee, and deserved,
If ever man might yet of all that served,
Since the first heartbeat bade the first man's knee
Bend, and his mouth take music, praising thee,
Some comfort; and some honey indeed of thine
Thou hast mixed for these with life's most bitter wine,
Commending to their passionate lips a draught
No deadlier than thy chosen of old have quaffed
And blessed thine hand, their cupbearer's: for not
On all men comes the grace that seals their lot
As holier in thy sight, for all these feuds
That rend it, than the light-souled multitude's,
Nor thwarted of thine hand nor blessed; but these
Shall see no twilight, Love, nor fade at ease,
Grey-grown and careless of desired delight,
But lie down tired and sleep before the night.
These shall not live till time or change may chill
Or doubt divide or shame subdue their will,
Or fear or slow repentance work them wrong,
Or love die first: these shall not live so long.
Death shall not take them drained of dear true life
Already, sick or stagnant from the strife,
Quenched: not with dry-drawn veins and lingering breath
Shall these through crumbling hours crouch down to death.
Swift, with one strong clean leap, ere life's pulse tire,
Most like the leap of lions or of fire,
Sheer death shall bound upon them: one pang past,
The first keen sense of him shall be their last,
Their last shall be no sense of any fear,
More than their life had sense of anguish here.
Weeks and light months had fled at swallow's speed
Since here their first hour sowed for them the seed
Of many sweet as rest or hope could be;
Since on the blown beach of a glad new sea
Wherein strange rocks like fighting men stand scarred
They saw the strength and help of Joyous Gard.

Within the full deep glorious tower that stands
Between the wild sea and the broad wild lands
Love led and gave them quiet: and they drew
Life like a God's life in each wind that blew,
And took their rest, and triumphed. Day by day
The mighty moorlands and the sea-walls grey,
The brown bright waters of green fells that sing
One song to rocks and flowers and birds on wing,
Beheld the joy and glory that they had,
Passing, and how the whole world made them glad,
And their great love was mixed with all things great,
As life being lovely, and yet being strong like fate.
For when the sun sprang on the sudden sea
Their eyes sprang eastward, and the day to be
Was lit in them untimely: such delight
They took yet of the clear cold breath and light
That goes before the morning, and such grace
Was deathless in them through their whole life's space
As dies in many with their dawn that dies
And leaves in pulseless hearts and flameless eyes
No light to lighten and no tear to weep
For youth's high joy that time has cast on sleep.
Yea, this old grace and height of joy they had,
To lose no jot of all that made them glad
And filled their springs of spirit with such fire
That all delight fed in them all desire;
And no whit less than in their first keen prime
The spring's breath blew through all their summer time,
And in their skies would sunlike Love confuse
Clear April colours with hot August hues,
And in their hearts one light of sun and moon
Reigned, and the morning died not of the noon:
Such might of life was in them, and so high
Their heart of love rose higher than fate could fly.
And many a large delight of hawk and hound
The great glad land that knows no bourne or bound,
Save the wind's own and the outer sea-bank's, gave
Their days for comfort; many a long blithe wave
Buoyed their blithe bark between the bare bald rocks,
Deep, steep, and still, save for the swift free flocks
Unshepherded, uncompassed, unconfined,
That when blown foam keeps all the loud air blind
Mix with the wind's their triumph, and partake

The joy of blasts that ravin, waves that break,
All round and all below their mustering wings,
A clanging cloud that round the cliff's edge clings
On each bleak bluff breaking the strenuous tides
That rings reverberate mirth when storm bestrides
The subject night in thunder: many a noon
They took the moorland's or the bright sea's boon
With all their hearts into their spirit of sense,
Rejoicing, where the sudden dells grew dense
With sharp thick flight of hillside birds, or where
On some strait rock's ledge in the intense mute air
Erect against the cliff's sheer sunlit white
Blue as the clear north heaven, clothed warm with light,
Stood neck to bended neck and wing to wing
With heads fast hidden under, close as cling
Flowers on one flowering almond-branch in spring,
Three herons deep asleep against the sun,
Each with one bright foot downward poised, and one
Wing-hidden hard by the bright head, and all
Still as fair shapes fixed on some wondrous wall
Of minster-aisle or cloister-close or hall
To take even time's eye prisoner with delight.
Or, satisfied with joy of sound and sight,
They sat and communed of things past: what state
King Arthur, yet unwarred upon by fate,
Held high in hall at Camelot, like one
Whose lordly life was as the mounting sun
That climbs and pauses on the point of noon,
Sovereign: how royal rang the tourney's tune
Through Tristram's three days' triumph, spear to spear,
When Iseult shone enthroned by Guenevere,
Rose against rose, the highest adored on earth,
Imperial: yet with subtle notes of mirth
Would she bemock her praises, and bemoan
Her glory by that splendour overthrown
Which lightened from her sister's eyes elate;
Saying how by night a little light seems great,
But less than least of all things, very nought,
When dawn undoes the web that darkness wrought;
How like a tower of ivory well designed
By subtlest hand subserving subtlest mind,
Ivory with flower of rose incarnadined
And kindling with some God therein revealed,
A light for grief to look on and be healed,

Stood Guenevere: and all beholding her
Were heartstruck even as earth at midsummer
With burning wonder, hardly to be borne.
So was that amorous glorious lady born,
A fiery memory for all storied years:
Nor might men call her sisters crowned her peers,
Her sister queens, put all by her to scorn:
She had such eyes as are not made to mourn;
But in her own a gleaming ghost of tears
Shone, and their glance was slower than Guenevere's,
And fitfuller with fancies grown of grief;
Shamed as a Mayflower shames an autumn leaf
Full well she wist it could not choose but be
If in that other's eyeshot standing she
Should lift her looks up ever: wherewithal
Like fires whose light fills heaven with festival
Flamed her eyes full on Tristram's; and he laughed
Answering, "What wile of sweet child-hearted craft
That children forge for children, to beguile
Eyes known of them not witless of the wile
But fain to seem for sport's sake self-deceived,
Wilt thou find out now not to be believed?
Or how shall I trust more than ouphe or elf
Thy truth to me-ward, who beliest thyself?"
"Nor elf nor ouphe or aught of airier kind,"
Quoth she, "though made of moonbeams moist and blind,
Is light if weighed with man's winged weightless mind.
Though thou keep somewise troth with me, God wot,
When thou didst wed, I doubt, thou thoughtest not
So charily to keep it." "Nay," said he,
"Yet am not I rebukable by thee
As Launcelot, erring, held me ere he wist
No mouth save thine of mine was ever kissed
Save as a sister's only, since we twain
Drank first the draught assigned our lips to drain
That Fate and Love with darkling hands commixt
Poured, and no power to part them came betwixt,
But either's will, howbeit they seem at strife,
Was toward us one, as death itself and life
Are one sole doom toward all men, nor may one
Behold not darkness, who beholds the sun."
"Ah, then," she said, "what word is this men hear
Of Merlin, how some doom too strange to fear
Was cast but late about him oversea,

Sweet recreant, in thy bridal Brittany?
Is not his life sealed fast on him with sleep,
By witchcraft of his own and love's, to keep
Till earth be fire and ashes?"
"Surely," said
Her lover, "not as one alive or dead
The great good wizard, well beloved and well
Predestinate of heaven that casts out hell
For guerdon gentler far than all men's fate,
Exempt alone of all predestinate,
Takes his strange rest at heart of slumberland,
More deep asleep in green Broceliande
Than shipwrecked sleepers in the soft green sea
Beneath the weight of wandering waves: but he
Hath for those roofing waters overhead
Above him always all the summer spread
Or all the winter wailing: or the sweet
Late leaves marked red with autumn's burning feet,
Or withered with his weeping, round the seer
Rain, and he sees not, nor may heed or hear
The witness of the winter: but in spring
He hears above him all the winds on wing
Through the blue dawn between the brightening boughs,
And on shut eyes and slumber-smitten brows
Feels ambient change in the air and strengthening sun,
And knows the soul that was his soul at one
With the ardent world's, and in the spirit of earth
His spirit of life reborn to mightier birth
And mixed with things of elder life than ours;
With cries of birds, and kindling lamps of flowers,
And sweep and song of winds, and fruitful light
Of sunbeams, and the far faint breath of night,
And waves and woods at morning: and in all,
Soft as at noon the slow sea's rise and fall,
He hears in spirit a song that none but he
Hears from the mystic mouth of Nimue
Shed like a consecration; and his heart,
Hearing, is made for love's sake as a part
Of that far singing, and the life thereof
Part of that life that feeds the world with love:
Yea, heart in heart is molten, hers and his,
Into the world's heart and the soul that is
Beyond or sense or vision; and their breath
Stirs the soft springs of deathless life and death,

Death that bears life, and change that brings forth seed
Of life to death and death to life indeed,
As blood recircling through the unsounded veins
Of earth and heaven with all their joys and pains.
Ah, that when love shall laugh no more nor weep
We too, we too might hear that song and sleep!"
"Yea," said Iseult, "some joy it were to be
Lost in the sun's light and the all-girdling sea,
Mixed with the winds and woodlands, and to bear
Part in the large life of the quickening air,
And the sweet earth's, our mother: yet to pass
More fleet than mirrored faces from the glass
Out of all pain and all delight, so far
That love should seem but as the furthest star
Sunk deep in trembling heaven, scarce seen or known,
As a dead moon forgotten, once that shone
Where now the sun shines—nay, not all things yet,
Not all things always, dying, would I forget."
And Tristram answered amorously, and said:
"O heart that here art mine, O heavenliest head
That ever took men's worship here, which art
Mine, how shall death put out the fire at heart,
Quench in men's eyes the head's remembered light,
That time shall set but higher in more men's sight?
Think thou not much to die one earthly day,
Being made not in their mould who pass away
Nor who shall pass for ever."
"Ah," she said,
"What shall it profit me, being praised and dead?
What profit have the flowers of all men's praise?
What pleasure of our pleasure have the days
That pour on us delight of life and mirth?
What fruit of all our joy on earth has earth?
Nor am I—nay, my lover, am I one
To take such part in heaven's enkindling sun
And in the inviolate air and sacred sea
As clothes with grace that wondrous Nimue?
For all her works are bounties, all her deeds
Blessings; her days are scrolls wherein love reads
The record of his mercies; heaven above
Hath not more heavenly holiness of love
Than earth beneath, wherever pass or pause
Her feet that move not save by love's own laws,
In gentleness of godlike wayfaring

To heal men's hearts as earth is healed by spring
Of all such woes as winter: what am I,
Love, that have strength but to desire and die,
That have but grace to love and do thee wrong,
What am I that my name should live so long,
Save as the star that crossed thy star-struck lot,
With hers whose light was life to Launcelot?
Life gave she him, and strength, and fame to be
For ever: I, what gift can I give thee?
Peril and sleepless watches, fearful breath
Of dread more bitter for my sake than death
When death came nigh to call me by my name,
Exile, rebuke, remorse, and—O, not shame.
Shame only, this I gave thee not, whom none
May give that worst thing ever—no, not one.
Of all that hate, all hateful hearts that see
Darkness for light and hate where love should be,
None for my shame's sake may speak shame of thee."
  And Tristram answering ere he kissed her smiled:
"O very woman, god at once and child,
What ails thee to desire of me once more
The assurance that thou hadst in heart before?
For all this wild sweet waste of sweet vain breath,
Thou knowest I know thou hast given me life, not death.
The shadow of death, informed with shows of strife,
Was ere I won thee all I had of life.
Light war, light love, light living, dreams in sleep,
Joy slight and light, not glad enough to weep,
Filled up my foolish days with sound and shine,
Vision and gleam from strange men's cast on mine,
Reverberate light from eyes presaging thine
That shed but shadowy moonlight where thy face
Now sheds forth sunshine in the deep same place,
The deep live heart half dead and shallower then
Than summer fords which thwart not wandering men.
For how should I, signed sorrow's from my birth,
Kiss dumb the loud red laughing lips of mirth?
Or how, sealed thine to be, love less than heaven on earth?
My heart in me was held at restless rest,
Presageful of some prize beyond its quest,
Prophetic still with promise, fain to find the best.
For one was fond and one was blithe and one
Fairer than all save twain whose peers are none;

For third on earth is none that heaven hath seen
To stand with Guenevere beside my queen.
Not Nimue, girt with blessing as a guard:
Not the soft lures and laughters of Ettarde:
Not she, that splendour girdled round with gloom,
Crowned as with iron darkness of the tomb,
And clothed with clouding conscience of a monstrous doom,
Whose blind incestuous love brought forth a fire
To burn her ere it burn its darkling sire,
Her mother's son, King Arthur: yet but late
We saw pass by that fair live shadow of fate,
The queen Morgause of Orkney, like a dream
That scares the night when moon and starry beam
Sicken and swoon before some sorcerer's eyes
Whose wordless charms defile the saintly skies,
Bright still with fire and pulse of blood and breath,
Whom her own sons have doomed for shame to death."
"Death — yea," quoth she, "there is not said or heard
So oft aloud on earth so sure a word.
Death, and again death, and for each that saith
Ten tongues chime answer to the sound of death.
Good end God send us ever — so men pray.
But I — this end God send me, would I say,
To die not of division and a heart
Rent or with sword of severance cloven apart,
But only when thou diest and only where thou art,
O thou my soul and spirit and breath to me,
O light, life, love! yea, let this only be,
That dying I may praise God who gave me thee,
Let hap what will thereafter."
So that day
They communed, even till even was worn away,
Nor aught they said seemed strange or sad to say,
But sweet as night's dim dawn to weariness.
Nor loved they life or love for death's sake less,
Nor feared they death for love's or life's sake more
And on the sounding soft funereal shore
They, watching till the day should wholly die,
Saw the far sea sweep to the far grey sky,
Saw the long sands sweep to the long grey sea.
And night made one sweet mist of moor and lea,
And only far off shore the foam gave light.
And life in them sank silent as the night.

VII

## THE WIFE'S VIGIL

But all that year in Brittany forlorn,
More sick at heart with wrath than fear of scorn
And less in love with love than grief, and less
With grief than pride of spirit and bitterness,
Till all the sweet life of her blood was changed
And all her soul from all her past estranged
And all her will with all itself at strife
And all her mind at war with all her life,
Dwelt the white-handed Iseult, maid and wife,
A mourner that for mourning robes had on
Anger and doubt and hate of things foregone.
For that sweet spirit of old which made her sweet
Was parched with blasts of thought as flowers with heat
And withered as with wind of evil will;
Though slower than frosts or fires consume or kill
That bleak black wind vexed all her spirit still.
As ripples reddening in the roughening breath
Of the eager east when dawn does night to death,
So rose and stirred and kindled in her thought
Fierce barren fluctuant fires that lit not aught,
But scorched her soul with yearning keen as hate
And dreams that left her wrath disconsolate.
When change came first on that first heaven where all
Life's hours were flowers that dawn's light hand let fall,
The sun that smote her dewy cloud of days
Wrought from its showery folds his rainbow's rays,
For love the red, for hope the gentle green,
But yellow jealousy glared pale between.
Ere yet the sky grew heavier, and her head
Bent flowerwise, chill with change and fancies fled,
She saw but love arch all her heaven across with red,
A burning bloom that seemed to breathe and beat
And waver only as flame with rapturous heat
Wavers; and all the world therewith smelt sweet,
As incense kindling from the rose-red flame:
And when that full flush waned, and love became
Scarce fainter, though his fading horoscope
From certitude of sight receded, hope
Held yet her April-coloured light aloft
As though to lure back love, a lamp sublime and soft.

But soon that light paled as a leaf grows pale
And fluttered leaf-like in the gathering gale
And melted even as dew-flakes, whose brief sheen
The sun that gave despoils of glittering green;
Till harder shone 'twixt hope and love grown cold
A sallow light like withering autumn's gold,
The pale strong flame of jealous thought, that glows
More deep than hope's green bloom or love's enkindled rose:
As though the sunflower's faint fierce disk absorbed
The spirit and heart of starrier flowers disorbed.
  That same full hour of twilight's doors unbarred
To let bright night behold in Joyous Gard
The glad grave eyes of lovers far away
Watch with sweet thoughts of death the death of day
Saw lonelier by the narrower opening sea
Sit fixed at watch Iseult of Brittany.
As darkness from deep valleys void and bleak
Climbs till it clothe with night the sunniest peak
Where only of all a mystic mountain-land
Day seems to cling yet with a trembling hand
And yielding heart reluctant to recede,
So, till her soul was clothed with night indeed,
Rose the slow cloud of envious will within
And hardening hate that held itself no sin,
Veiled heads of vision, eyes of evil gleam,
Dim thought on thought, and darkling dream on dream.
Far off she saw in spirit, and seeing abhorred,
The likeness wrought on darkness of her lord
Shine, and the imperial semblance at his side
Whose shadow from her seat cast down the bride,
Whose power and ghostly presence thrust her forth:
Beside that unknown other sea far north
She saw them, clearer than in present sight
Rose on her eyes the starry shadow of night;
And on her heart that heaved with gathering fate
Rose red with storm the starless shadow of hate;
And eyes and heart made one saw surge and swell
The fires of sunset like the fires of hell.
As though God's wrath would burn up sin with shame,
The incensed red gold of deepening heaven grew flame:
The sweet green spaces of the soft low sky
Faded, as fields that withering wind leaves dry:
The sea's was like a doomsman's blasting breath

From lips afoam with ravenous lust of death.
A night like desolation, sombre-starred,
Above the great walled girth of Joyous Gard
Spread forth its wide sad strength of shadow and gloom
Wherein those twain were compassed round with doom:
Hell from beneath called on them, and she heard
Reverberate judgment in the wild wind's word
Cry, till the sole sound of their names that rang
Clove all the sea-mist with a clarion's clang,
And clouds to clouds and flames to clustering flames
Beat back the dark noise of the direful names.
Fear and strong exultation caught her breath,
And triumph like the bitterness of death,
And rapture like the rage of hate allayed
With ruin and ravin that its might hath made;
And her heart swelled and strained itself to hear
What may be heard of no man's hungering ear,
And as a soil that cleaves in twain for drouth
Thirsted for judgment given of God's own mouth
Against them, till the strength of dark desire
Was in her as a flame of hell's own fire.
Nor seemed the wrath which held her spirit in stress
Aught else or worse than passionate holiness,
Nor the ardent hate which called on judgment's rod
More hateful than the righteousness of God.
"How long, till thou do justice, and my wrong
Stand expiate? O long-suffering judge, how long?
Shalt thou not put him in mine hand one day
Whom I so loved, to spare not but to slay?
Shalt thou not cast her down for me to tread,
Me, on the pale pride of her humbled head?
Do I not well, being angry? doth not hell
Require them? yea, thou knowest that I do well.
Is not thy seal there set of bloodred light
For witness on the brows of day and night?
Who shall unseal it? what shall melt away
Thy signet from the doors of night and day?
No man, nor strength of any spirit above,
Nor prayer, nor ardours of adulterous love.
Thou art God, the strong lord over body and soul:
Hast thou not in the terrors of thy scroll
All names of all men written as with fire?
Thine only breath bids time and space respire:

And are not all things evil in them done
More clear in thine eyes than in ours the sun?
Hast thou not sight stretched wide enough to see
These that offend it, these at once and me?
Is thine arm shortened or thine hand struck down
As palsied? have thy brows not strength to frown?
Are thine eyes blind with film of withering age?
Burns not thine heart with righteousness of rage
Yet, and the royal rancour toward thy foes
Retributive of ruin? Time should close,
Thou said'st, and earth fade as a leaf grows grey,
Ere one word said of thine should pass away.
Was this then not thy word, thou God most high,
That sin shall surely bring forth death and die,
Seeing how these twain live and have joy of life,
His harlot and the man that made me wife?
For is it I, perchance, I that have sinned?
Me, peradventure, should thy wasting wind
Smite, and thy sun blast, and thy storms devour
Me with keen fangs of lightning? should thy power
Put forth on me the weight of its awakening hour?
Shall I that bear this burden bear that weight
Of judgment? is my sin against thee great,
If all my heart against them burn with all its hate?
Thine, and not mine, should hate be? nay, but me
They have spoiled and scoffed at, who can touch not thee.
Me, me, the fullness of their joy drains dry,
Their fruitfulness makes barren: thou, not I,
Lord, is it, whom their wrongdoing clothes with shame,
That all who speak shoot tongues out at thy name
As all who hear mock mine? Make me thy sword
At least, if even thou too be wronged, O Lord,
At all of these that wrong me: make mine hand
As lightning, or my tongue a fiery brand,
To burn or smite them with thy wrath: behold,
I have nought on earth save thee for hope or hold,
Fail me not thou: I have nought but this to crave,
Make me thy mean to give them to the grave,
Thy sign that all men seeing may speak thee just,
Thy word which turns the strengths of sin to dust,
Thy blast which burns up towers and thrones with fire.
Lord, is this gift, this grace that I require,
So great a gift, Lord, for thy grace to give

And bid me bear thy part retributive?
That I whom scorn makes mouths at, I might be
Thy witness if loud sin may mock at thee?
For lo, my life is as a barren ear
Plucked from the sheaf: dark days drive past me here
Downtrodden, while joy's reapers pile their sheaves,
A thing more vile than autumn's weariest leaves,
For these the sun filled once with sap of life.
O thou my lord that hadst me to thy wife,
Dost thou not fear at all, remembering me,
The love that bowed my whole soul down to thee?
Is this so wholly nought for man to dread,
Man, whose life walks between the quick and dead,
Naked, and warred about with wind and sea,
That one should love and hate as I do thee?
That one should live in all the world his foe
So mortal as the hate that loves him so?
Nought, is it nought, O husband, O my knight,
O strong man and indomitable in fight,
That one more weak than foam-bells on the sea
Should have in heart such thoughts as I of thee?
Thou art bound about with stately strengths for bands:
What strength shall keep thee from my strengthless hands?
Thou art girt about with goodly guards and great:
What fosse may fence thee round as deep as hate?
Thou art wise: will wisdom teach thee fear of me?
Thou art great of heart: shall this deliver thee?
What wall so massive, or what tower so high,
Shall be thy surety that thou shouldst not die,
If that which comes against thee be but I?
Who shall rise up of power to take thy part,
What skill find strength to save, what strength find art,
If that which wars against thee be my heart?
Not iron, nor the might of force afield,
Nor edge of sword, nor sheltering weight of shield,
Nor all thy fame since all thy praise began,
Nor all the love and laud thou hast of man,
Nor, though his noiseless hours with wool be shod,
Shall God's love keep thee from the wrath of God.
O son of sorrows, hast thou said at heart,
Haply, God loves thee, God shall take thy part,
Who hath all these years endured thee, since thy birth
From sorrow's womb bade sin be born on earth?

So long he hath cast his buckler over thee,
Shall he not surely guard thee even from me?
Yea, but if yet he give thee while I live
Into mine hands as he shall surely give,
Ere death at last bring darkness on thy face,
Call then on him, call not on me for grace,
Cast not away one prayer, one suppliant breath,
On me that commune all this while with death.
For I that was not and that was thy wife
Desire not but one hour of all thy life
Wherein to triumph till that hour be past;
But this mine hour I look for is thy last."
  So mused she till the fire in sea and sky
Sank, and the northwest wind spake harsh on high,
And like the sea's heart waxed her heart that heard,
Strong, dark, and bitter, till the keen wind's word
Seemed of her own soul spoken, and the breath
All round her not of darkness, but of death.

## VIII

## THE LAST PILGRIMAGE

Enough of ease, O Love, enough of light,
Enough of rest before the shadow of night.
Strong Love, whom death finds feebler; kingly Love,
Whom time discrowns in season, seeing thy dove
Spell-stricken by the serpent; for thy sake
These that saw light see night's dawn only break,
Night's cup filled up with slumber, whence men think
The draught more dread than thine was dire to drink.
O Love, thy day sets darkling: hope and fear
Fall from thee standing stern as death stands here.
  For what have these to do with fear or hope
On whom the gates of outer darkness ope,
On whom the door of life's desire is barred?
Past like a cloud, their days in Joyous Gard
Gleam like a cloud the westering sun stains red
Till all the blood of day's blithe heart be bled
And all night's heart requickened; in their eyes
So flame and fade those far memorial skies,
So shines the moorland, so revives the sea,
Whereon they gazing mused of things to be

And wist not more of them than waters know
What wind with next day's change of tide shall blow.
Dark roll the deepening days whose waves divide
Unseasonably, with storm-struck change of tide,
Tristram from Iseult: nor may sorrow say
If better wind shall blow than yesterday
With next day risen or any day to come.
For ere the songs of summer's death fell dumb,
And autumn bade the imperial moorlands change
Their purples, and the bracken's bloom grow strange
As hope's green blossom touched with time's harsh rust,
Was all their joy of life shaken to dust,
And all its fire made ashes: by the strand
Where late they strayed and communed hand from hand
For the last time fell separate, eyes of eyes
Took for the last time leave, and saw the skies
Dark with their deep division. The last time—
The last that ever love's rekindling rhyme
Should keep for them life's days and nights in tune
With refluence of the morning and the moon
Alternative in music, and make one
The secrets of the stardawn and the sun
For these twain souls ere darkness held them fast;
The last before the labour marked for last
And toil of utmost knighthood, till the wage
Of rest might crown his crowning pilgrimage
Whereon forth faring must he take farewell,
With spear for staff and sword for scallop-shell
And scrip wherein close memory hoarded yet
Things holier held than death might well forget;
The last time ere the travel were begun
Whose goal is unbeholden of the sun,
The last wherewith love's eyes might yet be lit,
Came, and they could but dream they knew not it.
For Tristram parting from her wist at heart
How well she wist they might not choose but part,
And he pass forth a pilgrim, when there came
A sound of summons in the high king's name
For succour toward his vassal Triamour,
King in wild Wales, now spoiled of all his power,
As Tristram's father ere his fair son's birth,
By one the strongest of the sons of earth,
Urgan, an iron bulk of giant mould:

And Iseult in Tintagel as of old
Sat crowned with state and sorrow: for her lord
At Arthur's hand required her back restored,
And willingly compelled against her will
She yielded, saying within her own soul still
Some season yet of soft or stormier breath
Should haply give her life again or death:
For now nor quick nor dead nor bright nor dark
Were all her nights and days wherein King Mark
Held haggard watch upon her, and his eyes
Were cloudier than the gradual wintering skies
That closed about the wan wild land and sea.
And bitter toward him waxed her heart: but he
Was rent in twain betwixt harsh love and hate
With pain and passion half compassionate
That yearned and laboured to be quit of shame,
And could not: and his life grew smouldering flame.
And hers a cloud full-charged with storm and shower,
Though touched with trembling gleams of fire's bright flower
That flashed and faded on its fitful verge,
As hope would strive with darkness and emerge
And sink, a swimmer strangled by the swallowing surge.
  But Tristram by dense hills and deepening vales
Rode through the wild glad wastes of glorious Wales,
High-hearted with desire of happy fight
And strong in soul with merrier sense of might
Than since the fair first years that hailed him knight:
For all his will was toward the war, so long
Had love repressed and wrought his glory wrong,
So far the triumph and so fair the praise
Seemed now that kindled all his April days.
And here in bright blown autumn, while his life
Was summer's yet for strength toward love or strife,
Blithe waxed his hope toward battle, and high desire
To pluck once more as out of circling fire
Fame, the broad flower whose breath makes death more sweet
Than roses crushed by love's receding feet.
But all the lovely land wherein he went
The blast of ruin and ravenous war had rent;
And black with fire the fields where homesteads were,
And foul with festering dead the high soft air,
And loud with wail of women many a stream
Whose own live song was like love's deepening dream,

Spake all against the spoiler: wherefore still
Wrath waxed with pity, quickening all his will,
In Tristram's heart for every league he rode
Through the aching land so broad a curse bestrode
With so supreme a shadow: till one dawn
Above the green bloom of a gleaming lawn,
High on the strait steep windy bridge that spanned
A glen's deep mouth, he saw that shadow stand
Visible, sword on thigh and mace in hand
Vast as the mid bulk of a roof-tree's beam.
So, sheer above the wild wolf-haunted stream,
Dire as the face disfeatured of a dream,
Rose Urgan: and his eyes were night and flame;
But like the fiery dawn were his that came
Against him, lit with more sublime desire
Than lifts toward heaven the leaping heart of fire:
And strong in vantage of his perilous place
The huge high presence, red as earth's first race,
Reared like a reed the might up of his mace,
And smote: but lightly Tristram swerved, and drove
Right in on him, whose void stroke only clove
Air, and fell wide, thundering athwart: and he
Sent forth a stormier cry than wind or sea
When midnight takes the tempest for her lord;
And all the glen's throat seemed as hell's that roared;
But high like heaven's light over hell shone Tristram's sword,
Falling, and bright as storm shows God's bare brand
Flashed as it shore sheer off the huge right hand
Whose strength was as the shadow of death on all that land.
And like the trunk of some grim tree sawn through
Reeled Urgan, as his left hand grasped and drew
A steel by sorcerers tempered: and anew
Raged the red wind of fluctuant fight, till all
The cliffs were thrilled as by the clangorous call
Of storm's blown trumpets from the core of night,
Charging: and even as with the storm-wind's might
On Tristram's helm that sword crashed: and the knight
Fell, and his arms clashed, and a wide cry brake
From those far off that heard it, for his sake
Soul-stricken: and that bulk of monstrous birth
Sent forth again a cry more dire for mirth:
But ere the sunbright arms were soiled of earth
They flashed again, re-risen: and swift and loud

Rang the strokes out as from a circling cloud,
So dense the dust wrought over them its drifted shroud.
Strong strokes, within the mist their battle made,
Each hailed on other through the shifting shade
That clung about them hurtling as the swift fight swayed:
And each between the jointed corslet saw
Break forth his foe's bright blood at each grim flaw
Steel made in hammered iron: till again
The fiend put forth his might more strong for pain
And cleft the great knight's glittering shield in twain,
Laughing for very wrath and thirst to kill,
A beast's broad laugh of blind and wolfish will,
And smote again ere Tristram's lips drew breath
Panting, and swept as by the sense of death,
That surely should have touched and sealed them fast
Save that the sheer stroke shrilled aside, and passed
Frustrate: but answering Tristram smote anew,
And thrust the brute breast as with lightning through
Clean with one cleaving stroke of perfect might:
And violently the vast bulk leapt upright,
And plunged over the bridge, and fell: and all
The cliffs reverberate from his monstrous fall
Rang: and the land by Tristram's grace was free.
So with high laud and honour thence went he,
And southward set his sail again, and passed
The lone land's ending, first beheld and last
Of eyes that look on England from the sea:
And his heart mourned within him, knowing how she
Whose heart with his was fatefully made fast
Sat now fast bound, as though some charm were cast
About her, such a brief space eastward thence,
And yet might soul not break the bonds of sense
And bring her to him in very life and breath
More than had this been even the sea of death
That washed between them, and its wide sweet light
The dim strait's darkness of the narrowing night
That shuts about men dying whose souls put forth
To pierce its passage through: but south and north
Alike for him were other than they were:
For all the northward coast shone smooth and fair,
And off its iron cliffs the keen-edged air
Blew summer, kindling from her mute bright mouth;
But winter breathed out of the murmuring south,

Where, pale with wrathful watch on passing ships,
The lone wife lay in wait with wan dumb lips.
Yet, sailing where the shoreward ripple curled
Of the most wild sweet waves in all the world,
His soul took comfort even for joy to see
The strong deep joy of living sun and sea,
The large deep love of living sea and land,
As past the lonely lion-guarded strand
Where the huge warder lifts his couchant sides,
Asleep, above the sleepless lapse of tides,
The light sail swept, and past the unsounded caves
Unsearchable, wherein the pulse of waves
Throbs through perpetual darkness to and fro,
And the blind night swims heavily below
While heavily the strong noon broods above,
Even to the very bay whence very Love,
Strong daughter of the giant gods who wrought
Sun, earth, and sea out of their procreant thought,
Most meetly might have risen, and most divine
Beheld and heard things round her sound and shine
From floors of foam and gold to walls of serpentine.
For splendid as the limbs of that supreme
Incarnate beauty through men's visions gleam,
Whereof all fairest things are even but shadow or dream,
And lovely like as Love's own heavenliest face,
Gleams there and glows the presence and the grace
Even of the mother of all, in perfect pride of place.
For otherwhere beneath our world-wide sky
There may not be beheld of men that die
Aught else like this that dies not, nor may stress
Of ages that bow down men's works make less
The exultant awe that clothes with power its loveliness.
For who sets eye thereon soever knows
How since these rocks and waves first rolled and rose
The marvel of their many-coloured might
Hath borne this record sensible to sight,
The witness and the symbol of their own delight,
The gospel graven of life's most heavenly law,
Joy, brooding on its own still soul with awe,
A sense of godlike rest in godlike strife,
The sovereign conscience of the spirit of life.
Nor otherwhere on strand or mountain tower
Hath such fair beauty shining forth in flower

Put on the imperial robe of such imperious power.
For all the radiant rocks from depth to height
Burn with vast bloom of glories blossom-bright
As though the sun's own hand had thrilled them through with light
And stained them through with splendour: yet from thence
Such awe strikes rapture through the spirit of sense
From all the inaccessible sea-wall's girth,
That exultation, bright at heart as mirth,
Bows deeper down before the beauty of earth
Than fear may bow down ever: nor shall one
Who meets at Alpine dawn the mounting sun
On heights too high for many a wing to climb
Be touched with sense of aught seen more sublime
Than here smiles high and sweet in face of heaven and time.
For here the flower of fire, the soft hoar bloom
Of springtide olive-woods, the warm green gloom
Of clouded seas that swell and sound with dawn of doom,
The keen thwart lightning and the wan grey light
Of stormy sunrise crossed and vexed with night,
Flash, loom, and laugh with divers hues in one
From all the curved cliff's face, till day be done,
Against the sea's face and the gazing sun.
And whensoever a strong wave, high in hope,
Sweeps up some smooth slant breadth of stone aslope,
That glowed with duskier fire of hues less bright,
Swift as it sweeps back springs to sudden sight
The splendour of the moist rock's fervent light,
Fresh as from dew of birth when time was born
Out of the world-conceiving womb of morn.
All its quenched flames and darkling hues divine
Leap into lustrous life and laugh and shine
And darken into swift and dim decline
For one brief breath's space till the next wave run
Right up, and ripple down again, undone,
And leave it to be kissed and kindled of the sun.
And all these things, bright as they shone before
Man first set foot on earth or sail from shore,
Rose not less radiant than the sun sees now
When the autumn sea was cloven of Tristram's prow,
And strong in sorrow and hope and woful will
That hope might move not nor might sorrow kill
He held his way back toward the wild sad shore
Whence he should come to look on these no more,

Nor ever, save with sunless eyes shut fast,
Sail home to sleep in home-born earth at last.
　And all these things fled fleet as light or breath
Past, and his heart waxed cold and dull as death,
Or swelled but as the tides of sorrow swell,
To sink with sullen sense of slow farewell.
So surely seemed the silence even to sigh
Assurance of inveterate prophecy,
"Thou shalt not come again home hither ere thou die."
And the wind mourned and triumphed, and the sea
Wailed and took heart and trembled; nor might he
Hear more of comfort in their speech, or see
More certitude in all the waste world's range
Than the only certitude of death and change.
And as the sense and semblance fluctuated
Of all things heard and seen alive or dead
That smote far off upon his ears or eyes
Or memory mixed with forecasts fain to rise
And fancies faint as ghostliest prophecies,
So seemed his own soul, changefully forlorn,
To shrink and triumph and mount up and mourn;
Yet all its fitful waters, clothed with night,
Lost heart not wholly, lacked not wholly light,
Seeing over life and death one star in sight
Where evening's gates as fair as morning's ope,
Whose name was memory, but whose flame was hope.
For all the tides of thought that rose and sank
Felt its fair strength wherefrom strong sorrow shrank
A mightier trust than time could change or cloy,
More strong than sorrow, more secure than joy.
So came he, nor content nor all unblest,
Back to the grey old land of Merlin's rest.
　But ere six paces forth on shore he trod
Before him stood a knight with feet unshod,
And kneeling called upon him, as on God
Might sick men call for pity, praying aloud
With hands held up and head made bare and bowed;
"Tristram, for God's love and thine own dear fame,
I Tristram that am one with thee in name
And one in heart with all that praise thee — I,
Most woful man of all that may not die
For heartbreak and the heavier scourge of shame,
By all thy glory done our woful name

Beseech thee, called of all men gentlest knight,
Be now not slow to do my sorrows right.
I charge thee for thy fame's sake through this land,
I pray thee by thine own wife's fair white hand,
Have pity of me whose love is borne away
By one that makes of poor men's lives his prey,
A felon masked with knighthood: at his side
Seven brethren hath he night or day to ride
With seven knights more that wait on all his will:
And here at hand, ere yet one day fulfil
Its flight through light and darkness, shall they fare
Forth, and my bride among them, whom they bear
Through these wild lands his prisoner; and if now
I lose her, and my prayer be vain, and thou
Less fain to serve love's servants than of yore,
Then surely shall I see her face no more.
But if thou wilt, for love's sake of the bride
Who lay most loved of women at thy side,
Strike with me, straight then hence behoves us ride
And rest between the moorside and the sea
Where we may smite them passing: but for me,
Poor stranger, me not worthy scarce to touch
Thy kind strong hand, how shouldst thou do so much?
For now lone left this long time waits thy wife
And lacks her lord and light of wedded life
Whilst thou far off art famous: yet thy fame,
If thou take pity on me that bear thy name
Unworthily, but by that name implore
Thy grace, how shall not even thy fame grow more?
But be thy will as God's among us done,
Who art far in fame above us as the sun:
Yet only of him have all men help and grace."
 And all the lordly light of Tristram's face
Was softened as the sun's in kindly spring.
"Nay, then may God send me as evil a thing
When I give ear not to such prayers," he said,
"And make my place among the nameless dead
When I put back one hour the time to smite
And do the unrighteous griefs of good men right.
Behold, I will not enter in nor rest
Here in mine own halls till this piteous quest
Find end ere noon to-morrow: but do thou,
Whose sister's face I may not look on now,

Go, Ganhardine, with tiding of the vow
That bids me turn aside for one day's strife
Or live dishonoured all my days of life,
And greet for me in brother's wise my wife,
And crave her pardon that for knighthood's sake
And womanhood's, whose bands may no man break
And keep the bands of bounden honour fast,
I seek not her till two nights yet be past
And this my quest accomplished, so God please
By me to give this young man's anguish ease
And on his wrongdoer's head his wrong requite."
And Tristram with that woful thankful knight
Rode by the seaside moorland wastes away
Between the quickening night and darkening day
Ere half the gathering stars had heart to shine.
And lightly toward his sister Ganhardine
Sped, where she sat and gazed alone afar
Above the grey sea for the sunset star,
And lightly kissed her hand and lightly spake
His tiding of that quest for knighthood's sake.
And the white-handed Iseult, bowing her head,
Gleamed on him with a glance athwart, and said,
"As God's on earth and far above the sun,
So toward his handmaid be my lord's will done."
And doubts too dim to question or divine
Touched as with shade the spirit of Ganhardine,
Hearing; and scarce for half a doubtful breath
His bright light heart held half a thought of death
And knew not whence this darkling thought might be,
But surely not his sister's work: for she
Was ever sweet and good as summer air,
And soft as dew when all the night is fair,
And gracious as the golden maiden moon
When darkness craves her blessing: so full soon
His mind was light again as leaping waves,
Nor dreamed that hers was like a field of graves
Where no man's foot dares swerve to left or right,
Nor ear dares hearken, nor dares eye take sight
Of aught that moves and murmurs there at night.
But by the sea-banks where at morn their foes
Might find them, lay those knightly name-fellows,
One sick with grief of heart and sleepless, one
With heart of hope triumphant as the sun

Dreaming asleep of love and fame and fight:
But sleep at last wrapped warm the wan young knight;
And Tristram with the first pale windy light
Woke ere the sun spake summons, and his ear
Caught the sea's call that fired his heart to hear,
A noise of waking waters: for till dawn
The sea was silent as a mountain lawn
When the wind speaks not, and the pines are dumb,
And summer takes her fill ere autumn come
Of life more soft than slumber: but ere day
Rose, and the first beam smote the bounding bay,
Up sprang the strength of the dark East, and took
With its wide wings the waters as they shook,
And hurled them huddling on aheap, and cast
The full sea shoreward with a great glad blast,
Blown from the heart of morning: and with joy
Full-souled and perfect passion, as a boy
That leaps up light to wrestle with the sea
For pure heart's gladness and large ecstasy,
Up sprang the might of Tristram; and his soul
Yearned for delight within him, and waxed whole
As a young child's with rapture of the hour
That brought his spirit and all the world to flower,
And all the bright blood in his veins beat time
To the wind's clarion and the water's chime
That called him and he followed it and stood
On the sand's verge before the grey great flood
Where the white hurtling heads of waves that met
Rose unsaluted of the sunrise yet.
And from his heart's root outward shot the sweet
Strong joy that thrilled him to the hands and feet,
Filling his limbs with pleasure and glad might,
And his soul drank the immeasurable delight
That earth drinks in with morning, and the free
Limitless love that lifts the stirring sea
When on her bare bright bosom as a bride
She takes the young sun, perfect in his pride,
Home to his place with passion: and the heart
Trembled for joy within the man whose part
Was here not least in living; and his mind
Was rapt abroad beyond man's meaner kind
And pierced with love of all things and with mirth
Moved to make one with heaven and heavenlike earth

And with the light live water. So awhile
He watched the dim sea with a deepening smile,
And felt the sound and savour and swift flight
Of waves that fled beneath the fading night
And died before the darkness, like a song
With harps between and trumpets blown along
Through the loud air of some triumphant day,
Sink through his spirit and purge all sense away
Save of the glorious gladness of his hour
And all the world about to break in flower
Before the sovereign laughter of the sun;
And he, ere night's wide work lay all undone,
As earth from her bright body casts off night,
Cast off his raiment for a rapturous fight
And stood between the sea's edge and the sea
Naked, and godlike of his mould as he
Whose swift foot's sound shook all the towers of Troy;
So clothed with might, so girt upon with joy
As, ere the knife had shorn to feed the fire
His glorious hair before the unkindled pyre
Whereon the half of his great heart was laid,
Stood, in the light of his live limbs arrayed,
Child of heroic earth and heavenly sea,
The flower of all men: scarce less bright than he,
If any of all men latter-born might stand,
Stood Tristram, silent, on the glimmering strand.
Not long: but with a cry of love that rang
As from a trumpet golden-mouthed, he sprang,
As toward a mother's where his head might rest
Her child rejoicing, toward the strong sea's breast
That none may gird nor measure: and his heart
Sent forth a shout that bade his lips not part,
But triumphed in him silent: no man's voice,
No song, no sound of clarions that rejoice,
Can set that glory forth which fills with fire
The body and soul that have their whole desire
Silent, and freer than birds or dreams are free
Take all their will of all the encountering sea.
And toward the foam he bent and forward smote,
Laughing, and launched his body like a boat
Full to the sea-breach, and against the tide
Struck strongly forth with amorous arms made wide
To take the bright breast of the wave to his

And on his lips the sharp sweet minute's kiss
Given of the wave's lip for a breath's space curled
And pure as at the daydawn of the world.
And round him all the bright rough shuddering sea
Kindled, as though the world were even as he,
Heart-stung with exultation of desire:
And all the life that moved him seemed to aspire,
As all the sea's life toward the sun: and still
Delight within him waxed with quickening will
More smooth and strong and perfect as a flame
That springs and spreads, till each glad limb became
A note of rapture in the tune of life,
Live music mild and keen as sleep and strife:
Till the sweet change that bids the sense grow sure
Of deeper depth and purity more pure
Wrapped him and lapped him round with clearer cold,
And all the rippling green grew royal gold
Between him and the far sun's rising rim.
And like the sun his heart rejoiced in him,
And brightened with a broadening flame of mirth:
And hardly seemed its life a part of earth,
But the life kindled of a fiery birth
And passion of a new-begotten son
Between the live sea and the living sun.
And mightier grew the joy to meet full-faced
Each wave, and mount with upward plunge, and taste
The rapture of its rolling strength, and cross
Its flickering crown of snows that flash and toss
Like plumes in battle's blithest charge, and thence
To match the next with yet more strenuous sense;
Till on his eyes the light beat hard and bade
His face turn west and shoreward through the glad
Swift revel of the waters golden-clad,
And back with light reluctant heart he bore
Across the broad-backed rollers in to shore;
Strong-spirited for the chance and cheer of fight,
And donned his arms again, and felt the might
In all his limbs rejoice for strength, and praised
God for such life as that whereon he gazed,
And wist not surely its joy was even as fleet
As that which laughed and lapsed against his feet,
The bright thin grey foam-blossom, glad and hoar,
That flings its flower along the flowerless shore

On sand or shingle, and still with sweet strange snows,
As where one great white storm-dishevelled rose
May rain her wild leaves on a windy land,
Strews for long leagues the sounding slope of strand,
And flower on flower falls flashing, and anew
A fresh light leaps up whence the last flash flew,
And casts its brief glad gleam of life away
To fade not flowerwise but as drops the day
Storm-smitten, when at once the dark devours
Heaven and the sea and earth with all their flowers;
No star in heaven, on earth no rose to see,
But the white blown brief blossoms of the sea,
That make her green gloom starrier than the sky,
Dance yet before the tempest's tune, and die.
And all these things he glanced upon, and knew
How fair they shone, from earth's least flake of dew
To stretch of seas and imminence of skies,
Unwittingly, with unpresageful eyes,
For the last time. The world's half heavenly face,
The music of the silence of the place,
The confluence and the refluence of the sea,
The wind's note ringing over wold and lea,
Smote once more through him keen as fire that smote,
Rang once more through him one reverberate note,
That faded as he turned again and went,
Fulfilled by strenuous joy with strong content,
To take his last delight of labour done
That yet should be beholden of the sun
Or ever give man comfort of his hand.
   Beside a wood's edge in the broken land
An hour at wait the twain together stood,
Till swift between the moorside and the wood
Flashed the spears forward of the coming train;
And seeing beside the strong chief spoiler's rein
His wan love riding prisoner in the crew,
Forth with a cry the young man leapt, and flew
Right on that felon sudden as a flame;
And hard at hand the mightier Tristram came,
Bright as the sun and terrible as fire:
And there had sword and spear their soul's desire,
And blood that quenched the spear's thirst as it poured
Slaked royally the hunger of the sword,
Till the fierce heart of steel could scarce fulfil

Its greed and ravin of insatiate will.
For three the fiery spear of Tristram drove
Down ere a point of theirs his harness clove
Or its own sheer mid shaft splintered in twain;
And his heart bounded in him, and was fain
As fire or wind that takes its fill by night
Of tempest and of triumph: so the knight
Rejoiced and ranged among them, great of hand,
Till seven lay slain upon the heathery sand
Or in the dense breadth of the woodside fern.
Nor did his heart not mightier in him burn
Seeing at his hand that young knight fallen, and high
The red sword reared again that bade him die.
But on the slayer exulting like the flame
Whose foot foreshines the thunder Tristram came
Raging, for piteous wrath had made him fire;
And as a lion's look his face was dire
That flashed against his foeman ere the sword
Lightened, and wrought the heart's will of its lord,
And clove through casque and crown the wrongdoer's head.
And right and left about their dark chief dead
Hurtled and hurled those felons to and fro,
Till as a storm-wind scatters leaves and snow
His right hand ravening scattered them; but one
That fled with sidelong glance athwart the sun
Shot, and the shaft flew sure, and smote aright,
Full in the wound's print of his great first fight
When at his young strength's peril he made free
Cornwall, and slew beside its bordering sea
The fair land's foe, who yielding up his breath
Yet left him wounded nigh to dark slow death.
And hardly with long toil thence he won home
Between the grey moor and the glimmering foam,
And halting fared through his own gate, and fell,
Thirsting: for as the sleepless fire of hell
The fire within him of his wound again
Burned, and his face was dark as death for pain,
And blind the blithe light of his eyes: but they
Within that watched and wist not of the fray
Came forth and cried aloud on him for woe.
And scarce aloud his thanks fell faint and slow
As men reared up the strong man fallen and bore
Down the deep hall that looked along the shore,

And laid him soft abed, and sought in vain
If herb or hand of leech might heal his pain.
And the white-handed Iseult hearkening heard
All, and drew nigh, and spake no wifely word,
But gazed upon him doubtfully, with eyes
Clouded; and he in kindly knightly wise
Spake with scant breath, and smiling: "Surely this
Is penance for discourteous lips to kiss
And feel the brand burn through them, here to lie
And lack the strength here to do more than sigh
And hope not hence for pardon." Then she bowed
Her head, still silent as a stooping cloud,
And laid her lips against his face; and he
Felt sink a shadow across him as the sea
Might feel a cloud stoop toward it: and his heart
Darkened as one that wastes by sorcerous art
And knows not whence it withers: and he turned
Back from her emerald eyes his own, and yearned
All night for eyes all golden: and the dark
Hung sleepless round him till the loud first lark
Rang record forth once more of darkness done,
And all things born took comfort from the sun.

## IX

## THE SAILING OF THE SWAN

Fate, that was born ere spirit and flesh were made,
The fire that fills man's life with light and shade;
The power beyond all godhead which puts on
All forms of multitudinous unison,
A raiment of eternal change inwrought
With shapes and hues more subtly spun than thought,
Where all things old bear fruit of all things new
And one deep chord throbs all the music through,
The chord of change unchanging, shadow and light
Inseparable as reverberate day from night;
Fate, that of all things save the soul of man
Is lord and God since body and soul began;
Fate, that keeps all the tune of things in chime;
Fate, that breathes power upon the lips of time;
That smites and soothes with heavy and healing hand
All joys and sorrows born in life's dim land,

Till joy be found a shadow and sorrow a breath
And life no discord in the tune with death,
But all things fain alike to die and live
In pulse and lapse of tides alternative,
Through silence and through sound of peace and strife,
Till birth and death be one in sight of life;
Fate, heard and seen of no man's eyes or ears,
To no man shown through light of smiles or tears,
And moved of no man's prayer to fold its wings;
Fate, that is night and light on worldly things;
Fate, that is fire to burn and sea to drown,
Strength to build up and thunder to cast down;
Fate, shield and screen for each man's lifelong head,
And sword at last or dart that strikes it dead;
Fate, higher than heaven and deeper than the grave,
That saves and spares not, spares and doth not save;
Fate, that in gods' wise is not bought and sold
For prayer or price of penitence or gold;
Whose law shall live when life bids earth farewell,
Whose justice hath for shadows heaven and hell;
Whose judgment into no god's hand is given,
Nor is its doom not more than hell or heaven:
Fate, that is pure of love and clean of hate,
Being equal-eyed as nought may be but fate;
Through many and weary days of foiled desire
Leads life to rest where tears no more take fire;
Through many and weary dreams of quenched delight
Leads life through death past sense of day and night.
  Nor shall they feel or fear, whose date is done,
Aught that made once more dark the living sun
And bitterer in their breathing lips the breath
Than the dark dawn and bitter dust of death.
For all the light, with fragrance as of flowers,
That clothes the lithe live limbs of separate hours,
More sweet to savour and more clear to sight
Dawns on the soul death's undivided night.
No vigils has that perfect night to keep,
No fever-fits of vision shake that sleep.
Nor if they wake, and any place there be
Wherein the soul may feel her wings beat free
Through air too clear and still for sound or strife
If life were haply death, and death be life;

If love with yet some lovelier laugh revive,
And song relume the light it bore alive,
And friendship, found of all earth's gifts most good,
Stand perfect in perpetual brotherhood;
If aught indeed at all of all this be,
Though none might say nor any man might see,
Might he that sees the shade thereof not say
This dream were trustier than the truth of day.
Nor haply may not hope, with heart more clear,
Burn deathward, and the doubtful soul take cheer,
Seeing through the channelled darkness yearn a star
Whose eyebeams are not as the morning's are,
Transient, and subjugate of lordlier light,
But all unconquerable by noon or night,
Being kindled only of life's own inmost fire,
Truth, stablished and made sure by strong desire,
Fountain of all things living, source and seed,
Force that perforce transfigures dream to deed,
God that begets on time, the body of death,
Eternity: nor may man's darkening breath,
Albeit it stain, disfigure or destroy
The glass wherein the soul sees life and joy
Only, with strength renewed and spirit of youth,
And brighter than the sun's the body of Truth
Eternal, unimaginable of man,
Whose very face not Thought's own eyes may scan,
But see far off his radiant feet at least,
Trampling the head of Fear, the false high priest,
Whose broken chalice foams with blood no more,
And prostrate on that high priest's chancel floor,
Bruised, overthrown, blind, maimed, with bloodless rod,
The miscreation of his miscreant God.
That sovereign shadow cast of souls that dwell
In darkness and the prison-house of hell
Whose walls are built of deadly dread, and bound
The gates thereof with dreams as iron round,
And all the bars therein and stanchions wrought
Of shadow forged like steel and tempered thought
And words like swords and thunder-clouded creeds
And faiths more dire than sin's most direful deeds:
That shade accursed and worshipped, which hath made
The soul of man that brought it forth a shade
Black as the womb of darkness, void and vain,

A throne for fear, a pasturage for pain,
Impotent, abject, clothed upon with lies,
A foul blind fume of words and prayers that rise,
Aghast and harsh, abhorrent and abhorred,
Fierce as its God, blood-saturate as its Lord;
With loves and mercies on its lips that hiss
Comfort, and kill compassion with a kiss,
And strike the world black with their blasting breath;
That ghost whose core of life is very death
And all its light of heaven a shadow of hell,
Fades, falls, wanes, withers by none other spell
But theirs whose eyes and ears have seen and heard
Not the face naked, not the perfect word,
But the bright sound and feature felt from far
Of life which feeds the spirit and the star,
Thrills the live light of all the suns that roll,
And stirs the still sealed springs of every soul.
   Three dim days through, three slumberless nights long,
Perplexed at dawn, oppressed at evensong,
The strong man's soul now sealed indeed with pain,
And all its springs half dried with drought, had lain
Prisoner within the fleshly dungeon-dress
Sore chafed and wasted with its weariness.
And fain it would have found the star, and fain
Made this funereal prison-house of pain
A watch-tower whence its eyes might sweep, and see
If any place for any hope might be
Beyond the hells and heavens of sleep and strife,
Or any light at all of any life
Beyond the dense false darkness woven above,
And could not, lacking grace to look on love,
And in the third night's dying hour he spake,
Seeing scarce the seals that bound the dayspring break
And scarce the daystar burn above the sea:
"O Ganhardine, my brother true to me,
I charge thee by those nights and days we knew
No great while since in England, by the dew
That bathed those nights with blessing, and the fire
That thrilled those days as music thrills a lyre,
Do now for me perchance the last good deed
That ever love may crave or life may need
Ere love lay life in ashes: take to thee
My ship that shows aloft against the sea

Carved on her stem the semblance of a swan,
And ere the waves at even again wax wan
Pass, if it may be, to my lady's land,
And give this ring into her secret hand,
And bid her think how hard on death I lie,
And fain would look upon her face and die.
But as a merchant's laden be the bark
With royal ware for fraughtage, that King Mark
May take for toll thereof some costly thing;
And when this gift finds grace before the king,
Choose forth a cup, and put therein my ring
Where sureliest only of one it may be seen,
And bid her handmaid bear it to the queen
For earnest of thine homage: then shall she
Fear, and take counsel privily with thee,
To know what errand there is thine from me
And what my need in secret of her sight.
But make thee two sails, one like sea-foam white
To spread for signal if thou bring her back,
And if she come not see the sail be black,
That I may know or ever thou take land
If these my lips may die upon her hand
Or hers may never more be mixed with mine."
  And his heart quailed for grief in Ganhardine,
Hearing; and all his brother bade he swore
Surely to do, and straight fare forth from shore.
But the white-handed Iseult hearkening heard
All, and her heart waxed hot, and every word
Thereon seemed graven and printed in her thought
As lines with fire and molten iron wrought.
And hard within her heavy heart she cursed
Both, and her life was turned to fiery thirst,
And all her soul was hunger, and its breath
Of hope and life a blast of raging death.
For only in hope of evil was her life.
So bitter burned within the unchilded wife
A virgin lust for vengeance, and such hate
Wrought in her now the fervent work of fate.
  Then with a south-west wind the Swan set forth,
And over wintering waters bore to north,
And round the wild land's windy westward end
Up the blown channel bade her bright way bend

East on toward high Tintagel: where at dark
Landing, fair welcome found they of King Mark,
And Ganhardine with Brangwain as of old
Spake, and she took the cup of chiselled gold
Wherein lay secret Tristram's trothplight ring,
And bare it unbeholden of the king
Even to her lady's hand, which hardly took
A gift whereon a queen's eyes well might look,
With grace forlorn of weary gentleness.
But, seeing, her life leapt in her, keen to guess
The secret of the symbol: and her face
Flashed bright with blood whence all its grief-worn grace
Took fire and kindled to the quivering hair.
And in the dark soft hour of starriest air
Thrilled through with sense of midnight, when the world
Feels the wide wings of sleep about it furled,
Down stole the queen, deep-muffled to her wan
Mute restless lips, and came where yet the Swan
Swung fast at anchor: whence by starlight she
Hoised snowbright sails, and took the glimmering sea.
    But all the long night long more keen and sore
His wound's grief waxed in Tristram evermore,
And heavier always hung his heart asway
Between dim fear and clouded hope of day.
And still with face and heart at silent strife
Beside him watched the maiden called his wife,
Patient, and spake not save when scarce he spake,
Murmuring with sense distraught and spirit awake
Speech bitterer than the words thereof were sweet:
And hatred thrilled her to the hands and feet,
Listening: for alway back reiterate came
The passionate faint burden of her name.
Nor ever through the labouring lips astir
Came any word of any thought of her.
But the soul wandering struggled and clung hard
Only to dreams of joy in Joyous Gard
Or wildwood nights beside the Cornish strand,
Or Merlin's holier sleep here hard at hand
Wrapped round with deep soft spells in dim Broceliande.
And with such thirst as joy's drained wine-cup leaves
When fear to hope as hope to memory cleaves
His soul desired the dewy sense of leaves,

The soft green smell of thickets drenched with dawn.
The faint slot kindling on the fiery lawn
As day's first hour made keen the spirit again
That lured and spurred on quest his hound Hodain,
The breeze, the bloom, the splendour and the sound,
That stung like fire the hunter and the hound,
The pulse of wind, the passion of the sea,
The rapture of the woodland: then would he
Sigh, and as one that fain would all be dead
Heavily turn his heavy-laden head
Back, and close eyes for comfort, finding none.
And fain he would have died or seen the sun,
Being sick at heart of darkness: yet afresh
Began the long strong strife of spirit and flesh
And branching pangs of thought whose branches bear
The bloodred fruit whose core is black, despair.
And the wind slackened and again grew great,
Palpitant as men's pulses palpitate
Between the flowing and ebbing tides of fate
That wash their lifelong waifs of weal and woe
Through night and light and twilight to and fro.
Now as a pulse of hope its heartbeat throbbed,
Now like one stricken shrank and sank and sobbed,
Then, yearning as with child of death, put forth
A wail that filled the night up south and north
With woful sound of waters: and he said,
"So might the wind wail if the world were dead
And its wings wandered over nought but sea.
I would I knew she would not come to me,
For surely she will come not: then should I,
Once knowing I shall not look upon her, die.
I knew not life could so long breathe such breath
As I do. Nay, what grief were this, if death,
The sole sure friend of whom the whole world saith
He lies not, nor hath ever this been said,
That death would heal not grief—if death were dead
And all ways closed whence grief might pass with life!"
  Then softly spake his watching virgin wife
Out of her heart, deep down below her breath:
"Fear not but death shall come—and after death
Judgment." And he that heard not answered her,
Saying—"Ah, but one there was, if truth not err,

For true men's trustful tongues have said it — one
Whom these mine eyes knew living while the sun
Looked yet upon him, and mine own ears heard
The deep sweet sound once of his godlike word —
Who sleeps and dies not, but with soft live breath
Takes always all the deep delight of death,
Through love's gift of a woman: but for me
Love's hand is not the hand of Nimue,
Love's word no still smooth murmur of the dove,
No kiss of peace for me the kiss of love.
Nor, whatsoe'er thy life's love ever give,
Dear, shall it ever bid me sleep or live;
Nor from thy brows and lips and living breast
As his from Nimue's shall my soul take rest;
Not rest but unrest hath our long love given —
Unrest on earth that wins not rest in heaven.
What rest may we take ever? what have we
Had ever more of peace than has the sea?
Has not our life been as a wind that blows
Through lonelier lands than rear the wild white rose
That each year sees requickened, but for us
Time once and twice hath here or there done thus
And left the next year following empty and bare?
What rose hath our last year's rose left for heir,
What wine our last year's vintage? and to me
More were one fleet forbidden sense of thee,
One perfume of thy present grace, one thought
Made truth one hour, ere all mine hours be nought,
One very word, breath, look, sign, touch of hand,
Than all the green leaves in Broceliande
Full of sweet sound, full of sweet wind and sun;
O God, thou knowest I would no more but one,
I would no more but once more ere I die
Find thus much mercy. Nay, but then were I
Happier than he whom there thy grace hath found,
For thine it must be, this that wraps him round,
Thine only, albeit a fiend's force gave him birth,
Thine that has given him heritage on earth
Of slumber-sweet eternity to keep
Fast in soft hold of everliving sleep.
Happier were I, more sinful man, than he,
Whom one love-worthier then than Nimue

Should with a breath make blest among the dead."
And the wan wedded maiden answering said,
Soft as hate speaks within itself apart:
"Surely ye shall not, ye that rent mine heart,
Being one in sin, in punishment be twain."
And the great knight that heard not spake again
And sighed, but sweet thought of sweet things gone by
Kindled with fire of joy the very sigh
And touched it through with rapture: "Ay, this were
How much more than the sun and sunbright air,
How much more than the springtide, how much more
Than sweet strong sea-wind quickening wave and shore
With one divine pulse of continuous breath,
If she might kiss me with the kiss of death,
And make the light of life by death's look dim!"
And the white wedded virgin answered him,
Inwardly, wan with hurt no herb makes whole:
"Yea surely, ye whose sin hath slain my soul,
Surely your own souls shall have peace in death
And pass with benediction in their breath
And blessing given of mine their sin hath slain."
And Tristram with sore yearning spake again,
Saying: "Yea, might this thing once be, how should I,
With all my soul made one thanksgiving, die,
And pass before what judgment-seat may be,
And cry, 'Lord, now do all thou wilt with me,
Take all thy fill of justice, work thy will;
Though all thy heart of wrath have all its fill,
My heart of suffering shall endure, and say,
For that thou gavest me living yesterday
I bless thee though thou curse me.' Ay, and well
Might one cast down into the gulf of hell,
Remembering this, take heart and thank his fate—
That God, whose doom now scourges him with hate
Once, in the wild and whirling world above,
Bade mercy kiss his dying lips with love.
But if this come not, then he doth me wrong.
For what hath love done, all this long life long
That death should trample down his poor last prayer
Who prays not for forgiveness? Though love were
Sin dark as hate, have we not here that sinned
Suffered? has that been less than wintry wind

Wherewith our love lies blasted? O mine own,
O mine and no man's yet save mine alone,
Iseult! what ails thee that I lack so long
All of thee, all things thine for which I long?
For more than watersprings to shadeless sands,
More to me were the comfort of her hands
Touched once, and more than rays that set and rise
The glittering arrows of her glorious eyes,
More to my sense than fire to dead cold air
The wind and light and odour of her hair,
More to my soul than summer's to the south
The mute clear music of her amorous mouth,
And to my heart's heart more than heaven's great rest
The fullness of the fragrance of her breast.
Iseult, Iseult, what grace hath life to give
More than we twain have had of life, and live?
Iseult, Iseult, what grace may death not keep
As sweet for us to win of death, and sleep?
Come therefore, let us twain pass hence and try
If it be better not to live but die,
With love for lamp to light us out of life."
   And on that word his wedded maiden wife,
Pale as the moon in star-forsaken skies
Ere the sun fill them, rose with set strange eyes
And gazed on him that saw not: and her heart
Heaved as a man's death-smitten with a dart
That smites him sleeping, warm and full of life:
So toward her lord that was not looked his wife,
His wife that was not: and her heart within
Burnt bitter like an aftertaste of sin
To one whose memory drinks and loathes the lee
Of shame or sorrow deeper than the sea:
And no fear touched him of her eyes above
And ears that hoarded each poor word whence love
Made sweet the broken music of his breath.
"Iseult, my life that wast and art my death,
My life in life that hast been, and that art
Death in my death, sole wound that cleaves mine heart,
Mine heart that else, how spent soe'er, were whole,
Breath of my spirit and anguish of my soul,
How can this be that hence thou canst not hear,
Being but by space divided? One is here,

But one of twain I looked at once to see;
Shall death keep time and thou not keep with me?"
  And the white married maiden laughed at heart,
Hearing, and scarce with lips at all apart
Spake, and as fire between them was her breath;
"Yea, now thou liest not: yea, for I am death."
  By this might eyes that watched without behold
Deep in the gulfs of aching air acold
The roses of the dawning heaven that strew
The low soft sun's way ere his power shine through
And burn them up with fire: but far to west
Had sunk the dead moon on the live sea's breast,
Slain as with bitter fear to see the sun:
And eastward was a strong bright wind begun
Between the clouds and waters: and he said,
Seeing hardly through dark dawn her doubtful head,
"Iseult?" and like a death-bell faint and clear
The virgin voice rang answer—"I am here."
And his heart sprang, and sank again: and she
Spake, saying, "What would my knightly lord with me?"
And Tristram: "Hath my lady watched all night
Beside me, and I knew not? God requite
Her love for comfort shown a man nigh dead."
  "Yea, God shall surely guerdon it," she said,
"Who hath kept me all my days through to this hour."
  And Tristram: "God alone hath grace and power
To pay such grace toward one unworthier shown
Than ever durst, save only of God alone,
Crave pardon yet and comfort, as I would
Crave now for charity if my heart were good,
But as a coward's it fails me, even for shame."
  Then seemed her face a pale funereal flame
That burns down slow by midnight, as she said:
"Speak, and albeit thy bidding spake me dead,
God's love renounce me if it were not done."
  And Tristram: "When the sea-line takes the sun
That now should be not far off sight from far,
Look if there come not with the morning star
My ship bound hither from the northward back,
And if the sail be white thereof or black."
  And knowing the soothfast sense of his desire
So sore the heart within her raged like fire

She could not wring forth of her lips a word,
But bowing made sign how humbly had she heard.
And the sign given made light his heart; and she
Set her face hard against the yearning sea
Now all athirst with trembling trust of hope
To see the sudden gates of sunrise ope;
But thirstier yearned the heart whose fiery gate
Lay wide that vengeance might come in to hate.
And Tristram lay at thankful rest, and thought
Now surely life nor death could grieve him aught,
Since past was now life's anguish as a breath,
And surely past the bitterness of death.
For seeing he had found at these her hands this grace,
It could not be but yet some breathing-space
Might leave him life to look again on love's own face.
"Since if for death's sake," in his heart he said,
"Even she take pity upon me quick or dead,
How shall not even from God's hand be compassion shed?
For night bears dawn, how weak soe'er and wan,
And sweet ere death, men fable, sings the swan.
So seems the Swan my signal from the sea
To sound a song that sweetens death to me
Clasped round about with radiance from above
Of dawn, and closer clasped on earth by love.
Shall all things brighten, and this my sign be dark?"
  And high from heaven suddenly rang the lark,
Triumphant; and the far first refluent ray
Filled all the hollow darkness full with day.
And on the deep sky's verge a fluctuant light
Gleamed, grew, shone, strengthened into perfect sight,
As bowed and dipped and rose again the sail's clear white.
And swift and steadfast as a sea-mew's wing
It neared before the wind, as fain to bring
Comfort, and shorten yet its narrowing track.
And she that saw looked hardly toward him back,
Saying, "Ay, the ship comes surely; but her sail is black."
And fain he would have sprung upright, and seen,
And spoken: but strong death struck sheer between,
And darkness closed as iron round his head:
And smitten through the heart lay Tristram dead.
  And scarce the word had flown abroad, and wail
Risen, ere to shoreward came the snowbright sail,

And lightly forth leapt Ganhardine on land,
And led from ship with swift and reverent hand
Iseult: and round them up from all the crowd
Broke the great wail for Tristram out aloud.
And ere her ear might hear her heart had heard,
Nor sought she sign for witness of the word;
But came and stood above him newly dead,
And felt his death upon her: and her head
Bowed, as to reach the spring that slakes all drouth;
And their four lips became one silent mouth.
So came their hour on them that were in life
Tristram and Iseult: so from love and strife
The stroke of love's own hand felt last and best
Gave them deliverance to perpetual rest.
So, crownless of the wreaths that life had wound,
They slept, with flower of tenderer comfort crowned;
From bondage and the fear of time set free,
And all the yoke of space on earth and sea
Cast as a curb for ever: nor might now
Fear and desire bid soar their souls or bow,
Lift up their hearts or break them: doubt nor grief
More now might move them, dread nor disbelief
Touch them with shadowy cold or fiery sting,
Nor sleepless languor with its weary wing,
Nor harsh estrangement, born of time's vain breath,
Nor change, a darkness deeper far than death.
And round the sleep that fell around them then
Earth lies not wrapped, nor records wrought of men
Rise up for timeless token: but their sleep
Hath round it like a raiment all the deep;
No change or gleam or gloom of sun and rain,
But all time long the might of all the main
Spread round them as round earth soft heaven is spread,
And peace more strong than death round all the dead.
For death is of an hour, and after death
Peace: nor for aught that fear or fancy saith,
Nor even for very love's own sake, shall strife
Perplex again that perfect peace with life.
And if, as men that mourn may deem or dream,
Rest haply here than there might sweeter seem,
And sleep, that lays one hand on all, more good
By some sweet grave's grace given of wold or wood

Or clear high glen or sunbright wind-worn down
Than where life thunders through the trampling town
With daylong feet and nightlong overhead,
What grave may cast such grace round any dead,
What so sublime sweet sepulchre may be
For all that life leaves mortal, as the sea?
And these, rapt forth perforce from earthly ground,
These twain the deep sea guards, and girdles round
Their sleep more deep than any sea's gulf lies,
Though changeless with the change in shifting skies,
Nor mutable with seasons: for the grave
That held them once, being weaker than a wave,
The waves long since have buried: though their tomb
Was royal that by ruth's relenting doom
Men gave them in Tintagel: for the word
Took wing which thrilled all piteous hearts that heard
The word wherethrough their lifelong lot stood shown,
And when the long sealed springs of fate were known,
The blind bright innocence of lips that quaffed
Love, and the marvel of the mastering draught,
And all the fraughtage of the fateful bark,
Loud like a child upon them wept King Mark,
Seeing round the sword's hilt which long since had fought
For Cornwall's love a scroll of writing wrought,
A scripture writ of Tristram's hand, wherein
Lay bare the sinless source of all their sin,
No choice of will, but chance and sorcerous art,
With prayer of him for pardon: and his heart
Was molten in him, wailing as he kissed
Each with the kiss of kinship—"Had I wist,
Ye had never sinned nor died thus, nor had I
Borne in this doom that bade you sin and die
So sore a part of sorrow." And the king
Built for their tomb a chapel bright like spring
With flower-soft wealth of branching tracery made
Fair as the frondage each fleet year sees fade,
That should not fall till many a year were done.
There slept they wedded under moon and sun
And change of stars: and through the casements came
Midnight and noon girt round with shadow and flame
To illume their grave or veil it: till at last
On these things too was doom as darkness cast:

For the strong sea hath swallowed wall and tower,
And where their limbs were laid in woful hour
For many a fathom gleams and moves and moans
The tide that sweeps above their coffined bones
In the wrecked chancel by the shivered shrine:
Nor where they sleep shall moon or sunlight shine
Nor man look down for ever: none shall say,
Here once, or here, Tristram and Iseult lay:
But peace they have that none may gain who live,
And rest about them that no love can give,
And over them, while death and life shall be,
The light and sound and darkness of the sea.

## FROM *A CENTURY OF ROUNDELS* (1883)

### In Harbour

I

Goodnight and goodbye to the life whose signs denote us
As mourners clothed with regret for the life gone by;
To the waters of gloom whence winds of the day-spring float us
    Goodnight and goodbye.

A time is for mourning, a season for grief to sigh;
But were we not fools and blind, by day to devote us
As thralls to the darkness, unseen of the sundawn's eye?

We have drunken of Lethe at length, we have eaten of lotus;
What hurts it us here that sorrows are born and die?
We have said to the dream that caressed and the dread that smote us
    Goodnight and goodbye.

II

Outside of the port ye are moored in, lying
Close from the wind and at ease from the tide,
What sounds come swelling, what notes fall dying
    Outside?

They will not cease, they will not abide:
Voices of presage in darkness crying
Pass and return and relapse aside.

Ye see not, but hear ye not wild wings flying
To the future that wakes from the past that died?
Is grief still sleeping, is joy not sighing
    Outside?

**Plus Ultra**

Far beyond the sunrise and the sunset rises
Heaven, with worlds on worlds that lighten and respond:
Thought can see not thence the goal of hope's surmises
    Far beyond.

Night and day have made an everlasting bond
Each with each to hide in yet more deep disguises
Truth, till souls of men that thirst for truth despond.

All that man in pride of spirit slights or prizes,
All the dreams that make him fearful, fain, or fond,
Fade at forethought's touch of life's unknown surprises
    Far beyond.

**Plus Intra**

Insepulchred and deathless, through the dense
Deep elements may scarce be felt as pure
    Soul within sense.

From depth and height by measurers left immense,
Through sound and shape and colour, comes the unsure
Vague utterance, fitful with supreme suspense.

All that may pass, and all that must endure,
Song speaks not, painting shows not: more intense
And keen than these, art wakes with music's lure
    Soul within sense.

**On an Old Roundel** (Translated by D. G. Rossetti from the French of Villon.)

I

Death, from thy rigour a voice appealed,
And men still hear what the sweet cry saith,
Crying aloud in thine ears fast sealed,
    Death.

As a voice in a vision that vanisheth,
Through the grave's gate barred and the portal steeled
The sound of the wail of it travelleth.

Wailing aloud from a heart unhealed,
It woke response of melodious breath
From lips now too by thy kiss congealed,
Death.

II

Ages ago, from the lips of a sad glad poet
Whose soul was a wild dove lost in the whirling snow,
The soft keen plaint of his pain took voice to show it
Ages ago.

So clear, so deep, the divine drear accents flow,
No soul that listens may choose but thrill to know it,
Pierced and wrung by the passionate music's throe.

For us there murmurs a nearer voice below it,
Known once of ears that never again shall know,
Now mute as the mouth which felt death's wave o'erflow it
Ages ago.

## To Catullus

My brother, my Valerius, dearest head
Of all whose crowning bay-leaves crown their mother
Rome, in the notes first heard of thine I read
My brother.

No dust that death or time can strew may smother
Love and the sense of kinship inly bred
From loves and hates at one with one another.

To thee was Cæsar's self nor dear nor dread,
Song and the sea were sweeter each than other:
How should I living fear to call thee dead,
My brother?

## Envoi

Fly, white butterflies, out to sea,
Frail pale wings for the winds to try,
Small white wings that we scarce can see
Fly.

Here and there may a chance-caught eye
Note in a score of you twain or three
Brighter or darker of tinge or dye.

Some fly light as a laugh of glee,
Some fly soft as a low long sigh:
All to the haven where each would be
Fly.

## FROM *POEMS AND BALLADS, THIRD SERIES* (1889)

### To a Seamew

When I had wings, my brother,
   Such wings were mine as thine:
Such life my heart remembers
In all as wild Septembers
As this when life seems other,
   Though sweet, than once was mine;
When I had wings, my brother,
   Such wings were mine as thine.

Such life as thrills and quickens
   The silence of thy flight,
Or fills thy note's elation
With lordlier exultation
Than man's, whose faint heart sickens
   With hopes and fears that blight
Such life as thrills and quickens
   The silence of thy flight.

Thy cry from windward clanging
   Makes all the cliffs rejoice;
Though storm clothe seas with sorrow,
Thy call salutes the morrow;
While shades of pain seem hanging
   Round earth's most rapturous voice,
Thy cry from windward clanging
   Makes all the cliffs rejoice.

We, sons and sires of seamen,
   Whose home is all the sea,
What place man may, we claim it;
But thine—whose thought may name it?

Free birds live higher than freemen,
  And gladlier ye than we—
We, sons and sires of seamen,
  Whose home is all the sea.

For you the storm sounds only
  More notes of more delight
Than earth's in sunniest weather:
When heaven and sea together
Join strengths against the lonely
  Lost bark borne down by night,
For you the storm sounds only
  More notes of more delight.

With wider wing, and louder
  Long clarion-call of joy,
Thy tribe salutes the terror
Of darkness, wild as error,
But sure as truth, and prouder
  Than waves with man for toy;
With wider wing, and louder
  Long clarion-call of joy.

The wave's wing spreads and flutters,
  The wave's heart swells and breaks;
One moment's passion thrills it,
One pulse of power fulfils it
And ends the pride it utters
  When, loud with life that quakes,
The wave's wing spreads and flutters,
  The wave's heart swells and breaks.

But thine and thou, my brother,
  Keep heart and wing more high
Than aught may scare or sunder;
The waves whose throats are thunder
Fall hurtling each on other,
  And triumph as they die;
But thine and thou, my brother,
  Keep heart and wing more high.

More high than wrath or anguish,
  More strong than pride or fear,
The sense or soul half hidden
In thee, for us forbidden,
Bids thee nor change nor languish,

But live thy life as here,
More high than wrath or anguish,
More strong than pride or fear.

We are fallen, even we, whose passion
On earth is nearest thine;
Who sing, and cease from flying;
Who live, and dream of dying:
Grey time, in time's grey fashion,
Bids wingless creatures pine:
We are fallen, even we, whose passion
On earth is nearest thine.

The lark knows no such rapture,
Such joy no nightingale,
As sways the songless measure
Wherein thy wings take pleasure:
Thy love may no man capture,
Thy pride may no man quail;
The lark knows no such rapture,
Such joy no nightingale.

And we, whom dreams embolden,
We can but creep and sing
And watch through heaven's waste hollow
The flight no sight may follow
To the utter bourne beholden
Of none that lack thy wing:
And we, whom dreams embolden,
We can but creep and sing.

Our dreams have wings that falter,
Our hearts bear hopes that die;
For thee no dream could better
A life no fears may fetter,
A pride no care can alter,
That wots not whence or why
Our dreams have wings that falter,
Our hearts bear hopes that die.

With joy more fierce and sweeter
Than joys we deem divine
Their lives, by time untarnished,
Are girt about and garnished,
Who match the wave's full metre
And drink the wind's wild wine

With joy more fierce and sweeter
  Than joys we deem divine.

Ah, well were I for ever,
  Wouldst thou change lives with me,
And take my song's wild honey,
And give me back thy sunny
Wide eyes that weary never,
  And wings that search the sea;
Ah, well were I for ever,
  Wouldst thou change lives with me.

*Beachy Head: September 1886.*

**Neap-Tide**

Far off is the sea, and the land is afar:
  The low banks reach at the sky,
  Seen hence, and are heavenward high;
Though light for the leap of a boy they are,
  And the far sea late was nigh.

The fair wild fields and the circling downs,
  The bright sweet marshes and meads
  All glorious with flowerlike weeds,
The great grey churches, the sea-washed towns,
  Recede as a dream recedes.

The world draws back, and the world's light wanes,
  As a dream dies down and is dead;
  And the clouds and the gleams overhead
Change, and change; and the sea remains,
  A shadow of dreamlike dread.

Wild, and woful, and pale, and grey,
  A shadow of sleepless fear,
  A corpse with the night for bier,
The fairest thing that beholds the day
  Lies haggard and hopeless here.

And the wind's wings, broken and spent, subside;
  And the dumb waste world is hoar,
  And strange as the sea the shore;
And shadows of shapeless dreams abide
  Where life may abide no more.

A sail to seaward, a sound from shoreward,
And the spell were broken that seems
To reign in a world of dreams
Where vainly the dreamer's feet make forward
And vainly the low sky gleams.

The sea-forsaken forlorn deep-wrinkled
Salt slanting stretches of sand
That slope to the seaward hand,
Were they fain of the ripples that flashed and twinkled
And laughed as they struck the strand?

As bells on the reins of the fairies ring
The ripples that kissed them rang,
The light from the sundawn sprang,
And the sweetest of songs that the world may sing
Was theirs when the full sea sang.

Now no light is in heaven; and now
Not a note of the sea-wind's tune
Rings hither: the bleak sky's boon
Grants hardly sight of a grey sun's brow—
A sun more sad than the moon.

More sad than a moon that clouds beleaguer
And storm is a scourge to smite,
The sick sun's shadowlike light
Grows faint as the clouds and the waves wax eager,
And withers away from sight.

The day's heart cowers, and the night's heart quickens:
Full fain would the day be dead
And the stark night reign in his stead:
The sea falls dumb as the sea-fog thickens
And the sunset dies for dread.

Outside of the range of time, whose breath
Is keen as the manslayer's knife
And his peace but a truce for strife,
Who knows if haply the shadow of death
May be not the light of life?

For the storm and the rain and the darkness borrow
But an hour from the suns to be,
But a strange swift passage, that we
May rejoice, who have mourned not to-day, to-morrow,
In the sun and the wind and the sea.

## FROM *ASTROPHEL AND OTHER POEMS* (1894)

### A Nympholept

Summer, and noon, and a splendour of silence, felt,
 Seen, and heard of the spirit within the sense.
Soft through the frondage the shades of the sunbeams melt,
 Sharp through the foliage the shafts of them, keen and dense,
 Cleave, as discharged from the string of the God's bow, tense
As a war-steed's girth, and bright as a warrior's belt.
 Ah, why should an hour that is heaven for an hour pass hence?

I dare not sleep for delight of the perfect hour,
 Lest God be wroth that his gift should be scorned of man.
The face of the warm bright world is the face of a flower,
 The word of the wind and the leaves that the light winds fan
 As the word that quickened at first into flame, and ran,
Creative and subtle and fierce with invasive power,
 Through darkness and cloud, from the breath of the one God, Pan.

The perfume of earth possessed by the sun pervades
 The chaster air that he soothes but with sense of sleep.
Soft, imminent, strong as desire that prevails and fades,
 The passing noon that beholds not a cloudlet weep
 Imbues and impregnates life with delight more deep
Than dawn or sunset or moonrise on lawns or glades
 Can shed from the skies that receive it and may not keep.

The skies may hold not the splendour of sundown fast;
 It wanes into twilight as dawn dies down into day.
And the moon, triumphant when twilight is overpast,
 Takes pride but awhile in the hours of her stately sway.
 But the might of the noon, though the light of it pass away,
Leaves earth fulfilled of desires and of dreams that last;
 But if any there be that hath sense of them none can say.

For if any there be that hath sight of them, sense, or trust
Made strong by the might of a vision, the strength of a dream,
His lips shall straiten and close as a dead man's must,
His heart shall be sealed as the voice of a frost-bound stream.
For the deep mid mystery of light and of heat that seem
To clasp and pierce dark earth, and enkindle dust,
Shall a man's faith say what it is? or a man's guess deem?

Sleep lies not heavier on eyes that have watched all night
Than hangs the heat of the noon on the hills and trees.
Why now should the haze not open, and yield to sight
A fairer secret than hope or than slumber sees?
I seek not heaven with submission of lips and knees,
With worship and prayer for a sign till it leap to light:
I gaze on the gods about me, and call on these.

I call on the gods hard by, the divine dim powers
Whose likeness is here at hand, in the breathless air,
In the pulseless peace of the fervid and silent flowers,
In the faint sweet speech of the waters that whisper there.
Ah, what should darkness do in a world so fair?
The bent-grass heaves not, the couch-grass quails not or cowers;
The wind's kiss frets not the rowan's or aspen's hair.

But the silence trembles with passion of sound suppressed,
And the twilight quivers and yearns to the sunward, wrung
With love as with pain; and the wide wood's motionless breast
Is thrilled with a dumb desire that would fain find tongue
And palpitates, tongueless as she whom a man-snake stung,
Whose heart now heaves in the nightingale, never at rest
Nor satiated ever with song till her last be sung.

Is it rapture or terror that circles me round, and invades
Each vein of my life with hope—if it be not fear?
Each pulse that awakens my blood into rapture fades,
Each pulse that subsides into dread of a strange thing near
Requickens with sense of a terror less dread than dear.
Is peace not one with light in the deep green glades
Where summer at noonday slumbers? Is peace not here?

The tall thin stems of the firs, and the roof sublime
That screens from the sun the floor of the steep still wood,
Deep, silent, splendid, and perfect and calm as time,
Stand fast as ever in sight of the night they stood,
When night gave all that moonlight and dewfall could.

The dense ferns deepen, the moss glows warm as the thyme:
The wild heath quivers about me: the world is good.

Is it Pan's breath, fierce in the tremulous maidenhair,
That bids fear creep as a snake through the woodlands, felt
In the leaves that it stirs not yet, in the mute bright air,
In the stress of the sun? For here has the great God dwelt:
For hence were the shafts of his love or his anger dealt.
For here has his wrath been fierce as his love was fair,
When each was as fire to the darkness its breath bade melt.

Is it love, is it dread, that enkindles the trembling noon,
That yearns, reluctant in rapture that fear has fed,
As man for woman, as woman for man? Full soon,
If I live, and the life that may look on him drop not dead,
Shall the ear that hears not a leaf quake hear his tread,
The sense that knows not the sound of the deep day's tune
Receive the God, be it love that he brings or dread.

The naked noon is upon me: the fierce dumb spell,
The fearful charm of the strong sun's imminent might,
Unmerciful, steadfast, deeper than seas that swell,
Pervades, invades, appals me with loveless light,
With harsher awe than breathes in the breath of night.
Have mercy, God who art all! For I know thee well,
How sharp is thine eye to lighten, thine hand to smite.

The whole wood feels thee, the whole air fears thee: but fear
So deep, so dim, so sacred, is wellnigh sweet.
For the light that hangs and broods on the woodlands here,
Intense, invasive, intolerant, imperious, and meet
To lighten the works of thine hands and the ways of thy feet,
Is hot with the fire of the breath of thy life, and dear
As hope that shrivels or shrinks not for frost or heat.

Thee, thee the supreme dim godhead, approved afar,
Perceived of the soul and conceived of the sense of man,
We scarce dare love, and we dare not fear: the star
We call the sun, that lit us when life began
To brood on the world that is thine by his grace for a span,
Conceals and reveals in the semblance of things that are
Thine immanent presence, the pulse of thy heart's life, Pan.

The fierce mid noon that wakens and warms the snake
Conceals thy mercy, reveals thy wrath: and again
The dew-bright hour that assuages the twilight brake

Conceals thy wrath and reveals thy mercy: then
Thou art fearful only for evil souls of men
That feel with nightfall the serpent within them wake,
And hate the holy darkness on glade and glen.

Yea, then we know not and dream not if ill things be,
Or if aught of the work of the wrong of the world be thine.
We hear not the footfall of terror that treads the sea,
We hear not the moan of winds that assail the pine:
We see not if shipwreck reign in the storm's dim shrine;
If death do service and doom bear witness to thee
We see not,—know not if blood for thy lips be wine.

But in all things evil and fearful that fear may scan,
As in all things good, as in all things fair that fall,
We know thee present and latent, the lord of man;
In the murmuring of doves, in the clamouring of winds that call
And wolves that howl for their prey; in the midnight's pall,
In the naked and nymph-like feet of the dawn, O Pan,
And in each life living, O thou the God who art all.

Smiling and singing, wailing and wringing of hands,
Laughing and weeping, watching and sleeping, still
Proclaim but and prove but thee, as the shifted sands
Speak forth and show but the strength of the sea's wild will
That sifts and grinds them as grain in the stormwind's mill.
In thee is the doom that falls and the doom that stands:
The tempests utter thy word, and the stars fulfil.

Where Etna shudders with passion and pain volcanic
That rend her heart as with anguish that rends a man's,
Where Typho labours, and finds not his thews Titanic,
In breathless torment that ever the flame's breath fans,
Men felt and feared thee of old, whose pastoral clans
Were given to the charge of thy keeping; and soundless panic
Held fast the woodland whose depths and whose heights
were Pan's.

And here, though fear be less than delight, and awe
Be one with desire and with worship of earth and thee,
So mild seems now thy secret and speechless law,
So fair and fearless and faithful and godlike she,
So soft the spell of thy whisper on stream and sea,
Yet man should fear lest he see what of old men saw
And withered: yet shall I quail if thy breath smite me.

Lord God of life and of light and of all things fair,
Lord God of ravin and ruin and all things dim,
Death seals up life, and darkness the sunbright air,
And the stars that watch blind earth in the deep night swim
Laugh, saying, "What God is your God, that ye call on him?
What is man, that the God who is guide of our way should care
If day for a man be golden, or night be grim?"

But thou, dost thou hear? Stars too but abide for a span,
Gods too but endure for a season; but thou, if thou be
God, more than shadows conceived and adored of man,
Kind Gods and fierce, that bound him or made him free,
The skies that scorn us are less in thy sight than we,
Whose souls have strength to conceive and perceive thee, Pan,
With sense more subtle than senses that hear and see.

Yet may not it say, though it seek thee and think to find
One soul of sense in the fire and the frost-bound clod,
What heart is this, what spirit alive or blind,
That moves thee: only we know that the ways we trod
We tread, with hands unguided, with feet unshod,
With eyes unlightened; and yet, if with steadfast mind,
Perchance may we find thee and know thee at last for God.

Yet then should God be dark as the dawn is bright,
And bright as the night is dark on the world—no more.
Light slays not darkness, and darkness absorbs not light;
And the labour of evil and good from the years of yore
Is even as the labour of waves on a sunless shore.
And he who is first and last, who is depth and height,
Keeps silence now, as the sun when the woods wax hoar.

The dark dumb godhead innate in the fair world's life
Imbues the rapture of dawn and of noon with dread,
Infects the peace of the star-shod night with strife,
Informs with terror the sorrow that guards the dead.
No service of bended knee or of humbled head
May soothe or subdue the God who has change to wife:
And life with death is as morning with evening wed.

And yet, if the light and the life in the light that here
Seem soft and splendid and fervid as sleep may seem
Be more than the shine of a smile or the flash of a tear,
Sleep, change, and death are less than a spell-struck dream,
And fear than the fall of a leaf on a starlit stream.

And yet, if the hope that hath said it absorb not fear,
What helps it man that the stars and the waters gleam?

What helps it man, that the noon be indeed intense,
The night be indeed worth worship? Fear and pain
Were lords and masters yet of the secret sense,
Which now dares deem not that light is as darkness, fain
Though dark dreams be to declare it, crying in vain.
For whence, thou God of the light and the darkness, whence
Dawns now this vision that bids not the sunbeams wane?

What light, what shadow, diviner than dawn or night,
Draws near, makes pause, and again—or I dream—draws near?
More soft than shadow, more strong than the strong sun's light,
More pure than moonbeams—yea, but the rays run sheer
As fire from the sun through the dusk of the pinewood, clear
And constant; yea, but the shadow itself is bright
That the light clothes round with love that is one with fear.

Above and behind it the noon and the woodland lie,
Terrible, radiant with mystery, superb and subdued,
Triumphant in silence; and hardly the sacred sky
Seems free from the tyrannous weight of the dumb fierce mood
Which rules as with fire and invasion of beams that brood
The breathless rapture of earth till its hour pass by
And leave her spirit released and her peace renewed.

I sleep not: never in sleep has a man beholden
This. From the shadow that trembles and yearns with light
Suppressed and elate and reluctant—obscure and golden
As water kindled with presage of dawn or night—
A form, a face, a wonder to sense and sight,
Grows great as the moon through the month; and her eyes embolden
Fear, till it change to desire, and desire to delight.

I sleep not: sleep would die of a dream so strange;
A dream so sweet would die as a rainbow dies,
As a sunbow laughs and is lost on the waves that range
And reck not of light that flickers or spray that flies.
But the sun withdraws not, the woodland shrinks not or sighs,
No sweet thing sickens with sense or with fear of change;
Light wounds not, darkness blinds not, my steadfast eyes.

Only the soul in my sense that receives the soul
Whence now my spirit is kindled with breathless bliss

Knows well if the light that wounds it with love makes whole,
If hopes that carol be louder than fears that hiss,
If truth be spoken of flowers and of waves that kiss,
Of clouds and stars that contend for a sunbright goal.
And yet may I dream that I dream not indeed of this?

An earth-born dreamer, constrained by the bonds of birth,
Held fast by the flesh, compelled by his veins that beat
And kindle to rapture or wrath, to desire or to mirth,
May hear not surely the fall of immortal feet,
May feel not surely if heaven upon earth be sweet;
And here is my sense fulfilled of the joys of earth,
Light, silence, bloom, shade, murmur of leaves that meet.

Bloom, fervour, and perfume of grasses and flowers aglow,
Breathe and brighten about me: the darkness gleams,
The sweet light shivers and laughs on the slopes below,
Made soft by leaves that lighten and change like dreams;
The silence thrills with the whisper of secret streams
That well from the heart of the woodland: these I know:
Earth bore them, heaven sustained them with showers and beams.

I lean my face to the heather, and drink the sun
Whose flame-lit odour satiates the flowers: mine eyes
Close, and the goal of delight and of life is one:
No more I crave of earth or her kindred skies.
No more? But the joy that springs from them smiles and flies:
The sweet work wrought of them surely, the good work done,
If the mind and the face of the season be loveless, dies.

Thee, therefore, thee would I come to, cleave to, cling,
If haply thy heart be kind and thy gifts be good,
Unknown sweet spirit, whose vesture is soft in spring,
In summer splendid, in autumn pale as the wood
That shudders and wanes and shrinks as a shamed thing should,
In winter bright as the mail of a war-worn king
Who stands where foes fled far from the face of him stood.

My spirit or thine is it, breath of thy life or of mine,
Which fills my sense with a rapture that casts out fear?
Pan's dim frown wanes, and his wild eyes brighten as thine,
Transformed as night or as day by the kindling year.
Earth-born, or mine eye were withered that sees, mine ear
That hears were stricken to death by the sense divine,
Earth-born I know thee: but heaven is about me here.

The terror that whispers in darkness and flames in light,
The doubt that speaks in the silence of earth and sea,
The sense, more fearful at noon than in midmost night,
Of wrath scarce hushed and of imminent ill to be,
Where are they? Heaven is as earth, and as heaven to me
Earth: for the shadows that sundered them here take flight;
And nought is all, as am I, but a dream of thee.

## FROM *A CHANNEL PASSAGE AND OTHER POEMS* (1904)

### The Lake of Gaube

The sun is lord and god, sublime, serene,
  And sovereign on the mountains: earth and air
Lie prone in passion, blind with bliss unseen
  By force of sight and might of rapture, fair
  As dreams that die and know not what they were.
The lawns, the gorges, and the peaks, are one
Glad glory, thrilled with sense of unison
In strong compulsive silence of the sun.

Flowers dense and keen as midnight stars aflame
  And living things of light like flames in flower
That glance and flash as though no hand might tame
  Lightnings whose life outshone their stormlit hour
  And played and laughed on earth, with all their power
Gone, and with all their joy of life made long
And harmless as the lightning life of song,
Shine sweet like stars when darkness feels them strong.

The deep mild purple flaked with moonbright gold
  That makes the scales seem flowers of hardened light,
The flamelike tongue, the feet that noon leaves cold,
  The kindly trust in man, when once the sight
  Grew less than strange, and faith bade fear take flight,
Outlive the little harmless life that shone
And gladdened eyes that loved it, and was gone
Ere love might fear that fear had looked thereon.

Fear held the bright thing hateful, even as fear,
  Whose name is one with hate and horror, saith
That heaven, the dark deep heaven of water near,
  Is deadly deep as hell and dark as death.
  The rapturous plunge that quickens blood and breath

With pause more sweet than passion, ere they strive
To raise again the limbs that yet would dive
Deeper, should there have slain the soul alive.

As the bright salamander in fire of the noonshine exults and is
  glad of his day,
The spirit that quickens my body rejoices to pass from the sunlight
  away,
To pass from the glow of the mountainous flowerage, the high
  multitudinous bloom,
Far down through the fathomless night of the water, the gladness
  of silence and gloom.
Death-dark and delicious as death in the dream of a lover and
  dreamer may be,
It clasps and encompasses body and soul with delight to be living
  and free:
Free utterly now, though the freedom endure but the space of a
  perilous breath,
And living, though girdled about with the darkness and coldness
  and strangeness of death:
Each limb and each pulse of the body rejoicing, each nerve of the
  spirit at rest,
All sense of the soul's life rapture, a passionate peace in its
  blindness blest.
So plunges the downward swimmer, embraced of the water
  unfathomed of man,
The darkness unplummeted, icier than seas in midwinter, for
  blessing or ban;
And swiftly and sweetly, when strength and breath fall short, and
  the dive is done,
Shoots up as a shaft from the dark depth shot, sped straight into
  sight of the sun;
And sheer through the snow-soft water, more dark than the roof
  of the pines above,
Strikes forth, and is glad as a bird whose flight is impelled and
  sustained of love.
As a sea-mew's love of the sea-wind breasted and ridden for
  rapture's sake
Is the love of his body and soul for the darkling delight of the
  soundless lake:
As the silent speed of a dream too living to live for a thought's
  space more

Is the flight of his limbs through the still strong chill of the
  darkness from shore to shore.
Might life be as this is and death be as life that casts off time as
  a robe,
The likeness of infinite heaven were a symbol revealed of the lake
  of Gaube.

Whose thought has fathomed and measured
  The darkness of life and of death,
The secret within them treasured,
  The spirit that is not breath?
Whose vision has yet beholden
  The splendour of death and of life?
Though sunset as dawn be golden,
  Is the word of them peace, not strife?
Deep silence answers: the glory
  We dream of may be but a dream,
And the sun of the soul wax hoary
  As ashes that show not a gleam.
But well shall it be with us ever
  Who drive through the darkness here,
If the soul that we live by never,
  For aught that a lie saith, fear.

### In a Rosary

Through the low grey archway children's feet that pass
Quicken, glad to find the sweetest haunt of all.
Brightest wildflowers gleaming deep in lustiest grass,
Glorious weeds that glisten through the green sea's glass,
Match not now this marvel, born to fade and fall.

Roses like a rainbow wrought of roses rise
Right and left and forward, shining toward the sun.
Nay, the rainbow lit of sunshine droops and dies
Ere we dream it hallows earth and seas and skies;
Ere delight may dream it lives, its life is done.

Round the border hemmed with high deep hedges round
Go the children, peering over or between
Where the dense bright oval wall of box inwound,
Reared about the roses fast within it bound,
Gives them grace to glance at glories else unseen.

Flower outlightening flower and tree outflowering tree
Feed and fill the sense and spirit full with joy.
Nought awhile they know of outer earth and sea:
Here enough of joy it is to breathe and be:
Here the sense of life is one for girl and boy.

Heaven above them, bright as children's eyes or dreams,
Earth about them, sweet as glad soft sleep can show
Earth and sky and sea, a world that scarcely seems
Even in children's eyes less fair than life that gleams
Through the sleep that none but sinless eyes may know.

Near beneath, and near above, the terraced ways
Wind or stretch and bask or blink against the sun.
Hidden here from sight on soft or stormy days
Lies and laughs with love toward heaven, at silent gaze,
All the radiant rosary—all its flowers made one.

All the multitude of roses towering round
Dawn and noon and night behold as one full flower,
Fain of heaven and loved of heaven, curbed and crowned,
Raised and reared to make this plot of earthly ground
Heavenly, could but heaven endure on earth an hour.

Swept away, made nothing now for ever, dead,
Still the rosary lives and shines on memory, free
Now from fear of death or change as childhood, fled
Years on years before its last live leaves were shed:
None may mar it now, as none may stain the sea.

PART TWO

# *Collected Prose*

## "THE MONOMANIAC'S TRAGEDY, AND OTHER POEMS," BY ERNEST WHELDRAKE (1858)

Nothing is so tenacious of life as a bad poet. The opossum, we are credibly informed, survives for hours after its brains are blown out by a pistol. The author of "The Monomaniac's Tragedy" lives, writes, and finds a publisher; nay, it should appear, admirers also. Nevertheless, the chastisement inflicted for his first offence was severe enough to have killed a dozen rising prose writers. *Eve, a Mystery*, was anatomized "with a bitter and severe delight" by all the critics who noticed it, with the exception (we believe) of Mr. Wheldrake himself. But neither as poet nor as critic was the world worthy of that gentleman. Emboldened, however, by this very questionable success, he has dropped the anonymous veil which his modesty at first compelled him to assume. The reader of his new volume will not be agonized by doubts of the author's personality. It is indeed rumoured that he has adopted a pseudonym; from what we know of his modesty we might conceive it possible; but we ask our readers, what poet on earth would choose to appear before the world with such a substitute for John Smith or Timothy Brown? No; let us leave Mr. Ernest Wheldrake the full distinction of his christian name and patronymic.

The present volume, we are bound to say, is a decided advance upon the author's *Eve*. Those who do not remember that remarkable poem, may require to be informed that it represented the expiring moments of our first mother. The opening scene was laid in Pandemonium, where a conclave of devils was assembled to debate on the means of getting spiritual possession of the deceased. The speech in which Lucifer introduced the subject to their notice was a masterly exposition of facts; towards the end, however, the honourable gentleman becomes slightly tedious, not to say maudlin. Discovering, however, that Mammon had dropped asleep (at least, so we construe the lines—

Arouse thee, Mammon! is there room for sloth
In this contracted parallax of time?)

Lucifer rebukes him as a "thunder-winged sluggard" and a "starry drone." He is then dispatched to earth in a noticeably penitent condition: apparently to report proceedings, and ask leave to sit again.

We next find ourselves in the moon, which we are informed is

An extra-paradisal entity
Swung by a cord athwart the howling night,
Blackened with generations infinite,
Whose dust lies thick as winter's leafy tears.

Here we are introduced to "Adam and Belial." These gentlemen discourse for about twenty pages in the style of the foregoing extract: on what subject, we are unable to discover: after which Belial becomes more lively, but decidedly blasphemous; not to mention his evident disposition to dwell upon such unbecoming topics as "wine disheveled tresses," "globed sapphires of liquescent eyes, warmed with prenatal influx of rich love," "luscious sweetnesses of vintage-tinctured raiment," etc., etc. This behaviour Adam with great propriety rebukes, and puts to his companion the following query:

Spirit! know'st thou not
That the bad man is alien to the good
As conch-like lustres to the rayless pearl?

Belial remarks that such language "doth blast his preconception," and announces a resolution to "depart for the inane"; whither he accordingly betakes himself.

We shall not follow him. We might indeed relate how Adam on his return to earth

By starry passages
Thrilled down the plummet of a cherub's plume,

is startled by the news

That by the chill decrepitude of dawn
Sharp cold has caught his Eve—

in other words, that the lady has taken cold—how the invalid has yet breath to lecture him for two hundred lines on his past life, and on the prospects of humanity—how the solicitous husband requests her to

Dip her throat into this lunar bowl
And drink a little, only for his sake,
Lest med'cinable custom thwart itself,

how she positively refuses, and ultimately expires with the words,

Eternity, unhand me! Is it there?
Let me see—see—see; I feel very dead.

We at first, in common with other critics, took this Mystery as an irreverent parody of such poems as *Cain* and *Festus*. But we are now convinced that Mr. Wheldrake was in earnest; and so it seems are others. Certain periodicals, whose names we regret to say are new to us, have decided that *Eve* is "a happy overflow of young loveliness," "a green development" (this we entirely agree with), "a meridian imagining," and a "passionate revelation of purity"; also that it is "remarkable for nervous grace and [a] certain sinewy sweetness of expression." For one rash moment we did indeed believe that we had recognized here the fine Roman hand of a well-known North British critic; but we have since been given to understand that this advertisement is a hoax played off by Mr. Wheldrake and his publisher. If this be the case, such an impudent attempt at imposition cannot be too severely reprehended: it shews, indeed, a degree of moral turpitude which far outweighs the sin of writing absurd poetry. These gentlemen may consider the occupation of literary forgery as remarkably humorous and amusing; but we can tell them that all honourable men will be revolted by such a flagrant instance of dishonesty. Our language may appear strong, but we must remember that the question at issue is one of far higher importance than any literary merit or demerit.

Mr. Wheldrake's present publication is, as we have said before, decidedly superior to his *coup d'essai*. It abounds, indeed, in such flowers of language as "a seraph's rainbow-cinctured pieties," "thunder-spurred immensities of space Sun-beamed with arrowy sable," "violet-poisoned subtleties of breath," "lotus-begotten happiness of scent," "blue raptures of predominating larks"; it is impossible to discover the construction of nine sentences out of ten: and the main poem is about as comprehensible as *Eve, A Mystery*. We defy any man to make sense of the following extracts: —

"Dismally they skipped me up and down
In bloody famine; rents of life were torn
From the red culmination of my heart,
Cored with unspeakable despondencies,
And pulsed with meditations of despair,
Thro' all the stagnant seasons?"

"Futurity
Is the dull owl that croaks for any bone,
Ploughed over in the sepulchres of time."

"Love, crimson-hearted eagle, fed with stars,
Till he be potent (as my soul may be)
To brush the gold dust off the face of suns,
Assimilates all capability
In a mature parenthesis of thought.
Thought volatilatized by iris'd pain,
Thrice actuated by his own insolent sense,
Of muscular action, and destroyed disdain."

"By Heaven, had I the teeth of Caucasus
Red-hot from Promethean agonies,
And tusks more lucid than the lunar snows,
On those jagged lawns of Asia, cavernous
With many a dragon banquet-eyes like those

Minerva made of flint to shatter Jove—
I'd hurl their hate upon thee, and myself
Die in a red parabola of Fate!"

This may be dramatically proper from the lips of a maniac, although we think a compassionate keeper would speedily put a gag in the poor creature's mouth: but a whole poem composed of such materials is surely too much. Let Mr. Wheldrake read *King Lear* with attention; he will see that the ravings of that monarch, in themselves meaningless and uninteresting, are duly subordinate to the progress of the plot, and the development of character.

The story of "The Monomaniac's Tragedy," as far as we can make it out, is briefly this: The hero is engaged in writing *Iscariot, a Tragedy*; and naturally feeling that, while yet innocent, he cannot enter into the feelings of thieves and murderers, he determines to acquire the requisite experience. With this rational object in view, he organises a burglarious attempt upon his brother's house, and wrings the neck of that gentleman's infant son: after which he reflects as follows—

"Ay, I have seen the face of Theft,
And tasted the red kiss of murder still—
Large scope is yet for passion!
*(a very long pause)*
Oh! ah! oh!
Ha! ha! it burns me. Have I found him there?
Nay, thou dead pain, it shall not alter thee;
Tho' I hurled heaven into the reeling spume
Of thunder whitened ages, haled the moon
At some red meteor's palpitating heels,
A mangled residue of beams—what else?
*(a long pause)*

All this is a prelude to an attempt upon the life of his sister-in-law, whom he endeavours to poison in a Twelfth cake. He is, however, detected, and dispatched to Bedlam

With all the warmth of song
Bubbled within him, tremulous with hope,
Like a dead snow-drop.

Here he delivers himself of the interminable monologue which contains his life: and here we are happy to take leave of him.

The next poem is entitled "Keeping Cattle." One stanza we extract: —

These meadows, cowslip tinctured,
Fold-green dreams of May,
The lowlands, pinespur-cinctured,
Die into the day:

The cow's breath pains me,
The vapour stains me,
The sun disdains me;
I know not what I say.
Is it a bark far down? Hush! hark!
I heard him call the sweet old way
"Love, 'tis thy love overstrains me";
No! 'twas but the lark
And the red sunset hears the forest bray.

This idyl disposed of, we come to a Sonnet on the Emperor of the French, which we extract entire as a specimen of our author's saner mood.

Louis Napoleon.

He stands upon a rock that cleaves the sheath
Of blue sea like a sword of upward form;
Along the washing waste flows far beneath
A palpitation of senescent storm.
He, Lethean pilot of grim death,
Utters by fits a very potent breath.
He is the apex of the focussed ages,
The crown of all those labouring powers that warm
Earth's red hot core, when scoriac sorrow rages.
He is the breath Titanic—the supreme
Development of some presolar dream.
Owls, dogs, that bellow at him! is he not
More strong than ye? His intermittent love
The measure of your wretched hates keeps hot.
Ye are below him—for he is above.

We trust that Mr. Wheldrake's approbation will atone, in Imperial circles, for the publication of the "Châtiments." The English poet, indeed, seems determined to try for the post of Laureate at the Tuileries. In "A Dream of Ladies"—considerably altered from Tennyson—he is favoured with a glorified vision of

Her of the happy brows
Whom not in vain the Flemish sailor wooed;
First petal of our fair Imperial rose,
First dawn to France of good—

*i.e.* Madame de Saint-Leu! We trust the compliment will be as duly appreciated as it is happily chosen.

Of the other political poems in this volume we have not time to speak at length; but in passing we may recommend a lyric called "Flowers from Naples," to the attention of M. Veuillot, as a final refutation of the calumnies heaped by venal English and apostate Italian on his favorite monarch.

Next comes "Lines to ——." This person, it appears, died in Spring: and the result of her death to Mr. Wheldrake is described as follows:

I put a smile about my face;
Of tender doubts I cannot speak:
I shudder in a sunny place;
I tear a strip of tooth-shaped lace
And press her skirt against my cheek.
The luskish blossom near and far
In shadowy pulses palpitates;
The blooms that round her grave there are,
Blot noon's extremest coping star
With black my lost heart emulates.
A violet-vestured harmony
Caps the composure of her grave;
The voiced heaven's archæval sigh
In plenilunar agony
Dies round it like a broken wave.

We will go no further. The above remarks were uttered with no intention of giving pain to Mr. Wheldrake: if they do so we are sincerely sorry. But if such books are published they must be criticized; and we only hope it is not too late for our author to profit by advice which has been offered in no unfriendly spirit.

## FROM "CHARLES BAUDELAIRE: *LES FLEURS DU MAL*" (1862)

*"He has chosen to dwell mainly upon sad and strange things"*

To some English readers the name of M. Baudelaire may be known rather through his admirable translations, and the criticisms on American and English writers appended to these, and framing them in fit and sufficient commentary, than by his volume of poems, which, perhaps, has hardly yet had time to make its way among us. That it will in the long run fail of its meed of admiration, whether here or in France, we do not believe. Impeded at starting by a foolish and shameless prosecution, the first edition was, it appears, withdrawn before anything like a fair hearing had been obtained for it. The book now comes before us with a few of the original poems cancelled, but with important additions. Such as it now is, to sum up the merit and meaning of it is not easy to do in a few sentences. Like all good books, and all work of any original savour and strength, it will be long a debated point of argument, vehemently impugned and eagerly upheld.

We believe that M. Baudelaire's first publications were his essays on the contemporary art of France, written now many years since. In these early writings there is already such admirable judgment, vigour of thought and style, and appreciative devotion to the subject, that the worth of his own future work in art might have been foretold even then. He has more delicate power of verse than almost any man living, after Victor Hugo, Browning, and (in his lyrics) Tennyson. The sound of his metres suggests colour and perfume. His perfect workmanship makes every subject admirable and respectable. Throughout the chief part of this book, he has chosen to dwell mainly upon sad and strange things — the weariness of pain and the bitterness of pleasure — the perverse happiness and wayward sorrows of exceptional people. It has the languid lurid beauty of close and threatening weather — a heavy heated temperature, with dangerous hothouse scents in it; thick shadow of cloud about it, and fire of molten light. It is quite clear of all whining and windy lamentation; there is nothing of the blubbering and shrieking style long since exploded. The writer delights in problems, and has a natural leaning to obscure and sorrowful things. Failure and sorrow, next to physical beauty and perfection of sound or scent, seem to have an infinite attraction for him. In some points he resembles Keats, or still more his chosen favourite among modern poets, Edgar Poe; at times, too, his manner of thought has a relish of Marlowe, and even the sincerer side of Byron. From Théophile Gautier, to whom the book is dedicated, he has caught the habit of a faultless and studious simplicity; but, indeed, it seems merely natural to him always to use the right word and the right rhyme. How supremely musical and flexible a perfect artist in writing can make the French language, any chance page of the book is enough to prove; every description, the slightest and shortest even, has a special mark on it of the writer's keen and peculiar power. The style is sensuous and weighty; the sights seen are steeped most often in sad light and sullen colour. As instances of M. Baudelaire's strength and beauty of manner, one might take especially the poems headed *Le Masque*, *Parfum Exotique*, *La Chevelure*, *Les Sept Vieillards*, *Les Petites Vielles*, *Brumes et Pluies*; of his perfect mastery in description, and sharp individual drawing of character and form, the following stray verses plucked out at random may stand for a specimen: —

"Sur ta chevelure profonde
Aux âcres parfums,
Mer odorante et vagabonde
Aux flots bleus et bruns,

Comme un navire qui s'éveille
Au vent du matin,
Mon âme réveuse appareille
Pour un ciel lointain.

Tes yeux où rien ne se révèle
De doux ni d'amer
Sont deux bijoux froids où se mêle
L'or avec le fer.

---

Et ton corps se penche et s'allonge
Comme un fin vaisseau
Qui roule bord sur bord et plonge
Ses vergues dans l'eau."

The whole poem is worth study for its vigorous beauty and the careful facility of its expression. Perhaps, though, the sonnet headed *Causerie* is a still completer specimen of the author's power. The way in which the sound and sense are suddenly broken off and shifted, four lines from the end, is wonderful for effect and success. M. Baudelaire's mastery of the sonnet form is worth remarking as a test of his natural bias towards such forms of verse as are most nearly capable of perfection. In a book of this sort, such a leaning of the writer's mind is almost necessary. The matters treated of will bear no rough or hasty handling. Only supreme excellence of words will suffice to grapple with and fitly render the effects of such material. Not the luxuries of pleasure in their simple first form, but the sharp and cruel enjoyments of pain, the acrid relish of suffering felt or inflicted, the sides on which nature looks unnatural, go to make up the stuff and substance of this poetry. Very good material they make, too; but evidently such things are unfit for rapid or careless treatment. The main charm of the book is, upon the whole, that nothing is wrongly given, nothing capable of being re-written or improved on its own ground. Concede the starting point, and you cannot have a better runner.

Thus, even of the loathsomest bodily putrescence and decay he can make some noble use; pluck out its meaning and secret, even its beauty, in a certain way, from actual carrion; as here, of the flies bred in a carcase.

"Tout cela descendait, montait comme une vague;
Ou s'élançaint en pétillant.
On eût dit que le corps, enflé d'un souffle vague,
Vivait en se multipliant.

Et ce monde rendait une étrange musique,
Comme l'eau courante et le vent,
Ou le grain qu'un vanneur d'un mouvement rhythmique
Agite et tourne dans son van."

Another of this poet's noblest sonnets is that *A une Passante*, comparable with a similar one of Keats, "Time's sea hath been five years at its slow ebb," but superior for directness of point and forcible reality. Here for once the beauty of a poem is rather passionate than sensuous. Compare the delicate emblematic manner in which Keats winds up his sonnet to this sharp perfect finale: —

"Fugitive beauté
Dont le regard m'a fait soudainement renaître,
Ne te verrai-je plus que dans l'éternité?
Ailleurs, bien loin d'ici, trop tard! Jamais peut-être!
Car j'ignore où tu fuis, tu ne sais o je vais,
O toi que j'eusse aimée, ô toi qui le savais!"

There is noticeable also in M. Baudelaire's work a quality of *drawing* which recalls the exquisite power in the same way of great French artists now living. His studies are admirable for truth and grace; his figure-painting has the ease and strength, the trained skill, and beautiful gentle justice of manner, which come out in such pictures as the *Source* of Ingres, or that other splendid study by Flandrin, of a curled-up naked figure under full soft hot light, now exhibiting here. These verses of Baudelaire's are as perfect and good as either.

"—Tes sourcils méchants
Te donnent un air étrange,
Qui n'est pas celui d'un ange,
Sorcière aux yeux alléchants,
* * * * *
"Sur ta chair le parfum rôde
Comme autour d'un encensoir;

Tu charmes comme le soir,
Nymphe ténébreuse et chaude.
* * * * *
"Le désert et la forêt
Embaument tes tresses rudes;
Ta tête a les attitudes
De l'énigme et du secret.

*"Tes hanches sont amoureuses*
*De ton dos et de les seins,*
Et tu ravis les coussins
Par tes poses langoureuses."

Nothing can beat that as a piece of beautiful drawing.

It may be worth while to say something of the moral and meaning of many among these poems. Certain critics, who will insist on going into this matter, each man as deep as his small leaden plummet will reach, have discovered what they call a paganism on the spiritual side of the author's tone of thought. Stripped of its coating of jargon, this may mean that the poet spoken of endeavors to look at most things with the eye of an old-world poet; that he aims at regaining the clear and simple view of writers content to believe in the beauty of material subjects. To us, if this were the meaning of these people, we must say it seems a foolish one; for there is not one of these poems that could have been written in a time when it was not fashion to dig for moral motives and conscious reasons. Poe, for example, has written poems without any moral meaning at all; there is not one poem of the *Fleurs du Mal* which has not a distinct and vivid background of morality to it. Only this moral side of the book is not thrust forward in the foolish and repulsive manner of a half-taught artist; the background, as we called it, is not out of drawing. If any reader could extract from any poem a positive spiritual medicine—if he could swallow a sonnet like a moral prescription—then clearly the poet supplying these intellectual drugs would be a bad artist; indeed, no real artist, but a huckster and vendor of miscellaneous wares. But those who will look for them may find moralities in plenty behind every poem of M. Baudelaire's; such poems especially as *Une Martyre*. Like a mediæval preacher, when he has drawn the heathen love, he puts sin on its right hand and death on its left. It is not his or any artist's business to warn against evil; but certainly he does not exhort to it, knowing well enough that the one fault is as great as the other.

But into all this we do not advise any one to enter who can possibly keep out of it. When a book has been so violently debated over, so hauled this way and that by contentious critics, the one intent on finding that it means something mischievous, and the other intent on finding that it means something useful, those who are in search neither of a poisonous compound nor of a cathartic drug had better leave the disputants alone, or take only such notice of them as he absolutely must take. Allegory is the dullest game and the most profitless taskwork imaginable; but if so minded a reader might extract most elaborate meanings from this poem of *Une Martyre*; he might discover a likeness between the Muse of the writer and that strange figure of a beautiful body with the head severed, laid apart.

> "Sur la table de nuit comme une renoncule".

The heavy "mass of dark mane and heap of precious jewels" might mean the glorious style and decorative language clothing this poetry of strange disease and sin; the hideous violence wrought by a shameless and senseless love might stand as an emblem of that analysis of things monstrous and sorrowful, which stamps the whole book with its special character. Then again, the divorce between all aspiration and its results might be here once more given in type; the old question re-handled: —

> "What hand and brain went ever paired?
> What heart alike conceived and dared?"

and the sorrowful final divorce of will from deed accomplished at last by force; and the whole thing summed up in that noble last stanza: —

> "Ton époux court le monde: et ta forme immortelle
>   Veille près de lui quand il dort;
> Autant que toi sans doute il te sera fidèle,
>   Et constant jusque à la mort."

All this and more might be worked out if the reader cared to try; but we hope he would not. The poem is quite beautiful and valuable enough as merely the "design of an unknown master."

## *NOTES ON POEMS AND REVIEWS* (1866)

> *"Je pense sur ces satires comme Épictète: 'Si l'on dit du mal de toi, et qu'il soit véritable, corrige-toi; si ce sont des mensonges, ris-en.' J'ai appris avec l'âge à devenir bon cheval de poste; je fais ma station, et ne m'embarrasse pas des roquets qui aboient en chemin."*
>
> —Frederic le Grand.

> *"Ignorance by herself is an awkward lumpish wench; not yet fallen into vicious courses, nor to be uncharitably treated: but Ignorance and Insolence, these are, for certain, an unlovely Mother and Bastard!"*
>
> —Carlyle.

It is by no wish of my own that I accept the task now proposed to me. To vindicate or defend myself from the assault or the charge of men whom, but for their attacks, I might never have heard of, is an office which I, or any writer who respects his work, cannot without reluctance stoop to undertake. As long as the attacks on my book—I have seen a few, I am told there are many—were confined within the usual limits of the anonymous press, I let them pass without the notice to which they appeared to aspire. Sincere or insincere, insolent or respectful, I let my assailants say out their say unheeded.

I have now undertaken to write a few words on this affair, not by way of apology or vindication, of answer or appeal. I have none such to offer. Much of the criticism I have seen is as usual, in the words of Shakespeare's greatest follower,

> "As if a man should spit against the wind;
> The filth returns in's face."

In recognition of his fair dealing with me in this matter, I am bound by my own sense of right to accede to the wish of my present publisher, and to the wishes of friends whose advice I value, that on his account, if not on mine, I should make some reply to the charges brought against me—as far as I understand them. The work is not fruitful of pleasure, of honour, or of profit; but, like other such tasks, it may be none the less useful and necessary. I am aware that it cannot be accomplished without some show of egotism; and I am perforce prepared to incur the consequent charge of arrogance. The office of commentator of my own works has been forced upon me by circumstances connected with the issue and re-issue of my last book. I am compelled to look sharply into it, and inquire what passage, what allusion, or what phrase can have drawn down such sudden thunder from the serene heavens of public virtue. A mere libeler I have no wish to encounter; I leave it to saints to fight with beasts at Ephesus or nearer. "For in these strifes, and on such persons, it were as wretched to affect a victory, as it is unhappy to be committed with them."

Certain poems of mine, it appears, have been impugned by judges, with or without a name, as indecent or as blasphemous. To me, as I have intimated, their verdict is a matter of infinite indifference: it is of equally small moment to me whether in such eyes as theirs I appear moral or immoral, Christian or pagan. But, remembering that science must not scorn to investigate animalcules and infusoria, I am ready for once to play the anatomist.

With regard to any opinion implied or expressed throughout my book, I desire that one thing should be remembered: the book is dramatic, many-faced, multifarious; and no utterance of enjoyment or despair, belief or unbelief, can properly be assumed as the assertion of its author's personal feeling or faith. Were each poem to be accepted as the deliberate outcome and result of the writer's conviction, not mine alone but most other men's verses would leave nothing behind them but a sense of cloudy chaos and suicidal contradiction. Byron and Shelley, speaking in their own persons, and with what sublime effect we know, openly and insultingly mocked and reviled what the English of their day held most sacred. I have not done this. I do not say that, if I chose, I would not do so to the best of my power; I do say that hitherto I have seen fit to do nothing of the kind.

It remains then to inquire what in that book can be reasonably offensive to the English reader. In order to resolve this problem, I will not fish up any of the ephemeral scurrilities born only to sting if they can, and sink as they must. I will take the one article that lies before me; the work (I admit) of an enemy, but the work (I acknowledge) of a gentleman. I cannot accept it as accurate; but I readily and gladly allow that it neither contains nor suggests anything false or filthy. To him therefore, rather than to another, I address my reclamation. Two among my poems, it appears, are in his opinion "especially horrible." Good. Though the phrase be somewhat "inexpressive," I am content to meet him on this ground. It is something—nay, it is much—to find an antagonist who has a sufficient sense of honesty and honour to mark out the lists in which he, the challenger, is desirous to encounter the challenged.

The first, it appears, of these especially horrible poems is *Anactoria*. I am informed, and have not cared to verify the assertion, that this poem has excited, among the chaste and candid critics of the day or hour or minute, a more vehement reprobation, a more virtuous horror, a more passionate appeal, than any other of my writing. Proud and glad as I must be of this distinction, I must yet, however reluctantly, inquire what merit or demerit has incurred such unexpected honour. I was not ambitious of it; I am not ashamed of it; but I am overcome by it. I have never lusted after the praise of reviewers; I have never feared their abuse; but I would fain know why the vultures should gather here of all places; what congenial carrion they smell, who can discern such (it is alleged) in any rosebed. And after a little reflection I do know, or conjecture. Virtue, as she appears incarnate in British journalism and voluble through that unsavoury organ, is something of a compound creature—

"A lump neither alive nor dead,
Dog-headed, bosom-eyed, and bird-footed;"

nor have any dragon's jaws been known to emit on occasion stronger and stranger sounds and odours. But having, not without astonishment and disgust, inhaled these odours, I find myself at last able to analyse their component parts. What my poem means, if any reader should want that explained, I am ready to explain, though perplexed by the hint that explanation may be required. What certain reviewers have imagined it to imply, I am incompetent to explain, and unwilling to imagine. I am evidently not virtuous enough to understand them. I thank Heaven that I am not. *Ma corruption rougirait de leur pudeur*. I have not studied in those schools whence that full-fledged phœnix, the "virtue" of professional pressmen, rises chuckling and crowing from the dunghill, its birthplace and its deathbed. But there are birds of alien feather, if not of higher flight; and these I would now recall into no hencoop or preserve of mine, but into the open and general field where all may find pasture and sunshine and fresh air: into places whither the prurient prudery and the virulent virtue of pressmen and prostitutes cannot follow; into an atmosphere where calumny cannot speak, and fatuity cannot breathe; in a word, where backbiters and imbeciles become impossible. I neither hope nor wish to change the unchangeable, to purify the impure. To conciliate them, to vindicate myself in their eyes, is a task which I should not condescend to attempt, even were I sure to accomplish.

In this poem I have simply expressed, or tried to express, that violence of affection between one and another which hardens into rage and deepens into despair. The key-note which I have here touched was struck long since by Sappho. We in England are taught, are compelled under penalties to learn, to construe, and to repeat, as schoolboys, the imperishable and incomparable verses of that supreme poet; and I at least am grateful for the training. I have wished, and I have even ventured to hope, that I might be in time competent to translate into a baser and later language the divine words which even when a boy could not but recognise as divine. That hope, if indeed I dared ever entertain such a hope, I soon found fallacious. To translate the two odes and the remaining fragments of Sappho is the one impossible task; and as witness of this I will call up one of the greatest among poets. Catullus "translated"—or as his countrymen would now say "traduced"—the Ode to Anactoria—*Είς Έρωμέναν:* a more beautiful translation there never was and will never be; but compared with the Greek, it is colourless and bloodless, puffed out by additions and enfeebled by alterations. Let any one set against each other the two first stanzas, Latin and Greek, and pronounce. (This would be too much to ask of all of my critics; but some among the journalists of England may be capable of achieving the not exorbitant task.) Where Catallus failed I could not hope to succeed; I tried instead to reproduce in a diluted and dilated form the spirit of a poem which could not be reproduced in the body.

Now the ode *Είς Έρωμέναν*—the "Ode to Anactoria" (as it is named by tradition)—the poem which English boys have to get by heart—the poem (and this is more important) which has in the whole world of verse no companion and no rival but the Ode to Aphrodite, has been twice at least translated or "traduced." I am not aware that Mr. Ambrose Phillips, or M. Nicolas Boileau-Despréaux, was ever impeached before any jury of moralists for his sufficiently grievous offence. By any jury of poets both would assuredly have been convicted. Now, what they did I have not done. To the best (and bad is the best) of their ability, they have "done into" bad French and bad English the very words of Sappho. Feeling that although I might do it better I could not do it well, I abandoned the idea of translation—*ἕκων ἀέκοντί γε θυμῷ.* I tried, then, to write some paraphrase of the fragment which the Fates and the Christians have spared us. I have not said, as Boileau and Phillips have, that the speaker sweats and swoons at sight of her favourite by the side of a man. I have abstained from touching on such details, for this reason: that I felt myself incompetent to give adequate expression in English to the literal and absolute words of Sappho; and would not debase and degrade them into a viler form. No one can feel more deeply than I do the inadequacy of my work. "That is not Sappho," a friend said once to me. I could only reply, "It is as near as I can come; and no man can come close to her." Her remaining verses are the supreme success, the final achievement, of the poetic art.

But this, it may be, is not to the point. I will try to draw thither; though the descent is immeasurable from Sappho's verse to mine, or to any man's. I have striven to cast my spirit into the mould of hers, to express and represent not the poem but the poet. I did not think it requisite to disfigure the page with a footnote wherever I had fallen back upon the original text. Here and there, I need not say, I have rendered into English the very words of Sappho. I have tried to work into words of my own some expression of their effect: to bear witness how, more than any other's, her verses strike and sting the memory in lonely places, or at sea, among all loftier sights and sounds—how they seem akin to fire and air, being themselves "all air and fire;" other element there is none in them. As to the angry appeal against the supreme mystery of oppressive heaven, which I have ventured to put into her mouth at that point only where pleasure culminates in pain, affection in anger, and desire in despair—as to the "blasphemies"* against God or Gods of which here and elsewhere I stand accused,—they are to be taken as the first outcome or outburst of foiled and fruitless passion recoiling on itself. After this, the spirit finds time to breathe and repose above all vexed senses of the weary body, all bitter labours of the revolted soul; the poet's pride of place is resumed, the lofty conscience of invincible immortality in the memories and the mouths of men.

What is there now of horrible in this? the expressions of fierce fondness, the ardours of passionate despair? Are these so unnatural as to affright or disgust? Where is there an unclean detail? where an obscene allusion? A writer as impure as my critics might of course have written, on this or any subject, an impure poem; I have not. And if to translate or paraphrase Sappho be an offence, indict the heavier offenders who have handled and rehandled this matter in their wretched versions of the ode. Is my poem more passionate in detail, more unmistakable in subject? I affirm that it is less; and what I affirm I have proved.

Next on the list of accusation stands the poem of *Dolores*. The gist and bearing of this I should have thought evident enough, viewed by the light of others which precede and follow it. I have striven here to express that transient state of spirit through which a man may be supposed to pass, foiled in love and weary of loving, but not yet in sight of rest; seeking refuge in those "violent delights" which "have violent ends," in fierce and frank sensualities which at least profess to be no more than they are. This poem, like *Faustine*, is so distinctly symbolic and fanciful that it cannot justly be amenable to judgment as a study in the school of realism. The spirit, bowed and discoloured by suffering and by passion (which are indeed the same thing and the same word), plays for awhile with its pleasures and its pains, mixes and distorts them with a sense of half-humorous and half-mournful, exults in bitter and doubtful emotions—

> "Moods of fantastic sadness, nothing worth."

It sports with sorrow, and jests against itself; cries out for freedom and confesses the chain; decorates with the name of goddess, crowns anew as the mystical Cotytto, some woman, real or ideal, in whom the pride of life with its companion

*As I shall not return to this charge of "blasphemy," I will here cite a notable instance of what does seem permissible in that line to the English reader. (I need not say that I do not question the right, which hypocrisy and servility would deny, of author and publisher to express and produce what they please. I do not deprecate, but demand for all men freedom to speak and freedom to hear. It is the line of demarcation which admits, if offence there be, the greater offender and rejects the less—it is this that I do not understand.) After many alternate curses and denials of God, a great poet talks of Christ "veiling his horrible Godhead," of his "malignant soul," his "godlike malice." Shelley outlived all this and much more; but Shelley wrote all this and much more. Will no Society for the Suppression of Common Sense—no Committee for the Propagation of Cant—see to it a little? or have they not already tried their hands at it and broken down? For the poem which contains the words above quoted continues at this day to bring credit and profit to its publishers—Messrs. Moxon and Co.

lusts is incarnate. In her lover's half-shut eyes, her fierce unchaste beauty is transfigured, her cruel sensual eyes have a meaning and a message; there are memories and secrets in the kisses of her lips. She is the darker Venus, fed with burnt-offering and blood-sacrifice; the veiled image of that pleasure which men impelled by satiety and perverted by power have sought through ways as strange as Nero's before and since his time; the daughter of lust and death, and holding of both her parents; Our Lady of Pain, antagonist alike of trivial sins and virtues: no Virgin, and unblessed of men; no mother of the Gods or God; no Cybele, served by sexless priests or monks, adored of Origen or of Atys; no likeness of her in Dindymus or Loreto.

The next act in this lyrical monodrame of passion represents a new stage and scene. The worship of desire has ceased; the mad commotion of sense has stormed itself out; the spirit, clear of the old regret that drove it upon such violent ways for a respite, healed of the fever that wasted it in the search for relief among fierce fancies and tempestuous pleasures, dreams now of truth discovered and repose attained. Not the martyr's ardour of selfless love, an unprofitable flame that burnt out and did no service—not the rapid rage of pleasure that seemed for a little to make the flesh divine, to clothe the naked senses with the fiery raiment of faith; but a stingless love, an innocuous desire. "Hesperia," the tenderest type of woman or of dream, born in the westward "islands of the blest," where the shadows of all happy and holy things live beyond the sunset a sacred and sleepless life, dawns upon his eyes a western dawn, risen as the fiery day of passion goes down, and risen where it sank. Here, between moonrise and sunset, lives the love that is gentle and faithful, neither giving too much nor asking—a bride rather than a mistress, a sister rather than a bride. But not at once, or not for ever, can the past be killed and buried; hither also the huntress follows her flying prey, wounded and weakened, still fresh from the fangs of passion; the cruel hands, the amorous eyes, still glitter and allure. *Qui a bu boira*: the feet are drawn back towards the ancient ways. Only by lifelong flight, side by side with the goddess that redeems, shall her slave of old escape from the goddess that consumes: if even thus one may be saved, even thus distance the bloodhounds.

This is the myth or fable of my poem; and it is not without design that I have slipped in, between the first and the second part, the verses called *The Garden of Proserpine*, expressive, as I meant they should be, of that brief total pause of passion and of thought, when the spirit, without fear of hope of good things or evil, hungers and thirsts only after the perfect sleep. Now, what there is in all this unfit to be written—what there is here indecent in manner or repulsive in matter—I at least do not yet see; and before I can see it, my eyes must be purged with the euphrasy and rue which keep clear the purer eyes of professional virtue. The insight into evil of chaste and critical pressmen, their sharp scent for possible or impossible impurities, their delicate ear for a sound or a whisper of wrong—all this knowledge "is too wonderful and excellent for me; I cannot attain unto it." In one thing, indeed, it seems I have erred: I have forgotten to prefix to my work the timely warning of a great poet and humorist;—

"J'en préviens les mères des familles,
Ce que j'écris n'est pas pour les petites filles
Dont on coupe le pain en tartines; mes vers
Sont des vers de jeune homme."

I have overlooked the evidence which every day makes clearer, that our time has room only for such as are content to write for children and girls. But this oversight is the sum of my offence.

It would seem indeed as though to publish a book were equivalent to thrusting it with violence into the hands of every mother and nurse in the kingdom as fit and necessary food for female infancy. Happily there is no fear that the supply of milk for babes will fall short of the demand for some time yet. There are moral milkmen enough, in all conscience, crying their ware about the streets and byways; fresh or stale, sour or sweet, the requisite fluid runs from a sufficiently copious issue. In due time, perhaps, the critical doctors may prescribe a stronger diet for their hypochondriac patient, the reading world; or the gigantic *malade imaginaire* called the public may rebel against the weekly draught or the daily drug of MM. Purgon and Diafoirus. We, meanwhile, who profess to deal neither in poison nor in pap, may not unwillingly stand aside. Let those read who will, and let those who will abstain from reading. *Caveat emptor*. No one wishes to force men's food down the throats of babes and sucklings. The verses last analysed were assuredly written with no moral or immoral design; but the upshot seems to me moral rather than immoral, if it must needs be one or the other, and if (which I cannot be sure of) I construe aright those somewhat misty and changeable terms.

These poems thus disposed of are (I am told) those which have given most offence and scandal to the venal virtue of journalism. As I have not to review my reviewers, I need not be at pains to refute at length every wilful error or unconscious lie which a workman that way inclined might drag into light. To me, as to all others who may read what I write, the whole matter must continue to seem too pitiable and trivial to waste a word or thought on it which we can help wasting. But having begun this task, I will add yet a word or two of annotation. I have heard that even the little poem of *Faustine* has been to some readers a thing to make the scalp creep and the blood freeze. It was issued with no such intent. Nor do I remember that any man's voice or heel was lifted against it when it first appeared, a new-born and virgin poem, in the *Spectator* newspaper for 1862. Virtue, it would seem, has shot up surprisingly in the space of four years or less—a rank and rapid growth, barren of blossom and rotten at root. *Faustine* is the reverie of a man gazing on the bitter and vicious loveliness of a face as common and as cheap as the morality of reviewers, and dreaming of past lives in which this fair face may have held a nobler or fitter station; the imperial profile may have been Faustina's, the thirsty lips a Mænad's, when first she learnt to drink blood or wine, to waste the loves and ruin the lives of men; through Greece and again through Rome she may have passed with the same face which now comes before us dishonoured and discrowned. Whatever of merit or demerit there may be in the verses, the idea that gives them such life as they have is simple enough; the transmigration of a single soul, doomed as though by accident from the first to all evil and no good, through many ages and forms, but clad always in the same type of fleshly beauty. The chance which suggested to me this poem was one which may happen any day to any man—the sudden sight of a living face which recalled the well-known likeness of another dead for centuries: in this instance, the noble and faultless type of the elder Faustina, as seen in coin and bust. Out of that casual glimpse and sudden recollection these verses sprang and grew.

Of the poem in which I have attempted once more to embody the legend of Venus and her knight, I need say only that my first aim was to rehandle the old story in a new fashion. To me it seemed that the tragedy began with the knight's return to Venus—began at the point where hitherto it had seemed to leave off. The immortal agony of a man lost after all repentance—cast down from fearful hope into fearless despair—believing in Christ and bound to Venus—desirous of penitential pain, and damned to joyless pleasure—this, in my eyes, was the kernel and nucleus of a myth comparable only to that of the foolish virgins and bearing the same burden. The tragic touch of the story is this: that the knight who has renounced Christ believes in him; the lover who has embraced Venus disbelieves in her. Vainly and in despair would he make the best of that which is the worst—vainly remonstrate with God, and argue on the side he would fain desert. Once accept or admit the least admixture of pagan worship, or of modern thought, and the whole story collapses into froth and smoke. It was not till my poem was completed that I received from the hands of its author the admirable pamphlet of Charles Baudelaire on Wagner's *Tannhaüser*. If any one desires to see, expressed in better words than I can command, the conception of the mediæval Venus which it was my aim to put into verse, let him turn to the magnificent passage in which M. Baudelaire describes the fallen goddess, grown diabolic among ages that would not accept her as divine. In another point, as I then found, I concur with the great musician and his great panegyrist. I have made Venus the one love of her knight's whole life, as Mary Stuart of Chastelard's; I have sent him, poet and soldier, fresh to her fierce embrace. Thus only both legend and symbol appear to me noble and significant. Light loves and harmless errors must not touch the elect of heaven or of hell. The queen of evil, the lady of lust, will endure no rival but God; and when the vicar of God rejects him, to her only can he return to abide the day of his judgment in weariness and sorrow and fear.

These poems do not seem to me condemnable, unless it be on the ground of bad verse; and to any charge of that kind I should of course be as unable as reluctant to reply. But I certainly was even less prepared to hear the batteries of virtue open fire in another quarter. Sculpture I knew was a dead art; buried centuries deep out of sight with no angel keeping watch over the sepulchre; its very grave-clothes divided by wrangling and impotent sectaries, and no chance anywhere visible of a resurrection. I knew that belief in the body was the secret of sculpture, and that a past age of ascetics could no more attempt or attain it than the present age of hypocrites; I knew that modern moralities and recent religions were, if possible, more averse and alien to this purely physical and pagan art than to the others; but how far averse I did not know. There is nothing lovelier, as there is nothing more famous, in later Hellenic art, than the statue of Hermaphroditus. No one would compare it with the greatest works of Greek sculpture. No one would lift Keats on a level with Shakespeare. But the Fates have allowed us to possess at once Othello and Hyperion, Theseus and Hermaphroditus. At Paris, at Florence, at Naples, the delicate divinity of this work has always drawn towards it the eyes of artists and poets.* A creature at once foul and dull enough to extract from a sight so lovely, from a thing so noble, the faintest, the most fleeting idea of impurity, must be, and must remain, below comprehension and below remark. It is incredible that the meanest of men should derive from it any other than the sense of high and grateful pleasure. Odour and colour and music are not more tender or more pure. How favourite and frequent a vision among the Greeks was this of the union of sexes in one body of perfect beauty, none need be told. In Plato the legend has fallen into a form coarse, hard, and absurd. The theory of God splitting in two the double archetype of man and woman, the original hermaphrodite which had to get itself bisected into female and male, is repulsive and ridiculous enough. But the idea thus incarnate, literal or symbolic, is merely beautiful. I am not the first who has translated into written verse this sculptured poem: another before me, as he says, has more than once "caressed it with a sculptor's love." It is, indeed, among statues as a lyric among tragedies; it stands below the Niobe as Simonides below Æschylus, as Correggio beneath Titian. The sad and subtle moral of this myth, which I have desired to indicate in verse, is that perfection once attained on all sides is a thing thenceforward barren of use or fruit; whereas the divided beauty of separate woman and man—a thing inferior and imperfect—can serve all turns of life. Ideal beauty, like ideal genius,

*Witness Shelley's version: —

"A sexless thing it was, and in its growth
It seemed to have developed no defect
Of either sex, yet all the grace of both;
In gentleness and strength its limbs were decked
The bosom lightly swelled with its full youth,
The countenance was such as might select
Some artist, that his skill should never die,
Imaging forth such perfect purity."

*Witch of Atlas*, st. xxxvi.

But Shelley had not studied purity in the school of reviewers. It is well for us that we have teachers able to enlighten our darkness, or Heaven knows into what error such as he, or such as I, might not fall. We might even, in time, come to think it possible to enjoy the naked beauty of a statue or a picture without any virtuous vision behind it of a filthy fancy; which would be immoral.

dwells apart, as though by compulsion; supremacy is solitude. But leaving this symbolic side of the matter, I cannot see why this statue should not be the text for yet another poem. Treated in the grave and chaste manner as a serious "thing of beauty," to be for ever applauded and enjoyed, it can give no offence but to the purblind and the prurient. For neither of these classes have I ever written or will I ever write. "Loathsome and abominable" and full of "unspeakable foulnesses" must be that man's mind who could here discern evil; unclean and inhuman the animal which could suck from this mystical rose of ancient loveliness the foul and rancid juices of an obscene fancy. It were a scavenger's office to descend with torch or spade into such depths of mental sewerage, to plunge or peer into subterranean sloughs of mind impossible alike to enlighten or to cleanse.

I have now gone over the poems which, as I hear, have incurred most blame; whether deservedly or not, I have shown. For the terms in which certain critics have clothed their sentiments I bear them no ill-will: they are welcome for me to write unmolested, as long as they keep to simple ribaldry. I hope it gives them amusement; I presume it brings them profit; I know it does not affect me. Absolute falsehood may, if it be worth while, draw down contradiction and disproof; but the mere calling of bad names is a child's trick, for which the small fry of the press should have a child's correction at the hands of able editors; standing as these gentlemen ought to do in a parental or pedagogic relation to their tender charges. They have, by all I see and hear, been sufficiently scurrilous — one or two in particular.

"However, from one crime they are exempt;
They do not strike a brother, striking *me*."

I will only throw them one crumb of advice in return; I fear the alms will be of no avail, but it shall not be withheld: —

Why grudge them lotus-leaf and laurel,
O toothless mouth or swinish maw,
Who never grudged you bells and coral,
Who never grudged you troughs and straw?

Lie still in kennel, sleek in stable,
Good creatures of the stall or sty;
Shove snouts for crumbs below the table;
Lie still; and rise not up to lie.

To all this, however, there is a grave side. The question at issue is wider than any between a single writer and his critics, or it might well be allowed to drop. It is this: whether or not the first and last requisite of art is to give no offence; whether or not all that cannot be lisped in the nursery or fingered in the schoolroom is therefore to be cast out of the library; whether or not the domestic circle is to be for all men and writers the outer limit and extreme horizon of their world of work. For to this we have come; and all students of art must face the matter as it stands. Who has not heard it asked, in a final and triumphant tone, whether this book or that can be read aloud by her mother to a young girl? whether such and such a picture can properly be exposed to the eyes of young persons? If you reply that this is nothing to the point, you fall at once into the ranks of the immoral. Never till now, and nowhere but in England, could so monstrous an absurdity rear for one moment its deformed and eyeless head. In no past century were artists ever bidden to work on these terms; nor are they now, except among us. The disease, of course, afflicts the meanest members of the body with most virulence. Nowhere is cant at once so foul-mouthed and so tight-laced as in the penny, twopenny, threepenny, or sixpenny press. Nothing is so favourable to the undergrowth of real indecency as this overshadowing foliage of fictions, this artificial network of proprieties. *L'Arioste rit au soleil, l'Arétin ricane à l'ombre*. The whiter the sepulchre without, the ranker the rottenness within. Every touch of plaster is a sign of advancing decay. The virtue of our critical journals is a dowager of somewhat dubious antecedents: every day that thins and shrivels her cheek thickens and hardens the paint on it; she consumes more chalk and ceruse than would serve a whole courtful of crones. "It is to be presumed," certainly, that in her case "all is not sweet, all is not sound." The taint on her fly-blown reputation is hard to overcome by patches and perfumery. Literature, to be worthy of men, must be large, liberal, sincere; and cannot be chaste if it be prudish. Purity and prudery cannot keep house together. Where free speech and fair play are interdicted, foul hints and evil suggestions are hatched into fetid life. And if literature indeed is not to deal with the full life of man and the whole nature of things, let it be cast aside with the rods and rattles of childhood. Whether it affect to teach or to amuse, it is equally trivial and contemptible to us; only less so than the charge of immorality. Against how few really great names has not this small and dirt-encrusted pebble been thrown! A reputation seems imperfect without this tribute also: one jewel is wanting to the crown. It is good to be praised by those whom all men should praise; it is better to be reviled by those whom all men should scorn.

Various chances and causes must have combined to produce a state of faith or feeling which would turn all art and literature "into the line of children." One among others may be this: where the heaven of invention holds many stars at once, there is no fear that the highest and largest will either efface or draw aside into its orbit all lesser lights. Each of these takes its own way and sheds its proper luster. But where one alone is dominant in heaven, it is encircled by a pale procession of satellite moons, filled with shallow and stolen radiance. Thus, with English versifiers now, the idyllic form is alone in fashion. The one great and prosperous poet of the time has given out the tune, and the hoarser choir takes it up. His highest lyrical work remains unimitated, being in the main inimitable. But the trick of tone which suits an idyl is easier to assume; and the note has been struck so often that the shrillest songsters can affect to catch it up. We have idylls good and bad, ugly and pretty; idyls of the farm and the mill; idyls of the dining-room and the deanery; idyls of the gutter and the gibbet. If the Muse of the minute will not feast with "gig-men" and their wives, she must mourn with costermongers and their trulls. I fear the more ancient Muses are guests at neither house of mourning nor house of feasting.

For myself, I begrudge no man his taste or his success; I can enjoy and applaud all good work, and would always, when possible, have the workman paid in full. There is much excellent and some admirable verse among the poems of the day: to none has it given more pleasure than to me, and from none, had I been a man of letters to whom the ways were open, would it have won heartier applause. I have never been able to see what should attract men to the profession of criticism but the noble pleasure of praising. But I have no right to claim a place in the silver flock of idyllic swans. I have never worked for praise or pay, but simply by impulse, and to please myself; I must therefore, it is to be feared, remain where I am, shut out from the communion of these. At all events, I shall not be hounded into emulation of other men's work by the baying of unleashed beagles. There are those with whom I do not wish to share the praise of their praisers. I am content to abide a far different judgment: —

"I write as others wrote
On Sunium's height."

I need not be over-careful to justify my ways in other men's eyes; it is enough for me that they also work after their kind, and earn the suffrage, as they labour after the law, of their own people. The idyllic form is best for domestic and pastoral poetry. It is naturally on a lower level than that of tragic or lyric verse. Its gentle and maidenly lips are somewhat narrow for the stream and somewhat cold for the fire of song. It is very fit for the sole diet of girls; not very fit for the sole sustenance of men.

When England has again such a school of poetry, so headed and so followed, as she has had at least twice before, or as France has now; when all higher forms of the various arts are included within the larger limits of a stronger race; then, if such a day should ever rise or return upon us, it will be once more remembered that the office of adult art is neither puerile nor feminine, but virile; that its purity is not that of the cloister or the harem; that all things are good in its sight, out of which good work may be produced. Then the press will be as impotent as the pulpit to dictate the laws and remove the landmarks of art; and those will be laughed at who demand from one thing the qualities of another—who seek for sermons in sonnets and morality in music. Then all accepted work will be noble and chaste in the wider masculine sense, not truncated and curtailed, but outspoken and full-grown; art will be pure by instinct and fruitful by nature, no clipped and forced growth of unhealthy heat and unnatural air; all baseness and all triviality will fall off from it, and be forgotten; and no one will then need to assert, in defence of work done for the work's sake, the simple laws of his art which no one will then be permitted to impugn.

## FROM "BYRON" (1866, 1875)

*"Splendid and imperishable excellence"*

The most delicate and thoughtful of English critics has charged the present generation of Englishmen with forgetfulness of Byron. It is not a light charge: and it is not ungrounded. Men born when this century was getting into its forties were baptized into another church than his with the rites of another creed. Upon their ears, first after the cadences of elder poets, fell the faultless and fervent melodies of Tennyson. To them, chief among the past heroes of the younger century, three men appeared as predominant in poetry; Coleridge, Keats, and Shelley. Behind these were effaced, on either hand, the two great opposing figures of Byron and Wordsworth. No man under twenty can just now be expected to appreciate these. The time was when all boys and girls who paddled in rhyme and dabbled in sentiment were wont to adore the presence or the memory of Byron with foolish faces of praise. It is of little moment to him or to us that they have long since ceased to cackle and begun to hiss. They have become used to better verse and carefuller workmen; and must be forgiven if after such training they cannot at once appreciate the splendid and imperishable excellence which covers all his offences and outweighs all his defects: the excellence of sincerity and strength. Without these no poet can live; but few have ever had so much of them as Byron. His sincerity indeed is difficult to discover and define; but it does in effect lie at the root of all his good works: deformed by pretension and defaced by assumption, masked by folly and veiled by affectation; but perceptible after all, and priceless.

. . . . . . . . . . .

*"The ebb and flow of actual life"*

Even at its best, the serious poetry of Byron is often so rough and loose, so weak in the screws and joints which hold together the framework of verse, that it is not easy to praise it enough without seeming to condone or to extenuate such faults as should not be overlooked or forgiven. No poet is so badly represented by a book of selections. It must show something of his weakness; it cannot show all of his strength. Often, after a noble overture, the last note struck is either dissonant or ineffectual. His magnificent masterpiece, which must endure for ever among the precious relics of the world, will not bear dissection or extraction. The merit of "Don Juan" does not lie in any part, but in the whole. There is in that great poem an especial and exquisite balance and sustenance of alternate tones which cannot be expressed or explained by the utmost ingenuity of selection. Haidée is supplanted by Dudù, the shipwreck by the siege, the Russian court by the English household; and this perpetual change, this tidal variety of experience and emotion, gives to the poem something of the breadth and freshness of the sea. Much of the poet's earlier work is or seems unconsciously dishonest; this, if not always or wholly unaffected, is as honest as the sunlight, as frank as the sea-wind. Here, and here alone, the student of his work may recognize and enjoy the ebb and flow of actual life. Here the pulse of vital blood may be felt in tangible flesh. Here for the first time the style of Byron is beyond all praise or blame: a style at once swift and supple, light and strong, various and radiant. Between "Childe Harold" and "Don Juan" the same difference exists which a swimmer feels between lake-water and sea-water: the one is fluent, yielding, invariable; the other has in it a life and pulse, a sting and a swell, which touch and excite the nerves like fire or like music. Across the stanzas of "Don Juan" we swim forward as over the "the broad backs of the sea"; they break and glitter, hiss and laugh, murmur and move, like waves that sound or that subside. There is in them a delicious resistance, an elastic motion, which salt water has and fresh water has not. There is about them a wide wholesome air, full of vivid light and constant wind, which is only felt at sea. Life undulates and death palpitates in the splendid verse which resumes the evidence of a brave and clear-sighted man concerning life and death. Here, as at sea, there is enough and too much of fluctuation and intermission; the ripple flags and falls in loose and lazy lines; the foam flies wide of any mark, and the breakers collapse here and there in sudden ruin and violent failure. But the violence and weakness of the sea are preferable to the smooth sound and equable security of a lake; its buoyant and progressive impulse sustains and propels those who would sink through weariness in the flat and placid shallows. There are others whom it sickens, and others whom it chills; these will do well to steer inshore.

. . . . . . . . . . .

*"These poems are coherent and complete as trees or flowers"*

Side by side with the growth of his comic and satiric power, the graver genius of Byron increased and flourished. As the tree grew higher it grew shapelier; the branches it put forth on all sides were fairer of leaf and fuller of fruit than its earlier offshoots had promised. But from these hardly a stray bud or twig can be plucked off by way of sample. No detached morsel of "Don Juan," no dismembered fragment of "Cain," will serve to show or to suggest the excellence of either. These poems are coherent and complete as trees or flowers; they cannot be split up and parcelled out like a mosaic of artificial jewellery, which might be taken to pieces by the same artisan who put it together. It must then be remembered that any mere selection from the verse of Byron, however much of care and of goodwill be spent upon the task, must perforce either exclude or impair his very greatest work. Cancel or select a leaf from these poems, and you will injure the whole framework equally in either case. It is not without reluctance that I have given any extracts from "Don Juan;" it is not without a full sense of the damage done to these extracts by the very act of extraction. But I could only have left them untouched with a reluctance even greater; and this plea, if it can, must excuse me. As fragments they are exquisite and noble, like the broken hand or severed foot of a Greek statue; but here as much is lost as there. Taken with their context, they regain as much of beauty and of force as the sculptured foot or hand when, reunited to the perfect body, they resume their place and office among its vital and various limbs. This gift of life and variety is the supreme quality of Byron's chief poem; a quality which cannot be expressed by any system of extracts. Little can here be given beyond a sample or two of tragic and serious work. The buoyant beauty of surrounding verse, the "innumerable laughter" and the profound murmur of its many measures, the fervent flow of stanzas now like the ripples and now like the gulfs of the sea, can no more be shown by process of selection than any shallow salt pool left in the sand for sunbeams to drain dry can show the depth and length of the receding tide.

## FROM "MATTHEW ARNOLD'S NEW POEMS" (1867, 1875)

*"A French critic"*

A French critic has expressed this in words which I may quote here, torn out from their context: — "Le côté fort du caractère d'un peuple fait souvent le côté faible de sa poésie. Ces poëtes anglais pèchent du côté de la raison religieuse. Ce n'est pas que les anglais soient effectivement ou trop religieux ou trop raisonnables. C'est qu'ils ont la manie de vouloir réconcilier les choses irréconciliables. On voit cela partout, dans la politique, dans les beaux arts, dans la vie pratique, dan la vie idéale. Leur république est juchée sur des échasses féodales, attifée des guenilles étincelantes d'une royauté usée jusqu'à la corde; tout le bric-à-brac monarchique lui plaît; ses parfums rances, ses lambris dédorés, sa défroque rapiécée; elle n'ose se montrer sans mettre son masque de reine, sans rajuster ses jupons de pairesse. Pourquoi se donne-t-elle cette peine? quel profit espère-t-elle en retirer? c'est ce qu'un anglais même ne saurait dire;* tout en répondant que Dieu le sait, il est permis de douter que Dieu le sache. Venons aux arts; que veut-on d'un peintre? de la peinture? fi donc! Il nous faut un peu de morale, un peu d'intention, le beau vrai, le vrai beau, l'idée actuelle, l'actualité idéale, mille autres choses très-recommandables dans ce genre-là. C'est ce malin espirit, très-peu spirituel, qui est venu souffler aux poëtes la belle idée de se poser en apôtres réconciliateurs entre le croyant et le libre penseur. L'un deux fait foudroyer M. Renan par Saint Jean expirant en pleine odeur de philosophie, écrase sous son talon le pauvre évêque Colenso, et démontre que si le Christ n'est pas 'le Dieu incommensurable,' il doit être tout bonnement un homme 'perdu' (c'est son mot); vu que d'asprès la tradition de sa parole écrite plusieurs millions de gens plus ou moins honnêtes sont morts dans cette foi, et que voilà apparemment le seul Dieu, et que voilà la seule religion, qui ait jamais produit un effet pareil. Sous des vers plus soigneusement

* This is a strange and sad instance of the ignorance and perversity as foreign to Englishmen as they are natural to foreigners. Any one could have answered him, and at any length. Envy doubtless as well as error must have inspired this blasphemy against the Constitution once delivered to the saints — that august result of a plenary inspiration above the reach of human wisdom, sent down direct from heaven, and vouchsafed alone to this chosen nation, this peculiar people; to which, as to Tyre or Jerusalem in the time past, the Supreme Powers have said by the sweet voices of their representative elect — elect of gods and men — "Thou sealest up the sum; full of wisdom, and perfect in beauty."

limés, plus coquettement ajustés, nous ne trouverons qu'une plus profonde stérilité de raisonnement. Voici une belle âme de poëte qui pleure, qui cherche, qui envisage la mort, le néant, l'infini; qui veut peser les faits, trier les croyances, vanner la foi; et voici son dernier mot: Croyons, afin de moins souffrir; tâchons au moins de nous faire accroire à nous-mêmes que nous croyons à quelque chose de consolant. Il est douloureux de ne pas croire qu'on doit revivre un jour, revoir ses amis morts, accomplir de nouveaux destins. Posons donc que cela est, que cela doit être, qu'il faut absolument y croire, ou du moins faire semblant à ses propres yeux d'y croire, se persuader, se rétiérer à haute voix que cela est. La vie sans avenir est impossible. Plus de raisonnements d'incrédule. Le cœur se lève comme un homme irrité et répond; J'ai senti! Vous manquez de foi, dites-vous, vous manquez de preuves, mais il suffit que vous ayez eu des sensations. À ce compte-là, il vaut bien la peine de faire rouler le wagon poétique sur les rails de la philosophie, de s'embourber les roues dans les ornières de la théologie. Aimez, souffrez, sentez, c'est très-bien; vous êtes là dans votre droit. Cela ne prouve rien, mais cela est fort joli, mis en de beaux vers. On perd un objet aimé, on désire le revoir, on épreuve des émotions douloureuses à songer qu'on ne le reverra point. Après? La mort, la douleur, l'oubli, la misère, voilà sans doute des choses pénibles, et que l'on voudrait éviter; il est clair que nous ferions tous notre possible pour y échapper. Cela prouve-t-il que ces choses-là n'existent pas? On est tenté de répondre une bonne fois à ces bonnes gens: Messieurs, vous raisonnez en poëtes, vous poétisez en raisonneurs. De grâce, soyez l'un ou l'autre: ou bien, si vous avez les deux dons réunis, raisonnez en raisonneurs, poétisez en poëtes. Faites-nous grâce en attendant de cette poésie démontée, de cette philosophie déraillée.

"Encore un mot. La poésie n'a que faire de tout cela. Il n'y a pas de religion possible dont elle ne sache prendre son parti. Toute croyance qui émeut, qui fait vibrer, résonner, tressaillir une seule corde intérieure—toute véritable religion, sombre ou radieuse, tragique ou riante, est une chose essentiellement poétique. Partout où puisse aller la passion, l'émotion, le sentiment qui fait les martyrs, les prophètes, les vierges mystérieuses, les apôtres effrayants du bien ou du mal, partout où puissent pénétrer les terreurs mystiques, les joies énormes, les élans obscurs de la foi, il y a pour les poëtes un milieu respirable. Vénus ou Moloch, Jésus ou Brahma, n'importe. Un poëte enfermé chez lui peut être le meilleur chrétien du monde, ou bien le plus affreux païen; ce son là des affaires de foyer où la critique n'a rien à voir; mais la poésie propre ne sera jamais ni ceci ni cela. Elle est tout, elle n'est rien. . . . Toute émotion lui sert, celle de l'anachorète ni plus ni moins que celle du blasphémateur. Pour la morale, elle est mauvaise et bonne, chaste et libertine; pour la religion, elle est incrédule et fidèle, soumise et rebelle. Mais l'impuissance religieuse ou morale, mais la pensée qui boite, l'espirit qui louche, l'âme qui a peur et de se soumettre et de se révolter, la foi manquée qui pleure des larmes sceptiques, les effluves fades, tristes, nauséabonds, de la caducité spirituelle, les plantes étiolées, les sources desséchees, les pousses sans sève d'une époque douteuse et crépusculaire—que voulez vous qu'elle fasse de tout cela? Pour elle, la négation même n'est pas stérile; chez elle, Lucrèce a sa place comme Moise, Omar* comme Job; mais elle ne saurait où glisser les petites questions d'évidence, les petites tracasseries théologiques. Même en cette époque cependant nous ne manquons pas de poëtes qui sachent manier des choses hautes et sombres. Nous ne renverrons pas des écrivains anglais au sixième livre des *Contemplations*, aux sommets pour eux inabordables de la poésie actuelle, où la lumière se mêle au vertige; sans citer le grand maître, nous pourrions leur indiquer un des leurs qui a mieux fait qu'eux." [Often a people's strength of character brings about the weakness of its poetry. These british poets exaggerate religious thinking. Not that the british are either too religious or too thoughtful. But they have a mania for trying to reconcile irreconcilables. It shows everywhere: in politics, in the arts, in their daily and their spiritual life. Their Republic is perched on feudal stilts and wears the brilliant rags of an old threadbare monarchy. It likes all the bric-a-brac of royalty: its rancid perfumes, giltless panneling, its old cast offs. It dislikes appearing without its royal mask or without properly-arranged royal petticoats. Why go to all that trouble? What's to be gained by it? Even an Englishman couldn't tell you; and to say that God knows only makes one doubt it. Consider the arts. What do we expect of a painter? Paintings of course. But no, we need some morality, some ideas, true beauty, beautiful truth, the actual idea, the ideal actuality, and lots of other respectable things of that kind. It is this perverse spirit, not very spiritual in fact, that has made poets want to proselytize for reconciliation between believers and freethinkers. Thus one of them has St. John dying in the odour of philosophy, striking down M. Renan, crushing under his heels poor bishop Colenso, and demonstrating that if Christ is not the "incommensurable God" he must simply be a soul "lost" (that's his word). For by following his written word several millions of more or less honest men have died in that faith, and here we have the only God and the only religion to bring about such a result. Even with their carefully crafted or smartly turned verses we only discover sterile reasoning. Here is the poet's beautiful soul crying, searching, considering death, infinity, emptiness, trying to weigh the facts, to sort out beliefs, to winnow faith; and his concluding idea is this: let's believe so as to suffer less or at least let's delude ourselves into believing in something that will bring us solace. It's too painful not to think that we will live again, see our dead friends, fulfill other destinies. Therefore let's decide that it is so, that it must be, that we must absolutely believe it or at least pretend to believe it, persuade ourselves of the fact by repeating it loudly and clearly. Life without a future is impossible. No more

* Far better than in the long literal version of Omar Khayyám which is all that the French language can show, may the soul and spirit of his thought be tasted in that most exquisite English translation, sovereignly faultless in form and colour of verse, which gives to those ignorant of the East a relish of the treasure and a delight in the beauty of its wisdom.

skeptical reasonings. Our heart lifts itself up and madly proclaims: "I have felt". You might say that you have no faith, no proofs, but you have had sensations and that's enough. Thinking like that, you can set the poetic train to run on philosophical tracks and get your wheels stuck in the ruts of religion; but it's worth it. Love, suffer, feel—very well, it's your prerogative, but it proves nothing. It can be nice if put in lovely verses. One loses a loved one, one wants to see him again and suffers realizing its impossibility. So what? Death, suffering, misery, are painful and one wants to avoid them, clearly we all want to escape such things. But does it prove that these things do not exist? One really wants to tell these folks: you sophisticate like poets and you make poetry like sophists. Just be one or the other, or if by chance you have both gifts, then think like a philosopher and poetize like a poet. But spare us this deranged poetry, this derailed philosophy.

One word more. Poetry has nothing to do with all that. Poetry can accommodate itself to any religion. Any belief that moves me, that sets an interior cord vibrating responsively—every true religion, dark or radiant, tragic or gay—is essentially poetic. Wherever passion, emotion, sentiment make martyrs, prophets, mysterious virgins, apostles of good or evil; wherever mystical terrors, great joys, and impulses of faith can go, there is for poets an inspiring milieu. Closeted in his house a poet can be the best christian in the world or the wickedest pagan; those are domestic questions beside the point for critics; poetry is neither this nor that. In fact poetry is everything and nothing. It makes use of any emotion: the anchorite's is no better than the blasphemer's. For poetry, morality can be good or bad, chaste or libertine; religion can be incredulous and faithful, rebellious or submissive. But ineffectual religion or moral, lame thought, squinting spirits, the soul afraid to submit or revolt, the missed faith that sheds septic tears, the sad, the insipid, nauseating exhalations of spiritual decrepitude, the wilted plants, the dried springs, the sapless shoots of a dubious and decadent period: what can poetry do with all that? For poetry even negation is not sterile; Lucretia has her place as much as Moses, Omar as much as Job. But poetry doesn't deal with trivial factual problems or irksome theological pettinesses. So it is that now we have no dearth of poets capable of addressing high and serious subjects. We will not refer british writers to the 6th. book of *Contemplations*—to the summit, for them inaccessible, of contemporary poetry, the region of vertiginous light. We could, however, without naming the great master, cite one of their own who has done better than them.] Here follows the reference to Mr Arnold's poem and to the exact passages supposed to bear upon the matter at issue. "Ce monologue lyrique est d'une ampleur, d'une droiture poétique dont on ne saurait allieurs retouver une trace. C'est un rude évangile qu'on vient là nous prêcher; on sent dans cette cratère des flammes éteintes; c'est lugubre pour les âmes faibles, pour les espirits à l'œil chassieux; c'est une poésie froide et ferme et forte. Voici enfin quelqu'un qui a le regard haut, le pied sûr, la parole nette, la vue large; on sait ce qu'il nous veut. Sa philosophie âpre, escarpée, impassible, est après tout meilleure consolatrice que la théologie douteuse, pleureuse, tracassière de ses rivaux."* [The scope and poetic justice of this lyrical monologue are nowhere else to be found. A severe gospel is here being preached. Extinct flames rise from this crater, which will seem dismal to weak souls and rheumy-eyed spirits. It is a cold, firm and strong poetry. Here at last is someone whose vision is lofty, whose foot is firm, whose speech is clear and whose view is large. His unperturbed philosophical austerity brings finally a better consolation than his rivals' doubtful, whining, and irksome theology.] In spite of his flippancy and violence of manner, I am disposed in part to agree with this critic.

. . . . . . . . . . .

*"Thyrsis" and "The Forsaken Merman"*

There are in the English language three elegiac poems so great that they eclipse and efface all the elegiac poetry we know; all of Italian, all of Greek. It is only because the latest born is yet new to us that it can seem strange or rash to say so. The "Thyrsis" of Mr. Arnold makes a third with "Lycidas" and "Adonais." It is not so easy as those may think who think by rote and praise by prescription to strike the balance between them. The first however remains first, and must remain; its five opening lines are to me the most musical in all known realms of verse; there is nothing like them; and it is more various, more simple, more large and sublime than the others; lovelier and fuller it cannot be.

"The leader is fairest,
But all are divine."

The least pathetic of the three is "Adonais," which indeed is hardly pathetic at all; it is passionate, subtle, splendid; but "Thyrsis," like "Lycidas," has a quiet and tender undertone which gives it something of sacred. Shelley brings fire from heaven, but these bring also "the meed of some melodious tear." There is a grace ineffable, a sweet sound and sweet savour of things past, in the old beautiful use of the language of shepherds, of flocks and pipes; the spirit is none the less sad and sincere because the body of the poem has put on this dear familiar raiment of romance; because the crude and naked sorrow is veiled and chastened with

* There are varieties of opinion in this world; and the British critic's fond faith in the British thinker will not soon be shaken by the adverse verdict of any French heretic. Witness the words of a writer whom I once fell in with, heaven knows where; who, being far above the shallow errors of foolish "Greeks" and puerile "pagans," takes occasion to admonish their disciples that "*our* philosophers and poets will tell you that they have got far beyond *this* stage. The riddles *they* have to unravel involve finer issues" (and among these they might deign to expound what manner of thing may be the involution of an issue); no doubt, in a word, but they are the people and wisdom shall die with them. They may tell us so, certainly; thought and speech are free, and for aught I know they may be fully capable of the assertion. But it is for us to choose what amount of belief it may please us to accord them.

soft shadows and sounds of a "land that is very far off"; because the verse remembers and retains a perfume and an echo of Grecian flutes and flowers,

"Renews the golden world, and holds through all
The holy laws of homely pastoral,
Where flowers and founts, and nymphs and semi-gods,
And all the Graces find their old abodes."

Here, as in the "Scholar Gipsy," the beauty, the delicacy and affluence of colour, the fragrance and the freedom as of wide wings of winds in summer over meadow and moor, the freshness and expansion of the light and the lucid air, the spring and the stream as of flowing and welling water, enlarge and exalt the pleasure and power of the whole poem. Such English-coloured verse no poet has written since Shakespeare, who chooses his field-flowers and hedgerow blossoms with the same sure and loving hand, binds them in as simple and sweet an order. All others, from Milton downward to Shelley and onward from him, have gathered them singly or have mixed them with foreign buds and alien blooms. No poem in any language can be more perfect as a model of style, unsurpassable certainly, it may be unattainable. Any couplet, any line proves it. No countryman of ours since Keats died has made or has found words fall into such faultless folds and forms of harmonious line. He is the most efficient, the surest-footed poet of our time, the most to be relied on; what he does he is the safest to do well; more than any other he unites personality and perfection; others are personal and imperfect, perfect and impersonal; with them you must sometimes choose between inharmonious freedom and harmonious bondage. Above all, he knows what as a poet he should do, and simply does that; the manner of his good work is never more or less than right; his verse comes clean and full out of the mould, cast at a single jet; placed beside much other verse of the time, it shows like a sculptor's work by an enameller's. With all their wealth and warmth of flowers and lights, these two twin poems are solid and pure as granite or as gold. Their sweet sufficiency of music, so full and calm, buoys and bears up throughout the imperial vessel of thought. Their sadness is not chill or sterile, but as the sorrow of summer pausing with laden hands on the middle height of the year, the watershed that divides the feeding fountains of autumn and of spring; a grave and fruitful sadness, the triumphant melancholy of full-blown flowers and souls full-grown. The stanzas from the sixth to the fourteenth of "Thyrsis," and again from the sixteenth to the twentieth, are if possible the most lovely in either poem; the deepest in tone and amplest in colour; the choiceness and sweetness of single lines and phrases most exquisite and frequent.

"O easy access to the hearer's grace,
When Dorian shepherds sang to Proserpine!
    For she herself had trod Sicilian fields,

She knew the Dorian water's gush divine,
  She knew each lily white which Enna yields,
    Each rose with blushing face;
She loved the Dorian pipe, the Dorian strain.
  But, ah! of our poor Thames she never heard!
  Her foot the Cumnor cowslips never stirred;
And we should tease her with our plaint in vain."

She has learnt to know them now, the river and the river-meadows, and access is as easy for an English as a Dorian prayer to the most gentle of all worshipped gods. It is a triumphal and memorial poem, a landmark in the high places of verse to which future travellers studious of the fruits and features of the land may turn and look up and see what English hands could rear.

This is probably the highest point of Mr. Arnold's poetry, though for myself I cannot wholly resign the old preference of things before familiar; of one poem in especial, good alike for children and men, the "Forsaken Merman;" which has in it the pathos of natural things, the tune of the passion we fancy in the note of crying birds or winds weeping, shrill and sweet and estranged from us; the swift and winged wail of something lost midway between man's life and the life of things soulless, the wail overheard and caught up by the fitful northern fancy, filling with glad and sad spirits and untravelled ways of nature; the clear cry of a creature astray in the world, wild and gentle and mournful, heard in the sighing of weary waters before dawn under a low wind, in the rustle and whistle and whisper of leaves or grasses, in the long light breaths of twilight air heaving all the heather on the hills, in the coming and going of the sorrowful strong seas that bring delight and death, in the tender touch and recoil of the ripple from the sand; all the fanciful pitiful beauty of dreams and legends born in grey windy lands on shores and hill-sides whose life is quiet and wild. No man's hand has pressed from the bells and buds of the moors and downs by cape or channel of the north a sweeter honey than this. The song is a piece of the sea-wind, a stray breath of the air and bloom of the bays and hills: its mixture of mortal sorrow with the strange wild sense of a life that is not after mortal law—the childlike moan after lost love mingling with the pure outer note of a song not human—the look in it as of bright bewildered eyes with tears not theirs and alien wonder in the watch of them—the tender, marvellous, simple beauty of the poem, its charm as of a sound or a flower of the sea—set it and save it apart from all others in a niche of the memory. This has all the inexplicable inevitable sweetness of a child's or a bird's in its note; "Thyrsis" has all the accomplished and adult beauty of a male poem. In the volume which it crowns there is certainly no jewel of equal water.

## FROM "NOTES ON DESIGNS OF THE OLD MASTERS AT FLORENCE" (1868, 1875)

*Michelangelo: "Fairer than heaven and more terrible than hell"*

But in one separate head there is more tragic attraction than in these: a woman's, three times studied, with divine and subtle care; sketched and re-sketched in youth and age, beautiful always beyond desire and cruel beyond words; fairer than heaven and more terrible than hell; pale with pride and weary with wrong-doing; a silent anger against God and man burns, white and repressed, through her clear features. In one drawing she wears a head-dress of eastern fashion rather than western, but in effect made out of the artist's mind only; plaited in the likeness of close-welded scales as of a chrysalid serpent, raised and waved and rounded in the likeness of a sea-shell. In some inexplicable way all her ornaments seem to partake of her fatal nature, to bear upon them her brand of beauty fresh from hell; and this through no vulgar machinery of symbolism, no serpentine or otherwise bestial emblem: the bracelets and rings are innocent enough in shape and workmanship; but in touching her flesh they have become infected with deadly and malignant meaning. Broad bracelets divide the shapely splendour of her arms; over the nakedness of her firm and luminous breasts, just below the neck, there is passed a band as of metal. Her eyes are full of proud and passionless lust after gold and blood; her hair, close and curled, seems ready to shudder in sunder and divide into snakes. Her throat, full and fresh, round and hard to the eye as her bosom and arms, is erect and stately, the head set firm on it without any droop or lift of the chin; her mouth crueller than a tiger's, colder than a snake's, and beautiful beyond a woman's. She is the deadlier Venus incarnate;

Πολλὴ μὲν θεοῖσι κοὐκ ἀνωνυμος θεά

for upon earth also many names might be found for her: Lamia re-transformed, invested now with a fuller beauty, but divested of all feminine attributes not native to the snake—a Lamia loveless and unassailable by the sophist, readier to drain life out of her lover than to fade for his sake at his side; or the Persian Amestris, watching the only breasts on earth more beautiful than her own cut off from her rival's living bosom; or Cleopatra, not dying but turning serpent under the serpent's bite; or that queen of the extreme East who with her husband marked every day as it went by some device of a new and wonderful cruelty. In one design, where the cruel and timid face of a king rises behind her, this crowned and cowering head might stand for Ahab's, and hers for that of Jezebel. Another study is in red chalk; in this the only ornaments are ear-rings. In a third, the serpentine hair is drawn up into a tuft at the crown with two ringlets hanging, heavy and deadly as small tired snakes. There is a drawing in the furthest room at the Buonarroti Palace which recalls and almost reproduces the design of these three. Here also the electric hair, which looks as though it would hiss and glitter with sparks if once touched, is wound up to a tuft with serpentine plaits and involutions; all that remains of it unbound falls in one curl, shaping itself into a snake's likeness as it unwinds, right against a living snake held to the breast and throat. This is rightly registered as a study for Cleopatra; but notice has not yet been accorded to the subtle and sublime idea which transforms her death by the aspic's bite into a meeting of serpents which recognise and embrace, an encounter between the woman and the worm of Nile, almost as though this match for death were a monstrous love-match, or such a mystic marriage as that painted in the loveliest passage of "Salammbô," between the maiden body and the scaly coils of the serpent and the priestess alike made sacred to the moon; so closely do the snake and the queen of snakes caress and cling. Of this idea Shakespeare also had a vague and great glimpse when he made Antony murmur, "*Where's my serpent of old Nile?*" mixing a foretaste of her death with the full sweet savour of her supple and amorous "pride of life." For what indeed is lovelier or more luxuriously loving than a strong and graceful snake of the nobler kind?

## FROM "NOTES ON SOME PICTURES OF 1868" (1868, 1875)

*D. G. Rossetti*

It is well known that the painter of whom I now propose to speak has never suffered exclusion or acceptance at the hand of any academy. To such acceptance or such rejection all other men of any note have been and may be liable. It is not less well known that his work must always hold its place as second in significance and value to no work done by any painter of his time. Among the many great works of Mr. D. G. Rossetti, I know of none greater than his two latest. These are types of sensual beauty and spiritual, the siren and the sibyl. The one is a woman of the type of Adam's first wife; she is a living Lilith, with ample splendour of redundant hair;

"She excels
All women in the magic of her locks;
And when she winds them round a young man's neck
She will not ever set him free again."

Clothed in soft white garments, she draws out through a comb the heavy mass of hair like thick spun gold to fullest length; her head leans back half sleepily, superb and satiate with its own beauty; the eyes are languid, without love in them or hate; the sweet luxurious mouth has the patience of pleasure fulfilled and complete, the warm repose of passion sure of its delight. Outside, as seen in the glimmering mirror, there is full summer; the deep and glowing leaves have drunk in the whole strength of the sun. The sleepy splendour of the picture is a fit raiment for the idea incarnate of faultless fleshly beauty and peril of pleasure unavoidable. For this serene and sublime sorceress there is no life but of the body; with spirit (if spirit there be) she can dispense. Were it worth her while for any word to divide those terrible tender lips, she too might say with the hero of the most perfect and exquisite book of modern times—"Mademoiselle de Maupin" —"Je trouve la terre aussi belle que le ciel, et je pense que la correction de la forme est la vertu." Of evil desire or evil impulse she has nothing; and nothing of good. She is indifferent, equable, magnetic; she charms and draws down the souls of men by pure force of absorption, in no wise or willful or malignant; outside herself she cannot live, she cannot even see: and because of this she attracts and subdues all men at once in body and in spirit. Beyond the mirror she cares not to look, and could not.

"Ma mia suora Rahel mia non si smaga
Dal suo miraglio, e siede tutto 'l giorno."

So, rapt in no spiritual contemplation, she will sit to all time, passive and perfect: the outer light of a sweet spring day flooding and filling the massive gold of her hair. By the reflection in a deep mirror of fervent foliage from without, the chief chord of stronger colour is touched in this picture; next in brilliance and force of relief is the heap of curling and tumbling hair on which the sunshine strikes; the face and head of the siren are withdrawn from the full stroke of the light.

The other picture gives the type of opposite to this; a head of serene and spiritual beauty, severe and tender, with full and heavy hair falling straight in grave sweet lines, not, like Lilith's, exuberant of curl and coil; with carven column of throat, solid and round and flawless as living ivory; with still and sacred eyes and pure calm lips; an imperial votaress truly, in maiden meditation: yet as true and tangible a woman of mortal mould, as ripe and firm of flesh as her softer and splendid sister. The mystic emblems in the background show her power upon love and death to make them loyal servants to the law of her lofty and solemn spirit. Behind this figure of the ideal and inaccessible beauty, an inlaid wall of alternate alabaster and black marble bears inwrought on its upper part the rival twin emblems of love and death; over the bare carven skull poppies impend, and roses over the sweet head with bound blind eyes: in her hand is the palm-branch, a scepter of peace and of power. The cadence of colour is splendid and simple, a double trinity of green and red, the dim red robe, the deep red poppies, the soft red roses; and again the green veil wound about with wild flowers, the green down of poppy leaves, the sharper green of rose-leaves.

An unfinished picture of Beatrice (the Beata Beatrix of the Vita Nuova), a little before death, is perhaps the noblest of Mr. Rossetti's many studies after Dante. This work is wholly symbolic and ideal; a strange bird flown earthward from heaven brings her in its beak a full blown poppy, the funereal flower of sleep. Her beautiful head lies back, sad and sweet, with fast-shut eyes in a death-like trance that is not death; over it the shadow of death seems to impend, making sombre the splendour of her ample hair and tender faultless features. Beyond her the city and the bridged river are seen as from far, dim and veiled with misty lights as though already "sitting alone, made as a widow." Love, on one side, comes bearing in his hand a heart in flames, having his eyes bent upon Dante's; on the other side is Dante, looking sadly across the way towards Love. In this picture the light is subdued and soft, touching tenderly from behind the edges of Beatrice's hair and raiment; in the others there is a full fervour of daylight.

The great picture of Venus Verticordia has now been in great measure recast; the head is of a diviner type of beauty; golden butterflies hover about the halo of her hair, alight upon the apple or the arrow in her hands; her face has the sweet supremacy of a beauty imperial and immortal; her glorious bosom seems to exult and expand as the roses on each side of it. The painting of leaf and fruit and flower in this picture is beyond my praise or any man's; but of one thing I will here take note; the flash of green brilliance from the upper leaves of the trellis against the somber green of the trees behind.

Another work, as yet incomplete, is a study of La Pia; she is seen looking forth from the ramparts of her lord's castle, over the fatal lands without; her pallid splendid face hangs a little forward, wan and white against the mass of dark deep hair; under her hands is a work of embroidery, hanging still on the frame unfinished; just touched by the weak weary hands, it trails forward across the lap of her pale green raiment, into the foreground of the picture. In her eyes is a strange look of wonder and sorrow and fatigue, without fear and without pain, as though she were even now looking beyond earth into the soft and sad air of purgatory: she presses the deadly marriage-ring into the flesh of her finger, so deep that the soft skin is bloodless and blanched from the intense imprint of it.

Two other studies, as yet only sketched, give promise of no less beauty; the subject of one was long since handled by the artist in a slighter manner. It also is taken from the Vita Nuova; Dante in a dream beholding Beatrice dead, tended by handmaidens, and Love, with bow and dart in hand, in act to kiss her beautiful dead mouth. The other is a design of Perseus showing to Andromeda the severed head of Medusa, reflected in water; an old and well-worn subject, but renewed and reinformed with life by the vital genius of the artist. In the Pompeian picture we see the lovers at halt beside a stream, on their homeward way; here we see them in their house, bending over the central cistern or impluvium of the main court. The design is wonderful for grace and force; the picture will assuredly be one of the painter's greatest.

## FROM *WILLIAM BLAKE: A CRITICAL ESSAY* (1868)

*"He was born and baptized into the church of rebels"*

He was born and baptized into the church of rebels; we can hardly imagine a time or scheme of things in which he could have lived and worked without some interval of revolt. All that was accepted for art, all that was taken for poetry, he rejected as barren symbols, and would fain have broken up as mendacious idols. What was best to other men, and in effect excellent of its kind, was to him worst. Reynolds and Rubens were daubers and devils. The complement or corollary of this habit of mind was that he would accept and admire even small and imperfect men whose line of life and action seemed to run on the same tramway as his own. Barry, Fuseli, even such as Mortimer—these were men he would allow and approve of. The devils had not entered into them; they worked, each to himself, on the same ground as Michael Angelo. To such effect he would at times prophesy, standing revealed for a brief glimpse on the cloudy and tottering height of his theories, before the incurious eyes of a public which had no mind to inhale such oracular vapour. It is hard to conjecture how his opinions, as given forth in his *Catalogue* or other notes on art, would have been received—if indeed they had ever got hearing at all. This they naturally never did; by no means to Blake's discouragement. He spoke with authority; not in the least like the Scribes of his day.

So far one may at least see what he meant; although at sight of it many would cover their eyes and turn away. But the main part of him was, and is yet, simply inexplicable; much like some among his own designs, a maze of cloudy colour and perverse form, without a clue for the hand or a feature for the eye to lay hold of. What he meant, what he wanted, why he did this thing or not that other, no man then alive could make out. Nevertheless it was worth the trying. In a time of critical reason and definite division, he was possessed by a fervour and fury of belief; among sane men who had disproved most things and proved the rest, here was an evident madman who believed a thing, one may say, only insomuch as it was incapable of proof. He lived and worked out of all rule, and yet by law. He had a devil, and its name was Faith. No materialist has such belief in bread and meat as Blake had in substance underlying appearance which he christened god or spectre, devil or angel, as the fit took him; or rather as he saw it from one or the other side. His faith was absolute and hard, like a pure fanatic's; there was no speculation in him. What could be made of such a man in a country fed and clothed with the teapot pieties of Cowper and the tape-yard infidelities of Paine? Neither set would have to do with him; was he not a believer? and was he not a blasphemer? His licence of thought and talk was always of the maddest, or seemed so in the ears of his generation. People remember at this day with horror and pity the impression of his daring ways of speech, but excuse him still on the old plea of madness. Now on his own ground no man was ever more sane or more reverent. His outcries on various matters of art or morals were in effect the mere expression, not of reasonable dissent, but of violent belief. No artist of equal power had ever a keener and deeper regard for the meaning and teaching—what one may call the moral—of art. He sang and painted as men write or preach. Indifference was impossible to him. Thus every shred of his work has some life, some blood, infused or woven into it. In such a vast tumbling chaos of relics as he left behind to get in time disentangled and cast into shape, there are naturally inequalities enough; rough sides and loose sides, weak points and helpless knots, before which all mere human patience or comprehension recoils and reels back. But in all, at all times, there is the one invaluable quality of actual life.

. . . . . . . . . . .

*"To him all symbolic things were literal, all literal things symbolic"*

In the light of his especial faith all visible things were fused into the intense heat and sharpened into the keen outline of vision. He walked and laboured under other heavens, on another earth, than the earth and the heaven of material life:

"With a blue sky spread over with wings,
And a mild sun that mounts and sings;
With trees and fields full of fairy elves
And little devils who fight for themselves;
With angels planted in hawthorn bowers,
And God Himself in the passing hours."

All this was not a mere matter of creed or opinion, much less of decoration or ornament to his work. It was, as we said, his element of life, inhaled at every breath with the common air, mixed into his veins with their natural blood. It was an element almost painfully tangible and actual; an absolute medium or state of existence, inevitable, inexplicable, insuperable. To him the veil of outer things seemed always to tremble with some breath behind it: seemed at times to be rent in sunder with clamour and sudden lightning. All the void of earth and air seemed to quiver with the passage of sentient wings and palpitate under the pressure of conscious feet. Flowers and weeds, stars and stones, spoke with articulate lips and gazed with living eyes. Hands were stretched towards him from beyond the darkness of material nature, to tempt or to support, to guide or to restrain. His hardest facts were the vaguest allegories of other men. To him all symbolic things were literal, all literal things symbolic. About his path and about his bed, around his ears and under his eyes, an infinite play of spiritual life seethed and swarmed or shone and sang. Spirits imprisoned in the husk and shell of earth consoled or menaced him. Every leaf bore a growth of angels; the pulse of every minute sounded as the falling foot of God; under the rank raiment of weeds, in the drifting down of thistles, strange faces frowned and white hair fluttered; tempters and allies, wraiths of the living and phantoms of the dead, crowded and made populous the winds that blew about him, the fields and hills over which he gazed. Even upon earth his vision was "twofold always;" singleness of vision he scorned and feared as the sign of mechanical intellect, of talent that walks while the soul sleeps, with the mere activity of a blind somnambulism. It was fourfold in the intervals of keenest inspiration and subtlest rapture; threefold in the paradise of dreams lying between earth and heaven, lulled by lighter airs and lit by fainter stars; a land of night and moonlight, spectral and serene. These strange divisions of spirit and world according to some dim and mythologic hierarchy were with Blake matters at once serious and commonplace. The worlds of Beaulah and Jerusalem, the existence of Los god of Time and Enitharmon goddess of Space, the fallen manhood of Theotormon, the imprisoned womanhood of Oothoon, were more to him even than significant names; to the reader they must needs seem less. This monstrous nomenclature, this jargon of miscreated things in chaos, rose as by nature to his lips, flowed from them as by instinct. Time, an incarnate spirit clothed with fire, stands before him in the sun's likeness; he is threatened with poverty, tempted to make himself friends of this world; and makes answer as though to a human tempter:

"My hands are laboured day and night
And rest comes never in my sight;
My wife has no indulgence given
Except what comes to her from heaven;
We eat little, we drink less;
This earth breeds not our happiness."

He beheld, he says, Time and Space as they were eternally, not as they are seen upon earth; he saw nothing as man sees: his hopes and fears were alien from all men's; and upon him and his the light of prosperous days and the terrors of troubled time had no power.

"When I had my defiance given
The sun stood trembling in heaven;
The moon, that glowed remote below,
Became leprous and white as snow;
And every soul of man on the earth
Felt affliction and sorrow and sickness and dearth."

In all this way we may see on one side the reflection and refraction of outer things, on the other side of the projection of his own mind, the effusion of his individual nature, throughout the hardest and remotest alien matter. Strangely severed from other men, he was, or he conceived himself, more strangely interwoven with them. The light of his spiritual weapons, the sound of his spiritual warfare, was seen, he believed and was heard in faint resonance and far reverberation among men who knew not what such sights and sounds might mean. If, worsted in this "mental fight," he should let "his sword sleep in his hand," or "refuse to do spiritual acts because of natural fears and natural desires," the world would be the poorer for his defection, and himself "called the base Judas who betrays his friend." Fear of this rebuke shook and wasted him day and night; he was rent in sunder with pangs of terror and travail. Heaven was full of the dead, coming to witness against him with blood-shedding and with shedding of tears:

"The sun was hot
With the bows of my mind and with arrows of thought."

In this spirit he wrought at his day's work, seeing everywhere the image of his own mood, the presence of foes and friends. Nothing to him was neutral; nothing without significance. The labour and strife of soul in which he lived was a thing as earnest as any bodily warfare. Such struggles of spirit in poets or artists have been too often made the subject of public study; nay, too often the theme of chaotic versifiers. A theme more utterly improper it is of course impossible to devise. It is just that a workman should see all sides of his work, and labour with all his might of mind and dexterity of hand to make it great and perfect; but to use up the details of the process as crude material for cruder verse—to invite spectators as to the opening of a temple, and show them the unbaked bricks and untempered mortar—to expose with immodest violence and impotent satisfaction the long revolting labours of mental abortion—this no artist will ever attempt, no craftsman ever so perform as to escape ridicule. It is useless for those who can carve no statue worth the chiselling to exhibit instead six feet or nine feet of shapeless plaster or fragmentary stucco, and bid us see what sculptors work with; no man will accept that in lieu of the statue. Not less futile and not less indecent is it for those who can give expression to no great poem to disgorge masses or raw incoherent verse on the subject of verse-making: to offer, in place of a poem ready wrought out, some chaotic and convulsive story about the way in which a poet works, or does not work.

To Blake the whole thing was too grave for any such exposure of spiritual nudity. In these letters he records the result of his "sore travail;" in these verses he commemorates the manner of his work "under the direction of messengers from heaven daily and nightly, not without trouble or care;" but he writes in private and by pure instinct; he speaks only by the impulse of confidence, in the ardour of faith. What he has to say is said with the simple and abstract rapture of apostles or prophets; not with the laborious impertinence and vain obtrusion of tortuous analysis. For such heavy play with gossamer and straws his nature was too earnest and his genius too exalted. This is the mood in which he looks over what work he has done or has to do: and in his lips the strange scriptural language used has the sincerity of pure fire. "I see the face of my Heavenly Father; He lays His hand upon my head, and gives a blessing to all my work. Why should I be troubled? why should my heart and flesh cry out? I will go on in the strength of the Lord; through hell will I sing forth His praises; that the dragons of the deep may praise Him, and that those who dwell in darkness and in the sea-coasts may be gathered into His kingdom." So did he esteem of art, which indeed is not a light thing; nor is it wholly unimportant to men that they should have one capable artist more or less among them. How it may fare with artisans (be they never so pretentious) is a matter of sufficiently small moment. One blessing there assuredly was upon all Blake's work; the infinite blessing of life; the fervour of vital blood.

. . . . . . . . . . .

*William Blake and Dante*

Among these late labours of Blake the "Dante" may take a place of some prominence. The seven published plates, though quite surprisingly various in merit, are worth more notice than has yet been spared them. Three at least, for poetical power and nobility of imaginative detail, are up to the artist's highest mark. Others have painted the episode of Francesca with more or less of vigour and beauty; once above all an artist to whom any reference here must be taken as especially apposite has given with the tenderest perfection of power, first the beauty of beginning love in the light and air of life on earth, then the passion of imperishable desire under the dropping tongues of flame in hell. To the right the lovers are drawn close, yearning one toward another with touch of tightened hands and insatiable appeal of lips; behind them the bower lattice opens on deep sunshine and luminous leaves; to the left, they drift before the wind of hell, floated along the misty and straining air, fastened one upon another among the fires, pale with perpetual division of pain; and between them the witnesses stand sadly, as men that look before and after. Blake has given nothing like this: of personal beauty and special tenderness his design has none; it starts from other ground. Often as the lovers had been painted, here first has any artist desired to paint the second circle itself. To most illustrators, as to most readers, and (one might say) to Dante himself, the rest are swallowed up in those two supreme martyrs. Here we see, not one or two, but the very circle of the souls that sinned by lust, as Dante saw it; and as Keats afterwards saw it in the dream embalmed by his sonnet; the revolution of infinite sorrowing spirits through the bitter air and grievous hurricane of hell. Through strange immense implications of snake-shaped fold beyond fold, the involved chain of figures that circle and return flickers in wan white outline upon the dense dark. Under their feet is no stay as on earth; over their heads is no light as in heaven. They have no rest, and no resting-place: they revolve like circles of curling foam or fire. The two witnesses, who alone among all the mobile mass have ground whereon to set foot, stand apart upon a broken floor-work of roots and rocks, made rank with the slime and sprawl of rotten weed and foul flag-leaves of Lethe. Detail of drawing or other technical work is not the strong point of the design; but it does incomparably well manage to render the sense of the matter in hand, the endless measured motion, the painful and fruitless haste as of leaves or smoke upon the wind, the grey discomforted air and dividing mist. Blake has thoroughly understood and given back the physical symbols of this first punishment in Dante; the whirling motion of his figures has however more of blind violence and brute speed than the text seems to indicate: they are dashed and dragged one upon another like weed or shingle torn up in the drift of a breaking sea: overthrown or beaten down, haled or crushed together, as if by inanimate strength of iron or steam: not moved as we expect to see them, in sad rapidity of stately measure and even time of speed. The flame-like impulse of idea natural to Blake cannot absolutely match itself against Dante's divine justice and intense innate forbearance in detail; nor so comprehend, as by dint of reproduction to compete with, that supreme sense of inward and outward right which rules and attunes every word of the *Commedia*.

. . . . . . . . . . .

*"Art for art's sake first of all"*

Art for art's sake first of all, and afterwards we may suppose all the rest shall be added to her (or if not she need hardly be overmuch concerned); but from the man who falls to artistic work with a moral purpose, shall be taken away even that which he has — whatever of capacity for doing well in either way he may have at starting. A living critic* of incomparably delicate insight and subtly good sense, himself "impeccable" as an artist, calls this "the heresy of instruction" (*l'hérésie de l'enseignement*): one might call it, for the sake of a shorter and more summary name, the great moral heresy. Nothing can be imagined more futile; nothing so ruinous. Once let art humble herself, plead excuses, try at any compromise with the Puritan principle of doing good, and she is worse than dead. Once let her

* I will not resist the temptation to write a brief word of comment on this passage. While my words of inadequate and now of joyless praise were in course of printing, I heard that a mortal illness had indeed stricken the illustrious poet, the faultless critic, the fearless artist; that no more of fervent yet of perfect verse, no more of subtle yet of sensitive comment, will be granted us at the hands of Charles Baudelaire: that now for ever we must fall back upon what is left us. It is precious enough. We may see again as various a power as was his, may feel again as fiery a sympathy, may hear again as strange a murmur of revelation, as sad a whisper of knowledge, as mysterious a music of emotion; we shall never find so keen, so delicate, so deep an unison of sense and spirit. What verse he could make, how he loved all fair and felt all strange things, with what infallible taste he knew at once the limit and the licence of his art, all may see at a glance. He could give beauty to the form, expression to the feeling, most horrible and most obscure to the senses or souls of lesser men. The chances of things parted us once and again; the admiration of some years, at last in part expressed, brought me near him by way of written or transmitted word; let it be an excuse for the insertion of this note, and for a desire, if so it must be, to repeat for once the immortal words which too often return upon our lips;

"Ergo in perpetuum, frater, ave atque vale!"

turn apologetic, and promise or imply that she really will now be "loyal to fact" and useful to men in general (say, by furthering their moral work or improving their moral nature), she is no longer of any human use or value. The one fact for her which is worth taking account of is simply mere excellence of verse or colour, which involves all manner of truth and loyalty necessary to her well-being. That is the important thing; to have her work supremely well done, and to disregard all contingent consequences. You may extract out of Titian's work or Shakespeare's any moral or immoral inference you please; it is none of their business to see after that. Good painting or writing, on any terms, is a thing quite sufficiently in accordance with fact and reality for them. Supplant art by all means if you can; root it out and try to plant in its place something useful or at least safe, which at all events will not impede the noble moral labour and trammel the noble moral life of Puritanism. But in the name of sense and fact itself let us have done with all abject and ludicrous pretence of coupling the two in harness or grafting the one on the other's stock: let us hear no more of the moral mission of earnest art; let us no longer be pestered with the frantic and flatulent assumptions of quasi-secular clericalism willing to think the best of all sides, and ready even, with consecrating hand, to lend meritorious art and poetry a timely pat or shove. Philistia had far better (always providing it to be possible) crush art at once, hang or burn it out of the way, than think of plucking out its eyes and setting it to grind moral corn in the Philistine mills; which it is certain not to do at all well. Once and again the time has been that there was no art worth speaking of afloat anywhere in the world; but there never has been or can have been a time when art, or any kind of art worth having, took active service under Puritanism, or indulged for its part in the deleterious appetite of saving souls or helping humanity in general along the way of labour and progress.* Let no artist or poet listen to the bland bark of those porter dogs of the Puritan kingdom even when they fawn and flirt with tongue or tail. *Cave canem*. That Cerberus of the portals of Philistia will swallow your honey-cake to no purpose; if he does not turn and rend you, his slaver as he licks your hand will leave it impotent and palsied for all good work.

. . . . . . . . . . .

This old war—not (as some would foolishly have it defined) a war between facts and fancies, reason and romance, poetry and good sense, but simply between the imagination which apprehends the spirit of a thing and the understanding which dissects the body of a fact—this strife which can never be decided

*There are exceptions, we are told from the first, to all rules; and the sole exception to this one is great enough to do all but establish a rival rule. But, as I have tried already to say, the work—all the work—of Victor Hugo is in its essence artistic, in its accident above philanthropic or moral. I call this the sole exception, not being aware that the written work of Dante or Shelley did ever tend to alter the material face of things; though they may have desired that it should, and though their unwritten work may have done so. Accidentally of course a poet's work may tend towards some moral or actual result; that is beside the question.

or ended—was for Blake the most important question possible. He for one, madman or no madman, had the sense to see that the one thing utterly futile to attempt was a reconciliation between two sides of life and thought which have no community of work or aim imaginable. This is no question of reconciling contraries. Admit all the implied pretensions of art, they remain simply nothing to science; accept all the actual deductions of science, they simply signify nothing to art. The eternal "Après?" is answer enough for both in turn. "True, then, if you will have it; but what have we to do with your good or bad poetries and paintings?" "Undeniably; but what are we to gain by your deductions and discoveries, right or wrong?" The betrothal of art and science were a thing harder to bring about and more profitless to proclaim than "the marriage of heaven and hell." It were better not to fight, but to part in peace; but better certainly to fight than to temporize, where no reasonable truce can be patched up. Poetry or art based on loyalty to science is exactly as absurd (and no more) as science guided by art or poetry. Neither in effect can coalesce with the other and retain a right to exist. Neither can or (while in its sober senses) need wish to destroy the other; but they must go on their separate ways, and in this life their ways can by no possibility cross. Neither can or (unless in some fit of fugitive insanity) need wish to become valuable or respectable to the other: each must remain, on its own ground and to its own followers, a thing of value and deserving respect. To art, that is best which is most beautiful; to science, that is best which is most accurate; to morality, that is best which is most virtuous. Change or quibble upon the simple and generally accepted significance of these three words, "beautiful," "accurate," "virtuous," and you may easily (if you please, or think it worth while) demonstrate that the aim of all three is radically one and the same; but if any man be correct in thinking this exercise of the mind worth the expenditure of his time, that time must indeed be worth very little. You can say (but had perhaps better not say) that beauty is the truthfullest, accuracy the most poetic, and virtue the most beautiful of things; but a man of ordinary or decent insight will perceive that you have merely reduced an affair of things to an affair of words—shifted the body of one thing into the clothes of another—and proved actually nothing.

. . . . . . . . . . .

*William Blake and Walt Whitman*

There can be few books in the world like these; I can remember one poet only whose work seems to me the same or similar in kind; a poet as vast in aim, as daring in detail, as unlike others, as coherent to himself, as strange without and as sane within. The points of contact and sides of likeness between William Blake and Walt Whitman are so many and so grave, as to afford some ground of reason to those who preach the transition of souls or transfusion of spirits. The great American is not a more passionate preacher of sexual or political freedom than the English artist. To each the imperishable form of a possible and universal Republic is equally requisite and adorable as the temporal and spiritual queen of ages as of men. To each all sides and shapes of life are alike acceptable or endurable. From the fresh free ground of either workman nothing is excluded that is not exclusive. The words of either strike deep and run wide and soar high. They are both full of faith and passion, competent to love and to loathe, capable of contempt and of worship. Both are spiritual, and both democratic; both by their works recall, even to so untaught and tentative a student as I am, the fragments vouchsafed to us of the Pantheistic poetry of the East. Their casual audacities of expression or speculation are in effect wellnigh identical. Their outlooks and theories are evidently the same on all points of intellectual and social life. The divine devotion and selfless love which make men martyrs and prophets are alike visible and palpable in each. It is no secret now, but a matter of public knowledge, that both these men, being poor in the sight and the sense of the world, have given what they had of time or of money, of labour or of love, to comfort and support all the suffering and sick, all the afflicted and misused, whom they had the chance or the right to succour and to serve. The noble and gentle labours of the one are known to those who live in his time; the similar deeds of the other deserve and demand a late recognition. No man so poor and so obscure as Blake appeared in the eyes of his generation ever did more good works in a more noble and simple spirit. It seems that in each of these men at their birth pity and passion, and relief and redress of wrong, became incarnate and innate. That may well be said of the one which was said of the other: that "he looks like a man." And in externals and details the work of these two constantly and inevitably coheres and coincides. A sound as of a sweeping wind; a prospect as over dawning continents at the fiery instant of a sudden sunrise; a splendour now of stars and now of storms; an expanse and exultation of wing across strange spaces of air and above shoreless stretches of sea; a resolute and reflective love of liberty in all times and in all things where it should be; a depth of sympathy and a height of scorn which complete and explain each other, as tender and as bitter as Dante's; a power, intense and infallible, of pictorial concentration and absorption, most rare when combined with the sense and enjoyment of the widest and the highest things; an exquisite and lyrical excellence of form when the subject is well in keeping with the poet's tone of spirit; a strength and security of touch in small sweet sketches of colour and outline, which bring before the eyes of their student a clear glimpse of the thing designed — some little inlet of sky lighted by moon or star, some dim reach of windy water or gentle growth of meadow-land or wood; these are qualities common to the work of either. Had we place or time or wish to touch on their shortcoming and errors, it might be shown that these too are nearly akin; that their poetry has at once the melody and laxity of a fitful storm-wind; that, being oceanic, it is troubled with violent groundswells and sudden perils of ebb and reflux, of shoal and reef, perplexing to the swimmer or the sailor; in a word, that it partakes the powers and the faults of elemental and eternal things; that it is at times noisy and barren and loose, rootless and fruitless and informal; and is in the main fruitful and delightful and noble, a necessary part of the divine mechanism of things. Any work or art of which this cannot be said is superfluous and perishable, whatever of grace or charm it may posses or assume. Whitman has seldom struck a note of thought and speech so just and so profound as Blake has now and then touched upon; but his work is generally more frank and fresh, smelling of sweeter air, and readier to expound or expose its message, than this of the prophetic books. Nor is there among these any poem or passage of equal length so faultless and so noble as his "Voice out of the Sea," or as his dirge over President Lincoln — the most sweet and sonorous nocturn ever chanted in the church of the world. But in breadth of outline and charm of colour, these poems recall the work of Blake; and to neither poet can a higher tribute of honest praise be paid than this.

## FROM "VICTOR HUGO" (1869, 1872, 1875)

*Crossing the Channel from Ostend*

Once only in my life I have seen the likeness of Victor Hugo's genius. Crossing over when a boy from Ostend, I had the fortune to be caught in midchannel by a thunderstorm strong enough to delay the packet some three good hours over the due time. About midnight the thundercloud was right overhead, full of incessant sound and fire, lightening and darkening so rapidly that it seemed to have life, and a delight in its life. At the same hour the sky was clear to the west, and all along the sea-line there sprang and sank as to music a restless dance or chase of summer lightnings across the lower sky: a race and riot of lights, beautiful and rapid as a course of shining Oceanides along the tremulous floor of the sea. Eastward at the same moment the space of clear sky was higher and wider, a splendid semicircle of too intense purity to be called blue; it was of no colour nameable by man; and midway in it between the storm and the sea hung the motionless full moon; Artemis watching with a serene splendour of scorn the battle of Titans and the revel of nymphs, from her stainless and Olympian summit of divine indifferent light. Underneath and about us the sea was paved with flame; the whole water trembled and hissed with phosphoric fire; even through the wind and thunder I could hear the crackling and sputtering of the water-sparks. In the same heaven and in the same hour there shone at once the three contrasted glories, golden and fiery and white, of moonlight and of the double lightnings, forked and sheet; and under all this miraculous heaven lay a flaming floor of water.

That, in a most close and exact symbol, is the best possible definition I can give of Victor Hugo's genius. And the impression of that hour was upon me the impression of his mind; physical, as it touched the nerves with a more vivid passion of pleasure than music or wine; spiritual, as it exalted the spirit with the senses and above them to the very summit of vision and delight. It is no fantastic similitude, but an accurate likeness of two causes working to the same effect. There is nothing but that delight like the delight given by some of his work. And it is because his recent book has not seldom given it me again, that I have anything here to say of it.

It is a book to be rightly read, not by the lamplight of realism, but by the sunlight of his imagination reflected upon ours. Only so shall we see it as it is, much less understand it. The beauty it has, and the meaning, are ideal; and therefore cannot be impaired by any want of realism. Error and violation of likelihood or fact which would damn a work of Balzac's or of Thackeray's cannot even lower or lessen the rank and value of a work like this. To put it away because it has not the great and precious qualities of their school, but those of a school quite different, is just as wise as it would be on the other hand to assault the fame of Bacon on the ground that he has not written in the manner of Shakespeare; or Newton's, because he has not written like Milton. This premised, I shall leave the dissection of names and the anatomy of probabilities to the things of chatter and chuckle so well and scientifically defined long since by Mr. Charles Reade as "anonymuncules who go scribbling about;" there is never any lack of them; and it will not greatly hurt the master poet of an age that they should shriek and titter, cackle and hoot inaudibly behind his heel. It is not every demigod who is vulnerable there.

This book has in it, so to say, a certain elemental quality. It is great because it deals greatly with great emotions. It is a play played out not by human characters only; wind and sea, thunder and moonlight, have their parts too to fill. Nor is this all; for it is itself a thing like these things, living as it were an elemental life. It pierces and shakes the very roots of passion. It catches and bends the spirit as Pallas caught Achilles and bent him by the hair. Were it not so, this would be no child of the master's; but so, as always, it is. Here too the birth-mark of the great race is visible.

. . . . . . . . . . .

*"The rule of art is not the rule of morals"*

A poem having in it any element of greatness is likely to arouse many questions with regard to the poetic art in general, and certain in that case to illustrate them with fresh lights of its own. This of Victor Hugo's at once suggests two points of frequent and fruitless debate between critics of the higher kind. The first, whether poetry and politics are irreconcilable or not; the second, whether art should prefer to deal with things immediate or with things remote. Upon both sides of either question it seems to me that even wise men have ere now been led from errors of theory to errors of decision. The well-known formula of art for art's sake, opposed as it has ever been to the practice of the poet who was so long credited with its authorship, has like other doctrines a true side to it and an untrue. Taken as an affirmative, it is a precious and everlasting truth. No work of art has any worth or life in it that is not done on the absolute terms of art; that is not before all things and above all things a work of positive excellence as judged by the laws of the special art to whose laws it is amenable. If the rules and conditions of that art be not observed, or if the work done be not great and perfect enough to rank among its triumphs, the poem, picture, statue, is a failure irredeemable and inexcusable by any show or any proof of high purpose and noble meaning. The rule of art is not the rule of morals; in morals the action is judged by the intention, the doer is applauded, excused, or condemned, according to the motive which induced his deed; in art, the one question is not what you mean but what you do. Therefore, as I have said elsewhere, the one primary requisite of art is artistic worth; "art for art's sake first, and then all things shall be added to her—or if not, it is a matter of quite secondary importance; but from him that has not this one indispensable quality of the artist, shall be taken away even that which he has; whatever merit of aspiration, sentiment, sincerity, he may naturally possess, admirable and serviceable as in other lines of work it might have been and yet may be, is here unprofitable and unpraiseworthy." Thus far we are at one with the preachers of "art for art;" we prefer for example Goethe to Körner and Sappho to Tyrtæus; we would give many patriots for one artist, considering that civic virtue is more easily to be had than lyric genius, and that the hoarse monotony of verse lowered to the level of a Spartan understanding, however commendable such verse may be for the doctrine delivered and the duty inculcated upon all good citizens, is of less than no value to art, while there is a value beyond price and beyond thought in the Lesbian music which spends itself upon the record of fleshly fever and amorous malady. We admit then that the worth of a poem has properly nothing to do with its moral meaning or design; that the praise of a Cæsar as sung by Virgil, of a Stuart as sung by Dryden, is preferable to the most magnanimous invective against tyranny which love of country and of liberty could wring from a Bavius or a Settle; but on the other hand we refuse to admit that art of the highest kind may not ally itself with moral or religious passion, with the ethics or the politics of a nation or an age. It does not detract from the poetic supremacy of Æschylus and of Dante, or of Milton and of Shelley, that they should have been pleased to put their art to such use; nor does it detract from the sovereign greatness of other poets that they should have had no note of song for any such theme. In a word, the doctrine of art for art is true in the positive sense, false in the negative; sound as an affirmation, unsound as a prohibition. If it be not true that the only absolute duty of art is the duty she owes to herself, then must art be dependent on the alien conditions of a subject and of aim; whereas she is dependent on herself alone, and on nothing above her or beneath; by her own law she must stand or fall, and to that alone she is responsible; by no other law can any work or art be condemned, by no other plea can it be saved. But while we refuse to any artist on any plea the license to infringe in the least article the letter of this law, to overlook or overpass it in the pursuit of any foreign purpose, we do not refuse to him the liberty of bringing within the range of it any subject that under these conditions may be so brought and included within his proper scope of work. This liberty the men who take "art for art" as their motto, using the words in an exclusive sense, would refuse to concede; they see with perfect clearness and accuracy that art can never be a "handmaid" of any "lord," as the moralist, pietist, or politician would fain have her be; and therefore they will not allow that she can properly be even so much as an ally of anything else.

. . . . . . . . . . .

*"Art knows nothing of time"*

The question whether past or present afford the highest matter for high poetry and offer the noblest reward to the noble workman has been as loudly and as long debated, but is really less debateable on any rational ground than the question of the end and aim of art. It is but lost labour that the champions on one side summon us to renounce the present and all its works, and return to bathe our spirits in the purer air and living springs of the past; it is but waste of breath for the champions of the other party to bid us break the yoke and cast off the bondage of that past, leave the dead to bury their dead, and turn from the dust and rottenness of old-world themes, epic or romantic, classical or feudal, to face the age wherein we live and move and have our being, to send forth our souls and songs in search of the wonderful and doubtful future. Art knows nothing of time; for her there is but one tense, and all ages in her sight are alike present; there is nothing old in her sight, and nothing new. It is true, as the one side urges, that she fears not to face the actual aspect of the hour, to handle if it please her the immediate matters of the day; it is true, as the other side insists, that she is free to go back when she will to the very beginnings of tradition and fetch her subject from the furthest of ancient days; she cannot be vulgarised by the touch of the present or deadened by the contact of the past. In vain, for instance, do the first poetess of England and the first poet of America agree to urge upon their fellows or their followers the duty of confronting and expressing the spirit and the secret of their own time, its meaning and its need; such work is worthy of a poet, but no worthier than any other work that has in it the principle of life. And a poem of the past, if otherwise as good, has in it as much of this principle as a poem of the present. If a poem cast in the mould of classic or feudal times, of Greek drama or mediaeval romance, be lifeless and worthless, it is not because the subject or the form was ancient, but because the poet was inadequate to his task, incompetent to do better than a flat and feeble imitation; had he been able to fill the old types of art with new blood and breath, the remoteness of subject and the antiquity of form would in no wise have impaired the worth and reality of his work; he would have brought close to us the far-off loveliness and renewed for us the ancient life of his models, not by mechanical and servile transcript as of a copying clerk, but by loving and reverent emulation as of an original fellow-craftsman. No form is obsolete, no subject out of date, if the right man be there to rehandle it. To the question "Can these bones live?" there is but one answer; if the spirit and breath of art be breathed upon them indeed, and the voice prophesying upon them be indeed the voice of a prophet, then assuredly will the bones "come together, bone to his bone;" and the sinews and the flesh will come up upon them, and the skin cover them above, and the breath come into them, and they will live. For art is very life itself, and knows nothing of death; she is absolute truth, and takes no care of fact; she sees that Achilles and Ulysses are even now more actual by far than Wellington and Talleyrand; not merely more noble and more interesting as types and figures, but more positive and real; and thus it is (as Victor Hugo has himself so finely instanced it) "that Trimalchio is alive, while the late M. Romieu is dead." Vain as is the warning of certain critics to beware of the present and abstain from its immediate vulgarities and realities, not less vain, however nobly meant or nobly worded, is the counter admonition to "mistrust the poet" who "trundles back his soul" some centuries to sing of chiefs and ladies "as dead as must be, for the greater part, the poems made on their heroic bones;" for if he be a poet indeed, these will at once be reclothed with instant flesh and reinspired with immediate breath, as present and as true, as palpable and as precious, as anything most near and real; and if the heroic bones be still fleshless and the heroic poems lifeless, the fault is not in the bones but in the poems, not in the theme but in the singer. As vain it is, not indeed to invite the muse to new spheres and fresher fields whither also she will surely and gladly come, but to bid her "migrate from Greece and Ionia, cross out those immensely overpaid accounts, that matter of Troy, and Achilles' wrath, and Æneas', Odysseus' wanderings;" forsake her temples and castles of old for the new quarters which doubtless also suit her well and make her welcome; for neither epic nor romance of chivalrous quest or classic war is obsolete yet, or ever can be; there is nothing in the past extinct; no scroll is "closed for ever," no legend or vision of Hellenic or feudal faith "dissolved utterly like an exhalation:" all that ever had life in it has life in it for ever; those themes only are dead which never were other than dead. "She has left them all, and is here;" so the prophet of the new world vaunts himself in vain; she is there indeed, as he says, "by thud of machinery and shrill steam-whistle undismayed—smiling and pleased, with palpable intent to stay;" but she has not needed for that to leave her old abodes; she is not a dependent creature of time or place, "servile to all the skiey influences;" she need not climb mountains or cross seas to bestow on all nations at once the light of her countenance; she is omnipresent and eternal, and forsakes neither Athens nor Jerusalem, Camelot nor Troy, Argonaut nor Crusader, to dwell as she does with equal good-will among modern appliances in London and New York. All times and all places are one to her; the stuff she deals with is eternal, and eternally the same; no time or theme is inapt for her, no past or present preferable.

We do not therefore rate this present book higher or lower because it deals with actual politics and matter of the immediate day. It is true that to all who put their faith and hope in the republican principle it must bring comfort and encouragement, a sense of strength and a specialty of pleasure, quite apart from the delight in its beauty and power; but it is not on this ground that we would base its claim to the reverent study and thankful admiration of men. The first and last thing to be noted in it is the fact of its artistic price and poetic greatness. Those who share the faith and the devotion of the writer have of course good reason to rejoice that the first poet of a great age, the foremost voice of a great nation, should speak for them in the ears of the world; that the highest poetry of their time should take up the cause they have at heart, and set their belief to music.

## FROM "THE POEMS OF DANTE GABRIEL ROSSETTI" (1870, 1875)

*"This 'House of Life' has in it so many mansions"*

This "House of Life" has in it so many mansions, so many halls of state and bowers of music, chapels for worship and chambers for festival, that no guest can declare on a first entrance the secret of its scheme. Spirit and sense together, eyesight and hearing and thought, are absorbed in splendour of sounds and glory of colours distinguishable only by delight. But the scheme is solid and harmonious; there is no waste in this luxury of genius: the whole is lovelier than its loveliest part. Again and again may one turn the leaves in search of some one poem or some two which may be chosen for sample and thanksgiving; but there is no choice to be made. Sonnet is poured upon sonnet, and song hands on the torch to song; and each in turn (as another poet has said of the lark's note falling from the height of dawn)

> "Rings like a golden jewel down a golden stair."

There are no poems of the class in English—I doubt if there be any even in Dante's Italian—so rich at once and pure. Their golden affluence of images and jewel-coloured words never once disguises the firm outline, the justice and chastity of form. No nakedness could be more harmonious, more consummate in its fleshly sculpture, than the imperial array and ornament of this august poetry. Mailed in gold as of the morning and girdled with gems of strange water, the beautiful body as of a carven goddess gleams through them tangible and taintless, without spot or default. There is not a jewel here but it fits, not a beauty but it subserves an end. There seems no story in this sequence of sonnets, yet they hold in them all the action and passion of a spiritual history with tragic stages and elegiac pauses and lyric motions of the living soul. Their earnest subtleties and exquisite ardours recall to mind the sonnets of Shakespeare; poems in their way unapproachable, and here in no wise imitated. Shakespeare's have at times a far more passionate and instant force, a sharper note of delight or agony or mystery, fear or desire or remorse—a keener truth and more pungent simpleness of sudden phrase, with touches of sound and flashes of light beyond all reach; Mr. Rossetti's have a nobler fullness of form, a more stately and shapely beauty of build: they are of a purer and less turbid water than the others are at time, and not less fervent when more serene then they; the subject-matter of them is sweet throughout, natural always and clear, however intense and fine in remote and delicate intricacy of spiritual stuff. There is nothing here which may not be felt by any student who can grasp the subtle sense of it in full, as a just thing and admirable, fit for the fellowship of men's feelings; if men indeed have in them enough of noble fervour and loving delicacy, enough of truth and warmth in the blood and breath of their souls, enough of brain and heart for such fellow-feeling. For something of these they must have to bring with them who would follow the radiant track of this verse through brakes of flowers and solitudes of sunlight, past fountains hidden under green bloom of leaves, beneath roof-work of moving boughs where song and silence are one music. All passion and regret and strenuous hope and fiery contemplation, all beauty and glory of thought and vision, are built into this golden house where the life that reigns is love; the very face of sorrow is not cold or withered, but has the breath of heaven between its fresh live lips and the light of pure sweet blood in its cheeks; there is a glow of summer on the red leaves of its regrets and the starry frost-flakes of its tears. Resignation and fruition, forethought and afterthought, have one voice to sing with in many keys of spirit. A more bitter sweetness of sincerity was never pressed into verse than beats and burns here under the veil and girdle of glorious words; there are no poems anywhere of more passionate meditation or vision more intense than those of "Lost Days," "Vain Virtues," "The Sun's Shame;" none of more godlike grace and sovereign charm than those headed "New-born Death," "A Superscription," "A Dark Day," "Known in Vain," "The One Hope." And of all splendid and profound love-poetry, what is there more luminous or more deep in sense and spirit than the marvellous opening cycle of twenty-eight sonnets, which embrace and express all sorrow and all joy of passion in union, of outer love and inner, triumphant or dejected or piteous or at peace? No one till he has read these knows all of majesty and melody, all of energy and emotion, all of supple and significant loveliness, all of tender cunning and exquisite strength, which our language can show at need in proof of its powers and uses. The birth of love, his eucharistic presence, his supreme vision, his utter union in flesh and spirit, the secret of the sanctuary of his heart, his louder music and his lower, his graver and his lighter seasons; all work of love and all play, all dreams and devices of his memory and his belief, all fuller and emptier hours from the first which longs for him to the last which loses, all change of lights from his midday to his moonrise, all his foreknowledge of evil things and good, all glad and sad hours of his night-watches, all the fear and ardour which feels and fights against the advent of his difference and dawn of his division, all agonies and consolations that embitter and allay the wounds of his mortal hour; the pains of breach and death, the songs and visions of the wilderness of his penance, the wood of desolation made beautiful and bitter by the same remembrance, haunted by shadows of the same hours for sorrow and for solace, and beyond all the light of the unaccomplished hour which missed its chance in one life to meet it in another where the sundered spirits revive into reunion; all these things are here done into words and sung into hearing of men as they never were till now. With a most noble and tender power all forms and colours of the world without are touched and drawn into service of the spirit; and this with no ingenious abuse of imagery or misuse of figures, but with such gracious force of imagination that they seem to offer voluntary service.

. . . . . . . . . . .

*"The sacred art of Mr. Rossetti"*

A certain section of Mr. Rossetti's work as poet and as painter may be classed under the head of sacred art: and this section comprises much of his most exquisite and especial work. Its religious quality is singular and personal in kind; we cannot properly bracket it with any other workman's. The fire of feeling and imagination which feeds it is essentially Christian, and is therefore formally and spiritually Catholic. It has nothing of rebellious Protestant personality, nothing of the popular compromise of sentiment which in the hybrid jargon of a school of hybrids we may call liberalized Christianism. The influence which plainly has passed over the writer's mind, attracting it as by charm of sound or vision, by spell of colour or of dream, towards the Christian forms and images, is in the main an influence from the mythologic side of the creed. It is from the sandbanks of tradition and poetry that the sacred sirens have sung to this seafarer. This divides him at once from the passionate evangelists of positive belief and from the artists upon whom no such influence has fallen in any comparable degree. There are two living and leading writers of high and diverse genius whom any student of their work—utterly apart as their ways of work lie—may and must, without prejudice or presumption, assume to hold fast, with a force of personal passion, the radical tenet of Christian faith. It is as difficult for a reasonable reader to doubt the actual and positive adherence to Christian doctrine of the Protestant thinker as of the Catholic doctrine of the Protestant thinker as of the Catholic priest; to doubt that faith in Christ as God—a tough, hard, vital faith which can bear at need hard stress of weather and hard thought—dictated "A Death in the Desert" or "Christmas Eve and Easter Day," as to doubt that it dictated the "Apologia" or "Dream of Gerontius:" though neither in the personal creed set forth by Mr. Browning nor in the clerical creed delivered by Dr. Newman do we find apparent or flagrant—however they may lurk, tacit and latent, in the last logical expression of either man's theories—the viler forms and more hideous outcomes of Christianity, its more brutal aspects and deadlier consequences; a happy default due rather to nobility of instinct than to ingenuity of evasion. Now the sacred art of Mr. Rossetti, for all its Christian colouring, has actually no more in common with the spirit of either than it has with the semi-Christianity of "In Memoriam" or the demi-semi-Christianity of "Dipsychus." It has no trace, on the other hand, of the fretful and fruitless prurience of soul which would fain grasp and embrace and enjoy a creed beyond its power of possession; no letch after Gods dead or unborn, such as vexes the weaker nerves of barren brains, and makes pathetic the vocal lips of sorrowing skepticism and "doubt that deserves to believe." As little can it be likened to another form of bastard belief, another cross-breed between faith and unfaith, which has been fostered in ages of doubt; a ghost raised rather by fear than love; by fear of a dead God as judge, than by love of a dead God as comforter. The hankering and restless habit of half fearful retrospect towards the unburied corpses of old creeds which, as we need not Shelley's evidence to know, infected the spiritual life and disturbed the intellectual force of Byron, is a mirage without attraction for this traveller; that spiritual calenture of Christianity is a sickness unknown to his soul; nor has he ever suffered from the distemper of minds fretted and worried by gnatstings and fleabites of belief and unbelief till the whole lifeblood of the intellect is enfeebled and inflamed. In a later poet, whose name as yet is far enough from inscription on the canonical roll of converts, there was some trace of a seeming recrudescence of faith not unlike yet not like Byron's. The intermittent Christian reaction apparently perceptible in Baudelaire was more than half of it mere repulsion from the philanthropic optimism of sciolists in whose eyes the whole aim or mission of things is to make the human spirit finally comfortable. Contempt of such facile free-thinking, still more easy than free, took in him at times the form of apparent reversion to cast creeds; as though the spirit should seek a fiery refuge in the good old hell of the faithful from the watery new paradise of liberal theosophy and ultimate amiability of all things.* Alone among the higher artists of his age, Mr. Rossetti has felt and given the mere physical charm of Christianity, with no admixture of doctrine or of doubt. Here as in other things he belongs, if to any school at all, to that of the great Venetians. He takes the matter in hand with the thorough comprehension of Tintoretto or Veronese, with their thorough subjection of creed and history to the primary purpose of art and proper bearing of a picture. He works after the manner of Titian painting his Assumption with an equal hand whether the girl exalted into goddess be Mary or Ariadne: but his instinct is too masterly for any confusion or discord of colours; and hence comes the spiritual charm and satisfaction of his sacred art. In this class of his poems the first place and the fairest palm belong to the "Blessed Damozel." This paradisal poem, "sweeter than honey or the honeycomb," has found a somewhat further echo than any of its early fellows, and is perhaps known where little else is known of its author's. The sweet intense impression of it must rest for life upon all spirits that ever once received it into their depths, and hold it yet as a thing too dear and fair for praise or price. Itself the flower of a splendid youth, it has the special charm for youth of fresh first work and opening love; "the dew of its birth is of the womb of the morning;" it has the odour and colour of cloudless air, the

* It is remarkable that Baudelaire always kept in mind that Christianity, like other religions which have a broad principle of popular life in them, was not and could not be a creature of philanthropy or philotheism, but of church and creed; and this gives its peculiar savour and significance to the Christian infusion in some of his poems; for such recollection is too rare in an age and country where semi-Christian sentiment runs loose and babbles aloud.

splendour of an hour without spot. The divine admixtures of earth which humanize its heavenly passion have the flavour and bloom upon them of a maiden beauty, the fine force of a pure first sunrise. No poem shows more plainly the strength and wealth of the workman's lavish yet studious hand. One sample in witness of this wealth, and in evidence of the power of choice and persistent search after perfection which enhance its price, may be cited; though no petal should be plucked out of this mystic rose for proof of its fragrance. The two final lines of the stanza describing the secret shrine of God have been reformed; and the form first given to the world is too fair to be wholly forgotten: —

"Whose lamps tremble continually
   With prayer sent up to God,
*And where each need, revealed, expects
   Its patient period.*"

Wonderful though the beauty may be of the new imagination, that the spirits standing there at length will see their "old prayers, granted, melt each like a little cloud," there is so sweet a force in the cancelled phrase that some students might grudge the loss, and feel that, though a diamond may have supplanted it, a ruby has been plucked out of the golden ring. Nevertheless, the complete circlet shines now with a more solid and flawless excellence of jewels and of setting. The sweetness and pathos and gracious radiance of the poem have been praised by those who have not known or noted all the noble care spent on it in rejection and rearrangement of whatever was crude or lax in the first cast; but the breadth and sublimity which ennoble its brightness and beauty of fancies are yet worthier of note than these. What higher imagination can be found in modern verse than this?

"From the fixed place of heaven she saw
   *Time like a pulse shake fierce
Through all the worlds.*"

This grandeur of scale and sweep of spirit give greatness of style to poetry, as well as sweetness and brightness. These qualities, together with the charm of fluent force and facile power, are apparent in all Mr. Rossetti's work; but its height of pitch and width of scope give them weight and price beyond their own.

## FROM *A NOTE ON CHARLOTTE BRONTË* (1877)

*Charlotte Brontë and George Eliot: "The great gulf between pure genius and pure intellect"*

The gift of which I would speak is that of a power to make us feel in every nerve, at every step forward which our imagination is compelled to take under the guidance of another's, that thus and not otherwise, but in all things altogether even as we are told and shown, it was and it must have been with the human figures set before us in their action and their suffering; that thus and not otherwise they absolutely must and would have felt and thought and spoken under the proposed conditions. It is something for a writer to have achieved if he has made it worth our fancy's while to consider by the light of imaginative reason whether the creatures of his own fancy would in actual fact and life have done as he has made them do or not; it is something, and by comparison it is much. But no definite terms of comparison will suffice to express how much more than this it is to have done what the youngest of capable readers must feel on first opening 'Jane Eyre' that the writer of its very first pages has shown herself competent to do. In almost all other great works of its kind, in almost all the sovereign masterpieces even of Fielding, of Thackeray, of the royal and imperial master, Sir Walter Scott himself—to whose glorious memory I need offer no apology for the attribution of epithets which I cannot but regret to remember that even in their vulgar sense he would not have regarded as other than terms of honour—even in the best and greatest works of these our best and greatest we do not find this one great good quality so innate, so immanent as in hers. At most we find the combination of event with character, the coincidence of action with disposition, the coherence of consequences with emotions, to be rationally credible and acceptable to the natural sense of a reasonable faith. We rarely or never feel that, given the characters, the incidents become inevitable; that such passion must needs bring forth none other than such action, such emotions cannot choose but find their only issue in such events. And certainly we do not feel, what it seems to me the highest triumph of inspired intelligence and creative instinct to succeed in making us feel, that the mainspring of all, the central relation of the whole, 'the very pulse of the machine,' has in it this occult inexplicable force of nature. But when Catherine Earnshaw says to Nelly Dean, 'I *am* Heathcliff!' and when Jane Eyre answers Edward Rochester's question, whether she feels in him the absolute sense of fitness and correspondence to herself which he feels to himself in her, with the words which close and crown the history of their twin-born spirits—'To the finest fibre of my nature, sir'—we feel to the finest fibre of our own that there are no mere words. On this ground at least it might for once be not unpardonable to borrow their standing reference or illustration from that comparative school of critics whose habit of comparison we have treated with something less than respect, and say, as was said on another score of Emily Brontë in particular by Sydney Dobell, in an admirable paper which we miss with regret and with surprise from among the costly relics of his genius, so lovingly set in order and so ably lighted up by the faithful friendship and the loyal intelligence of Professor Nichol—that either sister in this single point 'has done no less' than Shakespeare. As easily might we imagine a change of the mutual relations between the characters of Shakespeare as a corresponding revolution or reversal of conditions among theirs.

If I turn again for contrast or comparison with their works to the work of George Eliot, it will be attributed by no one above the spiritual rank and type of Pope's representative dunces to irreverence or ingratitude for the large and liberal beneficence of her genius at its best. But she alone among our living writers is generally admitted or assumed as the rightful occupant, or at least as the legitimate claimant, of that foremost place in the front rank of artists in this kind which none can hold or claim without challenging such comparison or such contrast. And in some points it is undeniable that she may claim precedence, not of these alone, but of all other illustrious women. Such wealth and depth of thoughtful and fruitful humour, of vital and various intelligence, no woman has ever shown—no woman perhaps has ever shown a tithe of it. In knowledge, in culture, perhaps in capacity for knowledge and for culture, Charlotte Brontë was no more comparable to George Eliot than George Eliot is comparable to Charlotte Brontë in purity of passion, in depth and ardour of feeling, in spiritual force and fervour of forthright inspiration. It would be rather a rough and sweeping than a loose or inaccurate division which should define the one as a type of genius distinguished from the intellect, the other of intellect as opposed to genius. But it would, as I venture to think, be little or nothing more or less than accurate to recognise in George Eliot a type of intelligence vivified and coloured by a vein of genius, in Charlotte Brontë a type of genius directed and moulded by the touch of intelligence. No better test of this distinction could be desired than a comparison of their respective shortcomings or failures. These will serve, by their difference in kind and import, in quality and in weight, to show the depth and width of the great gulf between pure genius and pure intellect, even better than a comparison of their highest merits and achievements.

That great genius is liable to great error the world has ever been willing, if not more than willing, to admit; that great genius not equally balanced by great intellect is not one half as liable to go one half as wrong as intellect unequally counterpoised by genius, is a truth less popular and less familiar, but neither less important nor less indisputable. That Charlotte Brontë, a woman of the first order of genius, could go very wrong indeed, there are whole scenes and entire characters in her work which afford more than ample proof. But George Eliot, a woman of the first order of intellect, has once and again shown how much further and more steadily and more hopelessly and more irretrievably and more intolerably wrong it is possible for mere intellect to go than it ever can be possible for mere genius. Having no taste for the dissection of dolls, I shall leave Daniel Deronda in his natural place above the ragshop door; and having no ear for the melodies of a Jew's harp, I shall leave the Spanish Gipsy to perform on that instrument to such audience as she may collect. It would be unjust and impertinent to dwell much on Charlotte Brontë's brief and modest attempts in verse; but it would be unmanly and unkindly to touch at all on George Eliot's; except indeed to remark in passing that they are about equally commendable for the one and for the other of those negative good qualities which I have commended in Miss Brontë's. And from this point of difference, if from no other point here discernible, those who will or who can learn anything may learn a lesson in criticism which may perhaps be worth laying to heart: that genius, though it can put forth no better claim than intellect may assert for itself to share the papal gift of infallibility, is naturally the swifter of the two to perceive and to retrieve its errors. Where genius takes one false step in the twilight and draws back by instinct, intelligence once misguided will take a thousand without the slightest diffidence; will put its best foot foremost in the pitchy darkness, step out gallantly through all brakes and quagmires till stuck fast up to the middle, and higher yet, in some blind Serbonian bog of blundering presumption, and thence will not improbably strike up a psalm of hoarse thanksgiving or shrill self-gratulation, to be echoed from afar by the thousand marshy throats of a Mæotian or Bœotian frog concert, for the grace here given it to have set a triumphant foot on the solid rock, and planted a steady flagstaff on the splendid summits of supreme and unsurpassable success.

. . . . . . . . . . .

*Charlotte and Emily Brontë: "The tragic use of landscape"*

This instinct (if I may so call it) for the tragic use of landscape was wellnigh even more potent and conspicuous in Emily than in Charlotte. Little need was there for the survivor to tell us in such earnest and tender words of memorial record how 'my sister Emily loved the moors': that love exhales, as a fresh wild odour from a bleak shrewd soil, from every storm-swept page of 'Wuthering Heights.' All the heart of the league-long billows of rolling and breathing and brightening heather is blown with the breath of it on our faces as we read; all the wind and all the sound and all the fragrance and freedom and gloom and glory of the high north moorland—'in winter nothing more dreary, in summer nothing more divine.' Even in Charlotte Brontë's highest work I find no touches of such exquisite strength and triumphant simplicity as here. There is nothing known to me in any book of quite equal or similar effect to that conveyed by one or two of these. Take for instance that marvellous note of landscape struck as it seems unconsciously by the heaven-born instinct of a supreme artist in composition and colour, in tones and shades and minor notes of tragic and magic sweetness, which serves as overture to the last fierce rapturous passage of raging love and mad recrimination between Heathcliff and the dying Catherine; the mention of the church-bell that in winter could just be heard ringing right across the naked little glen, but in summer the sound was lost, muffled by the murmur of blowing foliage and branches full of birds. The one thing I know or can remember as in some sort comparable in its effect to this passage is of course that notice of the temple-haunting martlet and its loved mansionry which serves as prelude to the entrance of Lady Macbeth from under the buttresses where its pendant bed and procreant cradle bore witness to the delicate air in which incarnate murder also was now to breed and haunt. Even more wonderful perhaps in serene perfection of subdued and sovereign power is the last brief paragraph of that stormy and fiery tale. There was a dark unconscious instinct as of primitive nature-worship in the passionate great genius of Emily Brontë, which found no corresponding quality in her sister's. It is into the lips of her representative Shirley Keeldar that Charlotte puts the fervent 'pagan' hymn of visionary praise to her mother nature — Hertha, Demeter, 'la déesse des dieux,' which follows on her fearless indignant repudiation of Milton and his Eve. Nor had Charlotte's less old-world and Titanic soul any touch of the self-dependent solitary contempt for all outward objects of faith and hope, for all aspiration after a changed heart or a contrite spirit or a converted mind, which speaks in the plain-song note of Emily's clear stern verse with such grandeur of antichristian fortitude and self-controlling self-reliance, that the 'halting slave' of Epaphroditus might have owned for his spiritual sister the English girl whose only prayer for herself, 'in life and death' — a self-sufficing prayer, self-answered, and fulfilled even in the utterance — was for 'a chainless soul, with courage to endure.' Not often probably has such a petition gone up from within the walls of a country parsonage as this: —

And if I pray, the only prayer
  That moves my lips for me,
Is — Leave the heart that now I bear,
  And give me liberty!

That word which is above every word might surely have been found written on that heart. Her love of earth for earth's sake, her tender loyalty and passionate reverence for the All-mother, bring to mind the words of her sister's friend, and the first eloquent champion of her own genius: —

I praise thee, mother earth! oh earth, my mother!
Oh earth, sweet mother! gentle mother earth!
Whence thou receivest what thou givest I
Ask not as a child asketh not his mother,
Oh earth, my mother!

No other poet's imagination could have conceived that agony of the girl who dreams she is in heaven, and weeps so bitterly for the loss of earth that the angels cast her out in anger, and she finds herself fallen on the moss and heather of the mid moor-head, and wakes herself with a sobbing for joy. It is possible that to take full delight in Emily Brontë's book one must have something by natural inheritance of her instinct and something by earliest association of her love for the same special points of earth — the same lights and sounds and colours and odours and sights and shapes of the same fierce free landscape of tenantless and fruitless and fenceless moor; but however that may be, it was assuredly with no less justice of insight and accuracy of judgment than humility of self-knowledge and fidelity of love that Charlotte in her day of solitary fame assigned to her dead sister the crown of poetic honour which she as rightfully disclaimed for herself. Full of poetic quality as her own work is throughout, that quality is never condensed or crystallized into the proper and final form of verse. But the pure note of absolutely right expression for things inexpressible in full by prose at its highest point of adequacy — the formal inspiration of sound which at once reveals itself, and which can fully reveal itself by metrical embodiment alone, in the symphonies and antiphonies of regular word-music and definite instinctive modulation of corresponsive tones — this is what Emily had for her birthright as certainly as Charlotte had it not. Here are a few lines to give evidence for themselves on that score.

He comes with western winds, with evening's wandering airs,
With that clear dusk of heaven that brings the thickest stars.
Winds take a pensive tone, and stars a tender fire,
And visions rise, and change, that kill me with desire.

Desire for nothing known in my maturer years,
When Joy grew mad with awe, at counting future tears.

. . . . . . . . . . .

Oh, dreadful is the check — intense the agony —
When the ear begins to hear, and the eye begins to see;
When the pulse begins to throb, the brain to think again,
The soul to feel the flesh, and the flesh to feel the chain.

If here is not the pure distinctive note of song as opposed to speech — the 'lyrical cry,' as Mr. Arnold calls it — I know not where to seek it in English verse since Shelley.

## "EMILY BRONTË" (1883, 1886)

To the England of our own time, it has often enough been remarked, the novel is what the drama was to the England of Shakespeare's. The same general interest produced the same incessant demand for the same inexhaustible supply of imaginative produce, in a shape more suited to the genius of a later day and the conditions of a changed society. Assuming this simple explanation to be sufficient for the obvious fact that in the modern world of English letters the novel is everywhere and the drama is nowhere, we may remark one radical point of difference between the taste of playgoers in the age of Shakespeare and the taste of novel-readers in our own. Tragedy was then at least as popular as either romantic or realistic comedy; whereas nothing would seem to be more unpopular with the run of modern readers than the threatening shadow of tragedy projected across the whole length of a story, inevitable and unmistakable from the lurid harshness of its dawn to the fiery softness of its sunset. The objection to a novel in which the tragic element has an air of incongruity and caprice—in which a tragic surprise is, as it were, sprung upon the reader, with a jarring shock such as might be given by the actual news of some unforeseen and grievous accident—this objection seems to me thoroughly reasonable, grounded on a true critical sense of fitness and unfitness; but the distaste for high and pure tragedy, where the close is in perfect and simple harmony with the opening, seems not less thoroughly pitiable and irrational.

A later work of indisputable power, in which the freshness of humour is as real and vital as the fervour of passion, was at once on its appearance compared with Emily Brontë's now famous story. And certainly not without good cause; for in point of local colour *Mehalah* is, as far as I know, the one other book which can bear and may challenge the comparison. Its pages, for one thing, reflect the sterile glitter and desolate fascination of the salt marshes, their minute splendours and barren beauties and multitudinous monotony of measureless expanse, with the same instinctive and unlaborious accuracy which brings all the moorland before us in a breath when we open any chapter of *Wuthering Heights*. But the accumulated horrors of the close, however possible in fact, are wanting in the one quality which justifies and ennobles all admissible horror in fiction: they hardly seem inevitable; they lack the impression of a logical and moral certitude. All the realism in the world will not suffice to convey this impression: and a work of art which wants it wants the one final and irreplaceable requisite of inner harmony. Now in *Wuthering Heights* this one thing needful is as perfectly and triumphantly attained as in *King Lear* or *The Duchess of Malfy*, in *The Bride of Lammermoor* or *Notre-Dame de Paris*. From the first we breathe the fresh dark air of tragic passion and presage; and to the last changing wind and flying sunlight are in keeping with the stormy promise of the dawn. There is no monotony, there is no repetition, but there is no discord. This is the first and last necessity, the foundation of all labour and the crown of all success, for a poem worthy of the name; and this it is that distinguishes the hand of Emily from the hand of Charlotte Brontë. All the works of the elder sister are rich in poetic spirit, poetic feeling, and poetic detail; but the younger sister's work is essentially and definitely a poem in the fullest and most positive sense of the term. It was therefore all the more proper that the honour of raising a biographical and critical monument to the author of *Wuthering Heights* should have been reserved for a poetess of the next generation to her own. And those who had already in their mind's eye the clearest and most definite conception of Emily Brontë will be the readiest to acknowledge their obligation and express their gratitude to Miss Robinson for the additional light which she has been enabled to throw upon a great and singular character. It is true that when all has been said the main features of that character stand out before us unchanged. The sweet and noble genius of Mrs. Gaskell did not enable her to see far into so strange and sublime a problem; but, after all, the main difference between the biographer of Emily and the biographer of Charlotte is that Miss Robinson has been interested and attracted where Mrs. Gaskell was scared and perplexed. On one point, however, the new light afforded us is of the very utmost value and interest. We all knew how great was Emily Brontë's tenderness for the lower animals; we find, with surprise as well as admiration, that the range of this charity was so vast as to include even her own miserable brother. Of that lamentable and contemptible caitiff—contemptible not so much for his commonplace debauchery as for his abject selfishness, his lying pretention, and his nerveless cowardice—there is far too much in this memoir: it is inconceivable how any one can have put into a lady's hand such a letter as one which defaces two pages of the volume, and it may be permissible to regret that a lady should have made it public; but this error is almost atoned for by the revelation that of all the three sisters in that silent home 'it was the silent Emily who had ever a cheering word for Branwell; it was Emily who still remembered that he was her brother, without that remembrance freezing her heart to numbness.' That she saved his life from fire, and hid from their father the knowledge of her heroism, no one who knows anything of Emily Brontë will learn with any mixture of surprise in his sense of admiration; but it gives a new tone and colour to our sympathetic and reverent regard for her noble memory when we find in the depth of that self-reliant and stoic nature a fountain so inexhaustible of such Christlike longsuffering and compassion.

I cannot however but think that Miss Robinson makes a little too much of the influence exercised on Emily Brontë's work by the bitter, narrow, and ignoble misery of the life which she had watched burn down into such pitiful ruin that its memory is hardly redeemed by the last strange and inconsistent flash of expiring manhood which forbids us to regard with unmixed contempt the sufferer who had resolution enough to die standing if he had lived prostrate, and so make at the very last a manful end of an abject history. The impression of this miserable experience is visible only in Anne Brontë's second work, *The Tenant of Wildfell Hall*; which deserves perhaps a little more notice than it has ever received. It is ludicrously weak, palpably unreal, and apparently imitative, whenever it reminds the reader that it was written by a sister of Charlotte and Emily Brontë; but as a study of utterly flaccid and invertebrate immorality it bears signs of more faithful transcription from life than anything in *Jane Eyre* or *Wuthering Heights*. On the other hand, the intelligent reader of *Wuthering Heights* cannot fail to recognize that what he is reading is a tragedy simply because it is the work of a writer whose genius is essentially tragic. Those who believe that Healthcliff was called into existence by the accident that his creator had witnessed the agonies of a violent weakling in love and in disgrace might believe that Shakespeare wrote *King Lear* because he had witnessed the bad effects of parental indulgence, and that Æschylus wrote the *Eumenides* because he had witnessed the uncomfortable results of matricide. The book is what it is because the author was what she was; this is the main and central fact to be remembered. Circumstances have modified the details; they have not implanted the conception. If there were any need for explanation there would be no room for apology. As it is, the few faults of design or execution leap to sight at a first glance, and vanish in the final effect and unimpaired impression of the whole; while those who object to the violent illegalities of conduct with regard to real or personal property on which the progress of the story does undeniably depend—'a senseless piece of glaring folly,' it was once called by some critic learned in the law—might as well complain, in Carlylesque phrase, that the manners are quite other than Belgravian.

It is a fine and accurate instinct that has inevitably led Miss Robinson to cite in chosen illustration of the book's quality at its highest those two incomparable pictures of dreamland and delirium which no poet that ever lived has ever surpassed for passionate and lifelike beauty of imaginative truth. But it is even somewhat less than exact to say that the latter scene 'is given with a masterly pathos that Webster need not have made more strong, nor Fletcher more lovely and appealing.' Fletcher could not have made it as lovely and appealing as it is; he would have made it exquisitely pretty and effectively theatrical; but the depth, the force the sincerity, recalling here so vividly the 'several forms of distraction' through which Webster's Cornelia passes after the murder of her son by his brother, excel everything else of the kind in imaginative art; not expecting, if truth may be spoken on such a subject, the madness of Ophelia or even of Madge Wildfire. It is hardly ever safe to say dogmatically what can or cannot be done by the rarest and highest genius; yet it must surely be borne in upon us all that these two crowning passages could never have been written by any one to whom the motherhood of earth was less than the brotherhood of man—to whom the anguish, the intolerable and mortal yearning, of insatiate and insuppressible homesickness, was less than the bitterest of all other sufferings endurable or conceivable in youth. But in Emily Brontë this passion was twin-born with the passion for truth and rectitude. The stale and futile epithet of Titaness has in this instance a deeper meaning than appears; her goddess mother was in both senses the same who gave birth to the divine martyr of Æschylean legend: Earth under one aspect and one name, but under the other Righteousness. And therefore was the first and last word uttered out of the depth of her nature a cry for that one thing needful without which all virtue is as worthless as all pleasure is vile, all hope as shameful as all faith is abject—a cry for liberty.

And therefore too, perhaps we may say, it is that any seeming confusion or incoherence in her work is merely external and accidental, not inward and spiritual. Belief in the personal or positive immortality of the individual and indivisible spirit was not apparently, in her case, swallowed up or nullified or made nebulous by any doctrine or dream of simple reabsorption into some indefinite infinity of eternal life. So at least it seems to me that her last ardent confession of dauntless and triumphant faith should properly be read, however capable certain phrases in it may seem of the vaguer and more impersonal interpretation. For surely no scornfuller or stronger comment on the 'unutterable' vanity of creeds could pass more naturally into a chant expressive of more profound and potent faith; a song of spiritual trust more grave and deep and passionate in the solemn ardour of its appeal than the Hymn to God of Cleanthes. Her infrangible self-reliance and lonely sublimity of spirit she had in common with him and his fellows of the Porch; it was much more than 'some shy ostrich prompting' which bade her assign to an old Stoic the most personal and characteristic utterance in all her previous poems; but the double current of imaginative passion and practical compassion which made her a tragic poet and proved her a perfect woman gives as it were a living warmth and sweetness to her memory, such as might well have seemed incompatible with that sterner and colder veneration so long reserved for her spiritual kinsmen of the past. As a woman we never knew her so well as now that we have to welcome this worthy record of her life, with deeper thanks and warmer congratulations to the writer than can often be due even to the best of biographers and critics. As an author she has not perhaps even yet received her full due or taken her final place. Again and again has the same obvious objection been taken to that awkwardness of construction or presentation which no reader of *Wuthering Heights* can undertake to deny. But, to judge by the vigour with which this objection is urged, it might be supposed that the rules of narrative observed by all great novelists were of an almost legal or logical strictness and exactitude with regard to probability of detail. Now most assuredly the indirect method of relation through which the story of Heathcliff is conveyed, however unlikely or clumsy it may seem from the realistic point of view, does not make this narrative more liable to the charge of actual impossibility than others of the kind. Defoe still remains the one writer of narrative in the first person who has always kept the stringent law of possibilities before the eye of his invention. Even the admirable ingenuity and the singular painstaking which distinguish the method of Mr. Wilkie Collins can only give external and transient plausibility to the record of long conversations overheard or shared in by the narrator only a few hours before the supposed date of the report drawn up from memory. The very greatest masters in their kind, Walter Scott and Charles Dickens, are of all narrators the most superbly regardless of this objection. From *Rob Roy* and *Redgauntlet*, from *David Copperfield* and *Bleak House*, we might select at almost any stage of the autobiographic record some instance of detail in which the violation of plausibility, probability, or even possibility, is at least daring and as glaring as any to be found in the narrative of Nelly Dean. Even when that narrative is removed, so to speak, yet one degree further back—even when we are supposed to be reading a minute detail of incident and dialogue transcribed by the hand of the lay figure Mr. Lockwood from Nelly Dean's report of the account conveyed to her years ago by Heathcliff's fugitive wife or gadding servant, each invested for the nonce with the peculiar force and distinctive style of the author—even then we are not asked to put such an overwhelming strain on our faculty of imaginative belief as is exacted by the great writer who invites us to accept the report drawn up by Mr. Pendennis of everything that takes place—down even to the minutest points of dialogue, accent, and gesture—in the household of the Newcomes or the Firmins during the absence no less than in the presence of their friend the reporter. Yet all this we gladly and gratefully admit, without demur or cavil, to be thoroughly authentic and credible, because the whole matter of the report, however we get at it, is found when we do get at it to be vivid and lifelike as an actual experience of living fact. Here, if ever anywhere, the attainment of the end justifies the employment of the means. If we are to enjoy imaginative work at all, we must 'assume the virtue' of imagination, even if we have it not; we must, as children say, 'pretend' or make believe a little as a very condition of the game.

A graver and perhaps a somewhat more plausible charge is brought against the author of *Wuthering Heights* by those who find here and there in her book the savage note or the sickly symptom of a morbid ferocity. Twice or thrice especially the details of deliberate or passionate brutality in Heathcliff's treatment of his victims make the reader feel for a moment as though he were reading a police report or even a novel by some French 'naturalist' of a latest and brutallest order. But the pervading atmosphere of the book is so high and healthy that the effect even of those 'vivid and fearful scenes' which impaired the rest of Charlotte Brontë is almost at once neutralized—we may hardly say softened, but sweetened, dispersed, and transfigured—by the general impression of noble purity and passionate straightforwardness, which removes it at once and for ever from any such ugly possibility of association or comparison. The whole work is not more incomparable in the effect of its atmosphere or landscape than in the peculiar note of its wild and bitter pathos; but most of all is it unique in the special and distinctive character of its passion. The love which devours life itself, which devastates the present and desolates the future with unquenchable and raging fire, has nothing less pure in it than flame or sunlight. And this passionate and ardent chastity is utterly and unmistakably spontaneous and unconscious. Not till the story is ended, not till the effect of it has been thoroughly absorbed and digested, does the reader even perceive the simple and natural absence of any grosser element, any hint or suggestion of a baser alloy in the ingredients of its human emotion than in the splendour of lightning or the roll of a gathered wave. Then, as on issuing sometimes from the tumult of charging waters, he finds with something of wonder how absolutely pure and sweet was the element of living storm with which his own nature has been for awhile made one; not a grain in it of soiling sand, not a waif of clogging weed. As was the author's life, so is her book in all things: troubled and taintless, with little rest in it, and nothing of reproach. It may be true that not many will ever take it to their hearts; it is certain that those who do like it will like nothing very much better in the whole world of poetry or prose.

PART THREE

# *Uncollected Poetry*

**Dies Irae**

Day of wrath, the years are keeping,
When the world shall rise from sleeping,
With a clamour of great weeping!

Earth shall fear and tremble greatly
To behold the advent stately
Of the Judge that judgeth straitly.

And the trumpet's fierce impatience
Scatter strange reverberations
Thro' the graves of buried nations.

Death and Nature will stand stricken
When the hollow bones shall quicken
And the air with weeping thicken.

When the Creature, sorrow-smitten,
Rises where the Judge is sitting
And beholds the doom-book written.

For, that so his wrath be slaked,
All things sleeping shall be waked,
All things hidden shall be naked.

When the just are troubled for thee,
Who shall plead for me before thee,
Who shall stand up to implore thee?

Lest my great sin overthrow me,
Let thy mercy, quickened thro' me,
As a fountain overflow me!

For my sake thy soul was moved;
For my sake thy name reproved,
Lose me not whom thou hast loved!

Yea, when shame and pain were sorest,
For my love the cross thou borest,
For my love the thorn-plait worest.

By that pain that overbore thee,
By those tears thou weptest for me,
Leave me strength to stand before thee.

For the heart within me yearneth,
And for sin my whole face burneth;
Spare me when thy day returneth.

By the Magdalen forgiven,
By the thief made pure for heaven,
Even to me thy hope was given.

Tho' great shame be heavy on me,
Grant thou, Lord, whose mercy won me,
That hell take not hold upon me.

Thou whom I have loved solely,
Thou whom I have loved wholly,
Leave me place among the holy!

When thy sharp wrath burns like fire,
With the chosen of thy desire,
Call me to the crowned choir!

Prayer, like flame with ashes blending,
From my crushed heart burns ascending;
Have thou care for my last ending.

## [The High Victorian Tone]

Thus runs our wise man's song:
Being dark, it must be light;
And most things are so wrong
That all things must be right;
God must mean well, he works so ill by this world's laws.

This, when our souls are drowning,
Falls on them like a benison;
This satisfies our Browning
And this delights our Tennyson:
And soothed Brittania simpers in serene applause.

## Sonnet

Ah face & hands & body beautiful,
Fair tender body, for my body's sake
Are you made faultless without stain or break,
Locks close as weed in river-water cool,
A purer throat and softer than white wool,
Eyes where sleep always seems about to wake.
No dead man's flesh but feels the strong sweet ache
And that sharp amorous watch the years annul
If his grave's grass have felt you anywhere.
Rain & the summer shadow of the rain
Are not so gentle to the feverous year
As your soft rapid kisses are to men
Felt here about my face, yea here & here,
Caught on my lips & thrown you back again.

## The Ballad of Villon and Fat Madge

"'Tis no sin for a man to labour in his vocation." Falstaff
"The night cometh, when no man can work."

What though the beauty I love and serve be cheap,
Ought you to take me for a beast or fool?
All things a man could wish are in her keep;
For her I turn swashbuckler in love's school.
When folk drop in, I take my pot and stool
And fall to drinking with no more ado.
I fetch them bread, fruit, cheese, and water, too;
I say all's right so long as I'm well paid;
"Look in again when your flesh troubles you,
Inside this brothel where we drive our trade."

But soon the devil's among us flesh and fell,
When penniless to bed comes Madge my whore;
I loathe the very sight of her like hell.
I snatch gown, girdle, surcoat, all she wore,
And tell her, these shall stand against her score.
She grips her hips with both hands, cursing God,
Swearing by Jesus' body, bones, and blood,
That they shall not. Then I, no whit dismayed,
Cross her cracked nose with some stray shiver of wood
Inside this brothel where we drive our trade.

When all's made up she drops me a windy word,
   Bloat like a beetle puffed and poisonous:
Grins, thumps my pate, and calls me dickey-bird,
   And cuffs me with a fist that's ponderous.
   We sleep like logs, being drunken both of us;
Then when we wake her womb begins to stir;
To save her seed she gets me under her
   Wheezing and whining, flat as planks are laid:
And thus she spoils me for a whoremonger
   Inside this brothel where we drive our trade.

Blow, hail or freeze, I've bread here baked rent free!
Whoring's my trade, and my whore pleases me;
   Bad cat, bad rat; we're just the same if weighed.
We that love filth, filth follows us, you see;
Honour flies from us, as from her we flee
   Inside this brothel where we drive our trade.*

*I bequeath likewise to fat Madge
   This little song to learn and study;
By God's head she's a sweet fat fadge,
   Devout and soft of flesh and ruddy;
   I love her with my soul and body,
So doth she me, sweet dainty thing.
   If you fall in with such a lady,
Read it, and give it her to sing.

## A Ballad of Dead Creeds

Car ou sont ly sain et l'apostoles,
D'albes vestur, d'amys coeffen
ui ne sont ceinets fors que d'estoles
. . .
Autant en emporte ly vens.
Villon.

Where are God's holy men of old
      With alb & stole & amice clad?
The saints who cast out devils bold
      In faith more foul than filth, more mad
      Than madness? All the hope they had
In God, who bade them curse & pray,
      Where is it? Where is he who bade?
Borne down the wind & blown away.

Where is the gracious God whose fold
Shuts out all sheep that browse & gad?
Where is the Judge, as hot & cold
As Dante found his hell, as glad
As kings his servants, & as sad,
Who sent his Son on earth to pay
The debt men owed not, good or bad?
Borne down the wind & blown away.

Where is the lying tongue that told
Of murderous mercy—lass & lad
Damned & redeemed & bought & sold
By birth & baptism? (Fear forbade
Love's answer, lest the soul, unclad
Of raiment woven with lies, should slay
The living Lord, faith's ambling pad.)
Borne down the wind & blown away.

Where are the saints, from Paul to Chad,
Who made man's life, their godhead's prey
And Athens less than Dan or Gad?
Borne down the wind & blown away.

**The Cannibal Catechism**
**(versified from the writings of a Father of the Church)**

Preserve us from our enemies,
Thou who art Lord of suns & skies,
Whose meat & drink is flesh in pies
And blood in bowls!
Of thy sweet mercy, damn their eyes,
And damn their souls!

The cannibal of just behavior
Acknowledges the Lord his saviour,
With gifts of whose especial favour
He hath been crammed,
To whom an offering of sweet savour
Are all the damned.

O Lord, thy people know full well
That all who eat not flesh & fell,
Who cannot rightly speak or spell
Thy various names,

Shall be for ever boiled in hell
  Among the flames.

Glad tidings of great exultation
Proclaim we to the chosen nation;
To all men else in every station
  The joyful story
That they are going to damnation
  And we to glory.

In pits of sulfur thou wilt cram them,
In chains of burning brimstone jam them,
Squeeze them like figs, like wadding ram them,
  With flame surround them;
O Lord of love, confound & damn them
  Damn & confound them!

Grind them to pieces small & gritty,
O thou whose names are love & pity!
Roast brown all faces that were pretty,
  All black even blacker;
Strip off the trappings of their city,
  Paint, plumes, & lacquer.

The foes thy people seek to kill,
Even as a devil do thou grill!
O let thy stormy anger still
  Shake them like jellies!
Give thou their carcases to fill
  Thy servants' bellies!

The heathen, whose ungodly lip
Doth in ungodly pewter dip,
Curse his gin, whiskey, rum, & flip,
  Strong ale & bumbo!
Scourge him with anger as a whip
  O Mumbo-Jumbo!

The men who eat their neighbours not,
For all such has the Lord made hot
(To boil their souls as in a pot)
  The fire of hell:
But if thou leave not me to rot
  Then all is well.

The milky, vegetable race
Of such as have not seen thy face,

Lord, damn them by thy special grace
Thou who art gracious.
And raise into the holy place
Me, Athanasius.

## Cleopatra

"Her beauty might outface the jealous hours,
Turn shame to love and pain to a tender sleep,
And the strong nerve of hate to sloth and tears;
Make spring rebellious in the sides of frost,
Thrust out lank water with hot August growths,
Compel sweet blood into the husks of death,
And from strange beasts enforce harsh courtesy."
T. Hayman, *Fall of Antony*, 1655.

I
Her mouth is fragrant as a vine,
A vine with birds in all its boughs;
Serpent and scarab for a sign
Between the beauty of her brows
And the amorous deep lids divine.

II
Her great curled hair makes luminous
Her cheeks, her lifted throat and chin.
Shall she not have the hearts of us
To shatter, and the loves therein
To shred between her fingers thus?

III
Small ruined broken strays of light,
Pearl after pearl she shreds them through
Her long sweet sleepy fingers, white
As any pearl's heart veined with blue,
And soft as dew on a soft night.

IV
As if the very eyes of love
Shone through her shutting lids, and stole
The slow looks of a snake or dove;
As if her lips absorbed the whole
Of love, her soul the soul thereof.

V

Lost, all the lordly pearls that were
  Wrung from the sea's heart, from the green
Coasts of the Indian gulf-river;
  Lost, all the loves of the world — so keen
Towards this queen for love of her.

VI

You see against her throat the small
  Sharp glittering shadows of them shake;
And through her hair the imperial
  Curled likeness of the river snake,
Whose bite shall make an end of all.

VII

Through the scales sheathing him like wings,
  Through hieroglyphs of gold and gem,
The strong sense of her beauty stings,
  Like a keen pulse of love in them,
A running flame through all his rings.

VIII

Under those low large lids of hers
  She hath the histories of all time;
The fruit of foliage-stricken years;
  The old seasons with their heavy chime
That leaves its rhyme in the world's ears.

IX

The poised hawk, quivering ere he smote,
  With plume-like gems on breast and back;
The asps and water-worms afloat
  Between the rush-flowers moist and slack;
The cat's warm black bright rising throat.

X

The purple days of drouth expand
  Like a scroll opened out again;
The molten heaven drier than sand,
  The hot red heaven without rain,
Sheds iron pain on the empty land.

XI

She sees the hand of death made bare,
  The ravelled riddle of the skies,

The faces faded that were fair,
  The mouths made speechless that were wise,
The hollow eyes and dusty hair;

XII
The shape and shadow of mystic things,
  Things that fate fashions or forbids;
The staff of time-forgotten Kings
  Whose name falls off the Pyramids,
Their coffin-lids and grave-clothings;

XIII
Dank dregs, the scum of pool or clod,
  God-spawn of lizard-footed clans,
And those dog-headed hulks that trod
  Swart necks of the old Egyptians,
Raw draughts of man's beginning God;

XIV
All Egypt aches in the sun's sight;
  The lips of men are harsh for drouth,
The fierce air leaves their cheeks burnt white,
  Charred by the bitter blowing south,
Whose dusty mouth is sharp to bite.

XV
All this she dreams of, and her eyes
  Are wrought after the sense hereof.
There is no heart in her for sighs;
  The face of her is more than love—
A name above the Ptolemies.

XVI
Her great grave beauty covers her
  As that sleek spoil beneath her feet
Clothed once the anointed soothsayer;
  The hallowing is gone forth from it
Now, made unmeet for priests to wear.

XVII
She treads on gods and god-like things,
  On fate and fear and life and death,
On hate that cleaves and love that clings,
  All that is brought forth of man's breath
And perisheth with what it brings.

XVIII
She holds her future close, her lips
  Hold fast the face of things to be;
Actium, and sound of war that dips
  Down the blown valleys of the sea,
Far sails that flee, and storms of ships;

XIX
The laughing red sweet mouth of wine
  At ending of life's festival;
That spice of cerecloths, and the fine
  White bitter dust funereal
Sprinkled on all things for a sign;

XX
His face, who was and was not he,
  In whom, alive, her life abode;
The end, when she gained heart to see
  Those ways of death wherein she trod,
Goddess by god, with Antony.

**from "Arthur's Flogging"**

I sing of Arthur's Flogging; I, who heard
  The boy himself sing out beneath the birch,
Louder and shriller than a singing bird,
  Or screaming parrot on its gilded perch;
He has had this week three floggings; this, the third,
  A good sound swishing, was for missing church.
And on this point no two boys ever differed,
That no boy gets more flogged than Arthur Clifford.

The time was noon; the flogging room the scene;
  And all the boys in Arthur's form were there;
And in they brought the culrit of thirteen,
  A boy with bright dark eyes and bright gold hair,
Of slender figure and of careless mien,
  Though now his flushed face wore a cloud of care,
And with eyes downcast like a shrinking girl's,
He came on blushing right up to his curls.

To him the doctor, in judicial wise,
  "What kept you, Clifford Minor, out of church?"
Then the boy lifted his dark violet eyes,

And saw the flogging block, and saw the birch,
And felt the blood to cheeks and forehead rise,
And wistfully looked round him as in search
Of any pretext to ward off his fate,
And answered boldly, "Please, sir, I was late."

"What made you late, sir?" with a smile and frown
Of outward wrath and cruel inward joy,
Replied the master, "Were you not up town
On some vain errand for some foolish boy?"
No answer. "Clifford, take your trousers down."
With piteous eyes uplifted, the poor boy
Just faltered, "Please, sir," and could get no farther.
Again, that voice, "Take down your trousers, Arthur."

Then smiles were seen on many small boys' faces,
And smothered laughs on many a big boy's lips,
With stifled whispers and subdued grimaces,
While Arthur, with cold trembling finger tips,
Stood fumbling at his waistband and his braces,
Then bared the fleshy parts about his hips,
And let his trousers fall about his heels,
And showed a pair of buttocks full of weals.

A pretty pair of buttocks, round and plump,
With red points here and there, that seemed to dot 'em,
And here and there a broken twig or stump
Of birch still sticking in the flesh to spot 'em;
And many a red ridge right across the rump,
And many a half-healed scar on Arthur's bottom;
There might you see in fair and open sight
The red rose making war upon the white.

So with his parti-coloured bottom bare,
With all its wounds for all the school to mock,
With naked haunches delicately fair,
The parts unscarred as white as lady's smock,
A boy with violet eyes and yellow hair
Knelt, with his shirt up, on the flogging block;
And o'er him stood his master, fresh from church,
With a long, strong, lithe, new, green, sappy birch.

Once – twice – he whirled it whistling round his head,
Then struck with all a strong man's utmost might,
And Arthur's bottom blushed one burning red

All over, not an inch was left of white,
And from a score of weals at once it bled,
Great tingling weals that sprang up left and right
Under the birch, and from them every one
The drops of blood as thick as raindrops spun.

And all the cuts his bottom had before,
The parts where bits of birch were sticking still
Like spearheads in the wounds they had made of yore,
When last the birch had all its cruel will,
Began to bleed afresh and smart once more
As sheer through the air the whistling twigs swept shrill,
There, they're very sharp and straight, and smote afresh
The tingling space of naked quivering flesh.

The first cut made the flogged boy flinch and start,
And from his lips pain forced a short sharp cry,
So hard it fell on such a tender part,
Still sore from floggings felt so recently;
Right through his flesh he felt the bitter smart,
Like a snake's sting down darted from on high,
And writhed, and roared out at the second blow —
"Oh! please, sir; oh! sir! Oh! oh! oh! oh! oh!"

Swift as the birch on Arthur's bottom fell,
Hard as the birch on Arthur's bottom rung,
Like the deep notes of a funeral bell,
The master's words of keen rebuke were flung,
"I'll flog you well for crying—flog you well;
I'll have no crying here, boy; hold your tongue;
I'll give you more to cry for, you young dog, you!
I'll flog you—flog you—flog, flog, flog, flog, flog you."

At every pause, at every word, a blow
Fell, and made Arthur's bottom smart and bleed.
"Take that, sir," "Oh! sir, please, it hurts me so;
You don't know how you hurt me, sir, indeed;
Oh! sir, I'll never— Oh! sir, please, sir, Oh!"
And many a blood flake like a crimson bead,
At each fresh cut showed where each twig or bud
Had fallen, and drawn its one drop more of blood.

At each cut, Arthur, while his hands were free,
Pulled down his shirt and rubbed his bottom; but
Though some relief from torture it might be,

The gate of mercy was that instant shut;
And Arthur felt all through, but could not see,
How hard the doctor laid on the next cut,
And as the sharp twigs were afresh applied,
Fresh blood ran from fresh weals on his backside.

And over him in front stood Philip Shirley
And Edward Beauchamp, holding up his shirt;
And if he plucked it from them, they looked surly,
As they drew up again the blood-stained skirt,
And shook their fists aside at Arthur's curly
Head, or else grinned, and whispered, "Does it hurt?"
And only held the spotted shirt up higher,
Till the birch seemed to set his bum on fire.

He clapped his hands behind—the birch twigs caught 'em
Across, and made them tingle too and bleed;
And harder still the birch fell on his bottom,
And left some fresh red letters there to read;
Weeks passed before the part inscribed forgot 'em,
The fleshy tablets, where the master's creed
Is written on boy's skin with birchen pen,
At each re-issue copied fair again.

This was the third edition, not the first,
Printed on Arthur's bottom in red text
That very week, with comments interspersed,
And cuts that left the student's eye perplexed,
Though in the love of flagellation versed,
You hardly could tell one cut from the next
All the smooth seamy paper, white and pink,
Was crossed and scored and blotted with red ink.

The fair full page of white and warm young flesh
Was ruled across with long thick lines of red,
And lettered on the engraved backside with fresh
Large characters, by all boys to be read,
In hieroglyphs fine as a spider's mesh,
With copious coloured cuts illustrated,
Warm from the hand of the artist that begot 'em,
To adorn the bare blank page of Arthur's bottom.

All down the cream white margins, line on line,
Ran the red tracery of the engraver's tool,
With many a capital and flourish fine,

And ere the characters had time to cool
The well-soaked birch, still supple from the brine,
Made a fresh score in sight of the whole school,
Who saw the inscription on the bare flesh scored,
While Arthur writhed with agony, and roared.

## [Sonnet: Between Two Seas]

Between two seas the sea-bird's wing makes halt
Wind-weary; while with lifting head he waits
For what may come of glory thro' the gates
That open still toward sunrise on the vault
High-domed of morning, & in flight's default
With spreading sense of spirit anticipates
What new sea now may lure beyond the straits
His wings exulting that her winds exalt
And fill them full as sails to seaward spread
Fulfilled with fair speed's promise. Pass, my song,
Forth to the heaven of thy desire & dread,
The presence of our lord, long loved & long
Far off above beholden, who to thee
Was as light kindling all a windy sea.

## Poeta Loquitur

If a person conceives an opinion
That my verses are stuff that will wash,
Or my Muse has one plume on her pinion,
That person's opinion is bosh.
My philosophy, politics, free-thought!
Are worth not three skips of a flea,
And the emptiest of thoughts that can be thought
Are mine on the sea.

In a maze of monotonous murmur
Where reason roves ruined by rhyme,
In a voice neither graver nor firmer
Than the bells on a fool's cap chime,
A party pretentiously pensive,

With a Muse that deserves to be skinned,
Makes language and metre offensive
With rhymes on the wind.

A perennial procession of phrases
Pranked primly, though pruriently prime,
Precipitates preachings on praises
In a ruffianly riot of rhyme
Through the pressure of print on my pages:
But reckless the reader must be
Who imagines me one of the sages
That steer through Time's sea.

Mad mixtures of Frenchified offal
With insults to Christendom's creed,
Blind blasphemy, schoolboylike scoff, all
These blazon me blockhead indeed.
I conceive myself obviously some one
Whose audience will never be thinned,
But the pupil must needs be a rum one
Whose teacher is wind.

In my poems, with ravishing rapture
Storm strikes me and strokes me and stings:
But I'm scarcely the bird you might capture
Out of doors in the thick of such things.
I prefer to be well out of harm's way
When tempest makes tremble the tree,
And the wind with armipotent arm-sway
Makes soap of the sea.

Hanging hard on the rent rags of others,
Who before me did better, I try
To believe them my sisters and brothers,
Though I know what a low lot am I.
The mere sight of a church sets me yelping
Like a boy that at football is shinned!
But the cause must indeed be past helping
Whose gospel is wind!

All the pale past's red record of history
Is dusty with damnable deeds;
But the future's mild motherly mystery
Peers pure of all crowns and all creeds.
Truth dawns on time's resonant ruin,

Frank, fulminant, fragrant, and free
And apparently this is the doing
Of wind on the sea.

Fame flutters in front of pretension
Whose flagstaff is flagrantly fine
And it cannot be needful to mention
That such beyond question is mine.
Some singers indulging in curses,
Though sinful, have splendidly sinned:
But my would-be maleficent verses
Are nothing but wind.

## Disgust: A Dramatic Monologue

A woman and her husband, having been converted from free thought to Calvinism, and being utterly miserable in consequence, resolve to end themselves by poison. I'he man dies, but the woman is rescued by application of the stomach-pump.

I.
Pills? talk to me of your pills? Well, that, I must say, is cool.
Can't bring my old man round? he was always a stubborn old fool.
If I hadn't taken precautions — a warning to all that wive —
He might not have been dead, and I might not have been alive.

II.
You would like to know, if I please, how it was that our troubles began?
You see, we were brought up Agnostics, I and my poor old man.
And we got same idea of selection and evolution, you know —
Professor Huxley's doing — where does he expect to go!

III.
Well, then came trouble on trouble on trouble — I may say, a peck —
And his cousin was wanted one day on the charge of forging a cheque —
And his puppy died of the mange — my parrot choked on its perch.
This was the consequence, was it, of not going weekly to church?

IV.
So we felt that the best if not only thing that remained to be done
On an earth everlastingly moving about a perpetual sun,
Where worms breed worms to be eaten of worms that have eaten their betters–
And reviewers are barely civil — and people get spiteful letters —

And a famous man is forgot ere the minute hand can tick nine—
Was to send in our P. P. C., and purchase a package of strychnine.

V.
Nay—but first we thought it was rational—only fair—
To give both parties a hearing—and went to the meeting-house there,
At the curve of the street that runs from the Stag to the old Blue Lion.
"Little Zion" they call it—a deal more "little" than "Zion."

VI.
And the preacher preached from the text, "Come out of her." Hadn't
  we come?
And we thought of the Shepherd in Pickwick—and fancied a flavour
  of rum
Balmily borne on the wind of his words–and my man said, "Well,
Let's get out of this, my dear—for his text has a brimstone smell."

VII.
So we went, O God, out of chapel—and gazed, ah God, at the sea.
And I said nothing to him. And he said nothing to me.

VIII.
And there, you see, was an end of it all. It was obvious, in fact,
That, whether or not you believe in the doctrine taught in a tract,
Life was not in the least worth living. Because, don't you see?
Nothing that can't be, can, and what must be must. Q. E. D.
And the infinitesimal sources of Infinite Unideality
Curve into the central abyss of a sort of a queer Personality
Whose refraction is felt in the nebulae strewn in the pathway of Mars
Like the parings of nails Aeonian—clippings and snippings of stars—
Shavings of suns that revolve and evolve and involve—and at times
Give a sweet astronomical twang to remarkably hobbling rhymes.

IX.
And the sea curved in with a moan—and we thought how once—before
We fell out with those atheist lecturers—once, ah, once and no more,
We read together, while midnight blazed like the Yankee flag,
A reverend gentleman's work—the Conversion of Colonel Quagg.
And out of its pages we gathered this lesson of doctrine pure—
Zephaniah Stockdolloger's gospel—a word that deserves to endure
Infinite millions on millions of infinite Aeons to come—
"Vocation," says he, "is vocation, and duty duty. Some."

X.
And duty, said I, distinctly points out—and vocation, said he,
Demands as distinctly—that I should kill you, and that you should kill me.

The reason is obvious—we can't exist without creeds—who can?
So we went to the chemist's—a highly respectable church-going man—
And bought two packets of poison. You wouldn't have done so. Wait.
It's evident, Providence is not with you, ma'am, the same thing as Fate.
Unconscious cerebration educes God from a fog,
But spell God backwards, what then ? Give it up? the answer is, dog.
(I don't exactly see how this last verse is to scan,
But that's a consideration I leave to the secular man.)

XI.

I meant of course to go with him—as far as I pleased—but first
To see how my old man liked it—I thought perhaps he might burst.
I didn't wish it—but still it's a blessed release for a wife—
And he saw that I thought so—and grinned in derision—and threatened my life
If I made wry faces—and so I took just a sip—and he—
Well—you know how it ended—he didn't get over me.

XII.

Terrible, isn't it? Still, on reflection, it might have been worse.
He might have been the unhappy survivor, and followed my hearse.
"Never do it again"? Why, certainly not. You don't
Suppose I should think of it, surely? But anyhow—there—I won't.

PART FOUR

# *Uncollected Prose*

## A CRIMINAL CASE. A SKETCH

In June 1836, the Andryot household consisted of M. Andryot père, aged fifty-four, thin, nervous, bilious, and speculative; Mme. Andryot mère, forty-two, fat, red, and fierce; the son René; the daughter Sylvie; the wife of René, Héloise Ducorneau her maiden name, presumably the heroine of this criminal case. M. Poulain, Mme. Andryot's father, died July 1836. His fortune, got by grocery, fell to his married daughter; the only legacy was one of 3000 francs to his grand-daughter-in-law. It is noticeable that Mlle. Ducorneau's early reputation was of the most equivocal. She had a coarse beauty and a broad fashion of insolent flattery to help her forward; she married at twenty-five René Andryot, aged twenty. The two Mmes. Andryot were open enemies from the first. In a year's time René was heard to express weariness and fear of his wife; M. Andryot senior was always on her side; he was nobody, had not a voice in the family, was less considered than a servant, etc. This young man had the shrill, querulous weakness of a sickly and ill-natured fool; he had married Héloise and her ill fame in a feeble spasm of self-assertion, and was disposed to take out the value of his sacrifice in small daily change. Mlle. Ducorneau had no such change at hand. She insulted him broadly and publicly for his weakness of character, taunted him with her own bad repute, spent his money, and battled with the mother and sister Andryot day and night. Jean Pierre Andryot, ex-silk-mercer, was her one friend and ally. These were the family relations of this household in 1836.

Sylvie Céleste Madeleine Andryot, the daughter, inherited from her mother the temper, morals, manners, face and figure of the religious bourgeoise in high development. Her complexion was iron-grey, her eyes olive green, her outlines bony, her skin dry and stiff. She was so dreadful that she might have won the prix Montyon for hideous virtue, if such a prize had been established for the two qualities together. It follows naturally that she hated her sister-in-law with all her might of hate. It also follows that M. Robinet, her directeur, partook of this feeling, and as this priest had afterwards some influence on the fortunes of this family, the point is worth noting. Héloise was, by the way, what may be called a professional atheist. She asserted her opinion so violently and with such little provocation that the most patient of the devout might have been forgiven some slight aversion.

A fortnight after M. Poulain's decease the fight began over his remains. Héloise dragged the body of this ancient Patroclus by the head, Sylvie and her mother by the feet. At last mother and daughter contrived to quash the legacy. The old man was doting—had been taken with a sickly fondness for his grandson's wife—she had swindled him out of this legacy. Their relations had been a perfect scandal, disgusting—"this woman, figure to yourself, my dear Madame Flicoteau" (Madame Andryot confided the cause of sorrow to the family attorney's wife, a devout woman and her friend), "she would sit with the poor old broken man reading, oh, the most infamous books!" (violent verbal italics). "He was an incredule of the ancient type, this poor father, and she would read to him out of his old books—mais tout ce qu'il y a de plus encyclopedique, de plus Diderot, et puis des saletés á faire rugir les hussards!" Such were the worthy woman's assertions, screeched out in a note "like the last rattle in the throat of a dying cockatoo," said Héloise. At last she went so far, in her triumph after the decision against her enemy, that Héloise and her father, M. Ducorneau, got. an action of slander against her, and she had to pay a fine, plus her costs. Worse remained: M. Andryot, indignant with his wife, settled the value of the original legacy on his daughter-in-law, payable out of his own resources. Fresh shrieks from the defeated wife and daughter; fresh insults on both sides. Presently Réne fled, and M. Andryot took to drinking. Deserted by her husband, who set up on his own small account in Paris, the provident Héloise Andryot cast about for new friends. M. Paul-Honoré Baptiste Foulard, a doctor, was the object of her choice. She fell into a habit of weak health, and took remedies innumerable. Foulard's visits became daily, and were prolonged for hours. Again the clatter of provincial scandal began. But this time the lady met it like a heroine. Forsaken and unhappy, she had found in this young doctor a noble soul to understand her own, a brother's hand to support her feebleness. For the rest, Foulard was gifted with so singular and exquisite an ugliness that scandal was compelled to presume in Héloise a monstrous preference for the repulsive, before it could pronounce upon her guilt. Within the next year M. Andryot, the father, fell ill. The three women and Foulard watched him constantly; but his progress for the worse was rapid, and he died in three weeks.

Madame veuve Andryot was now mistress of the field. She asserted with open violence, what her daughter hinted with a sad hesitation, that her husband's end was hastened by the tender cares of his son's wife. The fury of Héloise at this charge threw upon her a very unwise course. She declared that if there was any murderer in the case, it was the dead man's wife. Night and day, when quiet was most requisite, and after Foulard had declared that perfect rest of mind and body could alone save the patent, Madame veuve Andryot had hovered about the sick room with spiritual consolations and warnings more harassing than any sickness. On the very evening of the decease, the priest Robinet had been closeted with her and the dying man for the space of half an hour. M. Andryot had refused the viaticum: why was this priest there at all? Why was she, why was the doctor excluded? All this Héloise articulated in a harsh excited tone, summoning the widow to answer. The charge against the priest fell through at once. Madame Andryot, encouraged by her daughter, proceeded to lay a direct accusation against the bringer of it for the same offence. The trial was to come on shortly before the criminal courts.

Foulard on hearing of this displayed the most abject nervous terror. Displayed, we say advisedly, for his passion of alarm was so ostentatious and loud as to seem calculated beforehand with a view to general notice. This point also we invite the student of the case to observe. His supposed accomplice, eased perhaps by her own furious outbreak of spite, was calm, warm, sparing and moderate of speech. Many persons were conciliated by the patient sorrowful manners in her, new and noticeable. The two dévotes were shrill, clamorous, and reckless.

A week before the trial Madame veuve Andryot disappeared, and disappeared utterly and for ever. To this day no clue has been found to this singular riddle. All the other parties to these proceedings being dead, we cannot suppose one ever will be.

The case came on. Sylvie Andryot was the mainspring of the prosecution against Héloise. She swore positively to having seen arsenic in the medicine administered to her father by this latter, Jean Pierre Andryot had drunk three-quarters and put it away with the usual complaint of the taste. She had afterwards examined it and found what she now produced. This was analysed, and, to the astonishment of the whole court, found to be a perfectly innocent substance, a deposit which had been allowed to settle in the medicine. It would now have gone hard with Mlle. Andryot but for two considerations. First; a person not acting throughout in good faith, however biassed by personal antipathy, would have laid her plan too well to be upset by so absurdly simple an oversight. If she had substituted anything for the real draught, she must have taken care to substitute a real poison. Secondly; the other circumstances of the case were very strong against the accused. Foulard's extreme terror—her own dubious character—her ridiculous accusation of Madame Andryot—everything told against her. Finally, the unaccountable disappearance of Madame Andryot was laid hold of as a suspicious point. Whose interest was it that she should not be present to give evidence? Several witnesses spoke to the character of Héloise. Madame Flicoteau, the notary's wife, swore to the expressions cited above, as having been uttered by Madame A. in conversation with her shortly after old M. Poulain's decease. The affair of the legacy was brought up and so handled as to blacken still further the reputation of the accused. Réne Andryot was the next witness. He spoke with violence against his wife's character: his evidence was of little value in consequence, except insomuch as it gave fresh proof of the family relations. M. Robinet, the curé, bore witness to her bad repute, and to one scandalous detail he swore personally as an eye and ear witness. This detail we abstain from reproducing here. It has no direct bearing on the case.

All this time, the reader sees, not probably without wonder, not one tittle of proof was brought as to the actual criminality of Héloise. No ill will was proved against her father-in-law; he was her one friend in the family. It was not proved that his death was hastened by any external means. Foulard's medical evidence was perfectly satisfactory. Nothing was gained by Andryot's death to any one but his heirs. Neither Héloise nor Foulard were legatees: the will simply recommended her to her husband's care. The whole charge was dismissed; marked and indignant wonder was expressed that it should ever have been brought forward.

## DEAD LOVE

About the time of the great troubles in France, that fell out between the parties of Armagnac and of Burgundy, there was slain in a fight in Paris a follower of the Duke John, who was a good knight called Messire Jacques d'Aspremont. This Jacques was a very fair and strong man, hardy of his hands, and before he was slain he did many things wonderful and of great courage, and forty of the folk of the other party he slew, and many of these were great captains, of whom the chief and the worthiest was Messire Olivier de Bois-Percé; but at last he was shot in the neck with an arrow, so that between the nape and the apple the flesh was cleanly cloven in twain. And when he was dead his men drew forth his body of the fierce battle, and covered it with a fair woven cloak. Then the people of Armagnac, taking good heart because of his death, fell the more heavily upon his followers, and slew very many of them. And a certain soldier, named Amaury de Jacqueville, whom they called Courtebarbe, did best of all that party; for, crying out with a great noise, 'Sus, sus!' he brought up the men after him, and threw them forward into the hot part of the fighting, where there was a sharp clamour; and this Amaury, laughing and crying out as a man that took a great delight in such matters of war, made of himself more noise with smiting and with shouting than any ten, and they of Burgundy were astonished and beaten down. And when he was weary, and his men had got the upper hand of those of Burgundy, he left off slaying, and beheld where Messire d'Aspremont was covered up with his cloak; and he lay just across the door of Messire Olivier, whom the said Jacques had slain, who was also a cousin of Amaury's. Then said Amaury:

"Take up now the body of this dead fellow, and carry it into the house; for my cousin Madame Yolande shall have great delight to behold the face of the fellow dead by whom her husband has got his end, and it shall make the tiding sweeter to her."

So they took up this dead knight Messire Jacques, and carried him into a fair chamber lighted with broad windows, and herein sat the wife of Olivier, who was called Yolande de Craon, and she was akin far off to Pierre de Craon, who would have slain the Constable. And Amaury said to her:

"Fair and dear cousin, and my good lady, we give you for your husband slain the body of him that slew my cousin; make the best cheer that you may, and comfort yourself that he has found a good death and a good friend to do justice on his slayer; for this man was a good knight, and I that have revenged him account myself none of the worst."

And with this Amaury and his people took leave of her. Then Yolande, being left alone, began at first to weep grievously, and so much that she was heavy and weary; and afterward she looked upon the face of Jacques d'Aspremont, and held one of his hands with hers, and said:

"Ah, false thief and coward! it is great pity thou wert not hung on gallows, who hast slain by treachery the most noble knight of the world, and to me the most loving and the faithfullest man alive, and that never did any discourtesy to any man, and was the most single and pure lover that ever a married lady had to be her knight, and never said any words to me but sweet words. Ah, false coward! there was never such a knight of thy kin."

Then, considering his face earnestly, she saw that it was a fair face enough, and by seeming the face of a good knight; and she repented of her bitter words, saying with herself:

"Certainly this one, too, was a good man and valiant," and was sorry for his death.

And she pulled out the arrow-head that was broken, and closed up the wound of his neck with ointments. And then beholding his dead open eyes, she fell into a great torrent of weeping, so that her tears fell all over his face and throat. And all the time of this bitter sorrow she thought how goodly a man this Jacques must have been in his life, who being dead had such power upon her pity. And for compassion of his great beauty she wept so exceedingly and long that she fell down upon his body in a swoon, embracing him, and so lay the space of two hours with her face against his; and being awaked she had no other desire but only to behold him again, and so all that day neither ate nor slept at all, but for the most part lay and wept. And afterward, out of her love, she caused the body of this knight to be preserved with spice, and made him a golden coffin open at the top, and clothed him with the fairest clothes she could get, and had this coffin always by her bed in her chamber. And when this was done she sat down over against him and held his arms about her neck, weeping, and she said:

"Ah, Jacques! although alive I was not worthy, so that I never saw the beauty and goodness of your living body with my sorrowful ayes, yet now being dead, I thank God that I have this grace to behold you. Alas, Jacques! you have no right now to discern what things are beautiful, therefore you may now love me as well as another, for with dead men there is no difference of women. But, truly, although I were the fairest of all Christian women that now is, I were in nowise worthy to love you; nevertheless, have compassion upon me that for your sake have forgotten the most noble husband of the world."

And this Yolande, that made such complaining of love to a dead man, was one of the fairest ladies of all that time, and of great reputation; and there were many good men that loved her greatly, and would fain have had some favour at her hands; of whom she made no account, saying always, that her dead lover was better than many lovers living. Then certain people said that she was bewitched; and one of these was Amaury. And they would have taken the body to burn it, that the charm might be brought to an end; for they said that a demon had entered in and taken it in possession; which she hearing fell into extreme rage, and said that if her lover were alive, there was not so good a knight among them, that he should undertake the charge of that saying; at which speech of hers there was great laughter. And upon a night there came into her house Amaury and certain others, that were minded to see this matter for themselves. And no man kept the doors; for all her people had gone away, saving only a damsel that remained with her; and the doors stood open, as in a house where there is no man. And they stood in the doorway of her chamber, and heard her say this that ensues: —

"O most fair and perfect knight, the best that ever was in any time of battle, or in any company of ladies, and the most courteous man, have pity upon me, most sorrowful woman and handmaid. For in your life you had some other lady to love you, and were to her a most true and good lover; but now you have none other but me only, and I am not worthy that you should so much as kiss me on my sad lips, wherein is all this lamentation. And though your own lady were the fairer and the more worthy, yet consider, for God's pity and mine, how she has forgotten the love of your body and the kindness of your espousals, and lives easily with some other man, and is wedded to him with all honour; but I have neither ease nor honour, and yet I am your true maiden and servant."

And then she embraced and kissed him many times. And Amaury was very wroth, but he refrained himself: and his friends were troubled and full of wonder. Then they beheld how she held his body between her arms, and kissed him in the neck with all her strength; and after a certain time it seemed to them that the body of Jacques moved and sat up; and she was no whit amazed, but arose up with him, embracing him. And Jacques said to her:

"I beseech you, now that you would make a covenant with me, to love me always."

And she bowed her head suddenly, and said nothing.

Then said Jacques:

"Seeing you have done so much for love of me, we twain shall never go in sunder: and for this reason has God given back to me the life of my mortal body."

And after this they had the greatest joy together, and the most perfect solace that may be imagined: and she sat and beheld him, and many times fell into a little quick laughter for her great pleasure and delight.

Then came Amaury suddenly into the chamber, and brought his sword into his hand, and said to her:

"Ah, wicked leman, now at length is come the end of thy horrible love and of thy life at once"; and smote her through the two sides with his sword, so that she fell down, and with a great sigh full unwillingly delivered up her spirit, which was no sooner fled out of her perishing body, but immediately the soul departed also out of the body of her lover, and he became as one that had been all those days dead. And the next day the people caused their two bodies to be burned openly in the place where witches were used to be burned: and it is reported by some that an evil spirit was seen to come out of the mouth of Jacques d'Aspremont, with a most pitiful cry, like the cry of a hurt beast. By which thing all men knew that the soul of this woman, for the folly of her sinful and most strange affection, was thus evidently given over to the delusion of the evil one and the pains of condemnation.

## THE PORTRAIT

There was a certain woman in the city of Pistoja who loved a man that was a painter; but she was espoused to one that was a merchant, and on a day she was married to him with great solemnity.

For many weeks this painter would come to her, and she would find means to withdraw herself from her husband that she might be the more given up to his love.

Now he, that is the painter, was a man of very evil conversation, and the woman became by his means infected with much wickedness; so that once she said to him: "Now, little Peter" (for thus she called him often, and his name was Messer Pietro Guastagni Bocafoli), " I would have you paint me a little picture which a man shall not look upon without loving, and so if he touch it he shall certainly die." But this painter laughed greatly and said: "How shall I then live if I paint it?" "Now," she said, "I shall show you, little Peter. Take a mask of glass, and also thick gloves on your hands, and work always till you can paint well without putting them off; and then paint me holding three roses, two red and a white between, to signify how I abide always between two men that love me, but the sweetness of either is not alike. And when this picture is finished you shall give it to my husband; and for love of me he will certainly give it a kiss or twain on its mouth; and when he is dead we will burn the picture."

Then this Peter greatly commended her, for he was a man that rejoiced in all manner of shameful dealing, and was also unclean of his life, as is the fashion of men that paint and men that make songs and verses; for this Peter also made many amorous poems, and played upon stringed instruments marvellously well. And the lives of such men as are painters, or such as are poets, are most often evil and foolish; therefore it may be well conceived of this Peter that he twas a very lewd man.

Now in six weeks he had well-nigh finished this picture, and she sat to be painted in a little close gown of green sewn about with ornaments of gold, and the lining was of a tender and clouded colour between violet-blue and grey-blue. And all this the painter had painted very beautifully, for he put all his love and the strong lust of his evil will into the picture. Also he was used to paint the bodies of beautiful women that were naked, which is a very grievous thing in the opinion of God. And he had drawn her with her head a little stooped, as was the fashion for the weight of gold and heavy pearls that she wore above her hair, her husband being very rich, and also that she might show more fully the glorious turn of her throat; for it was very round and long, and wonderfully soft, for nothing was so delicate but the wearing of it would leave a mark in the tender flesh that was coloured like pearl colour. And in this wise was the painting done. She had her gown all ungirt on one side (I believe it was the left side) and the fastenings of it undone; so that all her body from the breast downward, and over against the flank, was naked between two edges of gold colour that met like two lips. And the beauty of her body was a great wonder. And one who saw this picture some way off says yet to this day that to behold it was like the hearing of strong music or the drinking of sweet wine; for not the wonder and hunger of the eyes only, but also the mouth and the ears were feasted and fully satisfied with the deliciousness of the painting of it; and to men beholding it it was as the burning of a great perfume which they smelt.

Therefore it is certain that the sinful delight of one sense draws after it, yea, plucks on as with a net, the delight which is in the whole body of sin; and it is well not to have one sense open to any sweet invasion of the abominable flesh wherein all sin abides and increases as in fat ground. For out of earth is all our flesh made, and earth is compounded of tears and sin, by reason whereof it is always feeble and sorrowful even until it returns to the unclean beginning. And when this grievous body of our enduring sin is wasted again into tears and dust, and the heaviness of it is become light, and the holiness of it is become naked, then the sinfulness of it does not pass into earth, neither is it used to compound any other body; but it abides as a great and blind beast that is tied with fetters and fast bound, and at the last it shall be loosed and shall prey upon the soul as with sharp teeth. And out of this death there shall be no afterbirth of redemption. And to the sad body there shall be no remission made, and to the weary and heavy soul there shall be no ease given. For this death, which begins upon the first and fleshly death, shall endure always and wax great, and increase when all things shall be utterly abolished. Alas, now, what profit shall any man gather of these unprofitable things? I beseech therefore of all beautiful and gracious women and tender ladies, and lordly men that are strong and cunning, that they take good heed of all this matter. For the end of such sweet feeding is very bitter and pitiful. Therefore shall many tears be wept out of eyes that wept never yet, to behold the end of all this, for the end is most bitter. And in the delicate and perfumed mouths that ate honey gladly, and were filled between lip and lip with the strong kisses of love, there shall be the taste of blood and sharp gall. And in the pleasant flesh shall be the burning of whips like as fire. And the eyes shall flow over, and the blood become weak, and the loins of one shall be bruised, and the sides of another shall be broken. And in no side of the body shall there be any breath, neither any savour of ease; but the body shall be thoroughly consumed.

Now in such a manner was this picture finished; and Messer Gian having a good will to see it came to the house of this Peter. And the lady sat over against them and played with a large cat; for both she and this aforesaid Peter loved such things much. Then said Messer Gian, "Might not one give this picture a kiss on its mouth?" And they laughed violently. Then he kissed it, and there was a bitter savour in his lips, and they smarted therewith. So he said, "Messer Pietro, this lady is not so sweet for one to kiss, but I shall find a means to take out this bitterness."

Alas the folly of this man! For he knew not that whereas St. Paul spake concerning the lust of the eye, he spake not only against the eye of a man, but also against his mouth and all his members, that all should be cleanly governed and washed in sweet water; and by the desire of his ignorant lips was this man destroyed.

Then afterwards he came to his wife, and kissed her suddenly. And she, feeling the savour of a violent death on his lips (for his mouth was not yet wiped), cried out and smote him on the said mouth. Then he marvelled, and she crying always out on him, and reviling him with the most grievous words in any way imaginable, besought the man that was her Lover to fetch some medicine for her kissed mouth. Then her husband would fain have taken hold of her to embrace her. But she cried and wept the more exceedingly, saying she was poisoned. Then the said Peter took her between his arms sadly, and said in this wise, "Seeing now, my beloved lady, and all the comfort of my body, that your life by my deed is brought in certain peril of a bitter end, I am resolved that I will not behold the time of your burial with my weeping eyes, but after death will be your friend with all the love and little wisdom that is in me. Therefore have courage, for I shall bring it certainly to pass that all good lovers of ladies shall say prayers for our sake." So full of a shameless wit was this man, and thus sweetly could he make use of his intolerable sin; but undoubtedly God hath before this time confuted his foolishness with a very sharp reason.

Then Messer Gian was so wroth that he would presently have slain them, but for the might of the poison that waxed in him he could not pull forth his sword, and so cursed at them with a great rage, and presently died.

Then the lady; bitterly weeping and embracing her said lover with her hands and body, yet so as her lips should nowise touch him, also yielded up her spirit without any feintence, as one certainly delivered over to the shameful possession and government of her extreme love. Which things becoming presently known, the said picture was cut in twain and burned, and the painter of it taken and hanged in sight of a great multitude; and this was all the wages that this Peter had for his good painting. Certainly therefore it may be supposed that this manner of craft, except it be of a chaste habit, and only employed in the likeness of holy things, is without doubt very displeasing to God.

. . . . . . . . . . .

*"And when this story was finished," says the author of the original "Triameron," "they all laughed more exceedingly than before, for they understood well that Messer Vittore was a very good painter, and feared God little, being a loose living man."*

## LES ABÎMES. PAR ERNEST CLOUËT. PARIS: SILVAIN, LIBRAIRE-EDITEUR, 1862.

In every age there is a certain quantity of moral force secretly at work, busied with whatever of skill and energy may be at hand to further it, in counteracting the tendencies of the time. Small bands of laborious believers gather in fierce heat and haste about some rallying-point of belief or disbelief, clutch hold of some weapon, blunt or sharp, anything to hit with—take to their fists even—use alike the flail and the rapier to hack or thrash withal at received opinions. Much chaff they do occasionally send flying from under the flails; occasionally too the flails recoil and thump the thrashers in the face. One quality these people have always in common; an infinite, indestructible belief in their own merit; a most supple, agile, vivacious, invincible confidence in themselves. They can wrestle, and they can wriggle; box, fence, leap, writhe, crawl to admiration. The muscles of their intellect are kept in excellent training by the sharp exigencies of their position. Apostles of the future, anatomists of the spiritual energy, regenerators of art or society—call them by what name one will—they must not rest on their oars. It is hard pulling against the stream. At times—for in every life of martyr or confessor there must be some soft rainy break of light, some breath from above or under of a sorrowful consolation—they get into the way of some groundswell or eddy setting against the main current which helps to keep them straight on their track, perhaps even lends them a shove towards the haven where they would be. They are much given at such seasons of intervening good luck to raise with unanimous hoarse voices, throats roughened and rasped with sea-wind and salt of drifted spray, some shrill acclamation or outcry of thanksgiving easily distinguishable from the rowing songs and signal cries of ordinary weather. A coxswain in this service, one of a French squadron given overmuch to cruising in dangerous waters among sharp straits and shoals, lately took occasion to define the members of his crew as "témoins effarés de l'infini, portefaix flamboyants de l'idéal, chiffonniers étoilés ayant pour crochet la pensée, qui tiennent dans leur hotte l'avenir encore tout ruisselant des fanges du passé." The duties, the day's work, and the day's wages of a starry rag-picker were then gone into at some length. One of their self-imposed tasks is, it appears, this: "ouvrir à coups de ciseau la matrice noire des siècles frémissants pour en dégager, fœtus radieux, la régénération humaine; éventrer le sphinx impitoyable, éviscérer Dieu." A labour in which we sincerely wish these male midwives of the infinite better success than we can in reason anticipate. A Caesarean operation performed upon the "Supreme Being" would be a feat worth chronicling in the annals of spiritual surgery.

It was not without some surprise that we came suddenly upon M. Ernest Clouët in his new character of a "radiant drayman of the ideal," fully equipped with the tools of his trade, and (we might say in his own florid symbolic style) employed mainly in shovelling stray rubbish into the rag-basket of journalism with the ragman's hook of bombast. We knew him merely as a writer of the musical articles in one paper, a collector of *faits-Paris* for another, a novelist in a very minor key for a third. A small and rickety book of his, touching on matters very common and rather unclean, called *Studies on England*, had also come once in our way. Three facts, notable and memorable, we gathered out of these *Etudes*; 1°: that the lamented Prince Consort at one time enjoyed among the lower classes the nickname of *le prince prolétaire*, owing to his strong Chartist leanings; 2°: that no laxity of prenuptial conduct is considered at all derogatory to the character of a jeune miss (a state of things which naturally ensures the fidelity and felicity of married people) but that a husband may dispose of his faithless wife to her lover for a sum of money not exceeding a thousand francs, or, on the lover's refusal to purchase, is free to blow out her brains on payment of a small fine to the Archbishop of Canterbury as national guardian of the sanctity of the marriage vow; 3°: that the Lord Chancellor is annually elected by the "Central Committee of Alderman" and that the grievances and Abuses of the "Chancéri" are in the main attributable to the awful jobbing system prevalent in that powerful body, at whose meetings (one regrets to hear) there may be seen "le sourire de Torquemada, près du ricanement de Talleyrand; Laubardemont coudoyé par Metternich."

With a brain yet reeling from the shock of these revelations we turned to this present volume by the same hand; and having read it with some care, are bound to declare, as we now do, that it is a more wonderful, and a more disgraceful, piece of work than even the *Etudes Anglaises*. The chapter in M. Clouët's former book headed *Egout de Londres* was nauseous enough; but this book of *Les Abîmes* is simply—we know no English word for it—*inqualifiable*. Under the head of *Les Éclaireurs* our friend has thought fit to class some of the most unmentionable names in literary history. He anoints with a rancid oil of consecration the heads of men too infamous for open reference. A writer of monstrous books is with him "a force of nature—a spark blown by the wind of creation from the great palpitating source of generative fire hidden at the heart of the world." One of the "studies" here reprinted has for its subject a parallel elaborately worked out between Joan of Arc and Gille de Rays. Starting from the historical fact that these two served together in the war against the English, M. Clouët proceeds to draw upon a fertile and fetid imagination for details of their after intimacy. We have observed with some sense of relief that a critic of high standing and an unblemished reputation has condescended publicly to rebuke and chastise the author of this incredible outrage. "Eclabousser de cette fange sanglante la robe blanchie par les feux de la Pucelle," says M. Adolphe Vigniote with as much force as justice, "ce n'est pas seulement manquer à la France, c'est frapper par derrière toutes les croyances qui puissent fortifier ou soulager l'humanité." But this eminent journalist, it is too evident, is not one of that sublime crew out of which the scavengers of the Ideal and the rag-pickers of the Infinite are selected.

To justify the ways of Satan to man is one of the great aims of M. Clouët. Having as a first step demolished "le Dieu ganache des eunuques et des bourgeois" he rushes into a rapid analysis of crime such as probably was never before set down in human language. "La vertu selon les philistins," he affirms in a trenchant way, "c'est tout bonnement l'étiage de l'âme humaine." Crime, on the other hand, is the canal (étier) which serves to flood with strong tidal influx the stagnating marshes that lie dry at ebb-tide, along the coast of life, swarming as they are with a hateful brood of half-living animalcules—"the vermin of virtue—the sterile and sickly spawn of sexless moralities." The doctrine of moralists is to him a "croassement de grenouilles"; their daily life and practice a "croupissement de crapauds." Virtue indeed is as a red rag to this philosophic bull. "La crapule et le cynisme" he exclaims with a devout rapture "sont des travailleurs sublimes." One would take all this for dull and monstrous irony, but that the context in which these gems are set has evidently been wrought out with a serious purpose. "Le mal a pour moi quelque chose de mystérieux et de saint." He contemplates "avec un tressaillement d'entrailles farouche et voluptueux" the ugliest miracles of vice and the most inexplicable phases of crime. The odour of all these moral drains and sewers leaves, he says, in his nostrils the titillation of a pungent pleasure. Sin is his mental snuff. We recommend him to try the use of a milder sort, to accustom his "sensitive nose" by degrees to an adulterated kind. The pure essence is rather too high in flavour to be convenient for taking in public.

It is really a matter to think over as well as to wonder at, that such imbecile atrocities as these of M. Clouët can find an expression and an audience at the present day. Paradox has run mad in this miserable little book. Long since, in the full swing of romantic revolution, an ingenious poet, Pétrus Borel alias Champavert by his name, attempted to pass himself off as an actual live instance of lycanthropy; was indeed at the pains to write a book in evidence of the fact and call it *Contes Immoraux*; even to kill himself in print shortly after it appeared: all in vain; an obdurate public bore up against both intimations with an admirable equanimity; did not seem very much to care whether or no a much-wronged poet, weary of long-suffering, took to devouring raw flesh as a stimulant (preferring, one would hope and suppose, the flesh of reviewers and publishers): and the result was that M. Pétrus, after a few more kicks, collapsed on a sudden; did not eat anybody; did not even choke, or cut his unfortunate wolfish throat, hairy on the inside as it was; but accepted an office under government (we think in Algeria), and died in the fulness of his time a peaceable Philistine. We sincerely wish M. Ernest Clouët as good an end as this. But such a book as *Les Abîmes* does look like the product of some disease—lycanthropy perhaps, or it might be hydrophobia: possibly, after all, it is but a determination of bad reading to the head, resulting in a case of moral sewerage or ditch-water on the brain.

Not that the whole book is made up of such stuff. There are passages here and there of real grace and power; at times too one gets glimpses of some vigour of invention. There is the making of a good critic in the man, if the mad and morbid spirit of paradox were once well charmed out of him. The best paper in the book is an essay on the *Fragoletta* of Henri de Latouche; how it came there, or why it was left there, the author of it only knows. At all events, it is the best review we have seen of that singular, incoherent, admirable novel, so various and vigorous in manner of work; full of southern heat, and coloured as with Italian air and light to the last page of it. Another specimen of M. Clouët's saner and better mood is the short chapter of description called "A Prose Idyl." This small fragment of an essay is so delicate in touch, so soft and clear in colour, so complete and pleasant in its slight way, that one remembers it with a sort of gratitude. But a weary student never finds a rest for the sole of his foot worth speaking of in such books as this. Stepping off the good firm sward, he plunges ear-deep into some unspeakable quagmire, to emerge therefrom defiled and stifled. The longest section of *Les Abîmes*, that inscribed as "Prométhée," is a deliberate attempt to explain and justify the work of a writer whom most people would shrink from naming as they would from touching one of his books—the Arch-Unmentionable of literature. This shamefully foolish article is dated 1800–1814; the new Prometheus of M. Clouët had, it appears, during thirteen years, "Bicêtre for a Caucasus and Napoleon for a vulture." Snuffing from afar off the carrion of this congenial topic, M. Clouët warms by rapid gradations into a style which recalls, in the dull shamelessness of its scientific obscenity, the Abbé Domenech's famous preface to his invaluable Red-Indian manuscript of last year. It is deplorable that the space of a few months should have witnessed the appearance of two such effusions on the same loathsome subject as Félicien Cossu's infamous poem of *Charenton*, and this abominable notice in *Les Abîmes*: it looks really as though there were now alive a small and unsavoury crew of writers who cannot keep their fingers from poking and paddling in this mire. We transcribe, as far as it is in any way presentable, the sentence in which our present author winds up his article to a climax; for without some quotation no English reader could be expected to take our word for the nature of it:

Au milieu de toute cette bruyante épopée impériale, on voit passer en flamboyant cette tête foudroyée, cette vaste poitrine sillonnée d'éclairs, l'homme-phallus, profil auguste et cynique, grimace de titan épouvantable et sublime; on sent circuler dans ces pages maudites comme un frisson d'infini, vibrer sur ces lèvres brûlées comme un souffle d'idéal orageux. Approchez, et vous entendrez palpiter dans cette charogne boueuse et sanglante des artères de l'âme universelle, des veines gonflées de sang divin. Ce cloaque est tout pêtri d'azur; il y a dans ces latrines quelque chose de Dieu. Fermez l'oreille au cliquetis des baïonnettes, au jappement des canons; détournez l'œil de cette marée montante de batailles perdues ou gagnées; alors vous verrez se détacher sur cette ombre un fantôme, immense, éclatant, inexprimable; vous verrez poindre au-dessus de toute une époque semée d'astres la figure énorme et sinistre du marquis de Sade.

After this one feels bounden, as it were, to wash one's hands and rince out one's mouth in eastern fashion; however, like Jean Valjean in the great sewer, we are now well past this deepest slough of all, and it is at least some comfort to have done with the Arch-Unmentionable. No one will now be surprised to find the writer devoting a briefer article to the celebration of a still living notoriety—the pseudonymous authoress of *Rosine et Rosette, Confidences d'un Fauteuil*, and other books of as questionable a kind. We who have no inclination that way just now, will take leave of M. Clouët with a word of kindly counsel. We recommend him to give up all idea of making headway against the tide of modern morals, even with that Titan-phantom of the Arch-Unmentionable pulling stroke-oar in his boat. We do not believe he is really the sort of man to end in Bicêtre. We implore him to think of some honest trade—say of grocery—as an opening in life, feeling convinced that he would sleep warmly and well under protection of the proverbial *bonnet de coton*; and very heartily wish him speedy repentance, timely silence, and compassionate oblivion.

## FROM *LUCREZIA BORGIA. THE CHRONICLE OF TEBALDEO TEBALDEI*

### CHAPTER IV. OF THE GIFT OF AMOROUS MERCY

. . . And behold, she lay there upon her couch bed, and was laughing a little to herself under her breath. There was nothing upon her, not a shred of silk or purple, but only the clothing of that adorable and supreme beauty of her flesh which God made her with for the delight of men. She lay along upon soft great pillows that were tumbled about under her body, and was turned clean over on her left side. That was the most wonderful thing to behold that ever came in the eyes of any man. She had one arm and hand lying down her side along to the thigh, and there it lay with the fingers spread out, a little redder than the bright tender flesh under, being all rose-colour at the sweet sharp tips of them. One of her knees was pushed softly into the hollow at the back of the other, the leg and foot a little thrust out and pressing the silk and indented linen of the couch bed; the left leg lay straight with its delicious kissable foot *(pedem suaviabilem delectabilem)* pointing down to the bed foot. Her other arm was curled back upon itself from the elbow and the closed hand had its back and the knuckles of it pressed against her left flank a little below the heart. A low delicate breath compressed and lightened the two fair fruits of her bosom, and about every fifth breath she took her whole body moved and quivered like a keen note of music. The way she was lying made her throat reach upwards a tittle when she breathed, and threw out the shape of her chin: moreover there went and came a certain thin and tremulous colour in the clear opening of her nostrils, and her mouth flickered, with its lips touching and departing, like a flame. Looking close upon her one could have seen the soft rapid action of her blood in the subsiding veins over her eyebrows and in her temples close up to the hair, which was all shed out and tumbled between the pillows and a great heavy piece of it lying over her right shoulder and across to the left between her breasts. Her eyes were almost covered, rather with the under than the upper lids, so that the bluer and darker threads in these could be well seen; and the delicate glorious shape of her cheeks, the splendid and sweet stateliness of them, was enough to divide the soul from man's body. Also the breath seemed now and then to lift and tighten her flanks tenderly, as a sharp sigh or sobbing might do, but more softly and in a pleasant way; and she seemed to be all of a pure warm colour as an angel seen naked against a great light might be.

The hollow heavy-looking clothes emptied of her beautiful and desirable body, lay all upon a great carven chair some way off, and all the soft silk and hard gold kept in them the sweetness of her limbs, that had been there before she put off her raiment. And when I came in and beheld all these things, and chiefly the fashion in which that adorable and marvellous body of my very perfect lady's was lying, the sight thereof so caught me as it were by the throat and made my breast and all my body throb and heave up and down, while my head and feet only seemed to be fixed and set fast as in a vice, and my brain and blood to go mad and I knowing of it, that I could neither speak for a little nor see anything, only I smelt acutely the soft and keen scent of her body and her clothes. And when I got my breath and could see again, I knew that my sweet and merciful lady had turned herself round off her left side, and lay looking full upon me, smiling a little. And seeing that my sense and breath were come back to me she put her two fair great arms out towards me and beckoned with a fluttering motion of her fingers: and I drew close up to her, and stooped, and fastened my lips upon the inside of her left arm, and my tears fell out upon it and ran down to her wrist; and she held up her wrist and shook it to let them drop off. And when I lifted my face, that was quivering and weeping with pleasure, up from the curve of her arm, I saw all the colour and shadow of her eyes turned upon mine, and a shudder in the lashes of them as if she could have wept as well. Then I threw my arms up and caught her under the armpits and pulled her almost off the couch bed and my mouth clung upon her mouth and held it. And presently through the middle of that great kiss I felt her lips curling and the bite of her teeth upon my lips. Then I clove to her so with my arms and all my face that she cried out softly and taking my shoulder in her hands pushed me a little way back. And after musing upon my face some while (and all that while her fingers kept tightening upon the flesh of my shoulders and neck) she said to me under her breath: My sweet soul, it was not well done to go away.

My head dropped again towards her, and my face was hidden upon her throat sideways with her chin touching my ear, when I said: O my life and my blood, the most heavenly lady in the world, I would not have gone but for the extreme love I had of you. Ah, my sweet perfect heart, have mercy upon me. I love you so much that I am quite mad and weak, and I thought it more fit you should have a man to serve you that had done a brave deed or twain than a boy that had no might or desert in him: for it seemed that a feeble or base fellow could not have that nobleness or that honour in him that would make him fit to love you. But I understand now that I was then but a fool, supposing that the best man could be the worthiest to undergo this pain of loving you; for before the face of your beauty the best man is no whit better than the worst. If you will, I will always stay by you, and be nothing but a page; nay, I will be a coward, and will never do any sort of fighting again.

And D. Lucretia laughed with that little sweet way she had of letting the laughter go on inside of her throat and at last break upon her lips and divide them as it went out, and pulled me against her: and said—It is written that Adonis would needs hunt wild beasts and let Venus be for awhile; and I am not as beautiful as Venus was; truly I should not have played her part in that masque. I must give my fair huntsman leave to go away. It is a great folly to look for any faith in men, and what should one think to find in boys?—And saying this she began again to kiss me and flatter me with her lips and sweet fingers, and all the words of her speech were broken up, full of laughter and short sighs. Then I, feeling all my blood shaken mightily with desire of delight, and a faintness in my head and eyes to see and understand how beautiful she was, asked of her under my breath, did she indeed love me at all? as one craven asks if he may depart with his life gotten. And she cast herself on me embracing me, and her lips clove to my cheek and I felt them like fire wandering over my face: and again drawing back she beheld me, searching me with the light of her looks gazing under mine eyelids till her own eyes dazzled me; then plunged her face into the hollow of my throat biting and kissing it, and as if in a rage rent off a part of my raiment with her hands; and each gathered the other close, and trembled at the meeting of our bodies and mouths. But of the pleasure ensuing who shall ever be worthy to speak? for before the face of that supreme sweetness are the faces of the very gods made pale and the lips of Delight too harsh to make songs of it. Yea, of the paradise of heaven itself let no man conceive as of a greater thing than this. For by no reach of wit and by no strength of spirit can one in any wise imagine or suppose that God has ever been able to think of anything better; except indeed he were minded to destroy and blot out at one stroke soul and body through the excess of a mortal and deadly pleasure: seeing that hardly sometimes can the human life in us endure to bear up against this extremity, the joy whereof devours us like a fierce and ravenous disease. And of what pleasure can anything alive be capable beyond this of having his soul made part of the soul of another and his body made part of another body through the marvellous work of the pleasure of love? but especially when the body and soul enjoyed by him are so infinitely more beautiful and noble than his own that he is actually and naturally received into a very present heaven, the which may be touched and handled and understood of all the fleshly senses. . . .

## CHAPTER VI. THE TREATISE OF NOBLE MORALS

Upon this fifth day of April in the year of Christian grace 1510, but in the thirty-fifth year of her life whose life is the perfect love and whose love is the supreme delight and sovereign sweetness of the world; in the name of Venus our lady which is in heaven, and by the desire of her servant our *lady* which is upon earth, I begin this my treatise of noble morals and of the excellent goodness which is above all other virtues. These morals are called pleasures, and this goodness is bodily beauty; than which there is nothing more good and gracious and profitable, and without which all just or merciful conduct and all kinds of virtuous behaviour are as rags and weeds and dust and dung. Also whosoever looks upon the face and form of this perfect goodness is at once drawn and caught up to it as with attraction of hands; or in such wise as when much heavy and beautiful hair is spread out loosely from the uncovered sweet head of some lady one lock thereof draws and lifts after it another lock. For no man can speak against this faith to blaspheme it but he shall immediately be smitten on the mouth; shame shall get hold of him, and the lie in his lips shall be as fire to burn him. And indeed I have often demanded of myself whether there be any such man in all the world: for it seems to me a thing to be in nowise readily believed.

Beauty is the beginning of all things, and the end of them is pleasure. The colours of things created are all of them virtues; thus the colour of red is love, and the colour of green is pity, and the colour of purple is nobleness of mind, and the colour of blue is desire of good things, and the colour of black is heat of heart and singleness of courage, and the colour of white is the freedom of the senses and the soul, and the colour of yellow gold is the true and faithful appetite of affection which when it is once crowned will never abdicate or decay. A beautiful soft line drawn is more than a life saved; and a pleasant perfume smelt is better than a soul redeemed. For all spiritual and lofty good comes to us only by perception and conception; which things by their very names are naturally of the flesh and the senses. Therefore though we do much good and though we become very virtuous, notwithstanding, to take pleasure and to give it again is better than all our good deeds. For the excellence of wellbeing includes and involves the excellence of welldoing; and if one enjoy greatly he is good after the fashion of the gods, but if he act greatly he is good only after the fashion of men. So that if one think to make himself godlike by mere action and abstinence, he is a fool. To refrain from evil and to labour in doing good are as it were the two feet and hands of a man wherewith he walks and climbs; but to enjoy the supreme and sovereign pleasure is to have the wings and the eyes of the angels of God.

But here will some ignorant and ludicrous person say, that between the beginning which is beauty and the end which is pleasure there is midways the beast evil, full of danger and pain, a thing foul to be looked at; and to overcome this neither sight of what is fair nor sense of what is pleasant will in anyway avail, but only spiritual virtue and the good salvation of God: therefore the one is not the beginning nor the other the end, but goodness and beauty are several and can very well live asunder. To which liar and obtrusive sophist I reply: Thou fool, what if this very evil be of its nature also necessary and beautiful? Knowest thou not that a thing unsavoury if it be chewed by itself may be used to flavour deliciously some delicate weak wine? that bitter perfumes will stab and sting with excess of delight, burning inside nose and mouth? that a taste wherewith the palate is curdled may be a pleasure beyond words or tears or laughter? that a nerve may quiver and be convulsed with actual pain while the blood is dancing and singing for joy like a nymph drunken? that to be pinched and bitten and torn by the lips and teeth and fingers of love is a delight enduring when one is past kisses and when caresses have no sting or savour left in them? that the ache and smart of the fleshly senses are things common alike to pleasure and to pain? If now this my poor fool (*questo mio povero sciocco*) answer that he knows nothing hereof and is thick of apprehension on that side, I have to say that I regard him as less than a dead dog: but if these things be allowed of as true, then I say that in like manner as bodily anguish makes up a good part of bodily enjoyment so also does all kind of evil serve to complete and set off all kind of good. For in the eye of the gods good and evil, and gold and brass, are of one value, and go equally to make up pleasure, being as it were the right and the left hand thereof. And this is the ultimate reason, the root of which is under the leaves and blossom of all things.

It befell me once upon a hot day in June that as I lay looking upon the beauty of my faultless lady I began to consider with myself, saying as it were to my soul, Doth any kind of evil desire or aught of a darker nature *(qualche cosa di più fosco)* inhabit in this body or spirit of hers. And my soul answered, speaking to my senses through the flesh, Assuredly the nature of her body and the likeness of her spirit are the most perfect in excellence of all things divinely devised by Love since the beginning of established day; notwithstanding if one were to speak after the foolish fashion of men, he would say that she were not a creature without sin. Then I, musing and looking at her, who was now sitting on the extreme edge of sleep with his fingers upon her eyelids, It is most certain, I made answer, that she is more just and gracious than righteousness itself, yea the righteousness of angels; howbeit I well know that the virtue of her is not according to the virtue of devout persons, neither is her goodness like the goodness of saints who are praised of the daily people. For her life is sweet and amorous, and her faith is the faith of the fair old gods in their pleasant centuries, and the taking of life seems to her a small thing, compared with a little pleasure. And men say of the goddess Venus that she is a perilous and poisonous goddess, a deadly lady; and the savour of destruction is in her lips; and her pleasure is a sorrow for everlasting. But of the saints they say that their way is perfect, and their labour a labour unto life; and that through their travail they shall have great comfort, and through their anguish they shall have rest. These things do they say, being evidently foolish. Wherefore it is clear that by the rule and measure of such men this my life's lady is not what is called good in the judgment and opinion of these.—And considering this my side began to be chafed with the anger of my heart at their folly, and I trembled and waxed hot up to the eyes; and beholding her inconceivable beauty and the sweetness of her sleep, and how her face and body were heavy with beauty, I began (as it were) to feed upon her with my whole might, and with pressure of hands and eyes and mouth to oppress her face and breast; for the blood winced in my pulses under the scourging of the snakes of love: yea the tooth of Venus bit hard into the veins of my heart. So she turned about and woke and had great joy of me: but the joy I had of her is not well to be imagined even of God.*

Now when she had fallen on sleep again, and only her mouth still quivered like a red flower that is rained upon (saving that her hair also vibrated like a golden coloured great serpent with many throats and each breathing softly), I, because I could not keep mine eyes close, began anew to enquire of my soul concerning the truth. For at such seasons if the soul be not overcome with sleep or choked dead with the hot honey of fulfilled desire, it is wonderfully keen and swift of eyeshot to discern the very life and certainty of things: neither is it then easy for any lie to delude it. So my soul shewed me the foolishness of such as dispraise pleasure and follow after the things which are called good only of those who know not what is verily good indeed. For it is matter of necessity, yea a thing proved and visible, that what she is must be certainly good. I would desire therefore of such a man only to behold her. But God knows my good fool had never such a turn of luck in his life, neither shall he till the end of time; for it would be the death of his soul and body. O disconsolate soul and forlorn body, cast out of love's eye and beyond sight of hope! for the holiness of them is but as one grain of dust blown for a breathing-space between the eyelids of pleasure.

Truly I could weep for compassion of these men, mixing the mouth's laughter with tears of the eyes. Is not this a most grievous thing and very pitiable, to think they will never attain to the sweet wisdom and knowledge of anything that is good?

Moreover the thing is easy to learn; neither does any child want beating to make him get by heart this most gracious lesson. It lies in the blood and in the eyes, and it may be smelt and handled of all manner of people, yea eaten and drunken of all kind of lips. For who is there so heavy of head or so hard of understanding that he cannot discern a sweet savour from a sharp? Verily no born fool is born such a fool as this; but the wont of them will seek after what is desirable and eschew that which is to be hated. For if one feed him he will eat, and if one sing to him he will laugh. But these men follow after things hateful, even abstinence and anguish and deadly labour; and they eschew most laudable and desirable things, namely pleasure and love and the beautiful possession of beauty; and they worship fear and shame and imagination, and their belief is as a mouth toothless and lipless, the mouth of an old woman and unlovable; but our faith endures in all things pleasant and gracious, being like the red and tender mouth of desire that kisses the kiss of the lover before it comes. A perfect and noble faith, worthy the love and labour of men.

Nevertheless if they reply that we worship things evil, let us not over hastily rebuke that saying of theirs. For we do indeed worship these things, even love and desire and delight, as was written aforetime. And that which is called of these men evil, without doubt we do also worship it, if so be it seem in our sight as a parcel of that which is good. Neither is this of any evil to us, but rather a great good. Notwithstanding we refuse not to be called sinful, if this please them; nay, it may be that we will desire and require it of them. For in reproach there is a delight also, even as there is in praise. Yea, and if the body be sweet shall not the raiment also smell sweetly? and if a thing be good shall the end of it be evil, or any part thereof? For they who hold to this saying, that pleasure is hateful at one end and that sorrow grows like a fruit on the branch of a glad beginning, hold fast to a lie. That which is hateful at last was never indeed to be loved; and sorrow comes of sorrow as delight grows out of delight. He that repents was never wholly glad of his deed, and he that finds a grievous savour between lip and tongue after he has to his thinking eaten sweet food, hath never eaten at all of that which was indeed sweet: or else by his own fault and fear he hath made that bitter and deadly which of itself was only composed of good things. Let a man therefore, if he will repent and be wise, repent not of his sin, but of his repentance whereby he hath made to himself both evil and good unprofitable. Penitence comes not of the sin done or the pleasure taken, neither can it one whit impair the excellence of a thing past nor make stuff and matter for men to preach or argue against it; it comes merely of the folly in a man, and can be matter of argument against the said man only. But he shall have fruit of his deeds and delight of his days, whosoever shall do a thing and cleave to it, and set his face and his heart against the way of repentance, and regret not anything nor rebuke himself for all that he hath done. Now if they say that we err because pleasure ends in fullness of flesh and in sleep and great heaviness of soul, I say that we err not, but they both err and also lie. For albeit this saying were true, that sloth and sorrow and loathing of lips comes upon men satiated with much desire and with overflowing excess of fruition, assuredly the evil thing herein is not pleasure, but that which makes war upon pleasure to destroy it, namely satiety. And if there were more pleasure there were not space or breath left for satiety to live in. Satiety comes not therefore of too much pleasure, but of too little. Now is this proved, that they err in that saying, albeit they should speak truth as concerning the end of pleasure; they smite themselves on the cheek and mouth, spitting as it were in their own teeth. But it is moreover evident that they speak not truth at all, yea rather lie. For of a thing perfect and supreme there cometh never any satiety, neither fullness of life and loathing of heart.

**(But here let the reader turn to the fourth chapter of my Chronicle~; for it is full of such matters. Which having read, let him give thanks for me, and great praise to my most wonderful lady.)*

## FROM *LESBIA BRANDON*, CHAPTER XV, "VIA DOLOROSA"

She arranged her hair and went down to the children. A great desire to devour the time till nightfall impelled her, passive as before a wind. It was already but an hour from twilight: she had suffered long, and lain long torpid. In two hours it would be time to expect the end. That all would not return who had gone forth she knew well enough. At any minute some evil and horror nameless to herself might be at point to happen. Alone and silent, she would surely fall ill or go mad. She had impulses, bitter and strong, blind and imperious, to sing and play the time through: since somehow it must needs be lived over and lived through. Far out of sight, deep down in her sense of things, intangible to reason and invisible to thought, there lived a cruel fear of every instant, lest this perhaps were the instant for him of agony and death. Such a one there must be, and soon. She did not fear a suicide, she did not fear a mischance; she felt a fate as one feels a blow. Whence or how it might come against her she did not exactly guess, and would not. She awaited the stroke as though with bared breast and half-shut eyes.

The children saw only the bright face and swift step with which she entered. They came about her gladly, and she caressed them.

"What shall I sing you, children? we are left to our own devices; suppose you make the best of yours, and choose."

She did not often sing to them, and they would have left any game to hear her; even the elders, aggrieved as Cecil especially was by the refusal of a gun.

"You would rather I chose, or made a start at random? Draw the curtains first, it's dark enough: I hate the dusk out of doors. Tell them not to bring lamps till we ring, and I'll play by firelight."

She settled herself at the pianoforte and began playing as they stood round her; the eldest leaning on a chair, chin on fist, his thin sombre face brightened about the eyes as he took his pleasure sadly; Cecil opposite, with hands still restless but fixed face and feet; the second Bertie and Rosamond on either hand of her. At first she played short random tunes of rapid and brilliant sound; then fell as if by chance upon an old French air of softer music and began singing the words; a double ballad of love, the first part April and the second February. This first part she sang in clear high notes, where a sense of pleasure and of fear seemed to hover and tremble as in a bird's song. . . . .

She ceased, with the full firelight on her sad bright face, as the last note faded from her voice; and watched them with eyes that were tender and grew bitter as they watched.

"You look touched; all of you. I must give you something to take the taste out: a better song, and better sense."

*Combien de temps, dis, la belle,*
*Dis, veux-tu m' être fidèle?*
*Pour une nuit, pour un jour,*
*Mon amour.*

*L'amour nous flatte et nous touche*
*Du doigt, de l'oeil, de la bouche,*
*Pour un jour, pour une nuit,*
*Et s'enfuit.*

"There, children, that's how people really look at things: but you don't understand. This hardly makes you laugh, and that hardly made you cry. Ethel, if you get between me and my arm, I can't play."

The child withdrew his head from beneath her left elbow, and looked up hungrily, with a smile.

"That means you've had enough of French songs, and want something you can follow as well as feel? You small elf! you understand one thing as well as another, I believe. But you shall have a ballad if you like. I think I know it by heart now; Herbert was so fond of the scraps left of it, he wrote them out and added a verse or two. I used to sing him the fragment long ago: he was a child and I was a girl. His modern touches don't improve it."

She spoke in a rapid vague voice, turning from one to another, with brilliant unquiet looks. The firelight played upon her pale cheeks, her shifting eyes and bright bound hair.

"It's in two parts like the French song; it's called the Weary Wedding. The woman who nursed me taught me the old part, but I can't sing it now as she did." (She drew her arm again round Ethel's head and went on, leaning over him.) "Look here: at first there's a girl and her mother: that's all. Her love!—her first husband is just dead, you see, children, and they want to marry her again. They have driven her to it, and made her give up her little child. You needn't cry, and you needn't laugh; any of you."

And what will you give for your father's love?
*One with another.*
Fruits full few and thorns enough,
*Mother, my mother.*

And what will you give for your mother's sake?
*One with another.*

Tears to brew and tares to bake,
*Mother, my mother.*

And what will you give your sister Jean?
*One with another.*
A bier to build and a babe to wean,
*Mother, my mother.*

And what will you give your sister Nell?
*One with another.*
The end of life and beginning of hell,
*Mother, my mother.*

And what will you give your sister Kate?
*One with another.*
Earth's door and hell's gate,
*Mother, my mother.*

And what will you give your brother Will?
*One with another.*
Life's grief and world's ill,
*Mother, nay mother.*

And what will you give your brother Hugh?
*One with another.*
A bed of turf to turn into,
*Mother, my mother.*

And what will you give your brother Ned?
*One with another.*
Death for a pillow and hell for a bed,
*Mother, my mother.*

And what will you give to your bridegroom?
*One with another.*
A barren bed and an empty room,
*Mother, my mother.*

And what will ye give your bridegroom's friend?
*One with another.*
A weary foot to the weary end,
*Mother, my mother.*

And what will ye give to your bridesmaid?
*One with another.*
Grief to sew and sorrow to braid,
*Mother, my mother.*

And what will you drink the day you're wed?
*One with another.*

But one drink of the wan well-head,
*Mother, my mother.*

And whatten a water is that to draw?
*One with another.*
We maun draw thereof a', we maun drink thereof a',
*Mother, my mother.*

And what shall ye pu' where the well rins deep?
*One with another.*
Green herb of death, fine flowers of sleep,
*Mother, my mother.*

Are there any fishes that swim therein?
*One with another.*
The white fish grace, and the red fish sin,
*Mother, my mother.*

Are there ony birds that sing thereby?
*One with another.*
O when they come thither they sing till they die,
*Mother, my mother.*

Is there ony draw-bucket to that well-head?
*One with another.*
There's a wee well-bucket hangs low by a thread,
*Mother, my mother.*

And whatten a thread is that to spin?
*One with another.*
It's green for grace and it's black for sin,
*Mother, my mother.*

And what will you strew on your bride-chamber floor?
*One with anoth*er.
But one strewing and no more,
*Mother, my mother.*

And whatten a strewing shall that one be?
*One with another.*
The dust of earth and sand of the sea,
*Mother, my mother.*

And what will you take to build your bed?
*One with another.*
Sighing and shame and the bones of the dead,
*Mother, my mother.*

And what will you wear for your wedding gown?
*One with another.*

Grass for the green and dust for the brown,
*Mother, my mother.*

And what will you wear for your wedding lace?
*One with another.*
A heavy heart and a hidden face,
*Mother, my mother.*

And what will you wear for a wreath to your head?
*One with another.*
Ash for the white and blood for the red,
*Mother, my mother.*

And what will you wear for your wedding ring?
*One with another.*
A weary thought for a weary thing,
*Mother, my mother.*

And what shall the chimes and the bell-ropes play?
*One with another.*
A weary tune on a weary day,
*Mother, my mother.*

And what shall be sung for your wedding song?
*One with another.*
A weary word of a weary wrong,
*Mother, my mother.*

The world's way with me runs back,
*One with another,*
Wedded in white and buried in black,
*Mother, my mother.*

The world's wrong and the world's right,
*One with another,*
Wedded in black and buried in white,
*Mother, my mother.*

The world's bliss and the world's keen,
*One with another,*
It's red for white and it's black for green,
*Mother, my mother.*

The world's will and the world's way,
*One with another,*
It's sighing for night and crying for day,
*Mother, my mother.*

The world's good and the world's worth,
*One with another,*

It's earth to flesh and it's flesh to earth,
*Mother, my mother.*

"That's the first part; then they marry her to the new man, and his mother receives her—you see? Herbert stuck in a quantity of lines hereabouts; they're not good, but they tell the story."

When she came out at the kirkyard gate,
*One with another,*
The bridegroom's mother was there in wait;
*Mother, my mother.*

—O mother, where is my great green bed,
*One with another,*
Silk at the foot and gold at the head,
*Mother, my mother.*

—Yea, it is ready, the silk and the gold,
*One with another.*
—But line it well that I lie not cold,
*Mother, my mother.*

She laid her cheek to the velvet and vair,
*One with another.*
She laid her arms up under her hair,
*Mother, my mother.*

The gold hair fell through her arms twain,
*One with another;*
—Lord God, bring me out of pain!
*Mother, my mother.*

The gold hair fell in the reeds green,
*One with another.*
—Lord God, bring me out of teen!
*Mother, my mother.*

She raised her eyes and seeing opposite the intent faces of the elder children laughed softly and turned to the youngest, who had drunk every note with eager lips and eyes full of fiery pleasure.

"Then you see, Ethel, the husband came and met his mother. It wasn't his fault. He didn't know where she was—or what like, as they say. All the last verses are old. You may come and stand close up to me as you did before; if you like, I mean the last twelve or so."

O mother, where is my lady gone?
*One with another.*
In the bride-chamber she makes sore moan,
*Mother, my mother.*

Her hair falls over the velvet and vair,
*One with another*;
Her great soft tears fall over her hair;
*Mother, my moth*er.

When he came into the bride's chamber,
*One with another*,
Her hands were like pale yellow amber;
*Mother, my mother*.

Her tears made specks in the velvet and vair,
*One with another*;
The seeds of the reeds made specks in her hair;
*Mother, my mother*.

He kissed her under the gold on her head,
*One with another*;
The lids of her eyes were like cold lead;
*Mother, my mother*.

He kissed her under the fall of her chin,
*One with another;*
There was right little blood therein;
*Mother, my mother*.

("Bertie stuck all this in a year or two ago—I think it was better before; wait, and you'll see when the old verses begin again.")

He kissed her under her shoulder sweet,
*One with another;*
Her throat was weak, with little heat;
*Mother, my mother*.

He kissed her down by her breast-flowers red,
*One with another;*
They were like river-flowers dead,
*Mother, my mother*.

What ails you now o' your weeping, wife?
*One with another.*
It ails me salt o' my very life,
*Mother, my mother*.

What ails you now o' your weary ways?
*One with another*.
It ails me sair o' my long life-days,
*Mother, my mother*.

Nay, ye are young, ye are over fair;
*One with another.*

Though I be young, what needs ye care?
*Mother, my mother.*

Nay, ye are fair, ye are over sweet;
*One with another.*
Though I be fair, what needs ye greet?
*Mother, my mother.*

Nay, ye are mine while I hold my life;
*One with another.*
O fool, will ye marry the worm for a wife?
*Mother, my mother.*

Nay, ye are mine while I have my breath
*One with another.*
O fool, will ye marry the dust of death?
*Mother, my mother.*

Yea, ye are mine, we are handfast wed,
*One with another.*
Nay, I am no man's; nay, I am dead,
*Mother, my mother.*

"Crying? You ought to have something to cry for. Look at Cecil, how round his eyes. And it's all a song; and silly. People don't die; not women. Little bits of heart are tough: the girl was no such fool. And suppose she died, Bertie, you little white wild animal, do you know what that means? She is asleep and has forgotten it all; wouldn't know one from the other if they came and called her and kissed her—so. Your lips are very hot; and your head: what lithe hair you have; I shall get you shaved. She remembers no more about it now than you remember being born. You were redder then: your small scalp was a bald rose-leaf: you were hot like the heat of a flower. Eh! you don't remember. And when you began talking you spoke broad Northumbrian: you were just a pure borderer. You said vai for very: Italian.

"I remember," said Arthur with implied self-applause.

"Yes: you remember. You are my changeling; I knew you as soon as the fairies put you in my bed. Because I was a witch, children; like the witch-mother."

*She's set her young son to her breast,*
*Her auld son to her knee;*
*Says, "Weel for you the night, bairnies,*
*And weel the morn for me."*

Then she killed them, Ethel, both, and put their blood in a little brass dish—ah! I heard somebody; no?—in some pot or pan, with the blood of a little white chicken, like you: and of a grey pigeon, like Rosamond; and of a yellow kite, like Cecil; and of a starling, like nobody—except another starling.

*Says — eat your fill of your flesh, my lord,*
*And drink your fill of your wine;*
*For a' thing's yours and only yours,*
*That has been yours and mine.*

"You see that she didn't kill them for fun at all. It's not every witch that kills little unweaned babies; yes, it was hard, that. I might kill you if I tried; take care; be good. You are the auld son that stands at my knee. I shall never have a younger one again; no little red round fat fragments of babies: ah, you were all such fun once.

Says — Drink your fill of your wine, my lord,
And eat your fill of your bread;
I would they were quick in my body again,
And my body were dead.

"Ah — ah — as if people could drink themselves back into love; they try sometimes now: eating and drinking won't do it. You can't make that verse out: you will some day, Ethie, my small bad boy; when you and I and Elaine go underground and keep house with elves and learn witches' tricks. You don't cry now? Yes, come close to me. You are more electric than I am, child, I can comb sparks out of your hair with my fingers. Things in verse hurt one, don't they? hit and sting like a cut. They wouldn't hurt us if we had no blood, and no nerves. Verse hurts horribly: people have died of verse-making, and thought their mistresses killed them — or their reviewers. You have the nerve of poetry — the soft place it hits on, and stings. Never write verses when you get big; people who do are bad, or mad, or sick. Herbert? but he doesn't count; he scribbles now and then when I tell him, for fun: I don' t mean that. How your under-curls hiss and sputter on the inside. It's odd that words should change so just by being put into rhyme. They get teeth and bite; they take fire and burn. I wonder who first thought of tying words up and twisting them back to make verses, and hurt and delight all people in the world for ever. For one can't do without it now we like it far too much, I suspect, you and I. It was an odd device: one can't see why this ringing and rhyming of words should make all the difference in them: one can't tell where the pain or the pleasure ends or begins. 'Who shall determine the limits of pleasure?' that is a grand wise word: you ought to find out what it means soon. Listen now again.

*'O where will ye gang to and where will ye sleep*
*Against the night begins?'*
*'My bed is made wi' cauld sorrows,*
*My sheets are lined wi' sins.*

*'And a sair grief sitting at my foot*
*And a sair grief at nay head;*
*And dool to mak' me my pillow*
*And teen till I be dead.*

*'And the rain is sair upon nay face*
*And sair upon my hair:*
*And the wind upon nay weary mouth*
*That never shall kiss mair:*

*'And the snow upon my heavy lips*
*That never shall drink nor eat:*
*And shame to cledding, and woe to wedding,*
*And pain to drink and meat!'*

"I never knew the rest of that, but it should be something rather horrid to match the first lines.

*'But what shall ye have to your marriage meat,*
*The day that ye are wed?'*
*'Meat of strong crying, salt of sad sighing,*
*And God restore the dead.'*

*'But what will ye have to your wedding wine*
*The day that ye are wed?'*
*'Wine of weeping, and draughts of sleeping,*
*And God raise up the dead.'*

"But he won't now; he knows better. You would rather not see ghosts, children, would you? If they came back with white crying faces and no hands to touch you, you wouldn't thank God exactly: you'd rather let them be, under ground or under water.

*The cockle-shells to be my bed*
*And the mussels in the sea;*
*And the easterin' wind and the westerin' wind*
*To mak' my sheets to me.*

*O when my bed was salt wi' silk,*
*Mine een were sair wi' weeping;*
*But now my bed is sair wi' stanes,*
*Mine een are saft wi' sleeping.*

*Its under faem and fathom now,*
*And fathom under sea;*
*And for a' gates the wind gangs,*
*The wind wakes na me.*

"But the sea-shells have sharp edges to lie down on the first time. Still, never to hear any manner of wind that blows, that must be a comfort when one gets to bed: and we all shall some day: you remember that nursery jingle that I wouldn't let them frighten you with twice, Atty?

*Fair of face, full of pride,*
*Sit ye down by a dead man's side.*

*Ye sang songs a' the day:*
*Sit down at night in the worm's way.*

*Proud ye were a' day long;*
*Ye'll be but lean at evensong.*

*Ye had gowd kells on your hair;*
*Nae man kens what ye were.*

*Ye set scorn by the silken stuff;*
*Now the grave is clean enough.*

*Ye sit scorn by the ruby ring;*
*Now the worm is a sweet thing.*

*Fine gold and fair face,*
*Ye are come to a grimly place.*

*Cold hair and grey een,*
*Nae man kens if ye have been.*

She had sung this with hands resting idle on the keys, never striking a note: as it ended, her hands dropped off them, and hung by her side; only the fingers quivered and curled. Then, having Ethelbert close and Rosamond near her, both silent and trembling with dim pleasure and soft fear, she looked towards the two elder and seeing a whisper stir between them, laughed lightly and sadly. "You schoolboys think the little ones are fools to cry? come, I know you do. Now listen, I mean to make you cry: as Ethel here did over the wedding song. I won't have my young birds pecked at. I'll do what the headmaster never did—at least you say so—make you cry. I don't care what you do at school, but you shall cry this time, and without being whipped. I know, Atty, Cecil did squeak the first time: I know, Cecil, it's an awful lie; never mind. Stand there now and let me sing."

Her face altered as the smile went off, leaving for a moment a grave silent motion in the lips and eyelids: then, with a few rare touches by way of interlude, she began to sing.

*There's mony a man loves land and life,*
  *Loves life and land and fee;*
*And mony a man loves fair women,*
  *But never a man loves me, my love,*
  *But never a man loves me.*

*O weel and weel for a' lovers,*
  *I wot weel may they be;*

*And weel and weel for a' fair maidens,*
*But aye mair woe for me, my love.*
*But aye mair woe for me.*

*O weel be wi' you, ye sma' flowers,*
*Ye flowers and every tree;*
*And weel be wi' you, a' birdies,*
*But teen and tears wi' me, my love,*
*But teen and tears wi' me.*

*O weel be yours, my three brethren,*
*And ever weel be ye:*
*Wi' deeds for doing and loves for wooing,*
*But never a love for me, my love,*
*But never a love for me.*

*And weel be yours, my seven sisters,*
*And good love-days to see,*
*And long life-days and true lovers,*
*But never a day for me, any love,*
*But never a day for me.*

*Good times wi' you, ye bauld riders,*
*By the hieland and the lee;*
*And by the leeland and by the hieland*
*It's weary times wi' me, my love,*
*It's weary times wi' me.*

*Good days wi' you, ye good sailors,*
*Sail in and out the sea;*
*And by the beaches and by the reaches*
*It's heavy days wi' me, my love,*
*It's heavy days wi' me.*

*I had his kiss upon my mouth,*
*His bairn upon my knee;*
*I would my soul and body were twain,*
*And the bairn and the kiss wi' me, my love,*
*And the bairn and the kiss wi' me.*

*The bairn down in the mools, my dear,*
*O saft and saft sleeps she;*
*I would the mools were ower my head,*
*And the young bairn fast wi' me, my love,*
*And the young bairn fast wi' me.*

*The father under the faem, my dear,*
*O sound and sound lies he;*

*I would the faem were ower my face,*
*And the father lay by me, my love,*
*And the father lay by me.*

*I would the faem were ower my face,*
*Or the mools on my ee bree;*
*And waking-time with a' lovers,*
*But sleeping-time wi' me, my love,*
*But sleeping-time wi' me.*

*I would the mools were meat in my mouth,*
*The saut faem in my ee;*
*And the land-worm and the water-worm*
*To feed fu' sweet on me, my love,*
*To feed fu' sweet on me.*

*My life is sealed with a seal of love,*
*And locked with love for a key;*
*And I lie wrang and I wake lang,*
*But ye tak nae thought for me, my love,*
*But ye tak nae thought for me.*

*We were weel fairy of love, my dear,*
*O fain and fain were we;*
*It was weel with a' the weary world,*
*But O, sae weel wi' me, my love,*
*But O, sae weel wi' me.*

*We were nane ower mony to sleep, my dear,*
*I wot we were but three*
*And never a bed in the weary world*
*For my bairn and my dear and me, my love,*
*For my bairn and my dear and me.*

Her singing rather than her song had fulfilled her threat; before she ended, the boys stood by shuffling, with cheeks that twitched and eyes that blinked, stung by the bitter sweetness of her soft keen voice. She lifted her face and laughed again; as though their tears had the power to dry her own.

"I said you would children: Herbert always cried over that, and he would have gone into seas where I should like to see Atty follow him: never mind crying, Bertie minor, your major did when he was older than Cecil. They call that song *The Tyneside Widow*, I think; it never made me cry. But you are a set of children, and Herbert was the oldest baby: and is. I suppose it's the burden. I like it much better in that song of a border thief whom his wife or some other woman betrayed into the hands of justice —you know?"

"Oh, I know," said Cecil, with eyes now dry and bright; 'Willie's neck-song': Bulmer used to pitch into the maid for singing it. Oh I say, do sing that."

She bowed to the boy, smiling, and played some loud rapid music as she sang: turning first towards the youngest with a word or two.

"You see, Ethel, this woman—his wife—he had come back out of hiding to see her. He was a reiver, you know what that is, and had lifted ever so many heads of kye; a thief, and they wanted to hang him. He was safe I suppose where he was, but he must needs have a look of her, poor man. Well, when she had him safe at home, she gave him up. And they made this song for him at the gallows. They say he made and sang it, but I doubt that."

*Some die singing, and some die swinging,*
*And weel mot a' they be:*
*Some die playing, and some die praying,*
*And I wot sae winna we, my dear,*
*And I wot sae winna we.*

*Some die laughing, and some die quaffing,*
*And some die high on tree;*
*Some die spinning, and some die sinning,*
*But faggot and fire for ye, my dear,*
*Faggot and fire for ye.*

*Some die weeping, and some die sleeping,*
*And some die under sea;*
*Some die ganging, and some die hanging,*
*And a rape and a tow for me, nay dear,*
*A rape and a tow for me.*

"There's a song for you; but you needn't laugh and make such eyes. I'd rather cry over that of the two. You look half frightened."

As the fierce fragments rang from her lips, their eyes glittered and their lips moved; now they stood abashed and troubled. The brilliance of her voice and face became stronger at each note; her features assumed a fierce and funereal beauty, her eves a look of insane and bitter foresight. The children began to flinch from her; all but Ethel, who clung to her side and caressed her face with his fixed eyes.

"Ah, children," she began again, laughing only with the lips. Do you think she saw ghosts afterwards? I think not. They don't come to such people. I'm sure there was some-body just coming in. It must be fearfully late. I wish I knew more songs, but I forget them all now. And my voice is going; ah, not now: but I shan't sing a note much longer. Come over and kiss me, Atty my old first child. No, don't you all come. Are you afraid, now! you'll never be a man after all: but never mind. I can't sing any more. Oh!" she sighed and shuddered, sitting with open hands and shining eyes.

"It must be so late—ever so late. I ought to have sent you off. But I'll try and play to you. Do you ever dream now, Arthur? you did once; the trouble you gave with your dreams, and the frights you got! poor child. Do you remember the little woman in red shoes who sang songs that you knew were wicked without hearing the words? there was a notion for a child's head to get hold of. And the cruelties you used to invent in your sleep and cry over when you awoke! Don't be ashamed of dreaming. I dreamt once that I was very old, in an empty house in winter, and it snowed and blew outside, and there were trees torn up in the garden. And there was a secret about the place I had once known and forgotten long ago: not a good secret. And I was very cold, and I dreamt I fell asleep by the fire, and a little child came into the room and sat down on the rug and made faces at me; and I woke. I felt old for a day after."

## TO E. C. STEDMAN [A *MEMOIR*]

February 20, 1875

My dear Mr. Stedman

I have just received your letter and the kindly and able article accompanying it. First of all, accept my cordial thanks for both and my assurance that I consider the latter the most powerful as well as the most gratifying to me personally I ever read on the subject. Then I must say how glad I am that you have done me the justice not to attribute my long neglect in writing to graceless and discourteous ingratitude. The enforced delay began through inability to write at the time with the proper fullness, being frequently too unwell to apply my hand or mind to writing and constantly distracted by various calls on my time and attention. Then, leaving London for change of air I put by as far and as long as possible all correspondence of business or of pleasure. These together do I hope make up a real and sufficient excuse to any one who will take into friendly account the general human experience how a duty put off for a day by necessity is sure to be put off by accident for months. Then, very unluckily for me, the mere physical act of writing which to some men, e.g. to Rossetti, seems a positive enjoyment is to me usually a positive and often a painful effort. I have often wished to have lived my life and sung my song in the times of unwritten and purely oral poetry. But I must resign myself to the curse of penmanship—and mine I fear, is a curse to my friends also. (How Shakespeare must have hated it! look at his villainous and laborious pothooks and Ben Jonson's (or Milton's) copperplate and vigorous perfection of hand.) Now let me at last tell you how truly and how much I have enjoyed the beautiful book of poems which you must long since have thought of as thrown away on the most thankless and ungracious of recipients. Your rebuke on the subject of American poetry is doubtless as well merited as it is kindly and gently expressed. Yet I must say that while I appreciate (I hope) the respective excellence of Mr. Bryant's Thanatopsis and of Mr. Lowell's Commemoration Ode I cannot say that either of them leaves in my ear the echo of a single note of song. It is excellent good speech but if given us as song its first and last duty is to sing. The one is most august meditation, the other a noble expression of deep and grave patriotic feeling on a supreme national occasion; but the thing more necessary though it may be less noble than these is the pulse, the fire, the passion of music—the quality of a singer, not of a solitary philosopher or a patriotic orator.

Now when Whitman is not speaking bad prose he sings, and when he sings at all he sings well. Mr. Longfellow has a pretty little pipe of his own, but surely it is very thin and reedy. Again, whatever may be Mr. Emerson's merits, to talk of his poetry seems to me like talking of the scholarship of a child who has not learnt its letters. Even Browning's verse always goes to a recognizable tune (I say not, to a good one), but in the name of all bagpipes what is the tune of Emerson's? Now it is a poor thing to have nothing but melody and be unable to rise above it into harmony, but one or the other, the less if not the greater, you *must* have. Imagine a man full of great thoughts and emotions and resolved to express them in painting, who has absolutely no power upon either form or colour. Wain[e]wright the murderer, who never had any thought or emotion above those of a pig or of a butcher, will be a better man for us than he. But (as Blake says) 'Enough! or Too much.'

I have no love of talking of my own or other men's personal or family matters, uninvited, but there can hardly be egotism or self-conceit in complying with the direct request of a friend (as I understand you to ask for some account of my 'birth and career'—I think you said in your last); so for once I will begin to prate (as Byron loved and I do not love to do*) of my parentage and personality. The application of a stranger like the editor of 'Men of the Time' I long ago civilly declined to entertain, conceiving that the public had no concern but with my published works, and leaving him to find out what he could or to invent what he pleased; with the happy result, that in his first two lines I found myself to my great delight born some years out of my time at a place which I never heard of till I was between twenty and thirty, and educated in a country in which I never set foot till my school days were over. My father, Admiral Swinburne, is the second son of Sir John Swinburne, a person whose life would be better worth writing than mine. Born and brought up in France, his father, (I believe) a naturalized Frenchman (we were all Catholic and Jacobite rebels and exiles) and his mother a lady of the house of Polignac (a quaint political relationship for me as you will admit), my grandfather never left France till called away at 25 on the falling in of such English estates (about half the original quantity) as confiscation had left to a family which in every Catholic rebellion from the days of my own Queen Mary to those of Charles Edward had given their blood like water and their lands like dust for the Stuarts. I assume that his Catholicism sat lightly upon a young man who in the age of Voltaire had enjoyed the personal friendship of Mirabeau; anyhow he had the sense to throw it to the dogs and enter the political life from which in those days it would have excluded him. He was (of course on the ultra-liberal side) one of the most extreme politicians as well as one of the hardest riders and the best art-patrons of his time. Take these instances; 1) he used to tell us that he and Lord Grey had by the law of the land repeatedly made themselves liable to be impeached and executed for high treason; and certainly I have read a

*though now my letter (or essay!) is finished I fear it must look as if I did—and very much!

speech of his on the Prince of Wales which if delivered with reference to the present bearer of that title would considerably astonish the existing House of Commons. 2) It was said that the two maddest things in the North country were his horse and himself; but I don't think the horse can have been the madder—or at least the harder to kill; for once when out shooting he happened to blow away his right eye with a good bit of the skull, but was trepanned and lived to see his children's children (and a good many of them) and after more than ninety-eight years of health and strength to die quietly of a week's illness. We all naturally hoped to see him fill up his century; but the Fates said no. 3) He was the friend of the great Turner, of Mulready, and of many lesser artists; I wish to God he had discovered Blake; but that no man did till our own day. —For the rest, he was most kind and affectionate to me always as child, boy, and youth. To the last he was far liker in appearance and manner to an old French nobleman (I have heard my mother remark it) than to any type of the average English gentleman. He said that Mirabeau as far excelled as a companion and a talker one other man as that other man did all men else he had ever known in his life, of any kind or station; the man thus distancing all the world beside and distanced as immeasurably by Mirabeau alone was Wilkes. This I always remembered with interest, and I thought it would interest you; considering how many famous and splendid persons an able and active public man must have seen and known, who all but completes his century, and whose clearness and activity of mind never fails him to his last hour. An ancestress of his (i.e. a Lady Swinburne) bore thirty children to one husband; people thronged about her carriage in the streets to see the living and thriving mother of thirty sons and daughters. I think you will allow that when this race chose at last to produce a poet, it would have been at least remarkable if he had been content to write nothing but hymns and idyls for clergymen and young ladies to read out in chapels and drawing-rooms. —My mother is daughter to the (late) Earl of Ashburnham, whose family, though one of them was the closest follower of Charles I. to his death, afterwards held sensibly aloof from the cause of the later Stuarts, and increased in wealth and titles; (there *was* a Swinburne peerage, but it has been dormant or forfeit since the thirteenth of fourteenth century).

So much for family history; which may be a stupid matter, but to write about my personality is to me yet more so. My life has been eventless and monotonous; like other boys of my class, I was five years at school at Eton, four years at college at Oxford; I never cared for any pursuit, sport, or study, as a youngster, except poetry, riding, and swimming; and though as a boy my verses were bad enough, I believe I may say I was far from bad at the two latter. Also being bred by the sea I was a good cragsman, and am vain to this day of having scaled a well-known cliff on the South coast, ever before and ever since reputed to be inaccessible. Perhaps I may be forgiven for referring to such puerilities, having read (in cuttings from more than one American journal) bitterly contemptuous remarks on my physical debility and puny proportions. I am afraid this looks like an echo of poor great Byron's notorious and very natural soreness about his personal defect; but really if I were actually of powerless or deformed body I am certain I should not care though all men (and women) on earth knew and remarked on it. I write all this rubbish because I really don't know what to tell you about myself, and having begun to egotize I go on in pure stupidity. I suppose you do not require a Rousseau-like record of my experiences in spiritual or material emotions; and knowing as you do the date and sequence of my published books you know every event of my life. (Note) The order of composition is not always that of publication. Atalanta was begun the very day after I had given the last touch to Chastelard.

(February 21st)

Here I left off last night being very tired and feeling myself getting stupid. I see I have already done much more than answer such of your questions as I could; and as you have induced me for the very first time in my life to write about myself, I am tempted, considering that I have probably been more be-written and belied than any man since Byron, to pour myself out to a sincere and distant friend a little more: telling any small thing that may come into my head to mention. I have heard that Goethe, Victor Hugo, and myself were all born in the same condition—all but dead, and certainly not expected to live an hour. Yet I grew up a healthy boy enough and fond of the open air, though slightly built, and have never had a serious touch of illness in my life. As for the sea, its salt *must* have been in my blood before I was born. I can remember no earlier enjoyment than being held up naked in my father's arms and brandished between his hands, then shot like a stone from a sling through the air, shouting and laughing with delight, head foremost into the coming wave—which could only have been the pleasure of a very little fellow. I remember being afraid of other things but never of the sea. But this is enough of infancy: only it shows the *truth* of my endless passionate returns to the sea in all my verse.

To make a long leap—for to be egotistic one must be desultory, and jump from a little-boyhood into young-manhood—I was about to tell you last night that I had once an opening into that public life which alone (I think) authorizes public curiosity into the details of a man's biography. Several years ago the Reform League (a body of extreme reformers not now extant I believe but of some note and power for a time) solicited me to sit in Parliament (offering to insure my seat and pay all expenses) as representative of more advanced democratic or republican opinions than were represented there. Now I never in my life felt any ambition for any work or fame but a poet's (except indeed while yet a boy for a soldier's, but my father resolutely stamped that out) and I appealed to the man I most loved and revered on earth (Mazzini being then luckily in London) to know if he thought it my duty to forego my own likings on the chance of being of use to the cause? Mazzini told me I need not—I was doing my natural kind of service as it was, and in parliament I should of course be wasting my time and strength for a year on the chance of being of service by one speech or vote on some great and remote occasion. I never was more relieved in my life than when I felt I could dismiss the application with a wholly clear conscience. (I have seen a report of this in print, but not quite accurate.)

As my antitheism has been so much babbled about, perhaps I may here say what I really do think on religious matters. Having been as child and boy brought up a quasi-Catholic, of course I went in for that as passionately as for other things (e.g. well-nigh to unaffected and unashamed ecstasies of adoration when receiving the Sacrament); then when this was naturally stark dead and buried, it was left nothing to me but a turbid nihilism: for a Theist I never was; I always felt by instinct and perceived by reason that no man could conceive of a *personal* God except by brute Calibanic superstition or else by true supernatural revelation; that a natural God was the absurdest of all human figments; *because* no man could by other than apocalyptic means—i.e. by other means than a violation of the laws and order of nature—*conceive* of any sort of divine person than man with a difference—man with some qualities intensified and some qualities suppressed—man with the good in him exaggerated and the evil excised. This, I say, I have always seen and avowed since my mind was ripe enough to think freely. <But now I have other and different> Now of course this is the exact definition of every God that has ever been worshipped under any revelation. Men give him the qualities they prefer in themselves or about them. E.g. the God of the Christians is good for domestic virtue, bad for patriotic. A consistently good Christian cannot, or certainly need not, love his country. Again, the god of the Greeks and Romans is not good for the domestic (or *personal* in the Christian sense) virtues, but gloriously good for the patriotic. But we who worship no material incarnation of any qualities, no person, may worship the divine <man> humanity, the ideal of human perfection and aspiration, without worshipping any God, any person, any fetish at all. Therefore I might call myself if I wished a kind of Christian* (of the Church of Blake and Shelley), but assuredly in no sense a Theist. Perhaps you will think this is only a clarified nihilism, but at least it is no longer turbid.

There is something of this, with much other matter, in Matthew Arnold's 'Literature and Dogma'—a book from which I cannot say that I learnt anything, since it left me much as it found me, not far from the point to which he tries to bring his reader: so that I was more than once struck by coming on phrases and definitions about 'God' almost verbally coincident with <those> such as I had myself used, though not in public print, years before this book appeared. But it is a *very* good and fine book and has done I believe great good already, especially of course among the younger sort. (Has it found any echo in America?) I think and hope that among the younger Englishmen who think at all just now Theism is tottering; Theism, which I feel to be sillier (if less dangerous) even than Theology.

*That is, taking the semi-legendary Christ as type of human aspiration and perfection, and supposing (if you like) that Jesus may have been the highest and purest sample of man on record.

To return to personality (by no means a divine one), I need not say that you are most welcome to show any part or all of this huge epistle to any one you please, but if you wish to make use of any *facts* in it in a public way, please do so *in the third person* as I really have told you none that you could not have learnt from any intimate old friend of my family or myself, and I should loathe to appear in print talking about either myself or it: and I am sure you would do nothing to pain or to make me feel or look absurd, in revenge for the long babble you have brought on yourself, which after all you need never read unless you like. Wishing to make up for my long and unseemly silence, I have now probably erred on the other side.

You will soon see the 'Poems and Ballads' in new edition, and all those written at college removed into the same volume with my two early plays and labelled all together as 'Early Poems.' Your guess at some among them is quite right, but of course there are more. It was good of you to find anything in that first book praiseworthy and notable; I had forgotten the verses you quote from it, and rather liked them. Of all I have done I rate *Hertha* highest as a single piece, finding in it the most of lyric force and music combined with the most of condensed and clarified thought. I think there really is a good deal compressed and concentrated into that poem.

I shall send you when ready two volumes of reprinted and now first collected prose and verse respectively, with something new in each, together with my Essay on old Chapman, in which I hope you will like the panegyric on Marlowe introducing the final passage on the two kinds of great poets. I am now writing in the form of an essay a sort of history of the style of Shakespeare and its progress through various stages of growth. This I hope to do well, as I have been studying Shakespeare ever since I was six years old.

When I tell you that I never was in France or Italy for more than a few weeks together, and that not more than three or four times in my life, and never was out of England at all till I was eighteen, I think I shall have told you about all you want to know, and answered your questions about as well as I can. There is a misprint, I feel sure, in the words of mine you cite in your article (p. 592), thanks to my damnable autograph—I must have talked of 'taking delight in the metrical forms' not 'poems' which is meaningless or nearly so 'of any language' etc. I should think Mr. Conway (whom I know slightly) would be an excellent man to edit your book in London. Possibly you might be able to give me some hint as to dealings of my own with American publishers. When Atalanta appeared in '65 I received (I *think* from Messrs. Osgood, but am not sure) a cheque for £20 with a courteous note proposing arrangements for any future books. This proposal, being ignorant of all business, I, out of deference and a sense of etiquette towards him, referred to my then acting publisher in London—a person who has since been tried and convicted on three several charges of fraud and robbery of the employers in whose name he acted. Of course he took the matter out of my hands, and of course for my two next books ('Chastelard' and 'Poems and Ballads') I received from America not one penny. Messrs. Ticknor and Fields who published 'Chastelard' wrote long afterwards to ask if I had received anything on their account—I replied I had not, and I have no doubt the money was embezzled—i.e. stolen by the now convicted thief in question. My political poems brought in a very little, and 'Bothwell' it seems nobody would take at any price. Pardon my intruding on you these financial matters, but Mr. Longfellow whom I once met in London asked me what I had received from America, and on hearing told me I had been robbed of a sum which sounded to me incredible (it was much more than I ever had at once in my life—though that is not saying much); so perhaps you may be able to do me a kindness in the matter.

I did mean to tell you about my present poetical projects, but being by this time as weary of the subject of myself as you must be I will give instead the name of one more friend. All my friends know and joke about my lifelong fondness (I am happy to say I have always found it naturally reciprocated) for very little children and very old persons. Of the later I had known already two sublime examples in my grandfather and Mr. Landor, and last summer I made and enjoyed the acquaintance of Mr. Trelawney (the old friend of Shelley, of Byron, and of Greece); a triad of Titans, of whom one was a giant of genius. The present piratical old hero calls me the last of the poets, who he thought all died with Byron. To hear him speak of Shelley is most beautiful and touching; at that name his voice (usually that of an old sea-king—as he is) *always* changes and softens unconsciously. 'There' he said to me 'was the very Best of men, and he was treated as the very Worst.' He professes fierce general misanthropy but is as ardent a republican (*and* atheist) as Shelley was at twenty; a magnificent old Viking to look at. Of the three, Landor must have been less handsome and noble-looking in youth than in age; my grandfather and Trelawney probably even more. At last I have done. If you ever get thus far, please let me know that this has reached you safely.
Ever yours faithfully,
A. C. Swinburne

P.S. I trust this will find you perfectly restored and fresh, or if still suffering under any head-complaint I fear it will be a shock by its length. I forgot this when I began writing yesterday. I hope to hear of you better.
A.C.S.

# EXPLANATORY NOTES

## COLLECTED POETRY

### *ATALANTA IN CALYDON*

Composed in 1863 and 1864, the play was published by Edward Moxon and Co. in 1865 in an edition of about 500 copies paid for by ACS's father. This edition has one of D. G. Rossetti's famous decorated cover designs. A trade edition followed immediately thereafter. A conscious imitation of Greek tragedy, the play involves a performative argument with contemporary religious ideology about ultimate things. Its act of spirit-raising is aesthetic and antitheistic, for resurrection in ACS's view involves continuous change and translation, as the "Argument" at the work's head emphasizes. A pastiche of Elizabethan English prose, this Argument sets ACS's work in a second layer of transmission, very much in the manner later made famous by Ezra Pound in the opening canto of his *Cantos*. *Atalanta* is thus a wholly nineteenth-century work, fashioned to set contemporary Christianity in sharp, critical relief with the ethos of pagan Greece. "Dead men rise up never" ("The Garden of Proserpine" 86), but their works return as they are remade in the image and likeness of living humans. ACS announces this central idea in a Greek epigraph (from Euripides' lost play *Meleager*) set beneath his title, which translates as follows: "Do good to the living; for each man in dying becomes earth and shadow; nothing returns to nothing." The second epigraph fronting the text of the play (from Aeschylus's *The Libation Bearers*) translates to a kind of Argument for the action: "if any there be who is not light-minded in his understanding, let him know this, when he hath learned of the device of a lighted brand, planned by Thestius' heartless daughter [i.e., Althaea], who wrought the ruin of her own child when that she consumed the charred brand, which was to be like-aged with him from the hour when he came forth from his mother's womb and cried aloud . . . until the day foredoomed by fate" (Loeb translation). ACS's text is famously punctuated with allusions to and echoes from both classical and biblical culture. Far from a blunder in the representation, this running contradiction lies at the very heart of the play's polemical brilliance. The work is so thick with these intertextual connections that, as Cecil Lang observed in his annotations to the play, most will escape notice by "a generation not nurtured in the classics [or the bible!]." Lang left them unglossed, but with this general—wickedly wry—comment: "No one reared on Yeats, Joyce, Pound, and Eliot will be intimidated by the labor of looking up Swinburne's allusions" (Lang, *The Pre-Raphaelites and their Circle*, 520). The present edition follows Lang's lead here: students looking for reading aids in this respect may consult the useful notes in Haynes (380–401) and the materials supplied in Lafourcade and Rutland.

The play was published with the Greek epigraph, an elaborate English dedication to the poet Walter Savage Landor, who died in 1864; and two dedicatory poems in Greek written by ACS in Landor's memory. These materials are omitted from the present edition.

### FROM *POEMS AND BALLADS* (1866)

*A Ballad of Life.* Written in 1862, published in *PB1*. The poem is another pastiche work, in this case a kind of dramatic monologue in that we are to imagine it as having been written by—and perhaps, then, here "translated" from—a court poet of Lucrezia Borgia, someone like the Tabaldeo Tebaldei ACS invented as the author of his remarkable "Chronicle" (see excerpts below) written at the same time as this work. The poem is an Italian canzone and was clearly inspired by ACS's reading of D. G. Rossetti's volume *The Early Italian Poets* (1861), one of the great works of English verse translation. ACS's fascination with Lucrezia Borgia was fed by his reading of Landor ("On Seeing a Hair of Lucretia Borgia"), Hugo (*Lucrèce Borgia*), and Dumas (*Crimes Célèbres*).

*Laus Veneris.* Written 1863, published in *PB1*. Given ACS's explication of his poem in the *Notes on Poems and Reviews*, the title, "praise of Venus," would have to be ironical. Based on the medieval German legend of Venus and Tannhäuser, the dramatic monologue is spoken by Tannhäuser after he has returned to Venus's Hörselberg following his pilgrimage to Rome to seek absolution from Pope Urban IV (1216–64). The poem is composed in the stanza of Fitzgerald's Rubaiyat, which Rossetti had been enthusiastically promoting since 1860, when he found a copy by accident. Walder (chapter 9) regards the poem as thoroughly Baudelairean and specifically in debt to Baudelaire's pamphlet *Richard Wagner et Tannhäuser in Paris* (1861), although ACS asserted in his *Notes on Poems and Reviews* that the poem was finished before he received a copy of the pamphlet from Baudelaire.

133 Adonis: beloved of Venus, he was slain by a boar. See Ovid's *Metamorphoses* X. 298ff. for the story.

195 for her sake: Helen of Troy

198 The queen: Cleopatra

200 Semiramis: semilegendary queen of ancient Assyria, infamous for her sexual appetites

253 bitter love: the love of Christ

284 the Dove: the Christian Holy Ghost

299 bay-leaf: the laurel, traditional crown for the poet

355–56 See Jeremiah 13:23.

357–68 Compare Baudelaire, "Correspondances," 5-14.

391 Venus was born from sea-foam, according to legend.

417 referring to the legend of the Christian Last Judgment

425 A pastiche of a medieval formula for closing a text, it means "The Praise of Venus is finished." ACS is clearly using it here ironically, as a satirical comment on social orders dominated by the "bitter love" of Christianity.

*The Triumph of Time.* Written 1863 or perhaps 1864, published in *PB1*. Although strictly a dramatic monologue, the poem is usually read autobiographically, as ACS's poetical account of his early disappointment in love. In this reading, ACS's "lost love" is taken to be his cousin Mary Gordon, who married Col. Robert Disney Leith in 1865. See the commentary on the poem in the *Notes on Poems and Reviews*, where ACS casts it as part of the romantic myth of how a poet comes into his vocation to art—a myth of regular resort throughout the nineteenth century and most famously articulated, perhaps, by Shelley: "Most wretched men / Are cradled into poetry by wrong, / They learn in suffering what they teach in song." Although the title recalls Petrarch's celebrated sequence of *Trionfi*, its most immediate locus of attention is Tennyson's "Locksley Hall," as is especially clear from lines 113ff., which recall lines 57–58 in Tennyson's poem. Both tell the story of the "triumph" of the quotidian world over the speaker's dream of establishing an earthly paradise of love. In ACS the triumph is a pyrrhic one because it results in the speaker's initial turn to the vocation of poetry, of which this very poem appears as the first fruit. Its "sick dreams and sad . . . dull delight[s]" are the speaker's, not the poem's.

29 a Eucharistic reference—a parodic move recurrent in ACS's work generally

30 Genesis 3:5. Biblical allusions appear throughout (see e,g, lines 30, 36, 102, 168, 304, 363).

62 mother: Aphrodite

83 According to legend, waves comes in triads, and the third is always the greatest. See Plato, Republic 472a.

156 the fates: Clotho, Lachesis, Atropos

237 Echoes *Hamlet* III.1.

253 referencing the Seven Sorrows of the Virgin Mary (see "Dolores").

257–320 This event symbolizes a secular baptism into an imaginative life dedicated to a knowledge of the elemental orders of reality.

295–96 These are emblems of Christianity for ACS.

319 Love: Eros, the boy-god, conventionally pictured with wings

321–44 ACS references the legend of the twelfth-century troubadour poet Jaufré Rudel, which is a variation on the Tristan legend. When he was at Oxford ACS wrote a sequence of poems on Rudel and his star-crossed love for the Lady of Tripoli. Rudel figures in Petrarch's "Triumph of Love." The "midland sea" is the Mediterranean.

*Itylus.* Written in Italy early in 1864; first published *PB1*. The source is Ovid, *Metamorphoses* VI. 424ff. The poem retails the gruesome story of the rape of Philomela by her brother-in-law King Tereus, married to her sister Procne. Tereus ripped out Philomela's tongue to prevent her from reporting his crime, but she wove a tapestry to reveal it in images. Procne avenged her sister by killing their son Itys and feeding the boy to his unsuspecting father, Tereus. The sisters then fled from Daulis, where the gruesome meal was served. Ovid says Tereus was turned into a hawk while Philomela became a nightingale and her sister a swallow. ACS played many variations on this legend, with its rich resources for exploring the relations of love and poetry and their marvelous investment in patterns of translation and transformation. In a letter written to Edmund Gosse in 1915, R. W. Raper reported a meeting with ACS in which he said, "'I don't know whether it has any meaning or not, and I don't care: I am quite sure it is the most musical, and that is what I do care about.' He said that after he had composed it, he went out and chanted it to the nightingales, and they fell into tune."

*Anactoria.* First drafted in 1863, the poem was later reworked, perhaps in 1865, when ACS added lines 155–88; first published *PB1*. One of the greatest poems of the nineteenth century, its intense eroticism shocked ACS's contemporaries, and the poem was pointedly denounced by hostile reviewers (see ACS's reply in his *Notes on Poems and Reviews*). ACS rightly pointed out (*Letters* II. 74) that its "scheme of movement and modulation" was "original in structure and combination," and he used this scheme as the metrical basis for *Tristram of Lyonesse*. "Anactoria" is a dramatic monologue addressed by Sappho to her lover Anactoria, whom Sappho berates for her infidelity. The poem is formally a set of "variations on a theme" established originally by Sappho. That ACS was aware of the musical analogy is apparent from the poem's own variations on the theme of musicality, where the poet's procedural "scheme" for his work is most clearly on exhibit. The monologue's specific point of departure is the Greek poet's famous (so-called) "Ode to Aphrodite," which ACS echoes and recalls, as he does other passages from Sappho's surviving fragmentary corpus. Besides the epigraph, the passages distinctly echoing Sappho are 63, 70, 73–74, 81–84, 189–200, 203–14. ACS regarded Sappho as the greatest poet who ever lived, and she inspired him to some of his most magnificent verse (see "Sapphics" and "On the Cliffs"). The best commentary on the poem's astonishing verbal pyrotechnics is by Lang (*Pre-Raphaelites and their Circle,* 522–24), who also observes that the poem's couplets fall into "four grand modulations of accelerating intensity (ll. 1–58, 59–152, 153–88, 189–304)." But neither Lang nor other scholars comment on the crucial set of mirror texts at lines 35–46 and 47–58 (and see below the commentary for *Tristram of Lyonesse*). This (double) passage indexes the central idea pervading the poem: that the poetic imagination has the power to generate infinite transformations and that it is, in this respect, the source and end and test of the ceaseless generative power displayed in the natural world.

Epigraph The text is emended (by ACS) from a corrupt line in the "Ode to Aphrodite." The emendation is the first of ACS's "variations." The epigraph translates, "From whom by persuasion have you vainly caught love" (i.e., who has seduced you to the hopelessness of loving?).

22 Erinna: a Greek poetess from Lesbos mentioned by Sappho, here made one of her lovers; Erotion: a male lover (see ACS's poem so titled)

45 Aphrodite's girdle, one of her most seductive habiliments

64 Paphos: the location of the shrine to Aphrodite on Cyprus

155–88 This passage has been sharply criticized by many. Early reviewers were appalled at the fierce attack on the sadomasochism of Judaeo-Christian ideology. Others, including later critics, fault the passage on formal grounds, as being out of keeping with Sappho's monologue. But ACS's monologues (like D. G. Rossetti's) are themselves variations on the strict model made famous by Browning. As the supreme type of the poet, Sappho is for ACS "now [i.e., in the nineteenth century] no more a singer, but a song" ("Thalassius" 474). In this sense, which is essential to ACS's argument, Sappho here becomes "one with" ACS and one with Anactoria (and with "Anactoria"): "one with all these things, / With all high things for ever" (276–77). That is the argument demonstrated in the poem's concluding section (see especially lines 243–304).

260–65 glancing at the legend that Sappho died in a fit of love-despair by hurling herself into the sea from a cliff in Leucadia

*Hymn to Proserpine.* ACS read the poem to William Bell Scott in December 1862; first published *PB1*. It is a dramatic monologue, what ACS called "the deathsong of spiritual decadence" spoken by a pagan believer living after the establishment of Christianity as the official religion of Rome in 379–85 by the emperor Theodosius. The poem's epigraph is the famous remark attributed to Julian, emperor from 361 to 363 and called the Apostate because he rejected the Christian faith that was coming to power in Rome. The source is Theodoret's *Ecclesiastical History* 3.20. The poem is largely governed by the contrast between the pagan queen, worshipped under various names (Proserpine, Venus, Cybele), and the Queen of Heaven of the Christians, the Blessed Virgin, called here a "slave among slaves" (85) in allusion to her son Jesus ("despised and rejected"), sometimes called (like his vicar on earth, the pope) the "servant of servants." Invoking a Nietzschean myth of "eternal return" (see line 46), the poem implicitly comments on contemporary Christianity's "spiritual decadence." The famous couplet (35–36) marks Christianity as a religion that makes death and forgetfulness ("things Lethean") the hallmarks of its living faith. Christianity works to forget its pagan inheritance, and it represents "the fullness of death" because it seeks to turn the brief space of a human life into a morbid experience. The speaker's pagan faith, by contrast, marks the death of the body as an unambiguous blessing given to men and women after the initial—ambiguous and testing—gift of life. ACS's poem may be usefully compared with D. G. Rossetti's "The Burden of Nineveh," which makes its contemporary application in more specific terms.

71 thy lords: i.e., the Romans, who ruled the world

80 Venus was the mother of Aeneas, who founded Rome.

108 The line echoes a famous remark by the Roman philosopher Epictetus (ca. A.D. 60–120): Thou art a little soul bearing up a corpse.

*Hermaphroditus.* Composed March 1863, published *PB1*. The four sonnets (Italian in form) construct an interpretation of the Hellenistic sculpture of the sleeping Hermaphrodite in the Louvre (see ACS's note to the poem). Ovid is the source of the legend (*Metamorphoses* IV. 285–388): that when the beautiful youth Hermaphroditus rejected the love of the nymph Salmacis, the gods answered her prayer that the two be joined by causing him to melt into her when he was swimming in her pool. While the androgyne is an ancient figure of human perfection, in the nineteenth century this union of opposites acquired a distinctly erotic character. The key texts impinging on ACS are Henri De Latouche's notorious novel *Fragoletta* (1829), Balzac's *Séraphita* and *La fille aux yeux d'or* (both 1835), Gautier's *Mademoiselle de Maupin* (1836), and Baudelaire's "Le Bijoux." See ACS's commentary on his sonnets in *Notes on Poems and Reviews*, in which he cites Shelley's "The Witch of Atlas," which features a hermaphrodite as the familiar spirit of the witch, who represents the power of imagination. ACS's poem "Fragoletta" was printed in *PB1* immediately after this work.

*Anima Anceps.* Composition date is unknown; first published *PB1*. The poem is a carpe diem response to the "divided soul" of the Latin title, which ACS seems to have lifted from a passage in Hugo's *Notre-Dame de Paris* (book VIII, chap. 6). In Hugo the Latin formula is a priestly prayer for a person being sent to execution—death presumably ending the soul's self-division. Obviously ACS argues that the divided soul should look for psychic healing not in death but in life. Although the poem inevitably recalls Arthur Clough's "Dipsychus," which ACS knew and admired, Byron's splendid "Stanzas. 'Could love for ever'" is clearly the most important source text.

*A Match.* Composed 1862, first published *PB1*. The poem lays out a series of six "matches," each introducing a way of defining a possible relation between the lover, who speaks the poem, and his beloved. These matches, conventional antitheses, introduce six sets of assertions that "would" be the outcome of these hypotheses. The poem is notable, however, for not organizing its six units as anything but an aggregate—the order of the stanzas scarcely matters so that ACS short circuits any "sense of an ending" for his poem. The effect is to make the text a demonstration of the lover / poet's imaginative powers, as if any type of relation between him and his lover would suffice, as if any type of relation would be both possible and desirable.

*Faustine.* Probably composed in 1862, first published in *The Spectator* (31 May 1862) and collected in *PB1*. The best gloss on this astonishing tour de force is still ACS's own comments in his *Notes on Poems and Reviews*, where "the elder Faustina" is identified as the poet's inspiration. Around A.D. 110 she married Antoninus Pius, who later (A.D. 137) became emperor. Like her daughter (also named Annia Galeria Faustina), the elder Faustina became, perhaps unfairly, a byword for a libidinous, epicene woman.

Epigraph "Hail, Empress Faustina, they who are about to die salute you" (the Roman gladiators' traditional salutation before their circus combats). The impish comic overtone of this epigraph emerges to view when we see that the word "Faustina" here refers not so much to the Roman empress as to ACS's poem and its titular, highly transformational central figure.
121 lesbian love (see "Sapphics")
146 Priapus, god of gardens and fertility, was born in Lampsacus in Asia Minor.

*Stage Love.* Date of composition uncertain, but the poem has a clear connection to "A Match," which was written in 1862. First published *PB1*. ACS writes the poem to complicate and explore the traditional contrast between "real" and "stage" love, which here figure the relation of any artistic action to its representations. The argument presents the consequences of a real love relationship being undertaken under the auspices of a stage model. As such, the poem distinctly recalls works like Laclos's *Les liaisons dangerouses* or various works by Gautier, not least of all *Mademoiselle de Maupin*.

*The Leper.* The earliest version of this poem, titled "A Vigil," was written in 1862; when ACS revised it to the form of its (initial) publication in *PB1* is uncertain, but he is known to have recited it at Fryston in the summer of 1862. The French endnote that ACS gives as the story's source is of course his invention and was translated by Lang as follows: "At that time there was in this country a large number of lepers, which greatly displeased the king, since because of them God must have been grievously angered. Now it happened that a noble damsel named Yolande de Sallières, being afflicted and utterly ravaged by this evil malady, all her friends and relatives, having before their eyes the fear of God, drove her out of their houses and never were willing to receive a thing accursed by God and stinking and abominable to all men. That Lady had been very beautiful and of graceful figure, goodly in stature and lascivious in her life. However, none of her lovers who had ever embraced and kissed her very tenderly was willing to harbor any longer so ugly a woman and so detestable a sinner. Only a clerk who had been at first her servant and go-between in matters of love took her with him and hid her in a small hut. There the wicked woman died an evil death in great misery. And after she died the clerk aforesaid, who out of his great love had for six months, cared for her, washed her, dressed and undressed her every day with his own hands. People even say that this wicked man and cursed clerk, remembering this woman's former great beauty, [now] ravaged, often delighted in kissing her foul and leprous mouth and in caressing her gently with his loving hands. Therefore, he died of this same abominable disease. This happened near Fontainbellant in Gastenois. And when King Philip heard the story he marveled greatly."

Lang's notes and commentary on the ballad will probably never be surpassed. They expose what he calls the poem's "functional ambiguities," "all part of a conspiracy luring the willing reader to interpretations that can neither be wholly sustained nor comfortably dismissed". He cites line 137 as a "safe" example of such ambiguities (it "may or may not suggest that the clerk 'died of this same abominable disease'") and line 12 as one with "other reverberations" than the most obvious one (see Lang, *The Pre-Raphaelites and their Circle,* 521–22). The poem should be compared with ACS's story "Dead Love."

*Before the Mirror.* A rare case of a poem which can be dated exactly. Composed 2 April 1865, published *PB1* (but ACS published stanzas 4 and 6 in the Royal Society Exhibition Catalogue (1865) to accompany James Whistler's picture *The Little White Girl,* which inspired the poem). When ACS sent Whistler a copy of the poem in a letter (*Letters* I. 118–20), he told him that he "brought [it] off at once." But an early manuscript (late 1850s) titled "The Dreamer" comprises a version of the last three stanzas plus a fourth (unpublished) stanza that comes third in this poem (and that would have been "Before the Mirror"'s penultimate stanza). Its relevance to the received poem is clear:

A painted dream, beholden,
  Of no man's eye,
Framed in far memories, golden
  As hope when nigh
Holds fast her soul that hears
Faint waters flow like tears
By shores no sunbeam cheers
  From all the sky.

Whistler's painting led ACS to work his early lines into an artistic expression of the function of art as a second-order phantasm (or "dream") constructed to expose the phantasms that organize so much of our ordinary worlds:. As he wrote to Whistler, "I found . . . the notion of sad and glad mystery in the face languidly contemplative of its own phantom and all other things seen by their phantoms."

*Dolores.* Composed in the spring and perhaps the summer, 1865; published *PB1*. The outrage of ACS's early reviewers at this poem has rarely been taken as seriously as it should. The poem *is* outrageous, consciously so, and is best read as the "parody" that Lafourcade long since declared it to be. Indeed, the poem's splendor falls from its deliberately ludic approach to its materials: not just to its Christian materials, but to its Sadean inversions as well. The poem's corrosive power rests in its implicit argument that the Christian and the Sadean economies are codependent functions of each other. The poem is a triumph of the comic spirit over what Blake called "the wastes of moral law." ACS's high-spirited letter to Charles Augustus Howell (May or June 1865) provides the best gloss the poem has ever had: "I have added four more jets of boiling and poisonous infamy to the perennial and poisonous fountain of Dolores," and he adds a PS to the letter with a sample, lines 173–80. A second PS immediately follows: "Since writing the above I have added ten verses to D. —très infâmes et très bien tournés. 'Oh! Monsieur—peut-on prendre du plaisir à telles horreurs? Tu le vois, Justine, je bande-oh! Putain, que tu vas souffrir' —."

Walder (chapter 13) and Haynes both supply a thorough account of ACS's many sources: from the Bible, the Book of Common Prayer, and the Roman Missal to Sade, Byron, Gautier, and Baudelaire. ACS's subtitle gives the French form of Our Lady of Sorrows, one of the appellations of the Virgin Mary (whose "mysteries"—Joyful, Sorrowful, and Glorious—all get celebrated in the "Litanies" to her that provide the basis for ACS's bravura exercise).

19, 21 "Tower of ivory" (see the Song of Songs 7: 4) and "mystical rose" are two appellations of the Virgin Mary in one of her litanies.

51 Libitina: ancient Italian goddess of death and fertility; Priapus: god of sexual potency

217–56 an evocation of the bloodthirsty spectacles of ancient Rome, culminating (249ff.) in an allusion to the legend that Nero set fire to Rome in A.D.64

223 Thalassa, one of Aphrodite's names, meaning "sea-born"

228 children of change: Christians

231 one: Nero

281 Vesta: goddess of the hearth

299 Alciphron: Greek poet and rhetorician (second century), famous for his "imaginary letters" supposed to have been written by persons of an earlier age. Arisbe: in this instance ACS must be thinking of the Lesbian Arisbe, daughter of Macar.

340 Catullus: the great Roman poet (87–54 B.C.); see below, "Hendecasyllabics")

371 Exodus 7: 8–10

375 prophet: the Marquis de Sade

406 Aphaca: in Asia Minor, a center for worship of Venus and Priapus

409–10 three of Aphrodite's names

438 tares: see Matthew 13: 25–40

*The Garden of Proserpine*. The date of composition is uncertain, but 1865 is perhaps not unreasonable; first published in *PB1*. Some years after the publication of *PB1*, ACS told a dinner party that this piece, "The Triumph of Time," and "Dolores" were related to each other and were "beyond all the rest [of the poems in *PB1*] autobiographical." According to this tale, after a period of sensual indulgence "with which he had sought relief" from the trauma of his "lost love," he came to Proserpine's garden "to find . . . a haven of undisturbed rest." Whatever the historical truth of this tale, the poem certainly, and exquisitely, identifies that "haven" with poetry itself. Standing behind the poem is a general allusion to one of ACS's favorite New Testament passages, Galatians 6:7–9, which of course is here translated into a secular humanist meaning. This flagrantly symbolic poem should be compared (and contrasted) with "A Forsaken Garden," in which the illusory stabilities of the natural world are exposed by a consummate artifice.

Title ACS leaves it ambiguous whether the garden references the legendary place in the upper world where Proserpine (Kore) was raped away by Hades while she was gathering "bloomless buds of poppies" (27) or the garden in the underworld where she ate the pomegranate from Hades' garden. The literary sources locate the upper world garden with many different places in the ancient world, Sicilian Enna and Attic Eleusis being the most common.

70–72 recalls the opening of Shelley's "Ode to the West Wind"

*Hendecasyllabics*. Composed 1865, first published *PB1*. A homage to Catullus, the poem specifically recalls Carmen XLVI, which is cast as a celebration of spring in the classical form of hendecasyllables. ACS's poem inverts and transforms Catullus in order to celebrate not nature but art and imagination. Like its companion "Sapphics," this poem is therefore far more than a formal imitation of or response to Catullus, whom ACS regarded as one of the three supreme masters of lyric verse in Western literature (after Sappho and on a par with Shelley). The inversion of Catullus is the framework for a whole set of related transformations. Particularly notable is the inverted echo of Milton ("Lycidas" 26) in line 6 and of the Song of Songs (2:11–13) at lines 19–25. The poem announces an entrance into the same world figured in "The Garden of Prosperpine" and its nonnatural flowers.

*Sapphics*. The date of composition is uncertain, but the poem's close relation to "Anactoria" suggests a date of 1863; first published *PB1*. As "Hendecasyllabics" reworked Catullus's Carmen XLVI into a myth of poetry, this poem reworks Sappho's "Ode to Aphrodite" in an even more spectacular way. The poem tells a story of how Sappho assumed her office and fame as "the tenth muse": by repudiating Aphrodite and the order of natural love and devoting herself to the order of impossible things. Sappho was from Mitylene, on Lesbos.

*Dedication, 1865.* Composed 1865, first published *PB1*, the concluding poem of the volume. The poem is addressed to Edward Burne Jones (later Burne-Jones), the painter. They met at Oxford and remained lifelong friends. The poem deliberately recapitulates the motifs and images that recur throughout *PB1* in order to make clear that all are in the end poetic transformations—literally, literal figures of the power of the poetic imagination.

### FROM *SONGS BEFORE SUNRISE* (1871)

*Prelude.* Composed 1871 and printed as the first poem in *SBS*. The poem announces ACS's intention to give an explicitly political cast to his antitheist humanism, which in *PB1* took a very different form and tone. The sociopolitical context of the book is signaled by its dedication to the Italian patriot Joseph Mazzini (1805–72), whom ACS had recently met and who urged him to dedicate his poetical gifts to world revolution and especially the Italian struggle for independence. The "Sunrise," in ACS's view, referenced the dawning of a new humanist day of intellectual (scientific) and political liberation.

1 green buds: the poems of *PB1*; red: the revolutionary political poems of *SBS*

102, 104 According to legend, the daughters of Thyas were the first worshippers of Bacchus; the inhabitants of Bassara, in Libya, were famous Bacchantes.

117–18 Cotytto, a fertility goddess, worshipped at Mt. Edon, in Thrace

*Hertha.* Composed late 1869 (completed January 1870); first published in *SBS*. The titular speaker of the poem is the Germanic goddess of the earth and fertility. As so often in ACS, the poem functions through a self-referencing conceit, so that ultimately the "speaker" is the poem itself. Like "Genesis," "Hertha" is an imaginative creation myth countering the traditional Judaeo-Christian myth. The intellectual argument of the poem grafts the thought of Schopenhauer and Compte's evolutionary positivism to a Blakean view of the creation myth as set forth in *The Marriage of Heaven and Hell* and *The Book of Urizen*.

15 see Exodus 3: 14 and John 8: 58

21–25 recalls Baudelaire, "L'Héautontimorouménos," 21–24

41–62 see Job 38–39

64 tripod: referring to the seat on which the oracle of Delphi issued prophecies

70 This thought is a Blakean transposition of the Old Testament's contempt for the many gods of paganism.

80 the colors of the flag of Italy

91–95 recollecting Blake's "Auguries of Innocence" 129–32

97 Yggdrasil is the mythic tree from Norse mythology that joins the heaven and the earth.

100 a telling allusion to Genesis 2: 17

181 referring to the Twilight of the Gods, or Ragnarok; ACS clearly has in mind his own age as the Ragnarok of the Christian epoch.

*Before a Crucifix.* Composed Nov. 1869 (see ACS's letter to William Michael Rossetti of 25 November).

*Genesis.* Composition date unknown. As the title suggests, the poem offers a (Lucretian) countermyth to the story of creation told in the book of Genesis. The poem exhibits throughout ACS's reading of Blake (see especially lines 20 and 32).

### FROM *SONGS OF TWO NATIONS* (1875)

*Locusta.* This is one of the "Dirae" sequence that ACS wrote to celebrate the death at Chislehurst in Jan. 1873 of the hated Napoleon III.

## FROM *POEMS AND BALLADS, SECOND SERIES* (1878)

*A Forsaken Garden.* First published in *The Athenaeum* (July 1876). The poem is inspired by the famous West Undercliff, near East Dene, ACS's family home on the Isle of Wight.

*Sestina.* ACS told Frederick Locker on 15 Nov. 1871 that he "scribbled [it] off this morning." First published in *Once-a-Week* (January 1872).

*The Complaint of Lisa (Double Sestina).* ACS wrote it in November 1869 (see *Letters* I. 57). First published in the *Fortnightly Review* (February 1870). ACS was justly proud of this remarkable work: "A reduplicated inter-rhyming sestina (dodicina, as Rossetti proposed to call it) — the twelve rhymes carried on even into the six line 'envoy,' as you will find if you look into the fourth and tenth syllables of each line of it — or simply if you . . . read it out" (*Letters* III. 317).

*Ave atque Vale.* ACS was writing this elegy for Charles Baudelaire in May 1867, after ACS heard a (false) report of the poet's death. Baudelaire in fact died in August 1867, at forty-six years old. ACS was a great admirer of Baudelaire from the early 1860s. In 1862 he reviewed the 1861 edition of *Fleurs du mal* and was well aware of the scandal and legal proceedings that followed the publication of the first edition in 1857. His elegy was first published in the *Fortnightly Review* (January 1868). Oddly, ACS never thought as highly of his poem as most readers always have (see *Letters* II. 282 and VI. 153). Like some of ACS's most important poems, this one responds antithetically to Tennyson — in this case, to the elegy for Arthur Hallam *In Memoriam* (compare stanzas V and X with the climactic section XCV of Tennyson's elegy). The title is taken from the famous last line of Catullus, Carmen CI.

2 this: i.e., *Fleurs du mal* (see stanza X)

15–18 Sappho

33 biblical usage (see Galatians 6: 7)

60 Baudelaire, "La Géante"

sts. XI–XII ACS references Orestes and Elektra at the tomb of their father, Agamemnon, in the opening passages of Aeschylus, *Choephore*.

134 Apollo

st. XV Baudelaire

st. XVI see "Laus Veneris"

177–79 forgive: This amounts to a plea that God be forgiven for the sufferings maintained through his economy of grace (see stanzas XI–XII).

*Sonnet (with a Copy of Mademoiselle de Maupin).* ACS wrote the sonnet and several other poems on the death of Gautier in November 1872. First printed in *Le Tombeau de Théophile Gautier* (1873). ACS greatly admired Gautier's poetry, prose, and general aesthetic outlook, but especially this notorious novel, first published in 1836. ACS probably came to an acquaintance with Baudelaire's work through Gautier, who presided at the center of the so-called Parnassian poets.

14 Because once seen, Beauty ever after consumes us with desire but eludes our pursuit.

*A Ballad of Dreamland.* First published in *Belgravia* (September 1876). Like the first stanza of "A Vision of Spring in Winter," the refrain for this poem, ACS said, came to him while he was sleeping.

*A Ballad of Francois Villon*

16 shift: A word play meaning both a woman's underwear and a trick. Both can "come short" in several senses.

32 a God: Villon's human father is unknown; ACS here means Apollo.

*A Vision of Spring in Winter.* The date of composition is uncertain. First published in the *Fortnightly Review* (April 1875). The poem is closely related to ACS's Proserpine poems and may be usefully read as if spoken not by the poet but by Demeter.

42 compare Shelley, "Prometheus Unbound" II. 5. 8–14

*The Complaint of the Fair Armouress.* This is the first of the set of ten translations from Villon that ACS published in *PB2*. The set excluded some of the best of his translations and imitations, however, including the incomparable "Ballad of Villon and Fat Madge" (printed below in part 3, Uncollected Poetry), as beyond the bounds of Victorian proprieties. "The Complaint" itself was expurgated in the *PB2* publication, asterisks standing in place of the missing lines 54–56 and 70–72. These were restored posthumously. Mallarmé told ACS that he was uniquely fitted to translate Villon since ACS understood how and why Villon and Baudelaire were poetic seers. ACS indeed saw Villon (1431–65?) as occupying a crucial historical position and role at the nexus of the Christian Middle Ages and the humanism of the Renaissance with its revival of pagan culture. He incorporates his own poetry into this cultural framework in the opening lines of "The Ballad of Villon and Fat Madge," in which the pronoun "I" doubly references Villon and ACS and in which "beauty" means both Madge and the aesthetic ideal that ACS's work—in particular this work—argues for. In the early 1860s ACS and Rossetti planned to collaborate on translating all of Villon, a project that never came to fruition. ACS wrote some translations at that time, but at least five of his translations were written in 1876–77 (see *Letters* III. 136). In 1863 ACS wrote an important essay on Villon that was first published by Lang (*New Writings,* 184–86). Villon's originals are the imbedded "complaint" in *Le Testament* ("Avis m'est que j'oy regrecter") and the "Ballade" there known traditionally as the "Ballade de Villon et de la Grosse Margot."

## FROM *SONGS OF THE SPRINGTIDES* (1880)

*On the Cliffs.* Composed between July and October 1879, first published in *Songs of the Springtides*. The epigraph, which means "nightingale of beautiful song," announces a poem that uses the figure of the nightingale as the focus for a series of linked imaginative transformations that comprise the substance of the poem. The key transformation involves the association of the myths of Philomela and of Sappho (see "Itylus," "Anactoria," and "Sapphics"). ACS generates a panoply of imaginative figurations as a demonstration of the art of poetry, and the first person convention integrates his own life into these figurations. The cliffs of the poem are not just a memory of Sappho's notorious Leucadian cliff: they make an autobiographical reference to the celebrated "undercliff" on the Isle of Wight near ACS's family home at Bonchurch. ACS's memory seems to have reverted to that locale, much-loved from his youth, because the other family house in Berkshire, Holmwood, was being sold, a traumatic event for ACS. He began writing the poem while he was on his last visit to Holmwood.

48ff. referring to the Furies and the myth of Orestes and the House of Atreus (see Aeschylus, *Eumenides* 321ff.)

141ff. ACS is translating the passage from Aeschylus's *Agamemnon* (ll. 1146–49) in which Cassandra foretells the imminent deaths of the king and of herself. Cassandra's prophetic powers were a gift of Apollo, but the gift came with the stipulation that her prophecies would not be credited.

161 thou: primarily Sappho, but the poem's transformational inertia works to multiply its references

167 hers: primarily Aphrodite

299–300 quoting Sappho

304 the elaborately decorated throne of Aphrodite

325–35 compare "Anactoria"; ACS is echoing passages from Sappho's verse.

340 The nightingale—bird, woman, and god—replaces the Christian trinity.

## FROM *STUDIES IN SONG* (1880)

*By the North Sea.* The poem was composed in 1880 and completed by 5 July. ACS told Edmund Gosse that "in metrical and antiphonal effect I prefer it . . . to all my others." The poem is inspired by the Suffolk landscape along the North Sea coast, where the once prosperous town of Dunwich was slowly lost to the sea's encroachment over a period of several hundred years. Little remained of the place in ACS's day (less remains now) except a small village and abbey ruin.

105–10 Joel 3: 14

379–402 Death, change, darkness: ACS here translates the Christian Trinity into secular terms, a common move in all his work. Another favorite is the trinity of sun, wind, and sea. Implicit in these moves is an argument that triadic forms are fundamental to human thinking. ACS wrote many verse triads.

## FROM *THE HEPTALOGIA* (1880)

ACS drafted the final couplet of "The Higher Pantheism in a Nutshell" in January 1870 in his copy of Tennyson's *The Holy Grail and other Poems* (1869). When he completed the parody of Tennyson's "The Higher Pantheism" is uncertain, though we know he added lines 15–16 after 1880; they first appear in the collected edition of 1904. "Sonnet for a Picture" parodies Rossetti, who wrote numerous sonnets under similar titles. "Nephelidia" and the even more brilliant "Poeta Loquitur" (see part 3, Uncollected Poetry) are self-parodies, the latter not published, however, until 1917. The choice of a Latin title ("The Poet Speaks") is a remarkably witty turn.

## *TRISTRAM OF LYONESSE*

ACS began the poem in the fall of 1869, and he completed the "Prelude" in February 1870. He published this work separately in 1871 under the title "Tristram and Iseult: Prelude of an Unfinished Poem." He worked on it from time to time during the next ten years, completing and then publishing canto I in March 1877. He returned to the composition in 1880–81 and published the work in July as the title poem of his 1882 volume. While in the midst of writing the "Prelude" he wrote a long, amusing, and insightful letter to Rossetti about his plans for the poem (see *Letters* II. 72–74), which was written in the same "original" prosodic "scheme" as "Anactoria." The story of Tristan and Iseult is too well known to require rehearsal here. What does need mention is that ACS's poem pursues a Blakean rewriting of the moral of Dante's Paolo and Francesca episode (*Inferno* canto V). As ACS remarks in his letter to Rossetti, "These two lovers [are brought to] everlasting hell and honour," not to Christian damnation. A poetic fate sweeps them beyond their own purposes and will so that they can be uplifted as a quasi-eternal sign of the dominion of Love—the "alma Venus genetrix" celebrated as well in Lucretius's *De rerum natura*. Unlike Arnold, Tennyson, and other English poets taking up the Tristan legends, ACS did not use Malory as his chief source, but turned instead to twelfth-century French sources as well as Walter Scott's edition (1804) of Thomas of Erceldoune's *Sir Trestram*.

I. 1–44 see canto IX. 1–44, which mirrors and echoes this opening passage (as in "Anactoria" 35–58)

I. 796 see Dante, *Inferno* V. 137. In a French romance treating the loves of Launcelot and Guinevere, Galahault is the man who urges them to their love.

IX. 464–65 the lark / Triumphant: recollecting the climactic moment in Blake's *Milton*

IX. 490 echoes canto I line 1064.

IX. 494 inverts the Christian tag "Requiescat in pace"

## FROM *A CENTURY OF ROUNDELS* (1883)

ACS modified the traditional French form to an eleven-line stanza that restricts itself to two rhymes and requires that the fourth and eleventh lines repeat the opening word or words of the poem. Within that form he left himself free to make different kinds of prosodic variations. The Rossetti translation marked by "On an Old Roundel" is "To Death—Of his Lady," which Rossetti withdrew at the last moment from publishing in his volume *Poems* (1870).

### FROM *POEMS AND BALLADS, THIRD SERIES* (1889)

*To a Seamew.* As ACS's note to the poem indicates, it was written at Beachy Head in 1886, first published in *PB3*. Like Shelley's "To a Skylark," which it echoes and subtly transforms, the poem constructs a myth of the idea of the poet. The distinctively Swinburnean stanza transports various phrases and lines in the Shelley poem. The seamew's bleak, monotonous call as well as its distinctively alert eyes are being held in an implicit contrast with Shelley's skylark.

*Neap-Tide.* Composed either in 1888 or early 1889, the poem records ACS's walk along the sands "from Lancing to Shoreham" where "the sea was so far out and the shore slopes so much that even the tops of the downs were out of sight behind the low sea-bank which shut out everything on shore. It was wonderfully lonely and striking" (*Letters* V. 261–62).

### FROM *ASTROPHEL AND OTHER POEMS* (1894)

*A Nympholept.* Date of composition is late but uncertain, perhaps around 1887 when ACS was writing some similar poems; first published in *Black and White* (May 1891). The poem's focus is on the pagan god Pan, who is, in ACS's words, "lord of the mystery of earth, and immortal godhead of—and in—the terrene All" (*Letters* V. 209). ACS goes on to remark "the folly and falsehood of the cry that 'Pan is dead' which was uttered on a certain occasion not necessary to specify, and over which premature cry the old wood-god chuckles satirically." The ecstatic physical experience of union with a pervasive natural order is the subject of the poem. See the "Dedicatory Epistle" to ACS's collected edition of 1904, in which he describes this poem as coming from a class that renders "the effect of inland or woodland solitude the splendid oppression of nature at noon which found utterance of old in words of such singular and everlasting significance as panic and nympholepsy." For another poem of that "class," which ACS cultivated in the last twenty-five years of his work, see below, "The Lake of Gaube."

54 I.e., Philomela. See "Itylus."

### FROM *A CHANNEL PASSAGE AND OTHER POEMS* (1904)

*The Lake of Gaube.* Date of composition is uncertain but it is a late work; it was first published in *The Bookman* (October 1899). The poem recollects and reimagines an intense experience of the spring of 1862, when ACS visited Cauterets in the Pyrenees at the border of France and Spain and swam in the Lake of Gaube, which is located high in the mountains and about eight miles from Cauterets. According to local legend, to swim in the lake was to court death. The poem should be compared with ACS's prose description of the same scene that he wrote in 1890 for a review of Hugo's posthumously published letters (the review was republished in 1894 as "Notes of Travel: Alps and Pyrenees," in *Studies in Prose and Poetry*). It is written in and (typically for ACS) against the tradition of Romantic poems of natural sublimity, which commonly use such landscapes to reify traditional religious mythologies. See also "A Nympholept" (above).

10 I.e., salamanders. ACS recollected the salamanders he saw when he visited the lake with his family in 1862.

*In a Rosary.* Nothing is known about the composition of this poem or the particular locus of its description. But in a late letter to Emily Pfeiffer ACS wrote that his "neighborhood [in Putney] supplies one with constant models" for studies of gardens—a "subject," he added, "as inexhaustible as the sea" (*Letters* V. 263–64). The letter glosses all of ACS's many garden poems but is especially pertinent to this poem because of its comments on the presence of children. The poem might be usefully contrasted with Yeats's "Among School Children."

## "THE MONOMANIAC'S TRAGEDY, BY ERNEST WHELDRAKE"

First published in *Undergraduate Papers*, February-March 1858, reprinted in *New Writings*, 81–87. An early example of ACS's taste and facility for parody and literary hoax. The target here is Spasmodic Poetry, so-called, which had a great vogue in the 1850s. "Ernest Wheldrake" (there is a Wheldrake parish in Yorkshire) is a mask for writers like Philip James Bailey (1816–1902), Sydney Dobell (1824–74), and Alexander Smith (1830?–67). The text is replete with allusions to Milton, Byron, Shelley, Keats, Tennyson, Mrs. Browning, Arnold, Carlyle, and other writers. ACS developed a low opinion of his contributions to *Undergraduate Papers* (see *Letters* 5.235–36).

337; 6 "a bitter and severe delight": Landor, *Count Julian* (1812) 1.4

338.10–12 "wine-dishevelled tresses . . . vintage-tinctured raiment": See Marlowe, *Tamburlaine the Great Part 1*, 5.2.76+.

339.4 the fine Roman hand: *Twelfth Night* 3.4.31

339.29 "the dull owl": Webster, *The White Devil* 5.3.32

341.1 "The cow's breath pains me": Arnold, "Balder Dead," 340

341:29 Châtiments: Hugo's poems written against Napoleon III, *Les Châtiments* (1853)

341.36 Madame de Saint-Leu: Mother of Napoleon III. It was widely rumored that her pregnancy resulted from her intrigue with the Dutch admiral Verhuel.

341.40 M. Veuillot: Louis Veuillot (1813–83), ultramontane polemicist and editor of *L'Univers*

## FROM "CHARLES BAUDELAIRE: *LES FLEURS DU MAL*"

First published in the *Spectator*, 6 September 1862. See commentary above for "Ave atque Vale." The three Baudelaire allusions are to "Le serpent qui danse," "Une Charogne," and "Chanson d'après-midi," in that order.

## *NOTES ON POEMS AND REVIEWS*

Composed September 1866; published shortly thereafter by Hotten. ACS's reply to the many critics of *PB1* recalls Gautier's preface to *Mademoiselle de Maupin*.

348.1 "Je pense sur ces satires ...": Frederick II of Prussia, responding to Voltaire in a letter dated 2 March 1775. Carlyle provides a translation in volume 21 of his *Frederick the Great* (1858–65), one of ACS's sources for the epigraph: "I think of such Satires, with Epictetus: 'If they tell any truth of thee, correct thyself; if they are lies, laugh at them.' I have learned, with years, to become a steady coach-horse; I do my stage, like a diligent roadster, and pay no heed to the little dogs that will bark by the way."

348.5 "Ignorance by herself ...": Carlyle, again from volume 21 of *Frederick the Great*.

348.20 "As if a man should spit against the wind": Webster, *The White Devil*, 3.2.150–51

349.7–9 Ephesus: 1 Corinthians 15:32

350.10 "a lump neither alive nor dead ...": Shelley, *The Witch of Atlas* 135–36

350.19 "Ma corruption . . . pudeur": "My depravity would blush at their modesty" (Hyder trans.)

351.15 Phillips: ACS references the minor poet Ambrose Philips (c.1675–1749) and Boileau's translation of Longinus's treatise on the sublime (chapter 8).

351.21 ἔκων ἀέκοντί γε θυμῷ: "'of my own will, yet with reluctant mind'—or 'willing, with heart unwilling'"—ACS's own translations of *Iliad* 4.43 (see *Letters* 4. 230–31)

351.40 "all air and fire": quoting Drayton on Marlowe in his "To My Most Dearly-Loved Friend Henry Reynolds, Esquire, of Poets and Poesy" (1627)

352.28 "Moods of fantastic sadness, nothing worth": Arnold, "To a Gypsy Child by the Seashore," 18

352.43 Messrs. Moxon and Co.: ACS notes ironically that Moxon published Shelley's *Poeti-*

*cal Works* but withdrew in fear from ACS's *Poems and Ballads* when it was abused by the critics. ACS quotes Shelley's *Queen Mab*, 7.164, 172, 180.

353.9 Origen: ascetic Christian and theologian (c.185–c. 254) who castrated himself

353.10 Dindymus . . . Loreto: i.e., neither Cybele nor the Virgin Mary

353.28 *Qui a bu boira*: "who has drunk will drink" (French proverb)

353.39 euphrasy and rue: medicinal herbs for the eyes (see Milton, *Paradise Lost*, 11.414–15)

353.44 great poet and humorist: Théophile Gautier (1811–72); ACS quotes from his early poem *Albertus* (1832), XCVIII, which Hyder translates as, "I warn the mothers of families that I am not writing for little girls, for whom one makes bread and butter; my verses are a young man's verses."

354.17 Purgon and Diafoirus: in Molière's *Le Malade Imaginaire*

355.17 foolish virgins: cf. Matthew 25: 1

355.25 pamphlet of Charles Baudelaire: *Richard Wagner et Tannhäuser à Paris* (1861)

356.17 In Plato the legend has fallen: see *Symposium*, 5.189–193e

357.3–4 "thing of beauty": Keats, *Endymion* I

357.23–24 "However . . . ": Landor, "Appendix to the *Hellenics*"

358.12 L'Arioste . . . l'ombre: "Ariosto laughs in the sun, Aretino sniggers in the shade" (Hyder trans.).

358.12–13 The whiter the sepulchre: Matthew 23: 27

358.17–18 "It is to be presumed ...": Ben Jonson, the song for *Epicoene*, I. 1

359.18–19 "I write as others wrote ...": Landor, from the poem beginning "Wearers of rings and chains!," in "Poems on Books and Writers," *The Complete Works of Walter Savage Landor*, ed. Stephen Wheeler, 15:227

### FROM "BYRON"

Composed December 1865–January 1866. First published as preface to ACS's selections from Byron (Moxon, March 1866); reprinted by ACS in his *Essays and Studies* (1875).

360.1 most delicate and thoughtful of English critics: Matthew Arnold. See his "Heinrich Heine," *Essays in Criticism* (1865).

361.14 lake-water and sea-water: See Byron, "Dedication," *Don Juan*, 39–40.

361.17 "the broad backs of the sea": *Iliad* 2.159

361.30 steer inshore: cf. *Don Juan*, IX, 137–44

362.14 "innumerable laughter": Aeschylus, *Prometheus Bound*, ll. 89–90

### FROM "MATHEW ARNOLD'S NEW POEMS"

Composed August 1867. First published in the *Fortnightly Review*, October 1867. Revised for *Essays and Studies* (1875). ACS reviewed Arnold's poems with eagerness—cf. *Letters*, 1. 253. It's important to see that the praise of Arnold is carried by a coded critique of Tennyson and Browning, whose religious ideologies both pervade and enervate their verse, in ACS's view.

363.1 A French critic: Arnold himself detected ACS's hoax—cf. *Letters*, 1. 269.

363.18–20 M. Renan . . . Colenso: A string of allusions to Browning's "A Death in the Desert," the "Epilogue" to *Dramatis Personae*, and "Gold Hair."

363.31–32 ACS takes his text from Ezekiel 28:12.

364.10–11 Le Coeur ...J'ai senti!: ACS is recalling Tennyson's *In Memoriam* (section cxxiv).

364.25 Encore un mot: The allusion here is to Browning's "One Word More."

367.19–20 *See Empedocles on Etna* 2. 447–48

### FROM "NOTES ON DESIGNS OF THE OLD MASTERS AT FLORENCE"

First published in the *Fortnightly Review*, July 1868; reprinted in *Essays and Studies* (1875). In his opening remarks, ACS recalled that originally he had penned some "hasty memorial notes" while visiting the Uffizi in 1864. He later told Arnold that the finished piece had cost him "some time and care to draw up," saying, "I can only answer for its cautious and literal accuracy" (*Letters*, 1. 301). The guardedness of the last remark is suggestive; perhaps it reveals ACS's awareness that the imaginative ardor of his essay laid bare a critical sensibility for which his readers might be unprepared. At least one reader, however, proved responsive and attentive. One year later, in the pages of the *Fortnightly Review*, Walter Pater published his "Notes on Leonardo da Vinci."

370.22 Πολλὴ μὲν θεοῖσι κοὐκ ἀνώνυμος θεά: Euripides, *Hippolytus*, ll. 1–2
370.27 Amestris: wife of the Persian king, Xerxes
370.29 ACS probably read of the debaucheries of the emperor Kié and his queen in Sade's *Justine*.
371.16 loveliest passage of Salammbô: ACS is alluding to the scene with the serpent in chapter 10 of Flaubert's novel.
371.19–20 "Where's my serpent of old Nile?": *Antony and Cleopatra*, 1.5.25

### FROM *NOTES ON SOME PICTURES OF 1868*

First published in 1868 as the second part of a pamphlet coauthored with William Michael Rossetti; reprinted with deletions as "Notes on Some Pictures of 1868" in *Essays and Studies* (1875). ACS directs his attention to several key Rossetti works, including *Lady Lilith* (1864–69), *Sibylla Palmifera* (1864–70), *Beata Beatrix* (1864), *Venus Verticordia* (1863–69), *La Pia* (1868–69), *Dante's Dream at the Time of the Death of Beatrice* (1856), and *Aspecta Medusa* (1865; unfinished).

372.10–13 "She excels / All women ...": Shelley, "Scenes from the *Faust* of Goethe," 2.317–21.
372.25–27 Mademoiselle de Maupin: "I find earth as beautiful as heaven, and I think correctness of form is virtue " (Hyder trans.).
373.1–2 "Ma mia suora Rahel ...": *Purgatorio*, 27.104–05: "But my sister Rachel never turns from her mirror, and sits all day."
373.13 maiden meditation: *A Midsummer-Night's Dream*, 2.1.163–64
373.33 "sitting alone, made as a widow": *Vita Nuova*, 31
374.11 the deadly marriage ring: cf. the words of Pia de' Tolomei, *Purgatorio*, 5

### FROM *WILLIAM BLAKE: A CRITICAL ESSAY*

Begun in 1863 as a review of Gilchrist's *Life of Blake*, then extended into a "small commentary of a running kind," explicating the span of Blake's work (*Letters*, 1. 59–60). Completed in 1865, it was not published until 1868 because of ACS's split with his publisher, Moxon. The passage here printed is heavily in debt to Blake's two letters to Butts of 22 November 1802 (see ACS's source, Gilchrist's *Life of Blake* 2:188–91)

375.15 *Catalogue*: published by Blake in 1809
379.12 "the Dante": Blake's Dante illustrations, published in 1824
379.17 an artist: an oblique reference to Dante Gabriel Rossetti, who obsessively revisited Dante's story of Francesca da Rimini in *Inferno*, 5.
380.21–22 *l'hérésie de l'enseignement*: "the didactic heresy." See Baudelaire's study of Poe, in *Nouvelles Histoires Extraordinaires* (1857).
383.21 "he looks like a man": apocryphal comment by Lincoln; ACS uses the same quote in his review "Walt Whitman's Poems," *London Sun*, 17 April 1868.

### FROM TWO ESSAYS OF "VICTOR HUGO"

"Victor Hugo: L'Homme Qui Rit" first published in the *Spectator*, 1869; "Victor Hugo: *L'Année Terrible*" was published first in the *Fortnightly Review*, September 1872. Both pieces were later collected for *Essays and Studies* (1875). Both reviews earned ACS letters of appreciation from Hugo (see *Letters*, 2.110, 186).

386.11 "anonymuncules who go scribbling about": ACS attributes this to Charles Reade.
386.20 as Pallas caught Achilles: *Iliad*, book 1
387.3 as I have said elsewhere: in *William Blake* (1868)
388.34 "Can these bones live?": Ezekiel 37: 3–7
389.2–3 "Trimalchio is alive ...": Hugo, *William Shakespeare* (1864)
389.5–7 "mistrust the poet . . . heroic bones": Browning, *Aurora Leigh*, book 5

389.18–19 No scroll is "closed for ever": Whitman, "Song of the Exposition"
389.25–26 "servile to all the skiey influences": *Measure for Measure*, 3.1.9

### FROM "THE POEMS OF DANTE GABRIEL ROSSETTI"

First published in the *Fortnightly Review*, May 1870; reprinted in *Essays and Studies* (1875). A key essay on Rossetti, strongly influencing Pater's famous appreciation.

390.10 another poet: Sydney Dobell (1824–74); ACS quotes from "Home, Wounded" 48.

### FROM *A NOTE ON CHARLOTTE BRONTË*

Composed winter 1876 to spring 1877. First published August 1877. Initiated in response to the appearance of T. Wemyss Reid's book *Charlotte Brontë, A Monograph*, the essay began as a "brief discourse" in 1876 (*Letters*, 3. 219, 260–61) and soon grew to length. ACS moves against the critical current of his day, championing the visionary and tragic "genius" of Brontë over the realist "intellect" of Eliot.

397.32 "my sister Emily loved the moors": See Charlotte Brontë's ("Currer Bell"'s) introduction to the 1850 edition of her sisters' novels, *Agnes Grey* and *Wuthering Heights*.

398.17 Shirley Keeldar: Brontë's heroine in *Shirley* (1849). Chapter 18 recounts her antinomian reading of Milton, to which ACS alludes here.

398.19 "la déesse des dieux": "the goddess of the gods"—Hugo, "Hymne," 106, in *La Légende des Siècles*, 1

398.25 "halting slave" of Epaphroditus: The Stoic Epictetus, the "lame philosopher"—see Arnold's sonnet "To a Friend" (1849) for the story glanced at here.

398.26–33 "in life . . . liberty": Emily Brontë, "The Old Stoic" (1841)

398.38–42 "I praise thee, mother Earth!": Sydney Dobell, *Balder*, 24.131

399.22–31 "He comes with western winds ...": Emily Brontë, "The Prisoner, 37–42, 53–56"

### "EMILY BRONTË"

Published in the *Athenaeum*, 16 June 1883, reprinted in *Miscellanies* (1886). Originally penned as a review of A. Mary F. Robinson's biography, *Emily Brontë* (1883). ACS clearly found a poetic sensibility akin to his own in Brontë's novel, with its Moor country filled with windstorms and tragic romance. In a letter to Wise, he reflected upon "her passion for the moors—which I, as a Borderer, have always thought the next best thing to the sea" (*Letters*, 6. 118).

400.24 *Mehalah*: novel of 1880 by S. Baring-Gould

401.24–26 "it was . . . numbness": Robinson, *Emily Brontë*, 125

402.33–35 "is given . . . appealing": Robinson, *Emily Brontë*, 125

402.38 Cornelia: Webster, *The White Devil*

402.38–39 Madge Wildfire: Scott, *Heart of Midlothian*

403.7 Aeschylean legend: In some accounts, Prometheus figured as the son of Iapetus and Themis; ACS extends the resonance of his allusion to include Gaea.

403.9 One thing needful: Luke, 10: 42

403.20 "unutterable": See Brontë's "No coward soul is mine."

403.25 "some shy ostrich prompting": Robinson, *Emily Brontë*, 136

404.28 "assume the virtue": *Hamlet*, 3.4.160

404.37 "vivid and fearful scenes": See Charlotte Brontë's ("Currer Bell") introductory remarks in her 1850 edition of *Wuthering Heights*.

### UNCOLLECTED POETRY

*Dies Irae*. Composed 1858, first published posthumously in *Posthumous Poems* (1917), collected in *Bonchurch* 1:113–14. This is the finest English translation ever made of the great medieval Latin hymn.

[The High Victorian Tone]. This brilliant epigram dates from about 1859 and is an epitome of Swinburne's work. The satire begins in the metric, which is borrowed from Arnold's *Empedocles on Etna*, the work that ACS saw as marking a definitive turn away from Victorian pomposities. When ACS wrote this poem Arnold had suppressed his own masterpiece. As Lafourcade (who first printed the epigram) rightly observes, these ten lines comprise "une satire de l'inspiration de la poésie victorienne toute entière" (Lafourcade II. 163).

*[Sonnet. Ah face & hands & body beautiful].* Composed early 1860s and first printed (incorrectly) in a private edition in 1915. The text here is taken from the manuscript in the British Library. The poem itself is closely related to the "Treatise of Noble Morals" in ACS's homage to Lucrezia Borgia, the *Chronicle of Tebaldeo Tebaldei*. ACS wrote an epigraph for the poem in the right margin: "And she shd love my body as if it were / A cross of Abraham & Mahamout." The sonnet has an interesting (canceled) set of final lines: "Kiss me now, love, & love me without fear / There is no sin but sorrow & soul's pain."

*The Ballad of Villon and Fat Madge.* Composed probably 1862–63 (see commentary above to "The Complaint of the Fair Armouress"). The second epigraph here is from John 9:4.

*A Ballad of Dead Creeds.* Composed (probably) in 1863, here first published from ACS's corrected draft (in the British Library). ACS canceled the original title, "The Wind's Work. / Imitated from the French of Villon." The poem is indeed not a translation but an "Imitation" (like Pope's *Imitations of Horace*). The epigraph is quoted from the first stanza of Villon's ballade (incorporated in *Le Testament*). The text here is purged of its canceled readings but otherwise reproduces the manuscript exactly. The penultimate line defines ACS's ideological position precisely.

*The Cannibal Catechism.* Privately printed by Gosse in 1913 (without the final two stanzas) and, as Gosse notes on the autograph manuscript, "written probably . . . to amuse the Anthropological Society's Cannibal Club," which used to meet at Bertolini's Hotel. Gosse dates it 1865, but it was written in 1863. The poem is a parody of Burns's "Holy Willie"s Prayer."

*Cleopatra.* Composed in 1866 to accompany a drawing by Frederick Shelds; both appeared in *The Cornhill* (September 1866). ACS thought little of the poem (see *Letters* V. 234) and did not collect it in his edition of 1904. Several unauthorized printings were made in ACS's lifetime, however. The epigraph is, of course, ACS's invention.

From *Arthur's Flogging.* Composed in the 1860s, the poem (52 stanzas in its complete form) was printed in a private edition around 1888 (in London) in the collection of prose and verse titled *The Whippingham Papers*, most of it ACS's work. The poem is a kind of meta-parody since its *ottava rima* verse is clearly playing off Byron's *Don Juan*. It's worth knowing that Whippingham Church is a celebrated landmark on the Isle of Wight. As in all of ACS's comic verse in this mode, the boy survives this ordeal and ends a kind of parodic Christ figure.

*Disgust: A Dramatic Monologue.* Another splendid parody, this one composed in November 1881 after reading Tennyson's "Despair: A Dramatic Monologue" in *The Nineteenth Century* (November 1881). ACS published his verses in *The Fortnightly Review* the following month but did not collect the poem in 1904; it was reprinted in 1917 in Gosse's edition of the *Posthumous Poems.*

18 P.P.C.: *pour prendre congé* (to take leave)

24 the shepherd: Stiggins (see Dickens's *Pickwick Papers*, chaps. 22, 27, 32).

42 George Augustus Sala's story "Colonel Quagg's Conversion" was published in *Household Words* (30 Dec. 1854).

### UNCOLLECTED PROSE

*A Criminal Case.* Written probably in 1861, first printed posthumously in a small pamphlet by T. J. Wise in 1910.

*Dead Love*. Written in 1861 for ACS's abandoned *Triameron*. Published in *Once a Week* (October 1862). A forged printing (dated 1864) was created by T. J. Wise in the late 1880s. Collected in *Bonchurch* 17:11–18. ACS sets the story sometime during the Hundred years War in the 15th century.

*The Portrait*. Composed in 1861 and printed for private circulation by Watts-Dunton in 1909, with an introductory note. Collected in *Bonchurch*17:3–10. In a note to his edition Watts-Dunton remarks, "It is probable that he was imitating the "little novels" of Agnolo Firenzuola, which were excessively popular in the sixteenth century. There is a considerable resemblance of style. The teller of *The Portrait* is evidently a priest, a dissolute abbe, who shows his calling by an ironical attack on art and beauty and nakedness, an attack so obviously ironical that it makes the soldiers and the ladies 'laugh more exceedingly than before.'" The tale was to have formed part of ACS's *Triameron* and stands second in the list of ten stories intended for the first day, to come right after "Dead Love."

*Les Abîmes. Par Ernest Clouet*. This burlesque review of the fictitious French decadent poet was written in the summer or early autumn 1862. It was accepted for publication in *The Spectator*, set in type, but finally rejected by the editor Richard Holt Hutton because ACS did not write with "real disgust" for the French verse: "There is a tone of raillery about [your review] which I think one should hardly use to pure obscenity." The parody is evidently in debt to Baudelaire (see "Un Carogne," e.g., in *Fleurs du Mal*, as well as Baudelaire's essay "Petrus Borel" (published in 1861). Cecil Lang believed that ACS was here also writing "under the direct influence of the Marquis de Sade" (*New Writings*, 224). Edmund Wilson's comment is worth recalling: "What is masterly in these burlesques is the contrast between the French decadents letting themselves go and the tone of the English reviewer, with his restrained but superior sarcasm" (Wilson, 17) Félicien Cossu is another fictitious creation of ACS, who created various works in poetry and prose under Cossu's name. The reference to *le prince proletaire* is equally hoaxing: ACS wrote a French tale under this title around 1861 (first printed privately in 1963).

*The Chronicle of Tebaldeo Tebaldei*. Composed in 1861, along with the set of stories that ACS planned to write for his abandoned *Triameron* project, an interlocked set of prose tales modeled on Boccaccio. See *Letters* 1. 38–39. This work was abandoned after he had written six chapters, from which part of chapter IV and all of chapter VI are here printed from the manuscript. It was first published in 1942 in an extraordinary edition with elaborate notes by Randolph Hughes.

From *Lesbia Brandon*. This is excerpted from the "Via Dolorosa" chapter of ACS's brilliant, uncompleted novel which he worked at intermittently from 1860 until 1866. He had the fragments typeset for correction in 1877 and as late as 1881 was still committed to finishing the work. He was well aware of the unusual nature of the work, both in form and content, as is clear from his letter to Sir Richard Burton (11 January 1867): "I have in hand a scheme of mixed verse and prose—a sort of *étude à la Balzac* plus the poetry— which I flatter myself will be more offensive and objectionable to Britannia than anything I have yet done." The passage here comes after Lady Wariston and her lover (and half-brother) Denham have made a desperate parting, with Denham intending to commit suicide (as he does). The series of English ballads Lady Wariston reads to her children were lifted from the novel by ACS, put in an orderly form, and published separately in *PB3* (1889), where they are titled, respectively, "The Weary Wedding," "The Witch Mother," "A Lyke-Wake Song," "The Tyneside Widow," and "The Reiver's Neck-Verse."

*Letter to E. C. Stedman (20–21 February 1875)*. The letter replies to one from Stedman which came with a copy of Stedman's laudatory notice of ACS in *Scribner's Monthly* (March 1875).

# Bibliography to the Introduction


Eliot, T. S. "Swinburne." In *Selected Essays. A New Edition*. New York: Harcourt Brace, 1950.

Empson, William. *Seven Types of Ambiguity*. 2d rev. ed. New York: New Directions, 1947.

Forrest-Thomson, Veronica. *Poetic Artifice: A Theory of Twentieth-Century Poetry*. Manchester: Manchester University Press, 1978.

Gilchrist, Alexander. *Life of William Blake, "Pictor Ignotus."* London: Macmillan, 1863.

Gosse, Edmund. "The First Draft of 'Anactoria.'" In *Aspects and Impressions*. London, 1922.

——, and T. J. Wise., eds. *The Complete Works of Algernon Charles Swinburne*. 20 vols. London: Heinemann, 1925–27.

Harrison, Antony H. *Swinburne's Medievalism: A Study in Victorian Love Poetry*. Baton Rouge: LSU Press, 1988.

Haynes, Kenneth, ed. *Poems and Ballads and Atalanta in Calydon*. London and New York: Penguin Books, 2000.

Henderson, Philip. *Swinburne: The Portrait of a Poet*. London: Routledge and Kegan Paul, 1974.

Hughes, Randolph, ed. *Lucrezia Borgia: The Chronicle of Tebaldeo Tebaldei*. London: Golden Cokerell Press, 1942.

——. *Lesbia Brandon by Algernon Charles Swinburne* . . . London: Falcon Press, 1952.

Hyder, C. K., ed. *Swinburne: The Critical Heritage*. London: Routledge and Kegan Paul, 1970.

——. *Swinburne Replies: Notes on Poems and Reviews; Under the Microscope; Dedicatory Epistle*. Syracuse: Syracuse University Press, 1966.

Lafourcade, Georges. *La Jeunesse de Swinburne*. 2 vols. London and New York: Oxford University Press, 1928.

Lang, Cecil Y., ed. *New Writings by Swinburne*. Syracuse: Syracuse University Press, 1964.

——. *The Pre-Raphaelites and Their Circle*. 2d rev. edition. Chicago: University of Chicago Press, 1975.

——. *The Swinburne Letters*. 6 vols. New Haven: Yale University Press, 1959–62.

——, ed. *Victorian Poetry* 9 nos. 1–2 (spring-summer 1971) [special issue devoted to Swinburne].

Louis, Margot K. *Swinburne and His Gods*. Montreal: McGill-Queens University Press, 1990.

Maturana, Humberto. *Autopoiesis and Cognition*. Boston: D. Reidel, 1980.

McGann, Jerome. *Swinburne: An Experiment in Criticism*. Chicago: University of Chicago Press, 1971.

McSweeney, Kerry. *Tennyson and Swinburne as Romantic Naturalists*. Toronto: University of Toronto Press, 1981.

Nicholls, Peter. "The Swinburne Nexus." *Parataxis* 10 (spring 2001): 33–53.

Riede, David G. *Swinburne: A Study of Romantic Mythmaking*. Charlottesville: University Press of Virginia, 1978.

Rooksby, Rikky. *A. C. Swinburne: A Poet's Life*. Aldershot: Scolar Press, 1997.

——, and Nicholas Shrimpton, eds. *The Whole Music of Passion: New Essays on Swinburne*. Aldershot: Scolar Press, 1993.

Rosenberg, John. "Swinburne." *Victorian Poetry* 11 (1967): 131–52.

Rutland, William R.. *Swinburne: A Nineteenth-Century Hellene.* Oxford: Blackwell, 1931.

[Swinburne, A. C., ed.]. *The Poems* [6 vols.] and *The Tragedies* [5 vols.]. London: Chatto and Windus, 1904–5.

Walder, Anne. *Swinburne's Flowers of Evil: Baudelaire's Influence on Poems and Ballads, First Series.* Acta Universitatis Upsalienses. Studia Anglistica Upsaliensa 25. Uppsala: University of Uppsala, 1976.

Varela, Francisco. *The Embodied Mind*. Cambridge: MIT Press, 1991.

Wilson, Edmund. "Introduction." *The Novels of A. C. Swinburne*. New York: Farrar, Stauss, and Cudahy, 1962.

# INDEXES

## Titles (Poetry and Prose)

Note: The titles of the ballads included in the selection from *Lesbia Brandon* are not included here since they are untitled in that text and since the texts and titles of the ballads are differently represented in the different places of their publication by ACS. Their first lines are included in the index of first lines.

## First Lines (Poetry)